The Body and
Its Symbolism

The Body and Its Symbolism

A Kabbalistic Approach

ANNICK de SOUZENELLE

Translated from the French by Christopher Chaplin and Tony James

This publication has been generously supported by
The Kern Foundation

QUEST
BOOKS

THEOSOPHICAL PUBLISHING HOUSE
WHEATON, ILLINOIS • CHENNAI, INDIA

Quest Books
PO Box 270
Wheaton, IL 60187-0270

www.questbooks.com

Cover image: *L'Arbre à pain*, by Pierre Jourda (1931–2007)
Cover and interior design and typesetting by Drew Stevens

Library of Congress Cataloging-in-Publication Data

Souzenelle, Annick de.
   [Symbolisme du corps humain. French]
The body and its symbolism: a kabbalistic approach / Annick de
Souzenelle; translated from the French by Christopher Chaplin and
Tony James.
   pages   cm
Includes index.
ISBN 978-0-8356-0932-6
1. Cabala—Miscellanea. 2. Human body—Religious aspects—
Miscellanea. I. Title.
BM525. S6713 2015
296.1'6—dc23   2015008157

Printed in the United States of America

5   4   3   2   1   *   15   16   17   18   19   20

Contents

List of Illustrations

Acknowledgments

THE TRANSLATORS WOULD LIKE TO THANK DENIS MARIER FOR a number of suggestions when he carefully reread the manuscript at an earlier stage; and Mme. Christiane Lamberbourg, osteopath, who kindly checked the anatomical details in chapter 20.

The author and the translators express thanks to Richard Smoley for his eagle-eyed attention to the Hebrew and his sterling work in editing the text. Last, but by no means least, they are profoundly grateful to Sharron Dorr for her thorough attention to the presentation of the book as a whole and the outstanding quality of her collaboration throughout the process of production.

Foreword

THIS BOOK WAS FIRST PUBLISHED IN PARIS IN 1974. SINCE THEN it has never been out of print and continues to sell about eight thousand paperback copies every year. It has been successfully translated into other Romance languages (Italian, Spanish, and Romanian), but until now not into English.

The author, Annick de Souzenelle, is a vivacious ninety-three-year-old lady who still travels regularly in France and elsewhere, giving weekend courses and occasional lectures. Born in 1922 in the aftermath of the First World War, she was soon struck, even as a child, by the apparent absurdity of the world she was born into. Nothing, and certainly not the kind of Roman Catholicism then taught to young children, seemed to offer any remedy to the meaninglessness of life.

Early on, she was intrigued by references to the body in fairy tale and myth, whether biblical or Greek. She learned how the children of Eve were fated to be bruised on the heel by the serpent; how the patriarch Jacob was born holding his brother Esau's heel and was later to be wounded in the thigh while wrestling with an angel; how Samson's hair was the source of his strength; and how Christ washed his disciples' feet. *Oedipus* means "swollen foot," and Prometheus's liver was eaten by an eagle during the day and renewed at night, only to go through the same process again and again. Why? What was behind these and other quite precise references to parts of the body?

Adults seemed embarrassed by her questions and either found her too curious or replied that there was nothing requiring explanation. These subjects were not in the school curriculum. Visits to museums were, on the other hand, and copies of Romanesque sculptures gave rise to further questions. Why the elongated hands of Christ in glory, why spiral shapes round knees, thighs, or bellies in the cathedral of Autun and the basilica in Vézelay, why little men with ears down to the ground or dogs' heads? At Vaison-la-Romaine there was even a Christ with horns.

The only answer she sometimes received was "Well, you know, people in those days couldn't draw properly," and her frustration turned into anger, like the anger she already felt about life and its absurdity. But there was still nowhere to turn for genuine answers.

Perhaps with a view to meeting head on the question of suffering and meaning, she became a nurse. Now patients would suppose she had answers ("Why is this—this cancer, this stomach ulcer, etc.—happening to me, Madame?"), and although still she had none, her intuitive sense was that if she had been able to give some meaning to the illness, this might in itself have pointed the way to recovery. Illness was perhaps a way of putting right or drawing attention to a "poor aim,"[1] perhaps even, in some cases, of bringing more abundant life. An answer from her might have helped the patient take his or her illness in hand and not make the doctor into some kind of magician. Patient-doctor relations might have become more human and collaborative, and the patient might have called on his or her inner resources (the "physician within") to help the doctor deal with the disease.

Feelings and hunches like these later became certainties, and this book is born of the process that brought them into being. A point came when the author's life changed radically, and there were two key factors in this change: the rediscovery of Christianity through Orthodoxy and the discovery of the Hebrew language.

She experienced the Orthodox tradition as life giving through the transformative power of symbols, the archetypal dimension from which they sprang and to which they led back, and the upward thrust that led to the Word. This Word, the Logos, was mediated through the language of biblical Hebrew, the twenty-two "dancing" letters whose combinations revealed previously unsuspected meanings and that were in themselves symbols and archetypes. These discoveries resonated with much that was being said in the social sciences, then in their infancy, and particularly with Jungian psychology.

The impact of this double encounter was so powerful that she felt she had to break with the life she was then leading. The experience was of an almost ecstatic joy: everything was related, everything lived and had meaning, and this included the body. Was it not an image of the "Divine Body" whose likeness was shown to Moses (Numbers 12:8)? The body's vocation was to return to its divine origin and be united, wedded with God. Life between birth and death is the story of this return from "man below" to "man above," from Adam to Elohim in the biblical myth. It is an irresistible call to this "wedding."

In this adventure each limb and organ of the body plays a part, revealed by its immediate physiological function. Now she knew why the first vertebrae were called the sacrum (sacred bone), why the cerebellum is called "the tree of life," why the optical layers, in French, are called "nuptial" (*couches nuptiales*). When its ultimate vocation is neglected or disturbed, the body speaks and points to the origin of the disorder through the organs affected. The more she listened to this language of the body, the more she received answers to her questions.

The Divine Body may be represented by the model Moses is traditionally supposed to have handed down, the Sefirotic Tree or Tree of Life. In this book the diagram of the Tree of Life is a map on which man's growth in body, mind, and spirit may be charted, from the feet to the skull. The first four chapters lay the groundwork for what follows by explaining the nature of myth and symbol, the nature of the Hebrew letters and language, and the kabbalistic Tree of Life, the ten Divine Energies after which the body is patterned (chapter 5). Starting then from the feet (chapter 7), we begin an ascension of this "ladder" to arrive in chapter 20 at the skull and the brain, before glimpsing (chapter 21) the Light beyond. Finally, in an afterword, the author reflects thirty years later on the themes of the book and on our present predicament.

Thus, with the Sefirotic Tree as the ground plan, the whole body is visited. The author's method is a combination of association from everyday expressions (French will here sometimes differ from English), deciphering the import of the Hebrew words for the parts of the body (sometimes recombining their letters) and referring when appropriate to mythology, especially, but not only, Hebrew and Greek. Her knowledge of Hebrew leads to fresh readings of biblical texts: for instance Adam's "rib" is shown not to be a rib, and the Tree of the Knowledge of Good and Evil (Genesis 2:17) becomes rather the knowledge of Light and what has not yet become Light. Stress is continually laid on the importance of personal experience and the need to descend into the depths before being able to rise higher and attain new fields of consciousness. Since the use of certain terms or concepts is likely to be unfamiliar, a glossary is provided. There is also an index for those wishing to use the book as a work of reference and look up the parts of the body in which they are interested.

The author is an Orthodox Christian. Some readers may be surprised by frequent references to other traditions, beginning with Hermes Trismegistus in the first chapter. Her conviction is that Tradition is universal, whatever the myths or vocabulary used to express it. This was borne out after the publication of her book, when a doctor specializing in Chinese medicine said, "Annick, you've written a book on acupuncture," and when, later, a North American Indian chief said it matched his own tradition.

Experience shows that all is unlikely to be clear on a first reading, but if readers are prepared to let suggestions fall out of the pages into their minds and work at whatever level of consciousness appears appropriate they will find, as many already have, that the book—like their own bodies—holds unsuspected treasures.

Tony James
February 2, 2013

Hebrew Alphabet, Numerical Correspondences, and Symbolism

Units	Tens	Hundreds	Symbolism of the Hebrew Letters
Realm of principles	*Level of incarnation*	*Cosmic level*	
א alef 1	י yod 10	ק qof 100	Initial creative power. Divine force. The divine creative "I." Principle. Father.
ב bet 2	כ kaf 20	ר resh 200	Receptivity. Created "thou" receiving the creative "I."
ג gimel 3	ל lamed 30	ש shin, sin 300	Movement. Dynamism.
ד dalet 4	מ mem 40	ת tav 400	Matter. Resistance. Death. Womb. Temptation. Trial.
ה heh 5	נ nun 50	ך final kaf 500	Breath of existence. Seed of life.
ו vav 6	ס samekh 60	ם final mem 600	Union. Fertilization. Symbol of Man (created on the sixth day).
ז zayin 7	ע ayin 70	ן final nun 700	Disappearance. Death. Nothing; which imply: Return. Rebirth. Everything.
ח ḥet 8	פ peh 80	ף final peh 800	Resurrection. Barrier. Opening. Return. Rebirth.
ט tet 9	צ tsadi 90	ץ final tsadi 900	Perfection of what is created. Completion of the feminine side.
		א final alef 1000	Transfiguration.

Hebrew Pronunciation and Transliteration Table

א	alef	Sound of associated vowel
ב	bet	b, v
ג	gimel	g
ד	dalet	d
ה	heh	h
ו	vav	v
ז	zayin	z
ח	ḥet	ḥ (like *ch* in Scottish *loch*, German *ach*)
ט	tet	t
י	yod	y, i
כ, ך	kaf	k, kh
ל	lamed	l
מ, ם	mem	m
נ, ן	nun	n
ס	samekh	s
ע	ayin	Sound of associated vowel
פ, ף	peh	p, f
צ, ץ	tsadi	ts
ק	qof	q
ר	resh	r
ש	shin, sin	sh, s
ת	tav	t

Note on Biblical Translations
and References

THE AUTHORIZED KING JAMES VERSION HAS BEEN TAKEN AS standard. However, frequent departures are made from it when the author's rereading of the original Hebrew so requires. Hebrew is a fluid language, written without vowels (pointing was introduced about the tenth century AD to facilitate reading), and several levels of meaning and ways of reading are recognized by tradition. References are given so that readers may see differences for themselves. A number of Jewish scholars agree with the readings proposed here.

Glossary of Words Used
in Particular Senses

About-turn (French *retournement*).

This refers to a radical reorientation of life (the Greek *metanoia*, often translated as "repentance") and a return to what is essential, i.e., the wellspring of the divine within us.

Accomplished / unaccomplished / accomplishment

(French *accompli / inaccompli / accomplissement*).

Accomplished means "brought to fulfillment" in the sense in which Christ said he came to fulfill the law and the prophets (Matthew 5:17) or St. Paul said that "love is the fulfilling of the law" (Romans 13:10). *Accomplissement* has not usually been translated "fulfillment," because the connotations of happiness appeared inappropriate. *Accomplishment* is not used here in the sense of an acquired aptitude, like playing the piano, but carries the earlier sense of fulfillment, completion, or consummation. The Tree of the Knowledge of Good and Evil (Genesis 2:9) refers in fact to what is accomplished and not yet accomplished, what is light and not yet light. The French words *accompli* and *inaccompli* also denote the two aspects of the Hebrew verb, known in English as the perfect and the imperfect.

Cinnabar Field (French *champs de cinabre*).

In the Taoist tradition, the Cinnabar Fields (*dantien*) are loci in the human body corresponding roughly to guts, heart, and head. The function of the organs they contain have precise correspondences in the spiritual work of accomplishment. They play a major role in breathing, meditation, and "internal alchemy" practices (cf. www. goldenelixir.com). See also "Matrix."

Create / Make (French *créer / faire*).

"To create" (Hebrew *bara*) is the work of God alone and, read literally, can mean "placing in sight," that is, establishing otherness. "To make" (Hebrew *asah*) is both human and divine: the "other" (than God) is called to live the process of going from image to likeness (Genesis 1:26: "Let us make an Adam in our image, capable of likeness: and let him have dominion over the fish of the sea").

Earth / Land (French *terre*).

Both words translate the Hebrew *adamah*, which is "Mother Earth," the feminine of the word *adam*. It also signifies the inner ground that "Adam" (each man or woman) must till. These words refer almost always to internal states: levels or "fields" of consciousness. Advancing on a spiritual path implies the conquering of successive unknown "lands" within oneself by descending into the depths and coming up again. The word for "earth" in Genesis 1:10 (אֶרֶץ, *erets*) expresses dryness, opposed to the wetness or humidity of the depths.

Nuptials / Wedding (French *épousailles / noces*).

Men and women are called to be united with God, becoming his spouse. In this marriage of God with the human soul, men as well as women are receptive and feminine in relation to God. This is the final stage of a process that must begin with men (and women) espousing their feminine side, that is, the immense reservoir of unaccomplished energies contained in the unconscious. In Hebrew the feminine (*neqevah*) is a "hole," a container, an abyss, whereas the masculine (*zakhor*) means remembering and attending to this other side (which is not a "rib," as in most translations).

Matrix (French *matrice*).

Used in the earlier sense of "womb," but figuratively designating a space within the body (matrix of water: the belly; matrix of fire: the thorax; matrix of the skull) that is the site of different trials or "baptisms." Comparable to the Cinnabar Fields.

Name (French *NOM*).

In the Bible the Name represents the essence or the personhood of God or man. Where God is concerned, the Name (capitalized in this text), in Hebrew spelled *yod-heh-vav-heh* and often printed here in Hebrew (יהוה), is known as the Tetragrammaton (Greek for "four letters"). It is so holy as to be unpronounceable except once a year by the High Priest in the Holy of Holies of the Temple at the feast of Yom Kippur. When it occurs in reading aloud from the Hebrew Bible the word *adonai* (my Lord) or *ha-Shem* (the Name) is substituted for it. The King James Bible renders it "the LORD" (in small capitals). Contemporary Christian translations that have "Yahweh" are unfaithful to the Judeo-Christian tradition.

Each of us is called to become fully the Name, that is, the divine principle whose seed is within us but has yet to grow. This is another way of putting the ancient and often-forgotten Christian adage "God became man that man might become God" or of saying that we are called to union with God.

Ontological (French *ontologique*).

From the present participle of the Greek verb *einai* (to be), the word is used here to mean "according to nature," where nature refers to man's original being when created, before the situation of exile in that he now finds himself (we call it the Fall, although this word has no biblical foundation) and before he received the "coat of skin" that then became his second nature. Thus an "ontological law" is a law that structures creation. Its transgression can only lead to disorders of various kinds.

Uprightness / Becoming Upright (French *verticalité / verticalisation*).

Becoming upright is first a stage in the evolution of the species: man is no longer on all fours. Here the term chiefly denotes leaving behind the animal state of confusion (identification with various passions or impulses) in favor of the emergence of consciousness, responsibility, and adulthood.

CHAPTER 1

The *Mi* and the *Ma*, or That Which Is Within and That Which Is Without

That which is above resembles that which is below, and that which is below resembles that which is above, to accomplish the miracles of one thing.
—The Emerald Tablet

HERMES TRISMEGISTUS—THE THRICE-GREATEST—SEALS A golden key in the Emerald Tablet. With this key, we will attempt to unlock the mystery of what appears essential to us as human beings, a mystery we are drawn to even when we do not attempt to grasp it, a mystery compelling us and, at the same time, eluding our powerless intellects.

Hitherto modern civilization has tried to unlock the world and its mysteries with the key of intellect. We look at the world the way a child looks at a toy when it wants to take it to pieces to find out how the mechanism works. Accordingly, we have placed the world, and man, as two objects different in kind, two distinct entities, believing the knower, the "one who knows" (man) and "the object to be known" (the world) to be irreducible to each other. And when "the object to be known" is dubbed "human sciences" (humanities and social sciences), it becomes clear that man has studied man without any idea about what set of instruments he could use in attempting to know himself. This is absurd.

Hermetic wisdom also says: "Know yourself, and you will know the universe and the gods." This second key invites us to regard man within

1

the world and the world within man as two sides of the same coin, the same hidden reality. What joins them is their inner core.

In this respect, the within and the without are foreign to any spatial concept; they are just links to an "outer layer," the "skin," as in a fruit the skin covers the pulp, which leads to the kernel. Man can only apprehend his individual pulp and kernel by accessing other planes of reality without, however, leaving the realm of his familiar surroundings. Otherwise the philosopher could well ask, as he has in the past, whether the world does not begin and end at the level of the skin . . . and he will stray into the land of absurdity.

With a new level of consciousness, we may learn how to unlock new doors.

Is not the skin associated with "that which is below" and the kernel with "that which is above"? The divine Hermes distinguishes these, but does not separate them. When man, like Hermes, participates in what is "above," he *distinguishes*. Man, who is "below," *separates* and comes ultimately to deny the existence of what he has separated himself from. He then remains alone, kicking against the non-sense of his life. He thinks it is inhuman, whereas it is merely human, "human" designating the layer of skin that is separated from its kernel.

How can we restore the whole of the fruit? How do we reinsert the kernel within the pulp and revive the flesh beneath the skin? How do we enable that which is "below" to recover the image of that which is "above"and find again the path leading to its model?

The different myths of Creation that humanity has entertained in its traditional schools all allude to this "above" and this "below" resulting from a separation or distinction within an archetypal unity.

The Judeo-Christian tradition in particular describes Creation arising from such a distinction. The Hebrew word made up of the three letters *bet*, *dalet*, *lamed* (in Hebrew characters, from right to left, בדל), which we translate "to separate," really means "to distinguish." God distinguishes light from darkness, day from night, and later man from woman; but above all, God distinguishes within the primeval waters *maiim*, "the waters which are above the firmament," from "the waters which are below the firmament" (Genesis 1:6–7). These waters are called respectively, in the Hebraic tradition, the *mi* and the *ma* (which mean "who?" and "what?"). *Mi* and *ma* are linked through the "firmament" called *shamaim* (שמים) in Genesis 1:8 and commonly translated as "heaven," which, while separating the *mi* from the *ma*, paradoxically reunites them around the letter shin (ש), a letter akin to what we call the "kernel" (see chapter 17, page 337).

Symbolically, we could say that *mi* contains the nonmanifested world of archetypal unity, and *ma*, the world of multiplicity, manifested in its different levels of reality. The root *mi* corresponds to the root *mu* in Greek, which forms words such as *múō*, "to close the mouth," "to be silent," and *muéō*, "to initiate" (into the mysteries)—words connected with the realm of archetypes. Every initiation is an introduction to the road connecting the manifested world to the realm of its corresponding archetypes. It is achieved in silence. The myth, *mûthos*, is the story chronicling the life of the archetypes (see chapter 2, page 9). The words **mu**rmur, **mu**te, **my**stery originate from the same root.

The root *ma* is the mother root of all words signifying a **ma**nifestation (such as **ma**n, **ma**nner, **ma**ternal, **ma**trix, **ma**tter, etc.). Each element of the *ma* is the outer breath, that which has been exhaled by its corresponding element in the *mi*. The latter ceaselessly resounds throughout the former, which bears not only its image but its power. In this sense, the *ma*, in each of its elements, is symbolic of the *mi*. The symbol (from the Greek *sumbállō*: to throw together, to unite) links the *ma* to the *mi*. By comparison, *dibállō* (to throw apart, to separate) separates the two realms. The realm of *ma* then goes adrift, deprived of its authentic reference and true power.

The Hebrews call Elohim the "Man above," and Adam, the "Man below."

This Man above is the realm of *mi*; he expresses himself in the realm of *ma*. In his image, Adam—"the Man below"—garners the totality of *ma* containing, in its seed and in the promise of its fruit, the totality of *mi*. In this sense, man is the meeting point of the universe and of the gods. He is called "Microcosmos" (little universe) and "Microtheos" (little god) in traditional knowledge. He is the starting point of all vibrations, the center mirroring every resonance.

"Know yourself and you will know the gods and the universe." I believe that no complete study of man can be made if such injunctions are left out of account. Moreover, if these premises are true, we should find traces of a dialogue linking together man and God, Adam and Elohim, the *ma* and the *mi*. How could we conceive of the existence of a language capable of participating in both categories, human and divine, apparently transcending each other, irreducible to one another? It would seem impossible, yet the gods, whose imagination is far greater than ours, provide this language: every people in the world can find it hidden in their legends, in their myths, in their rites, and in their symbols. The psychiatrist Carl Jung exclaimed: "The Western world has lost its myths!"

Human myths are still at hand; our sacred heritage is immense, but we cannot decipher it; we have never really experienced its language, or, more to the point, we have debased its language to fit our banal day-to-day existence, instead of allowing it to raise us to new levels of consciousness. Thus, because we perceived myths as puerile, we have eliminated them from our science. And because science has now established itself as the only secure and accurate framework, we have eradicated the language of myth from the heart of life itself.

Craving and thirsting for something more, we either look to those places still able to provide this language or else we remain empty right next to our own riches, incapable of recognizing them, subject to mental sicknesses that are nothing but a case of spiritual rickets.

Jung was right to sound the alarm. We urgently need the tale, the legend, the myth, the ritual in our lives; we need to let ourselves be informed by them. Here lies the path to Knowledge.

Secular science never acknowledges the knower. Rather, it declares that the knower must remain "objective," meaning he must remain on the same footing as all other knowing "objects" on the level of their mutual experiential possibilities, of their common degree of consciousness.

In this respect, the knower is more or less intelligent, more or less equipped with more or less refined tools, but his experience is verifiable by all. Knowledge gained through higher levels of consciousness is also always experiential, but the experience is no longer common to all. It can be verified only by those with an equal degree of evolved consciousness.

In other words, this knowledge implies the evolution of the knower, the acquiring of ever-higher levels of consciousness. Knowledge is objective for those on the same level. On the other hand, its data are felt as subjective by those who have not broken free from the restraining categories of the *ma* world. The dualistic expression of objectivity/subjectivity pertains solely to these categories and betrays a knowledge that denies the "act of climbing up the ladder" or reaching to the "firmament"—*raqiya ha-shamaim.* At the top of this ladder, all dualism disappears in a surpassing of oneself. I will return to this point. Ultimately, God is absolute objectivity.

Whatever the level of *ma* at which the knower arrives, the elements of this *ma* always have an intrinsic objectivity in that they refer to their archetypes in the realm of *mi.* Deprived of this reference, they are "illusion," *maya* for the Hindus, *hevel* (הבל, "vanity," "nothingness," also "Abel") for the Hebrews. They are said to be "subjective" by skeptics who have no consciousness of the world of *mi* and project onto others their own ignorance. But the experience of *mi* cut off from *ma* is also illusion. *Mi* and *ma,* although distinguished, are inseparable.

Let me emphasize that the quality of the knower that we are calling upon is the quality of his inner *being,* of his *being* reaching to his "inner core," which pertains to the world of *mi.* Only with this *being* can we approach the mystery of man—another facet of the Divine Mystery. I am speaking of a *being* who has dispensed with the "self," which is usually crystallized in the culture, the erudition, or the ethics of the exterior environment, has given up all intellectual intelligence, and enters a real life experience. Giving the object of his meditation all power of *being*, the knower, at some point in time, is seized by the known and becomes the object meditated on. Little by little, all distances between the known and the knower disappear.

The Hebrew verb "to know" is the verb that Moses uses to render carnal knowledge of man with woman.

Knowledge is a wedding, a union of the known and the knower.

Knowledge is love.

CHAPTER 2

Symbols and Myths:
The Symbolic Dimension of
the Hebrew Language

BEFORE MAKING THEM WORKING TOOLS FOR OUR MEDITATION, we need a clear understanding of what symbols and myths represent, especially those drawn from our own Judeo-Christian tradition or from the treasure chest of Greek mythology.

Symbols are the elements of our perceptible world, each signifying and imaging its archetypal correspondent "above": the signified. Thus the symbol carries in itself the power of the signified. They resonate in unison, sending out overtones reverberating from one to another, from the *mi* to the *ma*, on the same wavelength.

This simultaneity is closely linked to the law of synchronicity in Jung, based chiefly on the Chinese tradition, the Tao. He shows the correspondence existing between an archetype and the series of symbols drawn from it. This correspondence becomes clear with the emergence of several converging events in the perceptible, manifest world, which seem strange coincidences only to the unaware, who put them down to chance.

Chance is but a reality unrecognized, the reality of the ontological laws linking the archetypes with the manifest world.

I leave aside all phenomena described as metapsychological (or parapsychological) on which these laws throw light. "Science" will not be able to deny their existence much longer. How often have we not seen the same event (e.g., a major scientific discovery) happen in several countries at the same time? And what about the law of series, which all statisticians acknowledge even if it is not rationally explicable?

In a broader context, a similar kind of link could be made between:

Woman's reaffirmation of her role, which had already appeared in early Christian times, but was rapidly muffled;

The recent discovery of the personal and collective unconscious by the psychological sciences;

A reappraisal of sexuality, freeing it from its false moorings, even though it is not yet reconnected with its divine archetype; and

Man landing on the moon.

Of course, each of these events can be rationally explained, but their synchronicity falls under a law beyond the laws of the rational world.

Similarly,

Womanhood in the history of humanity;

The unconscious, as the obscure face of being, on the psychic level;

The urogenital area, on the physical level; and

The moon, the planet of night, on the cosmic level

correspond to the same symbolic wavelength, whose archetype must be very active. This leads me to infer, on the basis of another law to be discussed later, that humanity is about to experience a new birth.

But before exploring this, let us look a bit more closely at symbols. We shall see, for instance, that the animal kingdom symbolizes man's vital energies (the bull, fecundity; the serpent, wisdom; the eagle, knowledge) whereas the vegetable kingdom symbolizes other kinds of energy (the rose, return to the One; the acacia, androgyny; the almond, immortality; see chapter 21).

In all traditions "stone" resonates on the same symbolic wavelength as "man." On this wavelength, between "stone" and "man," Christian tradition places "bread" and "flesh" (the Devil suggests that Christ change stones into bread; the Christian mysteries are built on the changing of bread into the body of Christ). Similarly, water, wine, and blood are on a common wavelength, which leads in turn to the Spirit: "And there are three that bear witness in earth, the Spirit, and the Water, and the Blood: and these three agree in one" (1 John 5:8).

However, like a coin, symbols have two faces: the serpent, symbol of wisdom, is also a symbol of the Devil; water, the purifying agent, also represents our passions; fire expresses love, but also hate. Gradually this sort of ambiguity will become more familiar. But it is up to each of us to unravel these symbols, their meaning, and their overtones and let them emerge into consciousness so that they can renew us, for such is their power.

Initiation rituals everywhere, from time immemorial, are a "symbol therapy" in the true sense of the word "therapy": "that which brings back harmony," a discipline entrusted in the past to priests and initiates alone.

Myths are also agents of renewed creation that, when activated, allow the entire power of primeval forms—*archaí*—to well up within us with the energy they had from the beginning. Myths (from the Greek *mûthos*, "fable") translate a higher reality that is not readily transmissible to our everyday mental plane without the aid of a subterfuge.

Just as a blueprint will give a sectional view of a volume, one could say that myths inscribe in the phenomenal world the world of primeval forms. I disagree with those authors who are unable to break loose from their time-space continuum and see in myth a story happening at the dawn of time. In reality myth is a metahistory,[1] forever present.

Thus the book of Genesis is a perpetual present tense, even if, from its sixth chapter onward, history and metahistory are intertwined in a common narrative. Historical criticism will play a very secondary role in our study. We shall see, for example, the myth of the Deluge under various forms, but with an identical structure in almost every important traditional rendering.

Note that history, as a development of this metahistory in the manifest world, can be myth. Without this clue for reading events, we might lack an essential means of shedding light on our historical future.

History finds its significance in myth, and at the same time, myth can be corroborated in history.

Moreover, we shall discover layers of myth in the Gospels, without having to challenge the historicity of Jesus Christ. For example, the two Johns of the Gospel, St. John the Baptist and St. John the Evangelist, embody the ancient god Janus Bifrons, whose function I will discuss in chapter 6.

It is clear, however, that the first chapters of Genesis, particularly the story of Adam and Eve, relate only to myth. They are not our first parents chronologically but the cosmic man (man and woman) that we all are, in our masculine and feminine functions.

The word *bereshit*—the very first word of Genesis—is untranslatable; we can only approach its meaning, but each of us must try and understand its essence. *Bereshit* implies without a doubt the notion of "principle," but we cannot look upon it as a beginning, that is, the first step in a chronology. It is a primary mystery, existing beyond the notions of past and future. In this way, it touches the vital core of each being and there finds its resonance. Such is the scope of Genesis.

At this stage, I would like to speak of the Hebrew language as a vehicle for myth.

A translation may enable someone "who knows" and who relies on the oral tradition to enter the heart of myth. But a translation congeals the text at the level of the translator's interpretation. For me, it was the sacred language itself that served as the foundation for my meditation.

Hebrew tradition says that there are many levels (seventy, to be precise) in the Hebraic language. Symbolically, the number seventy implies a meditation without end, because it leads to the contemplation of God.[2]

What makes this language such a vehicle for myth? I am not a historian or a semanticist, but it seems to me from numerous works on the subject that the Hebrew language remains, like Sanskrit, one of the languages that comes closest to an earlier source, unique and unknown.

No other language has kept its original imprint so intact.

According to tradition, the first tongue was given to men by God. It was "one," says Genesis 11:1, until the construction of the tower of Babel. It was then shattered, and each of its fragments became a separate tongue. The Hebrew language, soon dedicated to the religious life, was subject to hardly any profane variations.

The different messages contained in a given word, if not a sentence, will only reveal themselves to those who allow the loving thrust of the letter's energy to operate within and who are prepared to die to their previously held concepts in order to be reborn to concepts belonging to an entirely new state of consciousness. (I have explained the traditional procedures—gematria, notarikon, and temurah—that give access to other levels of meaning in my book *La lettre: chemin de vie*).

For we carry within ourselves this "unique and unknown source." Unknown because it partakes of the inner depths of our being, the strata deep within ourselves, only accessible through inner births: the process of giving birth from oneself to oneself. This will be the focus of our study later. Our body is both task and tool. Yet this source also flows through the words of the prophet, the song of the poet, or the veiled language of the unconscious.

This single tongue, which we may call "divine" (the principle of unity is a divine name in Hebrew), is the same language that the apostles, intoxicated with the Holy Spirit, spoke on the day of Pentecost, and which was understood by all present that day in Jerusalem. It was the Shavuot (harvest) feast foreshadowing the feast of man's inner harvest, whose ultimate crop is the Divine Word itself.

CHAPTER 3

From the Sword to the Tree of Life:
On Good and Evil

AS THE WORD IS BEGOTTEN FROM DIVINE SILENCE, AND LIGHT arises from Darkness according to the same law, a word has been born and light has shone forth for me which I cannot "leave under a bushel" (Matthew 5:15). I believe it is time to bear witness.

The Prodigal Son suffers hunger and solitude in the desert before returning to the house of the Father—the One who begat him (Luke 15:11–32). Only at the bottom of the pit, on the edge of the absurd, in the heart of despair, can man discover inside this dark womb the seed that will eventually sprout and give rise to his divine dimension. The path he has chosen involves this difficult bringing to birth.

The Great Work is brought to perfection by successive moments of gestation. I have known some of these moments and suffered the pangs of several births, but all I can say about the process of bringing myself to birth is that partaking in life brings formidable joy. Life ceases to be the humdrum "daily round" and becomes the experience of conquest, conquest of our "kernel." It is a difficult road, with darkness and light, setbacks and victories, but from one stage to the next invisible guides constantly take over.

One of the first "guides" to reveal itself to me took the form of the Divine Name, יהוה. It is composed of four letters and is called the Tetragrammaton. Never pronounced, yet sometimes spelled—*yod-heh-vav-heh*—this Name was voiced once a year by the high priest in the

13

secrecy of the Holy of Holies, with vibrations lost since then. We no longer have any conscious appreciation of the power of a name—a living being informing the one who utters it—and cannot comprehend the sacred terror this Divine Name inspired in the Hebrews. A name—*shem* in Hebrew—is, as indicated by the English word derived from it ("schema"), a model with all the power of a blueprint suddenly expanded into a full-blown work. This gives us some inkling of the fear felt by God's people when confronted with the resonance of the power of the Divine Name revealing God.

So what is this Name, appearing for the first time in the second chapter of Genesis, right next to Elohim, after the world was created in its principle? I was asking myself this question, when the Tetragrammaton suddenly appeared to me in the following form:

$$\text{הוּה}$$

A few months later, I opened at random the *Sefer ha-Zohar* (Book of Splendor), which is, with the *Sefer Yetsirah* (Book of Formation) a sort of Kabbalist's Bible, and chanced upon this sentence: "The Sword of the Holy, blessed be He, is formed by the Tetragrammaton; the *yod* is the pommel, the *vav* is the blade, the two *hehs* are its cutting edges" (*Zohar*, III, 274b).

Words cannot convey the reality of such an experience to those who have not lived through it. When on the right path, the fruit of one's meditation is confirmed. The Word speaks, the Spirit confirms. Henceforth the Sword-Tetragrammaton became my guide.

Gradually I made out its face: in the *yod*, the pommel of the sword, I discovered man's head: the forehead the Christian touches by making the sign of the cross and naming the Father. In the *vav*, the blade, I detected the spine, made up of the energies of the Father in the eternal begetting of the Son. In the two *hehs*, the two sharp edges, were the lungs, with their extensions in man's arms and hands, filled by the Spirit with the breath of life.

The Tetragrammaton thus reveals the divine structure in its Trinitarian essence, and the Trinitarian structure of man, its image. It is the archetype par excellence from which "God becomes man so that man can become God." This axiom, apparently expressed for the first time by St. Irenaeus of Lyon, is confirmed by all the fathers of the first Christian millennium and by their heirs in the Christian East.

Man is, ontologically, the divine image. ("Ontologically" means "by nature." From here on, I will distinguish "ontology," man's original nature, from the "coat of skin," his second nature added on after the Fall. See the glossary and a fuller explanation in chapters 3, 6, and 7.) This image is not affected by the tribulations of man's history, not even by the drama that constitutes his "Fall." Eve, giving birth to her first son, Cain, says: "I have acquired [*qaniti*] a man of divine structure and vocation." At least, this is how I translate the meaning of *et* (את), which brings together the two words "man" and יהוה, the Tetragrammaton. Usually translated by "with the help of," this *et* (את) normally introduces a verb's direct object and here may be read as juxtaposing the Divine Name and the name of man.

Et is made up of the first and the last letters of the Hebrew alphabet. Consequently it also indicates a beginning and an end, the Alpha and the Omega. Through it, the Christ dimension proclaims its presence in the fabric of the Fall. Man still has the image of the divine archetype. He has lost the path to its likeness, but can recover it. This is where the eschatological dynamics are. Christ, the new Adam, says: "I am the way."

Further, we can replace the four letters of the Sword-Tetragrammaton with their corresponding numbers:

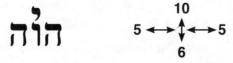

In this new diagram, the number 6 symbolizes man at the start of his development. Created on the sixth day of Genesis, he brings together in himself the first six days of Creation. The letter *vav* (ו), linked to the number six, brings together, for it is also the conjunction "and."

Man is conjunction.

On the one hand, man-*vav* links all the elements of the cosmos in their respective contradictions and complementarities (the two *hehs* [ה ו ה 5-6-5]), and on the other hand, heaven and earth (the combination הוה and the *yod*, whose value is 10, the sum of 5 and 5, hence unifying the two *hehs*). This unification is the subject matter of man's history, for his vocation is to pass from the 6 to the 10, taking on the 7, the 8, and the 9. This passage from the 6 to the 10 is accomplished, step by step, through every succeeding marriage of the two *hehs*.

Biologically, the same law is observed during the formation of a child in its mother's womb. In the sixth month of pregnancy, the child's basic form is there. Yet what happens in the womb during the seventh, eighth, and ninth months is symbolic of the child's whole life from birth to death. This is a cardinal stage that I shall discuss when studying blood (see chapter 12, page 206).

At birth, the child symbolizes the *yod*, the 10, the Divine Child he is called upon to bring to birth within himself; if we compare the whole of life to a period of gestation, this second birth will take place at the moment of death.

The 7 is a completion, a certain level of satisfaction (the two *hehs* are fully united); this involves in turn a withdrawal, a mutation, of which the 7 symbolizes the negative aspect.

The 8 that follows is a hurdle. Whoever passes it attains a new "birth/ resurrection," which is the positive aspect of the mutation.

The 9 symbolizes perfection, the culmination of the created realms.

In the 10, man attains deification and finds anew the wellspring in which the whole of creation, visible and invisible, including man, is restored. Giving birth to the Divine Child, the *yod*, he reaches in יהוה his very kernel and becomes his Name. All our Names, seeds of life into which Elohim breathes as with Adam (Genesis 2:7), are contained in יהוה.

From the source and all the way to the 6, during the first six days of Genesis, we witnessed the unfolding of the Divine Name יהוה, the out-breath from God to man. From the conclusion of the sixth day in man, until he recovers his ontological fullness in 10, that is, from Genesis to Revelation, we will witness the human inbreathing of the divine.

The Sword-Tetragrammaton, hidden from our awareness, will be beneath the surface during this second part of our journey. However, the symbol of the tree planted in the center of the Garden of Eden will shed the necessary light for man to rise toward God.

Let us contemplate this archetype, the Tree on which everything is structured.

Eden, the garden of delights, can only represent a particular state of being. This state is not permanent; the Hebrew letters, with their numerical values, say as much: עֶדֶן, 7-4-700. Between the 7 and the 700, the 4 symbolizes a halt, a door to go through. Man's paradisiac state in Eden is merely a seminal moment. In it, Adam undergoes transformation. He is a seed whose goal is to ripen into the *yod*, the fruit he must become.

This "ripening" seems to be brought about by the loving dialogue that then takes place between God and his Creation. The latter sends forth its vapors of desire that reach toward God, the Father-Husband. God responds by planting the tree in the midst of the garden. The tree extends into the river that flows beyond the boundaries of Eden to reach and fertilize the four worlds: *olam ha-atsilut* (archetypes); *olam ha-beriah* (creation); *olam ha-yetsirah* (formation); *olam ha-asiah* (the perceptible).

As the generative pillar of all Creation, the tree is actually two trees: the Tree of Life and the Tree of Knowledge of Good and Evil. Both planted "in the midst of the garden," these trees are one, according to tradition. This tree, the divine archetype of all Creation, is revealed to us by the Tetragrammaton. Its roots are in *yod*, its trunk is in *vav*. It manifests itself in its fruits, the two *hehs*. So, man, by taking hold of the two *hehs* that he is, is called to journey back to his root, the *yod*, the

unity from which he proceeds and which will become his fruit. Man
cannot eat of this fruit until he himself has become it. From Eden to
Eden, from matrix to matrix, he will beget himself in successive transformations on the way to the יהוה he must become.

He has been forewarned by God about this fundamental law. The
mythical form given to the injunction not to eat the fruit translates the
information Adam received concerning the structures of the different
worlds. He is henceforth aware of their workings: the penalty following
his choice illustrates the effect of these workings. The legalistic form of
the myth presents us, from the start, with a distorted view of the problem of good and evil. Let us try to penetrate the mystery of this Tree,
our archetype.

Translators of the Bible, limited by their dualistic outlook on the
world, speak of the Tree of the Knowledge of Good and Evil, *tov ve-ra*
(טוב ורע).

Are we to understand that evil, thus planted at the heart of the Garden of Eden, is ontological, an integral part of Creation?

Is evil then a reflection of the divine nature? We would have to ask
ourselves this question, were we to accept such premises. Is it not time
to rid men's hearts of this misapprehension?

Furthermore, *tov* (טוב), the "good," is the word encountered in the
very beginning of Genesis, which describes the light on the first day of
Creation. On each of the succeeding days it characterizes an emergence
into light, an achieved perfection. Perfection implies accomplishment,
completion, stabilization, even death. But since cessation annihilates
perfection, this is a logical dead end.

Leaving our rational logic on one side, let us engage in the Logos,
which can only give our consciousness an account of the divine world
through paradox: total immobility and absolute movement coexist in
God. This essential reality is what Chinese tradition expresses in the
symbolism of the wheel, whose central point is both completely im-
mobile and at the same time the source of all movement. It is notably
depicted in the vision of Ezekiel: the four living creatures accompanying

the four wheels of the divine chariot "went upon their four sides: and they turned not when they went" (Ezekiel 1:17).

Total immobility and absolute movement are one and the same reality conveyed in the biblical myth by developing the primordial unity of the Tree, the *yod*, the root of the Tree, into two apparently contradictory terms. Neither excluding each other nor making concessions, they express completely at once what is beyond each of them.

Man, having passed from the 6 to the 7, has thus begun his journey to the divine world, surpassing his own limits. The message leaves no doubt that he can enter into the mystery only by holding together simultaneously and completely both terms of the paradox in a right relation each to the other.[1] In God, Being and Nonbeing coexist. In defining himself as Being (Exodus 3:14), God is already limiting himself (this is the divine *kenōsis* of the Greek Fathers, the *tsimtsum* of the Hebrews), and the path to knowledge can only go beyond this definition by affirming equally forcefully its opposite, that is, Nonbeing.

In this perspective, the "good" and what we conventionally call the "evil" of the Tree are one, like two poles of a same inexpressible reality.

ורע, *ve-ra*, as the opposite of good, of perfection, of stabilization, does not have the meaning translators have given it, but implies the reality of a tremendous dynamic, a perpetual setting out toward this perfection, which paradoxically is already there.

In the biblical account, the word *ra* (רע) is prefixed with the letter *vav* (ו, the conjunction "and"), which turns it into a new word *ve-ra* (ורע). The letter *ayin* (ע) is always in a dialectical relation with the letter *alef* (א), a relation of darkness and light, because man can only go toward the light of the *alef* by going toward the "source" of his being, the *ayin*. The tension between these two energies creates the powerful active growth of the Tree.

If this growth has been achieved, the *alef* (א) will replace the *ayin* (ע) in the word ורע, which thus becomes ורא. These three letters spell the word "light" (אור, *aor*). The word *ve-ra* (ורע), so-called "evil," may accordingly be translated as "not-yet-light."

The balance of Creation as a living entity is only sustained because of the tension between these two realities, which, in the deepest sense, are one and the same: the light, *tov* (טוב), and what is not yet light, *ra* (רע): perfection and incompletion, the accomplished and the unaccomplished, harmony and confusion, etc.

A full cosmic syntropy is present, which can be verified by physics. This scientific discipline is undergoing its "7" with the paradigm shift brought about by Einstein's theory of relativity. Another physicist, O. Costa de Beauregard, said of this theory that it could be called "the theory of the Absolute veiled by appearances" (delivered in a private lecture in 1969).

These appearances—light and not-yet-light, the perfect and the not-yet-perfect, etc.—form the duality of the manifested realm. Anyone unaware of the unity that overlies them cannot apprehend these appearances except through the immediate opposition they express, or the split they give rise to.

Unless someone has lived through an experience, however limited, of going beyond the paradox toward the kernel that holds together its two poles, he cannot overcome this apparent dichotomy.

These two poles are constituent parts of the Adam created "male and female" (Genesis 1:27). He who is "male"—*zakhor* (זכר)—is he who "remembers" (the same word in Hebrew) his "female"— *neqevah* (נקבה)—his reserve of energy, a "container" that harbors the power of the Name. In this respect, whoever remembers his unaccomplished feminine side, and embarks on the journey to conquer his Name, is "male." That is the fundamental vocation of every Adam, be he physically man or woman. The Adam and his feminine are in the same dialectic pattern as *tov ve-ra*. Thus, our feminine side, our "shadow," harbors the secret of our Name. (The "rib" is in fact the "side," *tsela*, עלע, in Hebrew, the "dark" side, to be exact, from the root *tsel*, על. The letter ע intensifies the connotation of "darkness.")

The fruit of the Tree of Knowledge of duality is the knowledge of unity regained, the *yod* of the Divine Name הוֹה. When Adam eats the fruit before becoming the fruit (before the work on הוה, which entails a marriage of love with his feminine side), knowing that he is double in nature to begin with ("and they were both naked, the man and his wife, and were not ashamed," Genesis 2:25), he is under the illusion of having acquired unity, the illusion of having won his way to *yod*: "Behold, the man is become *as one*" (Genesis 3:22).[2] The illusion is complete. Believing himself to be One, Adam no longer aims to win that unity and therefore cannot attain it.

The exit from Eden, the putting on of "coats of skins," are protective measures, not punishments. They enable man to forget and leave behind the illusion that makes him sterile, so that taking up again the nuptial path, the path of fruitfulness, he justly wins back the *yod* of הוֹה.

What is this "coat of skin" with which God clothes Adam (Genesis 3:21)? The word "coat of skin"—*aor* (עוֹר)—is none other than the word *ve-ra* (ורע), non-light, if we transpose the order of the letters. We see how the "non-light"—*ve-ra* (ורע)—and the "coat of skin"—*aor* (עוֹר)—are connected by the same power! In other words, man is identified with "non-light."

If pronounced "*iver*," this same word (עוֹר) means "blind." Man, deprived of the *yod*—withdrawn since it is the very object of his illusion and identified only with הוה—is blind. He no longer knows his own profound reality. He can no longer name the energies that make him what he is, the "animals" that are part of his ontological structure. He is thus confused once again with his feminine, with his energy potential, which at the outset is animal in nature.

His "skin" is his opaqueness to any genuine consciousness. The two ה from the archetype הוֹה, deprived of the *yod* that unites them by the root, are left to wander by themselves. Man's energies are left to wander. They are checked in each of us by moral laws or strict observances, while waiting to be governed once more by the *yod*.

On the human level, the *vav* (ו), man, a conjunction of opposite poles, a rapport of love, becomes a rapport of power, and the strong crush the weak. Civic, social, and international laws place checks on this anarchy until the *yod* gives back the meaning of all things.

Man, existentially placed in the animal world, coated with his skin, deprived of the consciousness of his pole of "light," can only exist (*ex-esse*: "outside of being") and makes his way toward death. But opened again to his consciousness, moving toward this pole, set to win the coat of light, he enters into Being and embraces life.

The deathward movement will cease as soon as man redirects his desire toward the Father who made him and returns toward the *yod*, the 10, assuming the 7. Then he will exchange his coat of skin for the coat of light, which alone is authentically his.

CHAPTER 4

From the Tree of Life
to the Sefirotic Tree

HOW DID THE TREE OF LIFE COME TO BE CONTEMPLATED BY Jewish mystics in the form of the Sefirotic Tree?

Historically, this Tree is described for the first time in the *Sefer Yetsirah*, or Book of Formation. This and the *Sefer ha-Zohar*, or Book of Splendor, are the two most important texts for the esoteric doctrine of Judaism. Both have been preserved to this day. Their authors are unknown, but Hebrew tradition reports that they contain the "mysteries hidden since the dawn of time, mysteries that were transmitted from Moses to Joshua and from him to the Elders, the Prophets and to all those linked to this initiatory chain from then to now."[1] For a long time, this tradition was transmitted orally. When the scribe Ezra edited the Torah, it was known within the rabbinical college that these texts contained a mysterious meaning, entrusted only to a few initiates and hitherto transmitted only orally, in secret. The contents of this knowledge are enshrined in the Kabbalah, its root, *qabel*, meaning "to receive," "to contain." The *qab* is a measure of capacity. Over time, the word *Kabbalah* came to mean the container rather than the contents and was used to designate the tradition itself.

This tradition was therefore an oral teaching: the first written accounts of it date back to the thirteenth century, a period when numerous foreign contributions came to enrich—or possibly tarnish—the original data. What can we authentically retain from these writings?

It seems undeniable that, as they stand, these two books, the *Sefer ha-Zohar* and the *Sefer Yetsirah*, are an authoritative oral Torah. They are revered alongside the holy books of the written Torah.

If, however, we leave aside the historical perspective, there is another way by which we can recognize the authenticity of the Sefirotic Tree. I have myself experienced this way. And this experience enables me to testify to its unimaginable strength and power.

When the prophet—who does not predict the future, as is commonly believed, but sees events of an archetypal order—sees the "heavens open" (Ezekiel 1:1, Revelation 4:1, etc.), he can only convey this vision of the Splendor of Splendors through a desperately dry and elliptical outline compared to what he was given to experience. This outline is what remains of his vision, like the limp rubber of a deflated balloon that once rose in the sky, shiny, wholly light and colorful. It can be a simple geometrical figure. From it, the child in us painstakingly tries to reconstitute "the object," raising himself to the finest, highest point of his being, hoping to recapture what escapes him entirely.

The child takes a long time to understand that what he is left with is the symbol, which is the promise of the archetype merely glimpsed, the seed of the fruit, whose journey from seed to fruit he himself must make during this lifetime.

Might the Sefirotic Tree be a seed? Its first fruits will tell. My own appreciation of the justness and accuracy of this profile has certainly led me to write this book. Yet, though accurate, I also know what formidable power is contained in the Tree guarded by the Two-Edged Sword; it gives life to him who has become the sword, but death to him who cannot enter into its justice.

> Thus saith the Lord; Say, A sword, a sword
> is sharpened, and also furbished:
> It is sharpened to make a sore slaughter;
> it is furbished that it may glitter.
>
> (Ezekiel 21:9–10)

Indeed humanity, and each man in particular, must one day face up to it. That is what Judgment is about.

* * *

A *sefirah* (plural *sefirot*) is a receptacle: *sefer* is the "book" containing the tradition.

The ten sefirot of the Tree, reproduced in the next drawing (page 27), express ten Divine Energies, ten divine aspects, ten archetypes. They are not meant to limit the divine world, or enclose it in this number 10, but to translate through it its absolute unity and infinite diversity. Each sefirah receives the full measure of the Uncreated Light, but expresses it in its own way.

The first divine aspect to reveal itself is Keter, the Crown or summit of the Tree. But Hebrew Tradition teaches us that higher than Keter are *Ain Sof Aor*, meaning "infinite Light," then *Ain Sof*, meaning "without end, infinite," and at last *Ain*,[2] meaning "nothing" or the "point that is above." These three divine aspects, not inscribed on the Tree, express the Unknowable, the Unnameable who will nevertheless make himself known, and let himself be named, through the ten sefirot. All come from Keter, the very first sefirah, and unfold down to Malkhut, the last, which receives all their energies before they are taken back into Keter. According to tradition, this unfolding of the sefirotic unity is accomplished within three triads that flow into their common receptacle, Malkhut.

The first triad, composed of Keter, Hokhmah, Binah (Crown, Wisdom, Understanding), is the triad of divine transcendence.

The second triad, Hesed, Din, Tiferet (Grace, Justice, Beauty), expresses the plane of the principles of Creation, that is, the plane of law.

The third triad, Netsah, Hod, Yesod (Power, Majesty, Foundation), is Creation brought into being.

Malkhut (Kingdom) is Creation itself, the Divine Immanence. It is complete receptivity to God. In this sense, it is the Mother "below."

I cannot delve deeper here into the theological aspects of the mysteries hidden behind the Divine Energies. I shall only say what is essential to understand this study on the level of anthropology. But enough has already been said for the reader not to be astonished by what I now say: theology and anthropology are but two sides of the same coin, two inseparable facets of the same Reality. In the context of what has been presented above as a direct consequence of the Fall, to present these two sciences as being foreign to one another leads down a path that can only end in death. To grasp them both in their correct relationship constitutes the path to Life. This is the path I am attempting to take, and it is therefore essential that I consider, albeit briefly, the plane of the archetypes.

In Keter (the Crown), God remains hidden in his transcendence, and yet he crosses from Nonbeing into Being. He is the One without the two, known only to himself, containing the entire multiplicity yet without Unity being impaired.

In Hokhmah (Wisdom), God contemplates himself. Hokhmah is divine thought, which knows the unmanifest world. Wisdom is also called "Supreme Father."

Binah (Understanding) is the divine mirror that knows the Manifestation. Understanding is called "Supreme Mother."

These first three sefirot, united without confusion, distinct without separation, are called the Greater Countenance. The following seven, or the seven sefirot of construction, are called the Lesser Countenance. They are the archetypes of Creation on which the seven days of Genesis are structured. They comprise two triads, which are inverted compared to the first and which end in Malkhut.

The first energy that appears on the Lesser Countenance is Ḥesed (Mercy, Grace, Illumination), life that gives itself and can only give itself within the confines of the informal form expressed by Din (Justice, Justness, Rigor).

Ḥesed (Mercy) is the reflection of Wisdom; and Din (Rigor) is the reflection of Understanding. Both flow into Tiferet (Beauty), Divine Heart, the center of all divine harmonies. Fruitfulness is inscribed in

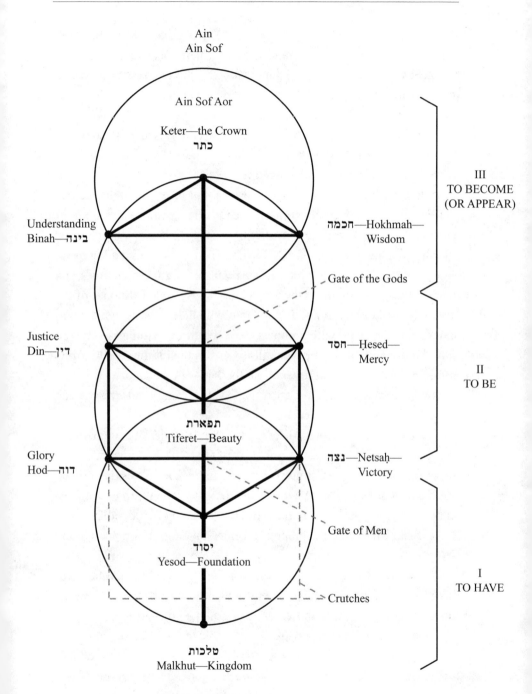

The Sefirotic Tree

Tiferet, which is the reflection of Keter. Divine Love, fruitful and creative, unfolds itself in Rigor and Mercy, which are paradoxically the
same. This is expressed in our fallen state by the two separate aspects
of the biblical God, "slow to anger, and plenteous in mercy" (Psalm
103:8). After that, Tiferet, in turn, extends into Netsaḥ and Hod.

Netsaḥ, itself a reflection of Hokhmah and Ḥesed (Wisdom and
Mercy), is Victorious Power, out of which comes Hod (Glory), Divine
Majesty, a reflection of Understanding and of Rigor.

Both give birth to Yesod (Foundation), the base, an unchangeable
equilibrium, as well as the eternally creative act. Yesod, a reflection of
Keter and Tiferet, is the very fertility of the realms contained in the last
sefirah, Malkhut, the Kingdom, which receives all the Divine Energies.

Malkhut, the junction and turning point linking these energies and
their cosmic emanations, is the Great Vessel, also called "Spouse of the
Divine King," or "Virgin of Israel," into which descend Keter, Tiferet,
and Yesod. Thus everything comes from Keter, everything is received
in Malkhut and returns to Keter. All is One, in the infinite wealth of its
unfolding. All is merciful diversity in the Rigor of the One.

Keter and Malkhut are also called the King and the Queen
respectively.

Three other triads can be discerned in the Sefirotic Tree, in the form
of columns. One is called "the right arm of God." This triad contains all
the sefirot of the right column: Wisdom, Mercy, and Victorious Power.
It is the arm of Mercy, archetype of the male, which in turn is completed by the archetype of the female, or "the left arm of God," the arm of
Rigor, that is, the column containing Understanding, Rigor, and Divine
Glory.

The Middle Column contains Crown, Beauty, and Foundation, with
the Crown and the Kingdom (Keter and Malkhut, King and Queen)
functioning as one. It is the column of balance, of harmony, through
which the Divine Unity expresses itself in the duality of Creation.

Are not these columns essentially the threefold axis of the
Sword-Tetragrammaton? The two side columns are its double edges,

the two *hehs*. The Middle Column is the blade, the *vav*. The *yod*, the sword's pommel, is inscribed in the Tree's superior triad, clearly distinguished from the others.

In this view, the Sefirotic Tree is the divine name יהוה, or הוֹה, the Tetragrammaton, in a scale symbolically reduced to ten energies expressing Unity at the same time as the infinite diversity of the divine harmonies.

Let us pause here. To elaborate further on these Divine Energies, and their method of revelation, would in effect imprison each one in a concept that would destroy it. These energies reveal themselves according to a form of knowledge that can only be experienced personally. Thus, it is up to each of us to go further, and to allow ourselves to be led by new guides.

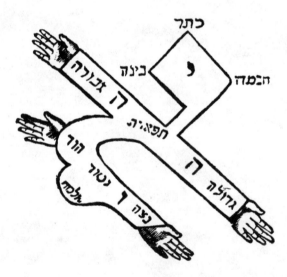

The Alef. The Sefirotic Tree is entirely contained in the divine Tetragrammaton, itself entirely contained in the *alef.* (Engraving taken from *Oedipus Aegyptiacus*, Athanasius Kircher, Rome, 1652.)

CHAPTER 5

From the Sefirotic Tree to the Pattern of the Body

ON THE OTHER HAND, TO SPEAK ABOUT THESE DIVINE ENERGIES, these archetypes, and to consider their reflections in the perceptible world is a matter of urgency.

Man's present-day state of consciousness means that he sees all elements of the perceptible world bereft of their primeval forms (*archai*), and hence either in confusion or in separation.

Anarchists do well to refuse society's false *archaí*. We could even maintain that their vision is the more accurate, given that the world is called to reinstate its true archetypes. Only then will they truly be "an-archists." (Their dream of *le grand soir* is none other than a dim foreshadowing of the heavenly Jerusalem.) As in the myth of Eden, our modern anarchists are in too much of a hurry. "Man's impatience has lost him paradise," said Kafka; "being lazy, he doesn't go back." For laziness leaves us in mortal ignorance. Instead of going back, we build with our own hands a labyrinth from which we need to free ourselves. We shall study the myth of the labyrinth and see that it is by Knowledge alone—in the nonintellectual sense we have already given that word (chapter 1, pages 4–5)—that man can find his way out.

Tibetans give such importance to the labyrinth that it is central to one of the basic meditations of monks. They draw a labyrinth (a mandala)—sometimes they even build it in space—and then begin to meditate. The object is to seek the gate, or rather be found by it. Like those monks poring over their mandalas, we question the Tree in order to be found and to discover within us this "below which resembles that which is above, to accomplish the miracle of Oneness."

Man's Body, Image of the Divine Body

Is there anything more familiar to us here below and yet more enigmatic than man's body? Is there anything more concrete, and yet more mysterious? Is there anything more complex, and yet perfectly knit together in fundamental unity?

For a thousand years, Western civilization was subject to what we know as Scholastic thought, which puts forth a dualistic and rationalistic vision of the universe. Since Augustine of Hippo (in the fourth century AD), who deeply influenced Western thought with the Manichaeism in which he was steeped, we have gradually set up good and evil as absolute values. So the Westerner, rooted in the idea that "man is a rational animal composed of soul and body" (from the traditional catechism of the diocese of Paris), rapidly came to identify evil with the body and good with the soul.

Have we not learned, over generations, to despise the body, even to maltreat it? Has our spirituality not been fed from early childhood by an emphasis on pain and suffering? Haven't we been shown that what pertains to the flesh—meaning the union of two bodies—is akin to the sin of all sins, equating "carnal knowledge" with "original sin"? We should note that the latter expression was originally coined by none other than Augustine of Hippo.

Until recently, Western thought had set up an unbridgeable divide between body and soul (adding to the confusion caused by the concept of soul). On one side, there is the grubby alleyway of the sinful body, on the other, the garden of the soul.

Psychology, a science still in its infancy, denouncing this taboo, countered the error, without, however, managing to introduce the truth.

Psychology remains a victim of its own contradictions. When one considers the Absolute—symbolized by the Divine Name *yod-heh-vav-heh*, יהוה—the two *hehs* find their true meaning only when they partake in the *yod* uniting them. With man, who reflects the Absolute, it is similar: the soma (body) and the psyche (soul) really *are* only when they participate in a third dimension of being. If this does not happen, body and psyche *exist*, but have no genuine being, and the body in particular exists only for the sake of better functioning for survival.

In the first case, the body is one element of a ternary (spirit-soul-body) called to find the harmony that enables the world above, the pure Truth, to be conveyed and shown. In the second, the body is alone, a slave to existence, and in the end is crushed by it.

For example: in the first case, man practices the art of yoga to cultivate a harmonious synthesis of the ternary as well as the link (which is the meaning of the word *yoga*) between this ternary and the world above.

In the second, man does gymnastics in order to oil the wheels of his machine—his body—which must operate in the most economical and efficient way.

What I have just said is a caricature, but its aim is to set out with some force the fundamentally opposed options open to man. Either the body is fully *lived*, and, as such, is an image of the Divine Body, tending to identify with it; or it is simply *maintained*, in which case it becomes identified with the commonplace nature of the world. There are those who "are their body" and those who "have a body," to quote from Karlfried Graf von Dürckheim's in-depth analysis.[1]

It is important here to insist on the phenomenon of *identification* just mentioned. It is simply a projection, in the mathematical sense, of the ontological law of image and likeness.

In the biblical myth, man "created in God's image" lives close to God and is called upon to grow into his likeness. Cut off from God, man lives close to the perceptible world, which he experiences through his senses. From now on this is natural for him, whereas living close to his

inner or spiritual world only becomes natural if he reaches the essential level of his being, in his approach to Knowledge as earlier defined
(chapter 1, page 6).

Man's Inner and Outer Worlds

Let us clarify these concepts of inner and outer worlds. They are distinct
from each other, but not separate. In chapter 1 (page 2), I have already
put forward the fundamental tenets of my work: on the one hand, man
within the cosmos, and on the other, the cosmos within man.

Man within the cosmos immediately entails the relational aspect of
life: the sense that, in his body and his psyche, man has of himself,
of other beings, of events and things; and then the communication he
establishes both with himself and with others. From these relationships
stems the life of thought, which may be apparent emotionally and/or
intellectually.

What I call here the inner world is not the world of thought, however
hidden it may be. Thought is still conditioned by the outward aspect of
things. Ultimately, these "things" belong to all dimensions, right down
to the one that reaches the very heart, the core, the spirit. At that point
these things are no longer simply in relation, but in communication, in
communion with the "kernel" of the one who has become capable of
experiencing them. This is what makes up the inner world of man. In
man, the heart of the cosmos finds its image, its resonance. The life of
thought that arises from this interior apprehension is part of the inner
world. We see thus that thought belongs to what is interior and to what is
exterior to man, according to whether it is fed by direct contact with the
psychophysical worlds, or by indirect contact with the spiritual world.

In the first case, the spiritual world remains below the threshold of
consciousness. The spiritual being is asleep. The direction of the identification is from the body and psyche to the outer world that sustains
them. It is common knowledge how, physically, man identifies with the

place he lives in. For example, a European who has settled in China will gradually come to look Chinese. There can be astonishing resemblances between those who live together, even between people and their pets.

As for the resounding impact of the body on the psyche, or the latter on the body, it is so well-documented that it now has become a new medical science: that of psychosomatic disorders. Generally, children model themselves body and soul by direct identification with their parents. Hence the important role played by the parent, not so much in doing but in *being*.

In the second case, man enters the spiritual world. His psyche and physical body are nurtured by it. The former is infused with spiritual content; the latter gradually identifies with the very substance of this content. The concrete fruits of the mystical experience prove it: certain Western Christian mystics, from a life of contemplating Christ suffering and dying on the cross, receive the stigmata. They carry the marks of the very wounds contemplated in the Person of Christ. Such was the experience of Francis of Assisi, Teresa of Avila, and, in more recent times, of Therese Neumann, Padre Pio, and many others.

Many have analyzed this phenomenon, which is foreign to other traditions, even to the Eastern Orthodox Christian tradition. The object contemplated by Orthodox Christian mystics is the icon of Christ in glory, the Risen Christ who has overcome death and clothed cosmic man with his body of light. Thus in this context, it is more common to come across phenomena of transfiguration. Nikolai Motovilov, a disciple of the Russian saint Seraphim of Sarov, describes at one point how his master enveloped him in the light that his body had become.

At this level, matter reverts to pure energy. Potentially, matter already is energy and gives out that on which it feeds. According to man's degree of participation in his divine being, his body, at various degrees, radiates the energy of the world above. Viewed thus, the human body seems to be our most concrete resource for reflecting the divine world. Is this not its fundamental purpose?

A difficult question!

If this suggestion is correct, the human body must reflect the Divine Body. It must be built according to the ontological blueprint of the divine structures; it must match the diagrams of the Sword-Tetragrammaton and the Sefirotic Tree. However, I must admit I reached this conclusion from the opposite direction, for it was by contemplating the Sefirotic Tree that I saw one day the Body of Man.

I was out walking one afternoon and suddenly saw a mental diagram. I was so violently shaken that I was sure I was on a royal path, a path of Truth. The street lit up. This vision was later confirmed by the same Kabbalistic tradition that says that the Adam, "the Man below" (as opposed to Elohim, the "Man above") corresponds in his bodily shape to the realms whose archetype is the Sefirotic Tree. But this was not information from an outside source; it was a matter of personal experience.

I was struck then no less forcibly by a conviction: we can verify the authenticity of the Tree by the way it matches the human body. In other words, if the body is not the Sefirotic Tree, the Tree is insignificant.

Today I can assert that the Tree is the diagram of the construction of the world and that, in its image, the human body is a diagram of how we are to become. The body is at once our tool, our laboratory, and our work, in order to enter into our true stature, which is divine.

The Structure of the Body
according to the Sefirotic Tree

The pattern of the body, imaging the "form of יהוה" (Numbers 12:8), appears to be essentially composed of three vertical axes. The spinal column, the central pillar or Middle Column, corresponds to the path Keter-Malkhut, which links the Crown to the Kingdom, the head to the feet. And both sides of the body, the lateral pillars, correspond respectively to the pillar of Rigor on the left and Mercy on the right. (See the reversal from right to left in relation to the divine archetype, in chapter 6.)

Three triangles are set on these vertical structures: the top triangle corresponds to the head; the first inverted triangle corresponds to the area of the heart and lungs; and the second inverted triangle corresponds to the urogenital plexus (lower abdomen and pubic area). These two inverted triangles appear as two heads pointing downward, and we can observe in men the presence of hair at the level of the epigastrium and of the pubic area, at the bottom respectively of the two inverted triangles. Other analogies come to light, which we shall look at later.

In the divine pattern, the two lateral pillars are the unfolding of duality arising from the original Unity. The divine manifests his Unity by limiting himself in two contradictory or paradoxical ways. Man can only reach the divine by going beyond the contradiction. God appears to us thus as principle of changelessness, absolute immobility, and at the same time the source of all movement. So man, "by grasping together in their just relationship these two paradoxical aspects,"[2] experiences their overarching unity and thus the divine.

On the level of creation, the principle of Immobility is manifest as form and structure: Rigor and Justice of the place and form of each element of the perceptible world. It is the uncompromising receptacle רע, ra. The feminine principle, in essence, is form, receptivity, and strength in abeyance. On the same level, the divine principle of movement, expressed in the fertilizing ray of Grace, or Mercy, is a dynamic force that will penetrate form, drawing from it the energy needed to structure new fields of light, טוב, tov. This is the dynamic and fertilizing force of the masculine.

The correct relationship uniting these opposing poles is displayed in the central pillar, the Middle Column of the Divine Pattern. It is the path of the One toward the Many. On the plane of creation it is the path of the Many toward the One.

The vertical structures of the human body are put together in the same way. Its balance is maintained in the axis of the spinal column through the tension spanning the opposite poles, the complementary and paradoxical aspects of its right and left sides.

Now the horizontal structures: in the Divine Pattern, the Upper Triangle reveals the very essence of Divinity, his transcendence and his principle, in Keter (the Crown), Hokhmah (Wisdom), and Binah (Understanding).

Likewise, on the level of the body, the head is the seat of the noblest human faculties. It symbolizes the divine in man and is thus a receptacle for the divine. It is in its image and has its power. The head is shaped like an egg. As such, it is the matrix of the deified human being, who must be born to perfect divine life, achieved in the return to the One, in the *yod* of the Sword-Tetragrammaton (the 10 in the scale going from 6 to 10).

Hindu iconography reveals this in its symbolism of the lotus flower blossoming at the crest of the skull. Other traditions use horns, rooted in the same crest, rising in half-moon shape. This is not foreign to Christian iconography, which sometimes presents Christ in glory with horns that become a crown.

The birth "above" is so represented. But it is also through this channel (the horn of plenty) that the Divine World descends within man. At every stage, there is a meeting between the world above and the world below, between the *mi* and the *ma*.

The first inverted triangle, when compared to the Upper Triangle, corresponds, on a divine level, to the triad Ḥesed-Din-Tiferet (Grace-Justice-Beauty). This triad contains the mystery of laws, laws that are ontological and hence liberating. On the level of the body, this first inverted triangle, reflecting the head, corresponds to the area of the heart and lungs. It is the seat of the spiritual being and the matrix of the divine being. Only a man moved by Spirit can enter into knowledge of the ontological laws.

Between these two triangles is the neck. When the biblical God is irritated by his "stiff-necked people," he is emphasizing the breach in

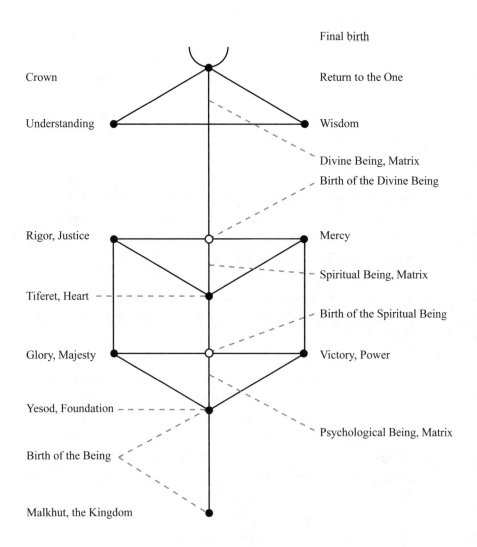

Stages of Being on the Sefirotic Tree

communication between heart and head. Tiferet (Heart, Beauty) can no longer reflect the summit of the triangle: Keter, the Crown. The heart is no longer creative Divine Love. Bereft of this communication, the empty heart turns to the second inverted triangle and becomes the tool of sentimental affect, a prey to the passions that bind it to the world of duality and tear it apart. As long as the heart reflects the Upper Triangle, beyond duality, it will master its affect. But when it feeds on its affect it becomes enslaved to it. This is confirmed by the break, on the level of the Sword-Tetragrammaton, between the *yod*, the divine, and the *vav*, man. Without his head, incapable of becoming God, man conjures up a false head, with all the deceptive values that he deifies. He will have to get rid of these false heads and be cleansed of these highly relative, erroneous values, represented by the understandings and wisdoms of these "masks." I shall discuss this later, when we consider the symbolism of decapitation (with John the Baptist and St. Denis in particular), which frequently occurs in dreams.

On the other hand, when "God goes forth *at the head* of his people, marching in the wilderness" (Psalm 68:7; emphasis added), the people of Israel truly embody the whole of humanity advancing toward deification.

When Moses comes down the mountain, where he has received the Tables of the Law for the first time, he finds a "stiff-necked people," which has replaced its real head with the head of a "molten calf" (Exodus 32:4). Moses then breaks the tables.

The symbolism is clear. Moses returns to a people caught up in the second, Lower Triangle, incapable of knowing and experiencing the ontological laws. These were to be replaced, on a lower level, by laws that govern the Jewish people to this day .

These laws of Moses are not only the moral laws of society, but a detailed codification of the smallest aspects of everyday life, all of which symbolize and signify the ontological laws. And, later, when Christ invited his people to pass from the signifier to the signified, from the Law to the archetype, Israel was still not ready to follow him. And, make no mistake about it, many of those who call themselves Christians are similarly enslaved to the Law in its reassuring and moralizing shape. Christianity is no moral code, but a tremendous liberation, giving access to consciousness of the ontological laws.

The second inverted triangle (the urogenital area) is a more distant reflection of the Upper Triangle. It is the seat of the psyche and a matrix for the spiritual being. It is the night of ignorance. But if it feeds on the Above, on the Divine World mirrored in the first triangle, as we have just seen, it will at length give birth to the spiritual being. If it feeds solely on what is below, sensual and emotional pleasures, it will keep the "stiff-necked man" wandering in psychosomatic darkness. Death is then the only escape; the matrix will not bear its fruit; there will be a sort of spiritual abortion.

The child inside the mother, surrounded by the dark waters of her womb, will be born to the physical world (Malkhut, the Kingdom) through the opening of the *cervix uteri*. The cervix (neck) of the uterus is none other than the lower counterpart of the neck supporting the head, which opens above "into a lotus flower" when giving birth to the deified being who has returned to the One.

On this road of development, of return, there are three stages whose overtones resonate on the cosmic plane:

1. Malkhut, the Kingdom (here the feet, the concrete bodily level, physical "feeling"), corresponds to the earth.
2. Yesod, the Foundation (here the sexual organs, the level of psyche), corresponds to the moon, symbol of night, whose crescent is the reflection below of the symbolic horns of the deified being above. (This same symbol is used by unconscious humanity to mean cuckoldry!)
3. Tiferet, Heart-Beauty (here the solar plexus, the spiritual plane), corresponds to the sun.

Our solar system, shaped (like all the others) in the image of the universal archetype, certainly has its Upper Triangle from which it takes its energy, energy that is transmitted to Yesod, then Malkhut—to the moon, then the earth. However, on the bodily level, observing the way we live, we recognize that it is not our spiritual being, our sun, that nourishes psychophysical being, but rather our sensations (the earth) and our emotions (the moon). They rule the roost in our solar plexus. If we experience joy, spring arrives and our heart is ready to dance. With sorrow, it rains, it is cold, and physically or psychologically we have "the blues." Joy can choke at the level of the chest, but sorrow contracts the stomach, sometimes inducing vomiting, or even a liver disorder such as jaundice. The whole of the solar plexus is overrun with emotion, whatever the source, and the heartbeat expresses it accordingly.

In other words, man is upside down. Not being nourished from above, his solar plexus is subservient to the information received from below. Psychiatric and psychosomatic medicine is based on this state of affairs. Instead of attempting to reverse it, it would rather give these values below the power of absolutes, capable of replacing the Absolute above. Thus Freudians are rightly engaged in freeing man from the constricting moral views linked with sexuality in the West. However, their work is more questionable when it sets up the latter as the touchstone for the highest human motivations.

According to our pattern, the best medicine would be to set the patient on an upright path. But such an attitude, were it adopted by medical science, would mean recognizing the reality of the spiritual level in man, his essential being, his divine calling. If medical science did share this view, our doctors would undoubtedly become the priests they formerly were, in the sense of teachers and masters, rather than moral judges or frustrated competitors with leaders of political opinion, as they are at present in the Western world.

Having effectively brought about a reversal (in the first instance within themselves), such teachers could enable others to stop their involutionary process and thus guide them into an evolutionary one. Any other type of medicine leads either to a dead end or to temporary solutions, necessary in the short term, but sooner or later calling for something more permanent.

* * *

The pattern of the body may also be considered a structure, a building.

From Malkhut to the path joining Hod and Netsaḥ, that is to say from the feet up to the level of the hips and kidneys, we can see a first floor. And from this horizontal path to the one higher up, parallel to it, joining Din and Ḥesed (the shoulders) a second floor is defined, consisting of a rectangle outlining the trunk. Finally, the Upper Triangle, the head, forms a third floor.

When we look at man's chronological development from birth to death, the first floor mirrors childhood; the second, adulthood; at the third, the head is determined by the new fields of consciousness that open up to man during the course of these different ages. The head is thus called to change until it is realized in the *yod* of the Sword-Tetragrammaton and receives the Crown.

On the first floor, which I call the stage of *Having*, the child does little but acquire: he acquires the knowledge of the world around him. He apprehends it through his senses, then through the development of his intellect, which is the extension of his senses. He studies it in greater depth, element by element, in time and space. He discerns the laws connecting the values that he little by little discovers. He acquires his bodily height, which will eventually stabilize around the age of twenty-one. Gradually he acquires psychological balance. Puberty and all the forces that come with it invade—sometimes assault—the child. In the face of such an onslaught, a young person cannot grow harmoniously, or establish a solid spinal column, physiologically or psychologically, without the framework of a set of right and safe values.

Of course, on this level values are just only inasmuch as they prolong and reflect the ontological, absolute, and essential values (see the dotted lines on the diagram), that is, the vertical structures of the second level. The child is not yet able to discover these vertical values, still less live by them. They will only be touched upon when man reaches his second floor, the dimension I call *Being*.

Parents are supposed to have reached it. Still, they are only parents insofar as they are genuinely an extension of the diagram's two vertical pillars, the masculine and the feminine, the duality returning to the One, from which, ontologically, they proceed.

The child matures in harmony between his mother and his father, insofar as these two reflect the One. Between the moral laws he needs to help him choose between what is good and what is bad, the future adult progresses toward his own structure. Parents and moral values, or others acting *in loco parentis* at different levels—civic and religious authorities for example—appear in the diagram as crutches that the child will soon discard, unless he permanently makes them his own legs. In this case he will never become an adult.

Generally, the child starts to question the validity of his crutches toward the age of puberty (on the level of Yesod, where two paths already link him directly to Hod and Netsaḥ, the roots of his future ontological structures). He then eagerly draws on those structures. Parents, meanwhile, must continue to be there, while taking care to withdraw gradually, in order to not encumber or perhaps even obstruct these two paths.

Parents who do not know how to let go are among those who will stay in a psychosomatic haze all their lives. They can only sustain themselves at the level of the Lower Triangle. With few exceptions, adolescents brought up by such parents are unable to reach the second level. Their parents will have kept them in the labyrinth they built for themselves, as Daedalus imprisoned his son Icarus (see chapter 10, page 150).

The parents' ascendancy is not the only reason young people become bogged down at this lower level. Any form of overprotection that reinforces the "crutches" is a barrier, preventing the spinal column—the only support needed for man to shift upward to a higher level—from forming properly.

Let us not delude ourselves: by offering all sorts of artificial security measures, our civilization is creating a world of cripples. Man, overprotected, remains under age. He becomes a cripple living in fear that one of his crutches will fall. He clings to them, giving them the value and power that rightly belongs to the spinal column. Unfortunately this type of man is all too common—only a minority shift upward to the higher level. To compensate for his state of dependency, this type of individual generally adopts an attitude that is seemingly strong but is subject to a merely conventional set of ethics.

Such an individual will, at the level of the head, show the mask of "appearance." This takes the place of the workshop where new forms of understanding and wisdom are fashioned for the evolving being. Such masks are made:

From the different roles with which the infantile man identifies (parental, professional, political, even ecclesiastical functions);

From compensations for lack, suffering, or psychological difficulties; or

More subtly, from ideologies to which he clings, confusing his identity, and from the roles he plays to appease his conscience.

But none of these result in a higher level. Man still lingers in the humdrum. Consciousness, in the luminous sense of the word (טוב, *tov*), does not come into being. Man remains submerged by רע, *ra*.

The second level to which the body pattern invites man to rise is formed by the rectangle Hod-Netsah-Din-Hesed. I call it the level of Being. Why?

This is the level where each of us is truly born. At this level, man develops his essential life, and, starting from Tiferet, a reflection of Keter, he enters into the experience of his ontological dimension.

On the first level man *exists*. On the second level, he *is*. By its very form (rectangular), the second level is characterized as a pause, a time of trial. The number 4 is a symbol of stability: four legs give balance to any solid shape; four walls provide the structure for a house. Beyond these practical examples, the value of four brings the idea of an enclosed, secret, and concealed place. Whoever stops there will undergo a trial.

All traditions point to this notion of trial linked with the number 4: the practice of quarantine is one example descended from the ontological law. Both in ancient Egypt and in the Judeo-Christian world, the forty days following a death indicate a passage that is difficult to cross.

The sacred tradition of ancient Egypt relates that Pharaoh, forty days after his own death, had to face a bull before being admitted into the dwelling place of the gods. The kings of France were never buried before the fortieth day following their death.

Our sacred texts say that the Hebrew people spent forty years in the desert after they came out of Egypt. Christ fasts for forty days in the desert after his baptism. Similarly, forty days of fasting prepare Christians for the coming of Easter, whose Hebrew equivalent (Passover, or Pesach) means "passage." In these same Christian mysteries, Ascension Day marks the fortieth day after Easter. In the mother's womb, the baby grows for seven times forty days. Many examples from other traditions would confirm this notion of a sojourn in a place of trial before a final passage, celebrated as a feast.

The rectangle, then, appears as a matrix, unless it becomes a tomb for those who do not know the true laws, or who simply do not have hope.

The law that governs this trial is inscribed in the Hebrew word for 4. This word, *dalet*, means "door." In this number symbolizing a trial, a matrix, a closed quarter from which no escape seems possible, the notion of a door is present: every matrix is a door. Every trial brings with it an outcome going beyond what was. The Hebrew word *dalet* is spelled דלת: *dalet, lamed, tav*, their numerical values being 4-30-400. The door is constructed as an opening framed by two 4s, two pillars, so to speak, allowing 30, a symbol of movement, of life, to pass between them. The 4 appears in its profound and paradoxical meaning as both a halt and a crossing.

Unfortunately, two opposing tendencies often push ordinary man into mistaken attitudes. One attitude sees in the 4 only the halt, which leads to a resigned frame of mind, unable to fully embrace life. This arrest leads to prison, death. Matter then inevitably becomes a tomb, burying all potential creativity, light, and happiness.

The other sees only the "crossing" aspect, refusing to acknowledge the substantial presence of the two pillars and considering only the movement leading "beyond" to new and promising vistas. I have in mind a widespread tendency amongst adepts of a half-baked Hinduism, which considers this formal, visible, and concrete world—which is, of course, the essential trial—solely as *maya* (illusion).

The 4, in this case the rectangle that constitutes our second level, is accurately perceived by those who fully appreciate the two poles of the trial in their correct relationship: on the one hand, the structures (the physical structures of our world, the psychosomatic structures of man in his coat of skin, and the ontological structures of his deeper being); on the other hand, the dynamics of life requiring the fulfillment of everything, from the seed to the fruit.

Between heaven and earth, man is in tension as if between two poles of a magnet. If he lets go of one of the poles, the "current" dies out. Then either man dissolves in a false spirituality, or he is bogged down in matter. But in neither case does he achieve his higher purpose.

It is essential to reach this level of consciousness as one enters the rectangle at the level of Being, the level of true incarnation. The lower level was only a preparatory step for this one.

The Hebrew language brings another reality to light through the similarity between the words "door" (*dalet*, דלת) and "knowledge" (*daat*, דעת). They are differentiated by only one letter, the middle one. The letter *ayin* (ע) in the word "knowledge" symbolizes the "source" from which man must draw, as well as the new "eye" he must acquire

when progressing on the path of the spiritual marriage. The letter *lamed*
(ל) in the word "door" symbolizes the "guide" on this path.

"He who knows" passes through the "door" between the two letters
dalet (ד) and *tav* (ת). Together these two letters make up the word דת,
which means "law." If man crosses this door without taking the law into
account, without observing it, he is annihilated by the new complex of
energy to which the door gives access. He is thunderstruck by the new
reality he encounters, and his acquired structures cannot sustain it.

So man can only open the door if he is in Knowledge which, again,
is not intellectual knowledge, but something lived.

To leave the first level of existence (Having) in order to penetrate
this new dimension of Being, to go through the "Strait Gate" (Matthew
7:13), traditionally known as the Gate of Men, means leaving ignorance
behind in order to live.

Who can go through this door?

The well-known story of Sleeping Beauty spells it out.

For a hundred years, a princess has been sleeping in a castle, buried
in the midst of a deep forest growing denser every day, year by year,
until it has become impenetrable, choking the dormant life within. The
princess, her dog, her servants, the entire castle, the garden are asleep.
After a hundred years, the son of a neighboring king learns of the existence of this sleeping beauty. His heart is aflame and he decides to go
and awaken her.

One can guess at the kind of adventures encountered by the young
prince while he blazes his way through the forest, penetrating ever deeper in order to get to its (his) heart. After a long ordeal, with innumerable
wounds, the prince, burning with love, comes to press upon the lips of
the princess the kiss that awakens her. She wakes up, and—a detail of
prime importance—the dog, the servants, the household, and the garden
wake up with her. They all awaken. In this little universe, everyone and
everything opens its eyes. What has happened?

The sleeping beauty is Beauty, Tiferet, the sun of being, which only
shines when man has ascended toward it. Man cannot reach it until he

rids himself of this psychological forest, conscious and unconscious, that invades and even smothers his being. He can only undertake this adventure once he is aware of the princess's presence, that is, of his essential, spiritual Being, a reflection of the divine, a promise of the divine, a buried seed, dormant.

Prince Charming, who learns of Beauty's presence, is none other than *informed consciousness*, capable of guiding man, insofar as he is inspired by a correct desire, on the path of this adventure. And man can only live this adventure from the impulse of love, from a dimension of love, a word which, sadly, is too hackneyed nowadays to convey what it should. Only true love enables the prince to pass through the ordeal of the forest. Once the kiss has been given, Being awakens within.

Note that the entire cosmos awakens simultaneously. The household, the dog, the garden are all kingdoms waiting for humanity to wake up so that their own colors may shine. Those who have made the journey can testify that the daily routine, previously experienced in the dullness of repetition, takes on new contours: "Behold, I make all things new" (Revelation 21:5).

I shall come back to this level in more detail. Suffice it to say now that after crossing the Lower Triangle, reaching beyond the ten degrees corresponding to the ten vertebrae (five sacral and five lumbar), perfectly illustrated—as we shall see—by the ten plagues of Egypt (Genesis 7–11), man knocks at the "Strait Gate" called the Gate of Men.

Once through this gate, he ascends the twelve steps of his twelve dorsal vertebrae. This passage into the rectangle—his only true incarnation—is accomplished, in all traditions, through the number 12: whether the twelve months of the year, the twelve labors of Hercules, or the twelve gates leading to the New Jerusalem, foreshadowed by the twelve tribes of Israel and, later, by the twelve apostles of Christ.

During his ascension of the twelve vertebrae, man plows, waters, and cultivates his inner gardens so that they each, gradually, yield all their fruit. When all the fruit is harvested, man will knock at the upper door of the rectangle, called the Gate of the Gods.

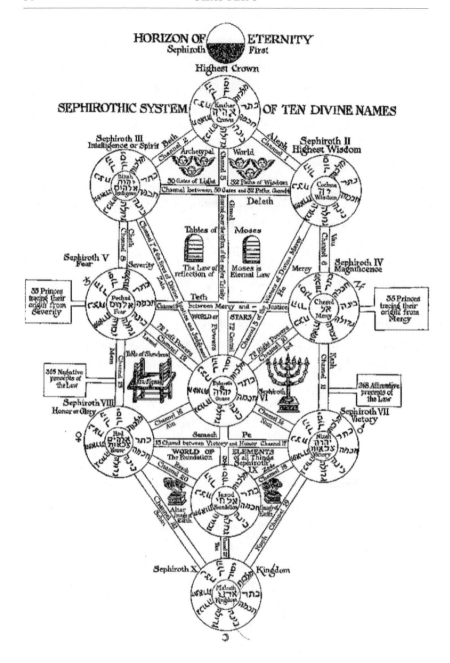

The Sefirotic Tree by Athanasius Kircher. (Engraving taken from *Oedipus Aegyptiacus*, Rome, 1652.)

Seven cervical vertebrae await him. They represent the septenary of the book of Revelation. The number 7 is very significant (see chapter 3, page 16). It symbolizes a totality, hence a death, a dissolving of self necessary to make way for a new birth experienced in the 8. The book of Revelation opens with the seven letters to the seven churches and continues with the book sealed with seven seals, the seventh of which reveals seven angels, to whom seven trumpets are given. When the seventh trumpet has sounded, a woman appears in the pangs of childbirth.

Here we come before the mystery of the final birth.

On the level of consciousness, this passage to the uppermost triangle determines the opening of a new world, where supraconsciousness is more important in relation to our conscious state than the conscious state is in relation to everyday knowledge. And just as consciousness sometimes crops up amid commonplace knowledge in a "state of awareness," or by means of a dream, similarly supraconsciousness, in rare flashes, breaches commonplace knowledge, which catches something of its light, while waiting to be born into it. Who can deny this potential for knowledge? Who can say that someone experiencing it is mad? Who has the right to use the categories of common knowledge to examine the experiences, whether in a waking or a dream state, that really belong to categories of supraconsciousness?

I am raising, briefly for the moment, an acute problem in our times. The psychoanalyst all too often acts as the sorcerer's apprentice, and the psychiatrist fails to recognize the divine experience and its corollary, the experience of darkness!

Between consciousness and supraconsciousness is what the Hebraic tradition calls the Reversal of Lights. This is a mysterious reversal by which man, who up to this point has been a mirror of God, goes through the mirror. His right arm becomes the left arm of God, his left arm, the right arm of God. Man, entering the divine, is turned inside out, and the inside becomes the outside. "For now we see through a glass, darkly; but then, face to face" (1 Corinthians 13:12).

This reversal can also be seen on the level of the body. The right cerebral hemisphere governs the left side of the body; the left cerebral hemisphere, the right side of the body. The crossing takes place near the medulla, where the nervous fibers from the right part of the brain travel to the left half of the spinal cord, and the fibers stemming from the left part of the brain travel to its right half (see chapter 6, page 55, and chapter 15, page 309).

The mediate image of this archetypal reversal is conveyed through symbols. Just as Hebraic tradition passes on this Reversal of Lights, likewise Christian tradition conveys it in its pontifical liturgy when the bishop advances toward the royal gathering, the *laós* (meaning "people," the Greek word from which *lay* and *laity* are derived), by crossing the torchlights. This reversal takes place by the Royal Gates in Orthodox churches (the communion table in Roman Catholic churches), which, in the traditional plan of a church as in the diagram of the Tree, are located at the level of the Gate of the Gods.

In the Egyptian tradition, the initiate holds the ankh in his right hand. On the frescoes in the Louvre representing scenes that take place after death in the abode of the elect, the elect hold this same ankh, cross of life, *in their left hands*. A reversal has occurred. The one who has crossed the Gate of the Gods is truly on the other side of the mirror.

This notion of reversal, intellectually unfathomable, can be expressed with the image of a glove turned inside out: the right glove will then fit onto the left hand, and the inside has become the outside.

This reversal goes along with the journey through the angelic hierarchies, the invisible worlds symbolized by the cervical vertebrae in the body. They lead to the ultimate mystery.

So my first guide revealed that the Sword-Tetragrammaton, the Tree of Life, the Tree of Knowledge of Good and Evil, and the Sefirotic Tree are one.

CHAPTER 6

The Two Sides of the Body; the Spinal Column

THE SPINE REFLECTS THE SEFIROTIC TREE'S MIDDLE COLUMN, the Tree of Life, the Sword's blade.

The two sides of the body reflect the column of Rigor on the left and the column of Mercy on the right. They reflect knowledge of *tov ve-ra* (good and evil), the two edges of the Sword.

Life shows itself to us through opposite or complementary features: darkness and light, silence and speech, cold and heat, feminine and masculine, etc. In essence, this manifestation results from a separation, in the sense of a "distinction," from primordial Unity. We have seen that this distinction is merely apparent. It is in the very image of the divine manifestation, which proceeds by paradox: immobility and source of all movement, Being and Nonbeing. The divine may only be apprehended when the knower takes these contradictions together in their correct relationship. But in the world as perceived by the senses, a world we "fallen men" see as separate and torn between its opposing aspects, our left and our right sides reflect the most contradictory aspects of our being.

The sefirah Hokhmah, Wisdom, also referred to as the Divine Father, presides over the right-hand side. It sheds its light on the column of Mercy, the sefirah Ḥesed, which is also Gedulah, Greatness. In the human body, it corresponds to the ontologically masculine right side;

on the level of the Tree of Knowledge, it corresponds to the *tov* (טוב)
side, the side of light.

Man's ability to make himself male comes from the extreme brightness of light he acquires at a given point in his evolution and the
greatness this bestows upon him. Yet man is only male when conscious
of his fragility, when he knows that his light is weak when compared
to the light he can and must become by penetrating his shadow, that
is his feminine side, the darkness, which holds new information, new
strength.

*Thus, being male consists in knowing oneself to be weak and becom-
ing a seed to go downward into a new earth beneath in order to bring
into being a new and still greater light.*

That is wisdom.

"O Lord, how manifold are thy works! In wisdom hast thou made
them all" sings the psalmist (Psalm 104:24).

In the image of Divine Wisdom, man can only build his inner cosmos by emptying himself and becoming weak, and by being full of
mercy, Ḥesed, for the weaknesses of his fellow men.

He is only able to make himself weak in relation to the new land
toward which he advances, because he knows he has gained strength
from the land previously conquered.

He can only become a seed because he has known Greatness.

The sefirah Binah, Understanding, also called the Divine Mother,
presides over the left-hand side. It sheds light on the column of Rigor,
the sefirah Din, which is also Gevurah, Strength.

It corresponds in the body to the ontologically feminine left side; on
the level of the Tree of Knowledge, to the *ra* (רע) side, the dark side,
the side yet to become light.

The kernel of energy, the Name that partakes of יהוה, symbolized
by the letter *yod* (י), is situated in the heart of the darkness. Each of our
inner heavens, with its corresponding level of energy, is made up of the
Name and partakes of it.

The feminine in each of us, in man, is the rigorous Strength born of a given degree of participation in the Name יהוה. Feminine strength is receptive to male penetration and awaits this penetration.

As the keeper of the Name, it is total Strength and total Knowledge. It is Intelligence, Binah (בינה), the one who, once penetrated, will "construct" (בנה, *banoh*) the "son" (בן, *ben*) who is the *yod* (י) dimension of יהוה.

Insofar as a person partaking of Divine Wisdom, aware of his weakness and ignorance, goes further and further into his inner heavens, understanding becomes in its depths a loving opening-out, which allows the energies of יהוה to be disseminated.

Such is the ontological order.

But the ontological order was disturbed by the drama of the Fall, which leaves man with the illusion that he has acquired unity in the conquest of his Name, even though he has not even begun the work of the inner marriage.

Adam is henceforth clothed in "coats of skin," and, so to speak, faces outward. We have seen that this second nature distributes the energies in such a way that the right has become the left and the left has become the right.

In the "skin-coated" man that each of us is today, the right part of the brain, corresponding to Wisdom, now conveys information to the left side of the body. This causes the feminine, which ontologically is profound Strength, to express itself as feminized pity, as emotional affect.

Divine Glory gives way to external victories, to the power of self-importance.

Likewise, the left part of the brain, corresponding to Understanding, now conveys information to the right side of the body. The masculine—ontologically Mercy—is conscious of its weakness. It becomes external, physical strength, a competitive, destructive strength, interested only in conquering the outside world.

Ontological power gives way to external glory, to the conquest of fame (an unconsciously externalized pole corresponding to the inner conquest of the Name) and to a glorified vanity.

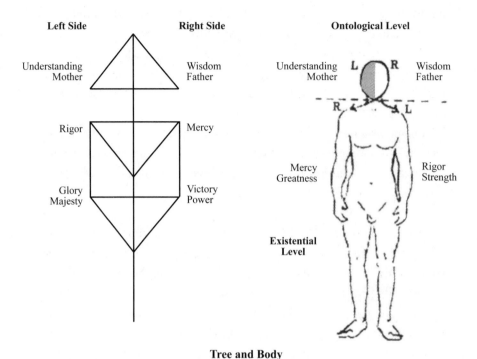

Tree and Body

In this light, we humans, clothed in our coats of skin, on the first level of consciousness, confuse the right-masculine-Wisdom side of the brain, which has not yet begun functioning, with the left-feminine-darkness side, meaning the unconscious. This is like confusing the male organ with the female womb. If the womb has not been penetrated, it is because man has not yet developed his Wisdom, his male ontological organ, whose function is to penetrate his inner earths and heavens.

The left, feminine side of the brain has developed by investing all of its Understanding in a quest to conquer the external world. Consequently, Understanding has given itself, so to speak, a spurious male organ. We have made our understanding masculine; it penetrates instead of being penetrated.

We have overdeveloped this pseudomasculine, with its array of forces dedicated to the external world. And denying weakness, we have feminized wisdom, forcing it to eke out its existence within safe moralistic categories.

Yet, in each of us, in man, these two dimensions, the one ontological, the other linked with the coat of skin, coexist and are superimposed one upon the other.

The Chinese confirm this view. According to their tradition, the energy body in its nonmanifest reality is masculine on the right, feminine on the left; but in its external, manifest reality, it is feminine on the right, masculine on the left.

They give the name "Earlier Heaven" to the ontological, nonmanifest world and the name "Later Heaven" to the manifest, biological world.

This inversion of orientations is situated at a very precise moment: that of conception. . . . The Earlier Heaven is everything before conception, the Later Heaven, everything after. Conception is thus the spatiotemporal site where the orientations change round. . . .

Nevertheless, these two orientations run together, because *birth is constant and permanent*, because every instant, Life, which follows its course in an individual, is a life which is born anew.[1]

Christ tells us: "You are in the world, but not of it" (John 17:16–18).

In mythology, these dimensions are often expressed by twinning. Pairs such as Cain and Abel, Jacob and Esau, are living symbols of this process.

Cain and Jacob correspond to ontological man. The one, *Qain* (קין), is "nest" (*qen*, קן) of the *yod*, the other, *Yaaqov* (יעקב), is "heel" (*aqov*, עקב) of the *yod*. And, as we shall see later, the heel is also a nest!

Abel and Esau correspond to the nature of man in a coat of skin, that is, a nature that has been added on. They are both identified with the animal world: Abel, the keeper of sheep; Esau, the hairy "Red Man," who likes to hunt.

Yet in each pair, the two men are brothers, and henceforth that deep nature that brings deification in the *yod* will only achieve fulfillment by

wholeheartedly taking on the animal coat. Cain's tragedy was to kill
Abel. The greatness of Jacob was to take on Esau, whose energies (the
birthright) he only reclaims when he is able to accomplish them ontologically, to bring the Messiah (יהוה) into the world.

In other words, we will be more like Abel-Esau during the first part
of our life, on the first level of our Tree, the level of Having. We are unable to tell our right from our left, because we are completely identified
with our energies on this level: the animal world.

Justifying Mercy, God says to Jonah, who has threatened the city of
Nineveh with divine Rigor, "And should not I spare Nineveh, that great
city, wherein are more than one hundred and twenty thousand people
who cannot discern between their right hand and their left, and countless animals?" (Jonah 4:11).

Here the animals represent the energies of the people who are not
yet conscious of them and hence are unable to conquer them.

The animals described on the sixth day of Genesis are the energies
that structure our inner lands, on each of the levels previously mentioned. As long as we are identified with them, we do not know them
and cannot conquer them.

To become men, to cross the Gate of Men, is to begin distinguishing
right from left, as well as discerning the male ontological right from
the female, existential[2] right and the female ontological left from the
male, existential left. It is to penetrate the true meaning of the "left side"
(Hebrew *smol*, שמאל, which may be read שם-אל, *shem-el*, Name of
Elohim), for the feminine left contains the *yod* (יהוה), the Divine Name,
in which Elohim is hidden, a seed at the heart of his creation. But this approach is a difficult one, as the Latin word for left, *sinister*, may suggest.

This side corresponds to the left column of the Temple of Solomon,
called *Boaz* (בעז, "in [ב] strength [עז])."

The Hebrew word for right is *yamiin* (ימיין), associated with the
right column of the Temple of Solomon, called *Yakhin* (יכין). These
two words contain the solar symbol of wine (*yayin*, יין). Therein lies
the male work, the source of intoxication.

Jacob's Ladder. (Great nave, Monreale Cathedral, Sicily.)

To become men is to become Jacob-Israel, to start building up the spinal column, experienced by Jacob in his dream of the ladder.

"Behold a ladder set up on the earth, and the top of it reached to heaven; and behold the angels of God ascending and descending on it. And, behold, יהוה stood above it" (Genesis 28:12–13).

In Hebrew, the word "ladder," *selam* (סלם, 60-30-600), is formed thus: guided (ל) by the tree of tradition, leaning (ס) on it, man progresses toward his accomplishment (ם).

In the body the ascending and descending angels are the energies moving along the spinal column, the energies ascending and descending, producing the dynamic force of man's encounter with the external world in the first part of his life, then of his encounter with himself as he crosses the Gate of Men, and finally of his encounter with his kernel, his Name, the divine marriage.

This is the force of eros at the level of the spinal column, which joins Keter with Malkhut, King with Queen (see chapter 4, page 28), husband with wife. Ever since the Fall, this force has been moving man exclusively outside himself, keeping him on the first level in an infantile situation.

Yet it can also obey anew the voice of the Spouse, return to the path leading to his Name, and rise like sap in a tree toward the heights of man. Every human being plays with his life when he plays with his energies. Either he raises his sap in order to "bring his tree to fruit," or he expends it, from birth, at the foot of the Tree, in the shoots or the low branches.

Many initiation rituals—particularly those of shamans from the far north—involve symbolically climbing a ladder; others involve climbing the Tree. They show that the meaning of man's life, the meaning of the mysterious and disturbing trial that makes up his passage on earth between birth and death, lies in the "rising of the sap."

Between the two opposite poles of birth and death, between these two "matrices," the Christian tradition proposes the Person of Christ, who reveals himself as "the way, the truth, and the life" (John 14:6). He also says, "I am the door" (John 10:7). Although he never actually said "I am the Tree," he did identify himself sufficiently with the tree of the cross for us to seek out its hidden meaning.

The tree appears for the first time in biblical myth in the shape of the Tree of Life and the Tree of Knowledge, planted in the midst of the garden.

In the third chapter of Genesis, when man is driven out of Eden, Cherubim with a flaming sword guard the entrance to the garden, so that no one can come near and eat of the fruit of the Tree of Life. And this marks the beginning of man's endless wandering about the earth. Man is driven from himself, driven from his divine axis; confused with his feminine side again, he is thrown down by the foot of the tree, at the base of his spinal column.

The laws structuring creation are turned against him. He has been warned of this by what is commonly known as the divine curse: God says to *ishah*, the woman: "In sorrow thou shalt bring forth children" (Genesis 3:16).

The expression "in pain" is *be-etsev* (בעצב). Between the two *bets* (ב), as between the two side columns, the Middle Column, *ets* (עץ) means the tree. *Ishah* here represents the Adam in his feminine function. The Adam, cut off from consciousness of the *yod*, is called to give birth to himself by himself by climbing back up the Tree, at whose foot he has fallen.

To recover consciousness of the *yod* within, and thus to give birth to oneself in one's divine dimension, remains man's only calling.

The book of Exodus, recounting the journey of the children of Israel through the desert, gives us a third symbol for humanity's spinal column: "And the Lord went before them by day in a pillar of cloud, to lead them the way; and by night in a pillar of fire, to give them light" (Exodus 13:21–22).

יהוה was that pillar.

In the darkness of this long desert that is our time on earth, our spinal column is the light-giving guide for whoever is able to see. It is the tool for the one who can work with it. It is the path for him who can ascend.

In India, the backbone is *brahmadanda* or "rod of Brahma." A serpent of fire—*kundalini*—must slowly rise up along this rod. This serpent of fire is much like the brazen serpent, a fiery serpent that Moses lifts up in the wilderness (Numbers 21:8–9), which cures all wounds, gives life, and with whom Christ identifies: "And as Moses lifted up the serpent in the wilderness, even so must the Son of Man be lifted up" (John 3:14).

In Christian mysteries the Son of God descends, the Son of Man rises. In Christianity this reality is experienced through the divine Person allowing himself to be taken into history in order to lift man up to deification.

In Hinduism, this reality is experienced through the spirit letting itself be caught in the body, so that it may open up the chakras, or energy centers, all along the spinal column. These energies, thus liberated, flow into man, enabling him by degrees to partake fully of the divine energy.

The seven principal chakras rise from the base of the spine—the basal, or root chakra—to the summit of the head, or crown chakra (compare the two sefirot, Foundation and Crown). Between them are the sacral, solar plexus, heart, throat, and brow chakras.

A ladder, a column, a tree in mythology; the Tao, the Way, the road leading to the reunification of contraries in the Chinese tradition—in the Christian tradition these are the Person of Christ, who says of himself: "I am the way, the truth, and the life" (John 14:6).

What the Chinese call *yin* and *yang*, what the Hebrews and other religious systems call principles or energies, are represented in the Christian tradition by living people, embodying duality.

Thus, in the Gospels, we find a detailed picture of different characters surrounding Christ two by two.

Foremost are Judah and Judas, whose name in Hebrew, *Yehudah* (יהודה), is the Divine Name itself, the Tetragrammaton, to which the letter ד, *dalet*, has been added. *Dalet*, the "door," corresponds to the number 4, which symbolizes a halt and here in particular the "door" of incarnation. The magnificent name of Judah-Judas indeed means "incarnation of יהוה," that is "יהוה written into history." Christ was born of the tribe of Judah, the fourth of the twelve sons of Israel, and put to death through the intervention of Judas, the last of the twelve apostles. Christ, between these two "doors" of birth and death, is Life: Life transcends history and becomes incarnate in it.

Then there are the two Josephs: first Joseph, husband of the Virgin Mary, who watches over the maternal womb through which God becomes man. And then Joseph of Arimathea, who takes the corpse of Christ, entombs him, and watches over the matrix of death, which becomes a matrix of resurrection, of rebirth, of man becoming God. Between them, Christ—God and man—is the perfect unity of heaven and earth, their right relationship.

The maternal womb and the tomb are two "limits"—*sof* (סוֹף) in Hebrew. The name Joseph, *Yosef* (יוֹסֵף, that is, *yod* becoming a limit), is also the verb *yasof*, "to increase." There can be no growth without first becoming a seed and allowing oneself to be captured for the necessary amount of time within the limits of a structure.

Again, there are the two thieves crucified on each side of the cross, symbolizing the Tree of Life; between two deviants stands the Truth. One of the thieves is identified with divine Mercy, the other with Rigor.

At the foot of the cross are Mary and John, archetypes of the feminine and the masculine. On the cross is the One who is "neither male nor female" (Galatians 3:28), for through this ultimate death he has recovered unity.

On Mount Tabor, Moses and Elijah appear around the transfigured Christ. Between the Rigor of the Law and the Fire of Prophecy, Christ is the living tradition.

I should like to deal at greater length with two figures: the two Johns, John the Baptist and John the Evangelist.

The god Janus was revered in ancient times, well before Christianity. He was depicted with a single head having two faces, one old, the other young, and was celebrated during the two yearly solstices.

This two-faced Janus symbolized time: the past in the face of the old man, the future in the face of the young. The face that was not and could not be represented was that of the elusive present, immaterial and timeless.

In the Person of Christ, the elusive is apprehended, the immaterial becomes incarnate, the present becomes reality, the eternal becomes historic, the immortal dies and rises again, reintroducing man to his divine dimension. Christ is the "instant," surrounded by the two Johns: John the Baptist, the "old man," the man in "a coat of skin" (he is clothed in camel's hair), and John the Evangelist, the future man, the one of whom the Master so mysteriously speaks ("If I will that he tarry till I come . . . " John 21:22–23), as if he means that John were already accomplished.

In the present man finds his true countenance and can experience his measure of eternity. In his Christlike dimension, he is out of time, while yet remaining in time; the instant is man's crux. Most human beings reject it, because it is most difficult to bear. Essentially linked with eternity, the present brings with it the Absolute.

Man lives a contradiction that consists of demanding the Absolute yet running away from it. He asks for it because in essence he is steeped in it. He flees it because he expects his own existence to deliver it, because he is looking for it not within but outside himself. He expects time to procure it for him: either from the past, which he idealizes and in which he takes refuge (many old people are like this), or from the future, which he hopes will fulfill him (the situation of young men and of many of us who live constantly reaching forward).

When the instant brings him joy, he demands that time take on the value of eternity: "O time, suspend your flight . . . " sings the poet Lamartine. Unable to grasp the true dimension of the present moment, man flees from it, and by fleeing he runs away from himself and hence destroys himself.

Western expressions of Christianity during the last ten centuries dramatically portray this experience. At present, torn between fundamentalists, who hold on to the customs of a very recent past, and progressives, who try to compete with the outward progress that they unconsciously worship, the church is forsaking its axis of tradition and destroying itself. Tradition is the fruit neither of the past nor of the future; it is prophetic time steeped in the timeless and embodied in the instant.

Political parties, right-wing or left-wing, lean on a crutch that unbalances the other side, causing the nation to limp and so keeping it from adulthood, which is centered on an authentic spinal column.

Returning to our ontological diagram of the body, we can see permanence, origins, and antiquity in the feminine left side; and in the right, masculine side, movement, and the future. Only the spinal column, which embodies the instant, the seed for growing beyond paradoxes and oppositions, is the life and the way that leads men, or groups, or nations, or even the whole of humanity, in the axis of its essential being, spiritual and divine.

Man does not live according to this axis. Consequently he uproots himself from life and is devoured by time.

This devouring aspect of time is conveyed in the myth of Cronus—central in the life of humanity. To retell it here would be lengthy. In brief, Cronus, son of the sky god, Uranus, dethroned his father with the help of the Titans.

Who is he in relation to his father?

He is time as against eternity. He presides over our birth, our development, our death. He embodies the symbols of continuity, succession, progression, repetition, in contrast with eternity.

Cronus devours all his children, that is to say every instant is annulled, devoured by the future, itself immediately becoming the past. Is this to say that all is lost, that there is nothing more in common between Uranus and Cronus, between eternity (also called the timeless) and time? The myth points to an answer: Rhea, Cronus's wife, saves the life of one of her children, one of these "instants," who is Zeus: he has divine dimension.

Every instant can be saved, can be restored to its dimension of eternity.

Zeus then reinstates the reign of Uranus. Zeus, this god within us, cannot let himself be devoured. With the help of the Cyclopes he battles against the Titans, who represent our instinctive forces, and against Cronus himself, in the volcano's fire. This fire from the earth's inner core corresponds to love in the inner folds of our being: the progressive love that burns at the core of the rectangle (see diagram, page 27), destroying everything that does not belong with divine being.

The Cyclopes are born with a frontal eye—the "third eye" of the Hindu tradition—also found in the Judeo-Christian tradition, when it mentions "the man whose eye is open" (Numbers 24:3). I shall return to this.

The Cyclopes are the forces of Knowledge. They remind us of Shiva, one of the three chief divinities in the Hindu pantheon, whose third eye, on the brow, destroys all manifestation. This destruction is the passing of time into eternity, of succession into permanence, which contains time and non-time.

Every instant is fraught with eternity.

Life is found within the instant and situated on the Middle Column. It follows that, symbolically, the spinal column is our path toward our inner self, by virtue of this potential we have to resemble God.

The Middle Column is the site of the *mi* and the meeting place of the *ma* and the *mi*, because it is the place where the right and the left, the masculine and the feminine in us, the "accomplished" and the "not yet accomplished,"[3] meet and marry.

This marriage with the feminine in us is only possible when man, with Adam, becomes conscious of his "left side" and so can distinguish between his right and his left.

This is why the spinal column, already rooted in the Lower Triangle on the first level, where man begins this process of discernment, undoing previous identifications, only begins to be genuinely constructed on the second level, when he becomes upright, through the straightening of the backbone.

Each vertebra of the spinal column then turns, as it were, into a nuptial bed, freeing and constructing the energies, so that two may become one, so that each ה of הוֹיה may wed its contrary and light, reaching into darkness, may completely turn that darkness into light.

The spinal column is therefore the place of choice, the site of all our liberations, our successive accomplishments, but also all our mental blocks, our fears, our refusals—refusal to evolve, refusal to wed, refusal to love—and all the tensions, all the suffering generated by them.

The spinal column also registers the necessary sufferings, those which are present each time we "give birth." To discern pathological suffering from initiatory suffering, as we shall see, should be the role of the true physician.

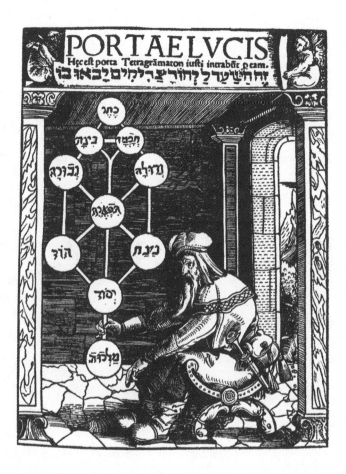

Gates of Light. In his right hand the wise man holds the Sefirotic Tree. His left hand points to the earth, in which the Tree must be planted to take root. (Engraving from *Portae Lucis* [Gates of Light] by Paulus Ricius, Augsburg, 1516.)

CHAPTER 7

Malkhut I: The Feet

FOR THE MEANING OF THE FEET, AND THE MYTHS CONCERNING them, we must return to the teaching of the Sefirotic Tree.

Let us remember (chapter 4, page 25) that the Tree first emerges from the invisible roots of the Ain Sof, becomes manifest in Keter, the first of the ten sefirot, and then blossoms in Malkhut, the tenth and last sefirah and seventh of the seven sefirot of Creation. In other words, this Tree, whose roots are above and whose foliage is below, is upside down. Similarly, the human body is an inverted tree.

Dr. Hubert Larcher recently pointed out that the popular French expression for doing a head stand is *faire l'arbre droit* (making a straight tree) and that this posture shows the amazing little universe that fits in the rib cage; for the tree of the lungs then blossoms upright under the influence of the heart, which stands for the sun and shines, so to speak, under the "celiac arch."

This solar triangle serves to show how true the image of the human Tree is. It is inverted in relation to the trees of the forests, which it undoubtedly complements. The Green Tree, by providing oxygen to the "tree" of the lungs, receives carbon dioxide in return, which, through the alchemy of chlorophyll (*khlôros*, green), again provides oxygen. Oxygen plays its well-known role in the blood. This enables us to notice the surprising complementarity between chlorophyll and blood. In fact, we can speak of the complementarity of "Green Tree" and "Red Tree" or "Green Man" and "Red Man."

Etymologically, there is no doubt that the Adam, in Hebrew, is the Red Man. (*Adamah* means "red earth," and *dam* means "blood.") On the other hand, the Green Man is no stranger to the three traditions of the Book: Judaism, Christianity, and Islam. In chapter 6, page 63, I spoke of St. John the Evangelist, forever young, who has made a bond with the divine. He is closely related to Elijah, who, taken up in the chariot of fire, knows not death. And, curiously, in Islam, Elijah is confused with the "man from God" who comes to instruct Moses in the eighteenth *sura* of the Qur'an, called "The Cave." This man is named Khadir in Muslim literature, which means "evergreen."

In the three traditions of the Book, the man who has accomplished every death and resurrection and has been born into his divine dimension is the Green Man. Gustav Meyrink immortalized the "green face" in his beautiful 1916 novel of the same name.

The Green Tree reflects the Green Man, that is, the divine man. So the tree symbolizes ourselves in our ontologically sound state. It represents what we are called to be in the end.

The Foot of Buddha. The foot—the first germ of existence—contains the whole body. From the heel to the tips of the toes, with the solar wheel in the center, it depicts the future development of man.

It is interesting to read (Mark 8:22–26) that the blind man cured by Christ, initially recovering sight, exclaims: "I see men as trees, walking." His eyes are then fully opened by Christ so that he sees the world. Such details are crucial for what follows.

Seen from the point of view of the inverted tree, the feet correspond to Malkhut. They are the roots of the human Tree and the leafage of the divine Tree, whose roots descend into the darkness of the Ain Sof.

Malkhut, the Kingdom, is the receptacle of all the Divine Energies from above. As the tenth sefirah, it is the uncreated and creative divine substance. Creating, it transforms itself into a seed inside the human Tree. The Hebrews call it the Queen. All the powers of the King (Keter) are entrusted to it (see chapter 4, page 28, and chapter 6, page 60).

The Queen is also called the Virgin of Israel. She is to give birth, and in this sense she is the mother of all life. She is the whole of Creation and of each one of us in particular, for we recapitulate the whole of Creation.

Malkhut, as the seventh sefirah of Creation, or of the Lesser Countenance (mentioned in chapter 4), corresponds to the seventh day of Genesis, day of the *shabbat* (שבת), when God withdraws as his work is completed and perfected. He withdraws and yet does not withdraw, for by making himself the "basis" (שת, *shet*) of his Creation (ב), he withdraws within it. He turns himself into the Seed, the symbol of which is the letter *yod* (י).

The *yod*, which is the tenth letter of the Hebrew alphabet, is the initial of the divine Tetragrammaton (יהוה), called *ha-Shem* (the Name) by the Hebrews, that is, the name that contains all names within it. These names are respectively written on all our hearts. Each constitutes our kernel, our "person," the person we are called to become. Each of us, man or woman, is Virgin of Israel, pregnant with the Name, called to bring it to birth.

This is consonant with the experience I mentioned earlier when contemplating the holy Name (יהוה).

Viewed thus, man's feet, corresponding to Malkhut, symbolize man as Virgin of Israel and mother, called upon to give birth to his Divine Name, thus participating in יהוה. The feet contain all the energies to be accomplished and hold the secret of the Name. They symbolize our feminine side, the shadow side (רע) of the Tree of Knowledge.

The foot is shaped like a seed, indicating man at his point of departure, with all his potentiality, still steeped in the waters of the womb. This shape is determined by the Divine Seed, the Name, which, through the umbilical cord, is linked with Elohim.

In the mother's womb, the placenta is a symbol of Elohim the nurturer. The placenta, the counterpart to the fetus, also separates itself from the initial egg and relates to the fetus in the same way as Elohim relates to יהוה. This relationship is mysterious, for the one God has two different functions, united and distinct, but this difference is the very object of Creation. After the expulsion of the actual placenta at birth, a virtual placenta connects Elohim with man, Elohim with יהוה sought within man.

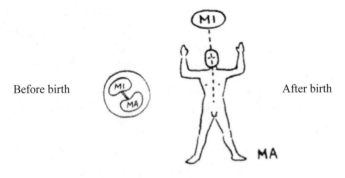

Before birth   After birth

Before and After Birth

In ontological terms, the Father seeks out the Son within man. Let us be clear about these different functions of the created in relation to the uncreated: Creation, daughter of Elohim-Father, is destined to become his Spouse.

Creation, entirely contained in Malkhut, is virgin, yet pregnant with the Divine Child, and called to bring him into the world.

Each one of us, man or woman, as Malkhut, is both virgin and mother. Each one of us is also symbolically the husband-spouse penetrating
Malkhut to give birth to our ontological selves, attaining at last the dimension of the Son-*yod*. Each one of us then becomes this Son.

Thus deified, we become the Bride (Malkhut fully accomplished) in
relation to God-as-Spouse. Espoused by God, we are crowned (Keter)
and enter into sovereignty.

The energies described in Genesis during the six days of Creation
represent our potential of accomplishment. They are the fundamental
erotic flow, which draws the bride toward her husband. This is why
foot, *regel* (רגל), is also "celebration" (a regale?). And in French a
number of popular expressions linked with the foot, such as "*c'est le
pied*" (meaning "it's great!") or "*prendre son pied*" (similar to the English "get a kick out of something"), express a celebration and often an
erotic celebration, which no longer has much to do with the encounter
of the Divine Spouse but ontologically foreshadows it.

The drama of the Fall, when these energies are violated by Satan,
the false spouse, is expressed in the biblical myth by the wounding of
the foot.

Man's Feet Are Wounded

Adam transgressed the ontological norms mentioned earlier (see chapter 3, page 15). He cut himself off from the *yod*, from the divine, from
his principle, from the Upper Triangle in the Sefirotic Tree. He beheaded himself. More precisely, he first rejected the information given by
the *yod* and then forgot his profound ontological dimension. He put
on a false head, a mask, a parody of the Upper Triangle. On his level,
understanding and wisdom are no longer divine. They no longer preside
over the accomplishment of man's calling, which is the conquest of the
divine kingdom within himself. Instead, this calling is changed into the
desire to conquer the kingdom without, the manifest world—in other

words, the conquest of Malkhut separated from Keter. Malkhut thus becomes merely the cosmos, and man no longer knows that it is also within himself and that he possesses its keys.

It is as if man's energies were pouring out through a gaping wound at the level of his feet—Malkhut—instead of rising up the Tree toward their proper realization.

Hence, in its sacred books, its tales and its myths, humanity painfully expresses its error through the symbol of the foot: a wounded foot with Oedipus, a vulnerable foot with Achilles, and a snake-bitten foot with Eve.

Later we shall discover the beginnings of a cure with Jacob, who at birth holds his brother Esau's heel in his hand. We shall see humanity's movement toward penitence with Mary Magdalene, the prostitute, who anoints the feet of Christ with perfume and wipes them with her hair. Finally we shall participate in humanity's total recovery with the apostles, whose feet are washed by Christ, the cosmic physician, before the Last Supper.

To heal the wound, separate from the false spouse, and reassemble the energies in their respective inner "earths," one must return Malkhut

Eve Wounded in the Foot. Satan's violation of the potential of energy symbolically contained in the feet, that is to say, the drama of the Fall, is portrayed in the biblical myth by the original wound: Eve has her heel crushed. (Vézelay Basilica; photo by Roger Viollet.)

to its feminine calling. Malkhut is the universal matrix and mother of all life. It is a force of germination that exalts the power of the divine. Malkhut is a dark, subterranean world, whose bowels go deep among abyssal archetypes. These reflect the divine archetypes, where the slow processes of death and resurrection—twin poles of the same reality—unfold.

Black Virgins, found in a number of French churches, are a symbol for Malkhut as the supreme substance, the infinite universal possibility of the Ain Sof, and the one called upon to give birth. Myths develop the image of Malkhut as queen and virgin of Israel and express the drama of the Fall by lamenting the father who is killed—the dead king, the widowed queen, and the orphaned son. The virgin of Israel has become empty, bereft of the Father-Spouse who calls out to her and whom she no longer hears.

In Egypt, she is Isis, weeping and desperately seeking Osiris. In Israel, she is the widow whose orphaned son dies (the *yod*-seed dies inside the sterile womb).

Biblical texts never cease to ask for the protection of "the widow and the orphan." Job, defending himself, reminds us that he "brought mercy to the orphan and filled the widow's heart with joy" (Job 29:12–13).

A widow's son is sent for by King Solomon to build the Temple (1 Kings 7:14). A widow's son from Zarephath (*Tsarfat* = "France" in Hebrew) is brought back to life by Elijah (1 Kings 17:21–24).

In Luke 7:12–17 Christ raises from the dead the son of a widow from Nain (in Hebrew, "the precious").

"To rebuild, to succor, to raise from the dead"—frequent expressions like these bear witness to the orphan's resurrection and to the return of joy to the widow's heart.

In the mystery of the Sword-Tetragrammaton, הוה, *yod*, has been killed, and *heh-vav-heh* (הוה) is widowed. We saw (chapter 3, page 15–16) that in הוה, the ו, *vav*, the 6, symbolizes man, that is, the Adam created on the sixth day. Consequently, האדמה, *ha-adamah*, the Mother Earth that gave birth to Adam, is a widow. Adam is an orphan.

In the body, the head has been removed; the feet are empty. Are they completely empty?

Using the language of myth, I alluded to the "murdered father." But murder can only be real in the world of the Fall, on the plane of existence. Adam cut himself off from the divine, yet the divine always is, and cannot die. Adam severed all links with the Father, but could not kill the Father except in his mind. He has left Eden and lost his knowledge of the divine, but the divine remains within him, like the transparent glass of a window set in visible leading.

The divine image is deeply repressed, masked—a leaden mask, whose symbolism we shall encounter later—but not altered. Yet the repression is so profound that an abyss now separates the human from the divine. The crossing of this abyss is the object of humanity's unfathomable anxiety. Art, songs, sacred literature, and folklore translate this anxiety in its purest form. It is projected onto the psychic plane and expressed with a tide of confusion and nostalgia, which rapidly becomes disorganized, giving way before long to a diabolical tide that an agnostic medicine cannot check.

The ontological nature of man is marriage.

This is particularly clear in biblical literature: the betrothed, the bride, the beloved, are terms constantly uttered by the psalmist or the prophet. But both psalmist and prophet also denounce the prostitute as having given herself to a false spouse. The true spouse, though rejected, is still there. The Upper Triangle, concealed by the mask, still continues to spread life through the whole body, insofar as it is able to receive it. Otherwise it would be reduced to nothingness.

"Thou couldest have no power at all against me, except it were given thee from above" (John 19:11).

No, the feet are not empty. Yet man is completely unaware of what they contain.

By looking at the names that conceal this mystery, we may become aware. Without separating the two poles of the ontological marriage, we shall study the two key words:

"Head": *resh* (ראש, 300-1-200) or "chief" (ריש, 300-10-200); and "foot": *regel* (רגל, 30-3-200).

Their numerical values are revealing. Both words are surrounded by 30 or 300 at one end (these two numbers express the same idea, one on the manifest level, the other on the cosmic) and by 200 at the other; only the middle numbers change.

At the level of the head, 1 or 10 expresses Divine Unity, which, passing through the prism of manifestation on the level of the feet, becomes 3. In all traditions, whether it concerns threefoldness of principles or triunity of persons, 3 is *One*. Thus seen, the head and the feet amount to the same word. If the head, above, recapitulates the whole body, the feet, below, do the same and are bearers of its potential "becoming." Even if man has lost awareness of the *alef*, the *alef* continues to inform the feet, which retain in the letter *gimel* (3) the hidden power of the divine (*alef*, 1, or *yod*, 10).

Much has been written about *gimel*, the letter "G," which is mysteriously engraved at the center of the initiate's five-pointed star and is also the letter gamma (Γ) dear to the Pythagoreans.

It seems clear that it represents the transfer of divine transcendence, which is One, into its triune immanence. *Yod* becomes "God," "Goth." Earlier we saw that, in the Sword-Tetragrammaton, if *yod* is killed, הוה (*heh-vav-heh*) is the widowed bride. We should also note that חוה (*hava*: 5-6-8 or 5-6-[5 + 3]), which means "Eve," could (numerologically) also be written גהוה (5-6-5-3).The name then becomes *Gheha*, Gaia, the Greek goddess of the earth.

The earth is widowed. Eve is widowed, yet she carries in her womb the very germ of the life of the Spouse. The letter "G" is shaped like a seed or germ. And the Christian mystery began to unfold, after the prophet Zechariah heard the angel of the Lord saying, near the end of the Old Testament: "For, behold, I will bring forth my servant the Germ" (Zechariah 3:8).

In the Christian perspective, Christ's incarnation is God descending into Malkhut, the cosmic feet (linked with the symbolism of the fish), to encounter man, dress his wound, and rescue him from deathly torpor, so that he may conquer his cosmic head and be brought to his true nuptials. Christ makes himself Seed in order to awaken in each of us our Divine Seed and enable us to become Green Trees, Trees of Life.

When man has achieved this, the *gimel* becomes *yod* once again, and one would be tempted to read ריל instead of רגל. The three letters ריל, read phonetically, spell "royal." This is no coincidence. The man who has returned to unity is king, he is "crowned."

The *yod* (value 10) can also be replaced by the *alef* א (value 1); the word then becomes "real."

Reality is royalty.

The figure in the Christian ecclesiastical hierarchy who has symbolically reached this stage is the bishop. We have seen (chapter 5, page 52) that this hierarch "crosses the torches" during the pontifical liturgy. This means that when he advances toward the *laos*, that is, the royal (lay) people, he crosses from the Upper Triangle that he embodies to the first inverted triangle, where the people are waiting (more precisely, are "in gestation"). The bishop, living the experience of the Upper Triangle—royalty—is crowned, "consecrated." At this level, the head meets the feet.

In the Western world, we see the bishop's miter, shaped like the head of a fish, climbing, as it were, vertically toward the sky.

The Bishop's Miter and Vertical Fish

In Chaldean culture, the bishop's ancestor is Oannes, the god-fish who taught men medicine, architecture, agriculture, etc. The origin of these astonishing heads of fish-men goes back 8000 years before Jesus Christ.

What do they mean?

Do they not relate to the fish, in whose shape the first avatar of Vishnu, the sustaining principle of the Hindu trinity, appears? Does not the seed, man's first avatar, live like a fish in the maternal waters? It seems that humanity, at whatever age, knew or knows the deep meaning of its vocation and expresses it through the flowering of its symbols and myths.

Man must grow like a tree, from his feet to his head, where his fruit will multiply.

"Be fruitful and multiply" is the injunction given to Adam from the moment of his creation.

The Tlatilco Acrobat. From the Olmec culture, the Tlatico Acrobat is a confirmation of the symbol of perfection of the feet touching the head known in other traditions. (National Museum of Anthropology, Mexico.)

Physically, the feet bring together the full potential of man's body. Hence, in acupuncture, one approach concentrates solely on the foot, whose points of energy, when accurately pricked, resound through the appropriate meridians all over the body.

Thus seen, the toes correspond to the head area of the body, and the heel, to its foundation.

By narrowing the object in view still further, the big toe can be seen as a small foot.

Some fine Babylonian frescoes represent a warrior kneeling in front of the king before going to battle. He is kneeling on one foot; the sole of this foot is turned toward the sky, except for the big toe. The big toe alone rests on the earth as if to receive from it the vital surge needed for the warrior. The earth then "pricks" the toe at that point of contact,which the Chinese call the "gushing spring."

The "Gushing Spring"

The Hindu master Sri Nisargadatta Maharaj seems to know about this acupuncture point. He says to his disciple, "In Marathi, the word 'foot' means 'the beginning of the moment.' . . . Find this very beginning, the *gushing of the source*, the first instant of consciousness." When the disciple finds this "first instant," he becomes the true "warrior" and is able to begin the conquest of his inner kingdom.

When man allows the precious energies contained in the feet to drain away by pouring them into vain motivations driven by a false sense of possession, his foot may indicate the swelling of his soul. Demotic French speaks ironically of "swollen ankles" (*chevilles enflées*). And many incidents occurring in this area—fractures, sprains, etc.—are none other than psychosomatic indications of a profound error.

All dis-ease is meaningful.

Foot problems indicate a false start on the way to growth.

All growth has its beginning in childhood. The foot is linked with childhood and specifically with intrauterine childhood.

What's more, in Greek, the word for "child" (*paîs, paidós*) is very close to the word for "foot" (*poús, podós*). If it were Hebrew, the words would be completely homonymous and would denote a close relationship.

Man's vocation is determined from the mother's womb. It is inscribed in the Name, which he receives there from the creative Word. It is also inscribed as a potential of fulfillment in the quality of the maternal vessel that enfolds him.

With the help of his mother, man can set himself on this path as early as his intrauterine childhood. Steeped still in the waters of his own genesis, man experiences Malkhut.

We cannot speak here of a conscious move, whereas the adult who has passed through the "Strait Gate" from Having to Being, on the Hod-Netsah path, and who consciously assumes the fullness of his incarnation, reaches the sefirah Tiferet.

In the diagram of the Divine Energies, Tiferet (Heart-Beauty) is a reflection of Keter and of Ain. It brings together and manifests all the divine possibilities in as many archetypes as there are sefirot and their opposites. Tiferet is the hub, the center of the solar wheel that links above with below, left with right, and embraces the whole in the divine fire of primordial harmony.

In the diagram of human energies, the one who enters this vortex is hurled along the spokes of the microcosmic and macrocosmic wheel into the experience of the center, which brings together all human possibilities. He experiences the marriage of the opposites and goes beyond them, which will lead him to the ineffable experience of the divine heart. Man then knows the greatest depth of the abyss in Malkhut before being lifted toward the highest peaks.

Of the "descent into the nether regions," I say only that at this conscious level of experience man truly encounters Malkhut. On this level alone he truly weds Malkhut, the Queen, Virgin, and Mother.

The mysteries of Israel, which Christ accomplishes, consist essentially in this: man must espouse the Mother of the Depths, whom every actual mother symbolizes, before being raised up toward the Father.

Every human being has this vocation.

Every individual woman is also called to embody Malkhut and be a matrix every moment of her life, a point of transformation for herself, for her own, and for humanity. To refuse this vocation is to refuse to enter the ontological plane.

In Greek mythology, Oedipus marries his mother.

Oedipus, or the Swollen Foot

Who is Oedipus?

His name means "swollen foot." He is the son of Laius ("the left-handed," "the gauche") and grandson of Labdacus ("the limping"), whose grandfather is Cadmus, the founder of Thebes.

Oedipus is the scion of a royal family. Every man, ontologically, is of royal stock. Thebes, to the Greeks, is the Holy City (like Jerusalem for the Hebrews). The man who dwells in his inner city is conscious of his lameness, his feminine shadow, his left side, which he must wed (see chapter 3, page 20).

Yet the royal couple, Laius-Jocasta, is sterile. Laius and Jocasta go to Delphi, to be told by the oracle that they will bear a son but that this son will kill his father and marry his mother.

At birth, Oedipus, this son, is entrusted to one of the palace servants, with orders to get rid of the child. Laius has decided to remove this son whose destiny he does not want to see fulfilled. The child is then suspended by his heel from a tree in the forest and exposed as prey to the wild beasts. Corinthian shepherds, passing by on their way to their homeland, are moved by compassion, rescue him, and then entrust him to the king and queen of their land, who in turn adopt him. Oedipus grows up with them until the day when, feeling different from their kin, he decides to find out the secret of his birth.

He departs for Delphi and learns from the oracle the fatal destiny that is to befall him. Refusing this dramatic lot, Oedipus does not return to Corinth, where he believes his parents dwell. Instead he heads for Thebes, towards his royal destiny.

Thebes is being ravaged by a monster that guards its entrance. Sitting on a huge rock, it devours all those who come to the city gates and cannot solve the riddle it asks.

Laius is making for Delphi, to consult the divine Apollo about this calamity, as Oedipus approaches Thebes. They meet in a defile. The king's chariot bruises Oedipus's foot. Oedipus turns in fury against the driver and kills him.

Unknowingly, Oedipus has killed his father.

Oedipus arrives at the gates of Thebes, where he learns of the king's death and Queen Jocasta's promise to give the crown, and hence her hand in marriage, to whoever delivers the city from the monster.

This formidable monster is a Sphinx. It is tetramorphic, with the feet of a bull, the body of a lion, the wings of an eagle, and the face of a woman.

Oedipus decides to confront it. "What animal, remaining the same, walks on four feet in the morning, on two feet at midday, and on three feet in the evening?" asks the Sphinx.

"Man," answers Oedipus, who is of royal essence and speaks from this deep level within him.

The Sphinx comes down from the rock and hands over her power to Oedipus, who enters the city of Thebes in triumph. He marries the queen, Jocasta.

Unknowingly, Oedipus has married his mother.

She bears him four children: two sons, Eteocles and Polyneices, and two daughters, Ismene and Antigone.

However, the joy from these births is soon overshadowed by a new affliction. The city has fallen prey to another formidable curse—sterility. The whole city is affected: women are barren, animals no longer give birth, the earth no longer bears fruit, trees are stricken with drought.

Oedipus determines to seek without respite the cause of this disastrous situation by going to the oracle. The oracle reveals that it is linked with the murder of King Laius. It thus becomes crucial for Oedipus to know who perpetrated this crime and is therefore the cause of the sterility.

Oedipus consults the renowned seer Tiresias, a wise old man, blind to the outside world but with inner insight. Tiresias refuses at first to reveal the terrible secret. However, he finally gives in after being hardpressed by the king: Oedipus has murdered King Laius, his father; Oedipus has married Queen Jocasta, his mother.

Oedipus enters into knowledge.

He gouges out his fleshly eyes, leaves Thebes, and, guided by Antigone, begins his long voyage in darkness toward Attica, while his two sons, Eteocles and Polyneices, divide the throne between themselves and end up killing each other.

At Colonus, Oedipus is stopped by the Erinnyes, snake-haired goddesses who guard the underworld. Here they are called the Eumenides, a new name by which they present their kindly face and allow the worthy to enter the abode of the gods.

Oedipus is introduced into this abode.

Note that Oedipus's foot, first crushed when he was hung from a tree in the forest, bears humanity's original wound. Oedipus, a son of Eve (so to speak), is wounded in the foot. He has already killed the Father. In the myth, Laius and Jocasta are the ontological parents, the

The Four Living Creatures. The four living creatures who surround Christ in Glory in Chartres Cathedral were already present in Ezekiel's vision (Ezekiel 1) and had been inscribed well before that in the collective unconscious.

archetypal king and queen. Thebes is the Greek equivalent of the heavenly Jerusalem. When driven out of the palace, out of his ontological norms, Oedipus leaves Eden.

With Oedipus's exposure to the wild beasts, the Greek myth depicts man's reidentification with the animal world after the Fall. Oedipus then becomes prey to his own energies.

But just as Adam, in the biblical myth, is covered by a coat of skin, Oedipus is protected by Corinthian shepherds who allow him to take on his energies, in other words, the animal world. These shepherds symbolize actual parents.

Oedipus, brought up by his Corinthian parents, represents each of us in relation to our actual parents. At a deep level, his essence is royal— for he is in God's image and is called to enter into his likeness—but in everyday life he is also a prey to energies—animal drives—which he has not begun to name, to know, to "marry." Our ontological dimension is overlaid by our existential, animal nature.

We have seen (chapter 6, page 57) that myths often express this double reality of man through the symbol of twinning: Cain and Abel, Jacob and Esau, to name the most famous in the Hebrew tradition; Castor and Pollux among the Greeks; and many others in Africa and elsewhere.

These twins always represent man in his ontological nature, carrying consciousness of the *yod*, and man's second nature (forgetfulness), when consciousness is erased (reidentified with animal nature).

This twin is man wounded in the foot!

At their birth we see Jacob holding Esau's foot in his hand, as if to check the leaking energies and cure it of its wound.

In the Greek myth both natures coexist in Oedipus-man: the ontological dimension is the one every man must regain (or remember) so as to realize it as he moves toward the Divine Likeness. Its symbol is the Green Tree of the forest. In this respect, the tree is the Green Man; and the Red Man, the man in a coat of skin, is Oedipus himself.

There is an odd symmetry between these two myths. The Green Tree in the forest holding the Red Man's foot at the time of the latter's birth corresponds to Jacob clasping the heel of his brother Esau in a similar circumstance.

We shall shortly look at these two brothers and their adventure (see chapters 7 and 11), but the similarity between these two myths already enables us to read, in Oedipus's story, the promise of this hero's recovery: his heel is seized by the Green Tree, maintaining the Red Man above the wild beasts of the forest (his energies), who thus cannot devour him. The Green Man, as the underlying force within Oedipus, will later come to the fore. Oedipus is swiftly moved away from his real parents so that he may ask himself the only real question about his being and his existence, the very question the Sphinx asks in her riddle. But before this, the oracle consulted at Delphi—the Green Man's consciousness—induces Oedipus to differentiate himself from the Red Man by leaving Corinth and proceed toward the royal city, Thebes, where his ontological parents reign.

The murder of Laius is simply a form of repetition of man's break with his ontological norms; and the wound on Oedipus's foot, inflicted by the royal chariot, is a form of repetition of the wound in the Garden of Eden.

In order to rediscover the image of the father in himself, to bring back to life the Father in his wounded consciousness, Oedipus must marry his mother.

Only by marrying the mother, "by returning to the *adamah* [the Mother Earth] from which he was taken" (Genesis 3:19), can Adam recover his ontological dimension and realize himself according to the original model.

Returning to Mother Earth, the royal mother, who governs the holy inner city with the king, means going through the Gate of Men.

A guardian of the threshold stands at the entrance and devours those who cannot answer its riddle. This guardian, related to all the devouring monsters found in mythology, is in turn devoured, that is to say, assimilated by whoever seizes the energy-information it embodies. He who has vanquished the monster is now informed and knows.

As long as we have not become, or integrated, these energies, the guardian remains a frightening dimension of ourselves. Its aim is for us to become the guardian itself. To this end, it obliges us to go toward our inner selves, to marry ourselves and the inner mother in order to access these energies within us. These guardians are often terrifying females because the inner feminine holds the strength that we are called upon to marry, which ultimately holds the kernel, the Name.

The tetramorphic Sphinx is Oedipus, whose accomplishment will be symbolized by the four children Jocasta bears him, four dimensions of himself, as he progresses through an ever-deepening marriage to his inner self—the energies of the mother.

"The Sphinx, according to some, was Laius's illegitimate daughter."[1]

This version confirms our interpretation: the Sphinx is "Oedipus's sister," meaning his as yet unaccomplished feminine side.

Ismene (vigorous strength) is the bull: the first stage of life, a grounding in the earth, the promise of fecundity, and the promise of the crown, symbolized by the animal's horns.

Polyneices (many victories) is the lion: the second stage of life, centered on the solar quality of true love, which makes possible all victories over oneself (marriage to one's energies).

Eteocles (true key) is the eagle, guardian of the Gate of the Gods, the holder of the power of the "keys" (the collarbones—clavicles—in the body; see chapter 14, page 283).

Antigone (before birth) is the restoration of ontological norms, the dimension in which man alone can accomplish the Name he embodies.

When the Sphinx asks the essential question, the Green Man in Oedipus clearly knows the answer:

On four feet in the morning, man is still identified with the animal and has not yet crossed the Gate of Men.

On two feet at midday, man is in the process of becoming vertical, of aligning with the axis from heaven to earth, connected to the two sustaining poles, Father and Mother, in his midday ("day of the *mi*").

On three feet in the evening, man has attained his kernel, his Name. By opening it, he liberates his threefold energy (see the study of the *yod* in chapter 9) and becomes One. He enters into the Divine Likeness.

Only the one who, through the Green Man, has established a link with his kernel can go through the first gate.

Oedipus goes through and marries the royal mother.

This couple is the only fertile one in Thebes. All other couples, and nature itself, are stricken with sterility. Clearly this sterility is linked with the murder of the father, and he who "does not remember" is sterile in the ontological sense of the word. (The Hebrew root זכר, *zakhor*, forms both the noun "male" and the verb "to remember"; see chapter 3, page 20). For he alone is fertile who brings *himself* to birth, who is reborn to different fields of consciousness, new lands. Therefore, what

The Archaic Sphinx. The Tetramorph symbolizes the four essential stages that man must realize within himself. The woman's face, last of these four stages, is the face of the celestial spouse. (Greece, sixth century BC; Acropolis Museum, Athens; photo by Giraudon.)

is stricken with sterility in Thebes is what Oedipus does not yet remember. He must become the Green Man in entirety, and to this end must remember the father.

Tiresias is his memory. Blind to the outside world, his inner eye is open; he is Oedipus's consciousness and male strength.

Only through total recollection of what he is can Oedipus wholly wed the Mother, and thus accomplish the descent into his own depths, into his own hell, where his kernel, his Name, awaits him.

Jocasta herself disappears from the story now, because the feminine side of Oedipus, which he must now marry, can only be married in the opening of a new vision, to which we are blind (see chapter 19, page 347).

Oedipus, guided by the daughter he has become—Antigone, who is the bearer of this vision of the depths—undertakes his descent into hell, into the thickest darkness. With Antigone ("before birth"), Oedipus recovers his ontological dimension, his "pristine heaven."

"In this operation, the eagle devours the lion," say the alchemists (see chapter 13, page 263). Antigone looks after the burials of her brothers, Polyneices, the lion, and Eteocles, the eagle, because she integrates them both.

Oedipus then arrives at Colonus, a "high place"—paradoxically we might say "deepest place"—before the three guardians of the Gate of the Gods, guardians of the Name.

Three and One.

Oedipus crosses over. He becomes his Name.

Achilles, or the Vulnerable Heel

The legendary wrath of "fiery Achilles" recalls the rage to which Oedipus gave vent in the defile.

The nymph Thetis, wanting her son Achilles to be invulnerable and therefore immortal, dips him at birth into the sacred waters of the Styx. The only part of the child's body not to be immersed is the heel by which Thetis holds him.

"Fleet-footed" Achilles remains a son of the earth, and mortal, because of his heel. In relation to the rest of his body, his divine essence, his heel is as if wounded. On this level, his energies spill out into warlike activities, alien to his conquest of himself. They spill out into wrath, ostensibly noble passions, and enormous conquests, but they are far from being invested in the construction of his divine being, his "immortal" nature.

At the siege of Troy, Paris, guided by the sky god Apollo, shoots an arrow that strikes vain Achilles in the heel. The hero has courage enough to pull out the arrow, but his blood pours out through the wound. The man collapses and dies. The Red Man dies.

That divine arrow is the divine ray. Man is visited by the *yod*, which obliges him to die to the Red Man in him in order to bring the Green Man back to life. The story of Achilles does not include this sequel.

Greek thought in general leads to it, but does not develop it. The Judeo-Christian tradition, however, displays this theme in all its grandeur.

In various myths, humanity, whose heel is wounded at the point where its energies arise, is none other than Eve, Adam's spouse, who, as the Bible has it, will give birth to the *yod*, the Messiah who will master the serpent. "And I will put enmity between you and *ishah* [the woman]," says God to the serpent, "between your seed and her seed; and her seed will bruise you as you are head, and you will wound *ishah*, as she is heel" (Genesis 3:15).

This to-and-fro movement between head and heel seems clearer as a result of what we have just seen.

The serpent designated here as "head" is the false spouse, to whom humanity has just surrendered, opened itself, and abandoned all its energies: the symbol of the foot with an open wound.

The genuine Divine Spouse feeds humanity so that it may grow and become the Bride, but the serpent gnaws at humanity's heel, whose wound he constantly chafes, draining it of its energy.

This wound is deep and deadly, and rivers of blood flow from it. This is where blind humanity loses its soul. Each and every one of us, unaware though warned, squander our strength and die when the bloodletting ceases.

Ontologically, man can only conquer the outside world by first conquering his inner cosmos. He can only become master of the earth outside himself by marrying the entire creation in the depths of its mystery and not by violating it from the outside, which brings about the bristling of its "brambles and thorns." To become gods is to marry the mother. Only then can one recapture the cosmos.

All else is mere activism, loss of energy, bloodletting, and death! The more noble or apparently useful the motive (nobility and usefulness belong to our psychological conditioning), the more subtle the danger. The majority of so-called "charitable works," carried out in the absence of spiritual awareness, are part of this bloodletting!

I will return to this later. For the moment, the essential questions are:

How to dress this wound?

How to staunch the flow of blood?

The path to recovery is found in the story of Jacob.

Jacob, or the Divine Heel; Healing of the Wound

We learn from Genesis that Jacob, even in his mother's womb, fights with his twin brother. His father, Isaac, is 40 years old when he marries Rebecca, so the second patriarch of Israel, the very symbol of this people, approaches the ordeal of the 4 in the rectangular part of the Tree under the auspices of this number 40. He gives up his crutches and chooses the woman, the 2, to become, with her, the 1.

Any marriage contracted before approaching this rectangle in the Tree is doomed to an agonizing duality, resulting in separation, unless husband and wife approach it together with the appropriate discipline.

With Isaac, the Hebrew people leave their crutches behind to enter the level of their Being, marked by the number 12 (the twelve dorsal vertebrae corresponding to the rectangle). Jacob, the third patriarch, having become Israel, is to experience this level through the twelve tribes he fathers.

In order to shift from a dimension of Having to one of Being, Isaac will have to wrestle with himself. His two sons fighting in their mother's womb are the heroes of this bout; they are man's double nature:

A primordial nature, in which there is potentiality for the divine *becoming*, symbolized by Jacob;

A "fallen" nature, in a coat of skin, symbolized by Esau.

Esau is the elder; he is the first one out of his mother's womb and hence the heir. He is "red, all over like an hairy garment" (Genesis 25:25). He is the Red Man, who has gone out of Eden. This man makes a nonentity of the man who is capable of becoming god. He holds the birthright, in other words, all power.

This is the turning point for the history of humanity: Jacob has no power, but nevertheless he holds his brother's heel in his hand, just as the Green Tree held Oedipus—the Red Man—by the foot.

"Heel," in Hebrew, is *aqev* (עָקֵב), hence the name Jacob–*Yaaqov* (יַעֲקֹב). The letter *yod* (י), placed before the word "heel," suggests that in Jacob the heel will meet the head and through him the Hebrew people will achieve their royalty. Man will recover his divine dimension.

The hand is a symbol of knowledge, and hence of power. Jacob's hand grasping his brother's heel means that Jacob will bring together all the human energies of the Adam that Esau contains, and accomplish them. He has complete power over them.

For this to happen, it is vital that within Isaac, the spiritual man, the Green Tree, should gain primacy over the Red Tree, the worldly man whom he loves ("Isaac loved Esau," Genesis 25:28). Isaac loves his coat of skin, even though he is on the way to unity.

Speaking of his wife, Rebekah, he says: "She is my sister" (Genesis 26:7). Now "Rebekah loved Jacob." She knows the seed she is carrying. Rebekah is a spiritual matrix, a point of change. Her name read backward is *haqever* (הקבר), "the tomb." She thus personifies the tomb in which the double process of death and resurrection takes place.

The first part of this change happens without her: Jacob must obtain primacy over his brother. In other words he must acquire the birthright: he prepares a soup, a *roux* ("red" in French; in Hebrew, *edom*). When Esau returns from the hunt, he, the Red Man, craves the dish. The exchange between the two brothers takes place around this red dish.

Symbolically, it means that Jacob abandons the "old Adam." He leaves him to his brother Esau, who eats him. Since eating is a symbol of identification, Esau becomes *Edom* (אדום = אדם + ו [6]), meaning, in Hebrew, the Adam fixed within the 6.

Esau, the Red Man, remains with his parents, and between these two "crutches" he stays at the child stage. Jacob departs; he must bring the house of Israel to the 7 so that it may regain unity. Esau abandons his birthright for the *roux* (pottage). Jacob now has complete power over

Isaac's inheritance. The new man has supplanted the old man ("to sup-plant" in Hebrew is again the same root: *aqev*).

With the complicity of his mother, Jacob puts on a false coat of skin, so that Isaac, now blind, is led to believe that Jacob is his first-born, the old Adam, who is to receive his blessing. In the Hebrew, there is a play on words between "first-born" and "blessing" (see chapter 8, page 101). This false coat of skin is clearly nonontological. Man's true nature is covered by this skin.

As for Isaac's blindness, it is curiously like the blindness of Oedipus. Jacob's evolution is a symbol for Isaac, who is himself in full progress, and his eyes are in the darkness of that journey that foreshadows spiritual light. He blesses his posterity in Jacob, whom he believes to be his first-born, giving him all power over his "brothers," the Red Men. Henceforward Jacob is prepared to bring this posterity back to the Promised Land by marrying successive Mother Earths until he meets the one containing the Name. Jacob's cunning counterbalances the cunning of the serpent in Eden.

So Jacob departs. He seeks a wife in the house of Laban, his mother's brother. He is to marry into his mother's lineage, a lineage of purification too, for *Laban* means "white." Once again, man through his *becoming* symbolically marries his mother, whereas Esau, who has become Edom, meaning fixed in the 6, in the commonplace, marries women "which were a grief of mind unto Isaac and to Rebekah" (Genesis 26:35).

Before we leave Jacob for now, let us also note that the word *aqev*, "heel" (עָקֵב 70-100-2), is close to the word *iqar* (עָקָר 70-100-200), which means "root," "belonging to the race."

There can thus be no doubt that Jacob's race is divine. The prophet Isaiah says: "He shall cause them that come of Jacob to take root, Israel shall blossom and bud, and fill the face of the world with fruit" (Isaiah 27:6).

The Green Tree was to blossom. The fruit that Israel was to bring forth is the one tradition speaks of as "the second Adam," the Christ.

In fact, Israel's whole lineage is Adam, the Adam Jacob artfully picked up from the dust where he was being devoured and raises to his true dimension.

But there is a crucial detail: Jacob not only puts on this coat of skin but receives with it the father's blessing. Later he is to transform the coat of skin into a garment of light.

Christ Washes the Apostles' Feet

The classic perception of Christ washing the feet of his apostles is that it represents humility. Though Master, he makes himself servant.

This is correct. But there is more to it.

First, the scene should be placed in context: Christ makes this gesture before sitting down to eat, to celebrate the Passover, the very heart of the mystery.

In our functional societies, where the sense of symbols is no longer alive, we wash our hands before a meal. When Pilate washes his hands, it means he refuses to know. Hands, we shall later see, are a symbol of knowledge. "I don't want to know, I don't want to be involved, it's not my jurisdiction" is what Pilate expresses as he declines all responsibility.

But the apostles must be brought back to their ontological norms before they can participate in the mystical supper that will give them a foretaste of the wedding banquet of man and God. Christ bends down before them and washes their feet. He thus cures the wound of humanity symbolically borne in the feet, for they carry the potential of the whole sick person.

"From the sole of the foot even unto the head, there is no soundness in it; but wounds and bruises, and putrifying sores: they have not been closed, neither bound up, neither mollified with ointment," says Isaiah (1:5–7), lamenting the sin of humanity symbolized by Israel.

But, speaking to Peter, Christ emphasizes the need to cure the

Christ Washing the Feet of His Apostles before the Last Supper. He cures the wound of his "spouse," humanity. Only then can she partake of the wedding banquet. (Early 13th century psalter; photo by Roger Viollet.)

wound by washing the feet alone: "If I then, your Lord and Master, have washed your feet, ye also ought to wash one another's feet" (John 13:14).

Similarly, Moses is ordered to take off his shoes before the burning bush. This bush is a symbol of the Tree of Life, ablaze with the Fire of Life, a fire that does not consume and has its roots in earth, which is pure. No foreign body must come between man's feet and Mother Earth.

Muslims remain conscious of this tradition and take off their shoes when entering the mosque. In various traditions, initiation into religious mysteries takes place barefoot. This physical stripping elicits a state of psychic and spiritual relinquishment.

This relinquishment requires laying down every burden at the foot of the Tree. Similarly, a man wanting to reach out to someone from whom he has been estranged as a result of some mistake "throws himself at his feet." This is what Mary Magdalene, the prostitute, did (Luke 7:37–38). She who had given herself to false lovers approaches the Spouse who awaits her. She represents humanity. Jeremiah had already lamented her sin:

How is she become as a widow! She that was great among the nations, and princess among the provinces, how she is become tributary!

She weepeth sore in the night, and her tears are on her cheeks: among all her lovers she hath none to comfort her: all her friends have dealt treacherously with her, they are become her enemies.

(Lamentations 1:1–2)

Mary Magdalene weeps; with her tears, she washes the feet of Christ; she wipes them with her hair and anoints them with perfume.

Here there are three new symbols—tears, perfume, and hair—to be studied in due course.

Might she not be the same woman whose name is not revealed by the Gospels, but who, on the night of the passion, anoints the head of Christ with a perfume of "pure nard, very precious" (Mark 14:3)?

From the feet to the head, the whole body becomes perfume.

CHAPTER 8

Malkhut II

The Knees

As far as I am aware, the only posture for prayer mentioned in the Bible is the following: "And Elijah went up to the top of Carmel; and he cast himself down upon the earth, and put his face between his knees" (1 Kings 18:42).

In this text, Elijah appears kneeling, with his head touching the earth between his knees. His prayer is fervent: he asks for rain for the parched earth—a shift to fertility! This posture for prayer, which is still that of Islam, may help us approach the meaning of the knees.

In astrology, the knees are linked with the sign of Capricorn, an earth sign in the heaviest and densest sense of earth, the sense of what is most secretly buried in its wintry depths.

The feet correspond to Malkhut as the water element. The knees also correspond to Malkhut, this time as the earth element. The feet are linked with the fetus in the mother's womb, and the knees are linked with the child at birth. More inwardly, the feet are linked with the not-yet-accomplished; the knees, with the accomplished. (Genesis expresses the unaccomplished with the symbol of water, or the moist; and the accomplished with the symbol of earth, or the dry.)

On the level of the Divine Energies, Malkhut (the Kingdom) is a receptacle for all these energies; Malkhut, at the end of the divine outbreath, is the seed of all Creation. On the cosmic level, Creation is the perfect receptivity of all created energies in the four elements that make it up. It is capable of giving forth the fifth element, the "quintessence," or divine inbreath, which brings Creation back to its original unity.

In Christian iconography, I have always been struck by the unexplained enigma of concentric circular lines around the knees of Christ in glory. The same concentric circles are found at other levels of the body. They appear to be important energy centers, each holding a specific power. What power do the knees hold?

The knees clasping the head, as in Elijah's posture, give the praying figure the shape of a seed, in which all forces are condensed. The head-knee relationship seems as powerful as the one we have just seen linking the head with the feet.

Elijah's Posture

Head and knees form a new pair in accomplishment. They are bound together by the "crown" quality that both possess.

The kneecaps are like two little crowns at the base of the Tree diagram, in which Keter (Crown) may be thought to find the confirmation of its promise.

In French both horses and children are said to "crown themselves" (*se couronner*) when wounded at the knee.

In Hebrew, "knee" is *berekh* (ברך). The head, ר, in the middle, is surrounded by the letters בך, which mean "within you"; as if this word ברך somehow also means "within you is the secret of your true head, the head that will be crowned." It can also be read as *bar* (בר)—the "young son"—on the way to the final *kaf* (ך), which will be his last seed

The Knees of Christ in Glory. The knees' vibrations spiral to form two crowns below, foreshadowing the single Crown (Keter) above. (Vézelay Cathedral, France.)

before entering the dimension of the "accomplished son," whose name is *ben* (בן), which has the same numerical value (702) as the knee.

In its numerical value, the knee already contains the energies of the Son. We know that if man realizes these energies, he enters the dimension of the crowned "bride." Thus man is blessed from the moment of his birth.

Pronounced *barukh*, the word ברך means the "blessed." For Arabs, *baraka* has the same meaning. Knee and blessing are the same word.

These three letters of the Hebrew word "knee," switched round (בכר), form the root of many words accounting for an initial birth. This seems to confirm that the child, linked with the feet in its fetal state, is born to the world and its cycles of time on the level of the knees. The word "knee" in French (*genou*) comes from the same root as the words *gene, generate, engender.* Certain initiatory rites require the one coming forward for a new birth to present himself with knee uncovered.

Pythagoras, who engendered knowledge, was called "the master with the golden knee."

If one again switches round the letters ברך, the word כרב is formed, and this is the root of "Cherub." The Cherubim are the eighth angelic hierarchy, of which Ezekiel was granted the vision: "Behold one wheel upon the earth by the living creatures. . . . The appearance of the wheels and their work was like unto the gemstones of Tarshish: As for their rings, they were so high that they were dreadful; and their rings were full of eyes round about them four" (Ezekiel 1:15–18).

The crown-wheel of the knees can be seen in Saturn, master of the sign of Capricorn, and Saturn is surrounded by rings.

Saturn—like the Capricorn sign—brings us to the other aspect of the prayer posture: the knees (and the head) in contact with the earth. When he is dubbed, the knight also puts one knee on the ground. Anyone who asks for strength from above anchors himself to the earth with his knees.

What exactly is this relationship between knee, Saturn, and earth?

Saturn is linked with lead. The child born into the cycles of time is nothing but "dross of lead" (Isaiah 1:25). Whoever can transmute this lead into gold will be born to the crown of eternity.

Transforming lead into gold is precisely the work of growth that man has to do, the work performed by the knight, the initiate, or any other human being experiencing his first inner birth.

Of Saturn, the alchemist Isaac Hollandus says:

Indeed, it contains the good Sun within it.
All the philosophers agree on this.
Truly, Saturn is the stone the ancient philosophers refused to name.
With a little work, one may convert Saturn into Moon; and with a
little more time or work one may convert it into Sun, then fix it and
turn it into the philosopher's stone.[1]

Hollandus describes in alchemical terminology the transmutation of our energies that, once freed from base material, are first raised to the level of Yesod (the moon), then to the level of Tiferet (the sun), which is the promise of the third level, Keter, the Crown.

"Saturn" and "lead" are the same word in Hebrew: *oferet* (עפרת). This word contains in essence the root *par* (פר), symbol of fecundity, caught in עת, *et*, "time." עת is Saturn's ring. The verb פרה, *paro*, is the verb "to grow, to be fruitful," which is found in the chapter where Adam is commanded by God to "be fruitful and multiply, and replenish the earth" (Genesis 1:28).

But at the beginning, man is just lead. His fecundity has not yet been released. This lead is all the heavier because in our world of darkness since the Fall it has nourished Satan, who is diametrically opposed to fecundity.

"And dust shalt thou eat all the days of thy life" (Genesis 3:14), says God to the serpent, Satan. Dust is the word *afar* (עפר), which, in the word עפרת (lead), is weighed down with the last letter of the alphabet, the *tav.*

Contrary to what undiscerning translations maintain, "dust" in the biblical text does not refer to the earth, but to Adam in his first fragmented state.

Literally: "And יהוה Elohim forms the Adam-dust out of the *adamah*" (Genesis 2:7). *Adamah* is the earth, made up on the sixth day of Genesis of all the beasts of the field. *Adamah* is Adam's inner earth, where countless energies abound.

"Dust," עפר, is a symbol of multiplicity, but not the multiplicity of the kind to which Adam is called in his fundamental vocation.

The call to "multiply" has nothing to do with the meaning usually given it, namely, "have many children," in other words, "make sure that there are births in the world." This interpretation of the divine command would nullify its first command: "Be fruitful, grow."

Genuine increase is promised as the outcome of inner growth, as the fruiting of the Tree that is Adam. This increase and fruiting of the Adamic Tree is inseparable from the paradoxical reality of its Unity. Adam, becoming One, breaks forth into fruit. An increase of descendants symbolizes this, but in itself still belongs to the dust that we unfortunately accumulate without cleaning up.

However, fecundity (פר) has been sealed into this dust we begin with, in this multiplicity symbolized by the teeming and swarming animals making up the *adamah* and all other earths to come.

And when Adam returns to dust after the Fall, he goes back to his first state, to his swarming multiplicity, forgetful of his first marriage with the *adamah* and thereby completely intermingled with it. It is even worse because man, returning to dust, is no longer aware of its power of fecundity. He is no longer conscious that he is the husband who is summoned to espouse his "earths." A curse has come between his earth-bride and him.

If we stay with this level of interpretation, however, we miss the deeper meaning of the text. God says: "In the sweat of thy nostrils shalt thou eat bread, till thou return unto the *adamah*, for out of it wast thou taken; for dust thou art, and towards thy dust, turn round" (Genesis 3:19).

The bread of sorrow is the enslavement that man experiences until he turns round and faces his *adamah*, his mother-bride; "for dust thou art"—literally "you dust," "you fecundity." Remember to emerge from the shroud of forgetfulness in which I have to bury you in order to save you from your illusion. Turn around!

The order is striking: *tashuv*, תשוב in Hebrew, is none other than *teshuvah*, "repentance," in the sense of the Greek word *metánoia*, "turning around."

Before being born, the child turns round in its mother's womb. On another level, deep in the waters of רע (the not-yet-accomplished), man has forgotten that these waters are also a fertile matrix and that he can turn round and be born to the light, טוב (the accomplished).

Kissing the ground, with knees and face touching it, "marrying" the external earth that symbolizes the inner *adamah*, is the posture of penitence.

Only in response to man's love will earth give water. Elijah knew this when seeking water for the earth. Man will only receive its strength for growth and its fruits for increase if, kneeling on the ground and humble (from *humus*, ground, earth), he "comes back to her" and once again becomes the loving spouse.

Christ accomplished this. He took away the curse resulting from the divorce of Adam and *adamah*.

Each one of us, knit to our kernel that is Christ, can remove this curse and come out of servitude. Then the knees will be able to be fertile once more.

From birth to inner birth, from the image of God that he is as בר, *bar* (young son), to the likeness to which he is called as בן *ben* (son), man transforms the cycles of time into a crown of eternity.

A Finnish creation myth, the *Kalevala*, describes the world as having arisen from the eggs of a teal deposited on the knee of the water goddess as she was momentarily lifting it above the waves.

> And her nest she there established,
> And she laid her eggs all golden,
> Six gold eggs she laid within it,
> And a seventh she laid of iron.
> O'er her eggs the teal sat brooding. . . .
> And she felt her skin was heated,
> Till she thought her knee was burning
> And that all her veins were melting.
> Then she jerked her knee with quickness,
> And her limbs convulsive shaking,
> Rolled the eggs into the water,
> Down amid the waves of ocean,
> And to splinters they were broken,
> And to fragments they were shattered. . . .
> From the cracked egg's lower fragment,

> Now the solid earth was fashioned,
> From the cracked egg's upper fragment,
> Rose the lofty arch of heaven.[2]

One might well imagine that on this same knee the upper and lower part of the eggshell, the *mi* and the *ma*, also join in marriage.

The Legs

From the feet to the knees, the legs symbolize the full power of realization of the seed from conception to birth, and until maturity.

Bearing in mind that our state at the moment of birth is that of a new seed within the cosmic matrix, our legs symbolize on the one hand the child's capacity for growth within the mother's womb, and on the other man's capacity for growth from his birth to his crowning.

Man's legs are certainly his tool for walking on the actual earth. But on a deeper level, they are also an image of other "legs" that will enable him to explore his inner earths and are supported by new "feet" for this purpose, new seeds that gather together his energies. These are the kidneys.

As man's power of realization, his legs are identified with his libido and with the horse's legs. If his libido is only invested on the first level— the level of Having—we have the bleeding illustrated in myths by descriptions of the wounded foot.

Thus the psalmist exclaims: "He delighteth not in the strength of the horse: he taketh not pleasure in the legs of a man" (Psalm 147:10).

Hiding away in man's unconscious, the libido takes on the role of master and furthers the activities of the slave, whom it leads to ruin.

The order of knights taught man how to mount his own horse, how to hold the reins, so that the animal may serve him. Its legs are then obedient to a conscious libido, a libido that is under control but above all is redirected toward its correct realization. The master horseman controls his horse almost entirely with his legs. He is at one with his horse, and the horse becomes, as it were, the legs and the accomplished energy of its master, who is still the head and the heart.

If the energy of the libido were to be truly realized, man would be free from the laws of the fallen world. Having explored all of his inner realms, he would no longer need a horse.

This is why God does not "delight in the horse" but in the accomplishment of what this animal symbolizes for man. It is also why man on horseback is fragile: his inner structures are not commensurate with the power of the steed. At this level he can only tame it, but not master it, and his unconscious forces run the risk of reverting to the animal at any moment.

At the other extreme, for someone who refuses or denies this animal nature, libido, or vital strength—for instance, someone who is completely cerebral—it would be as if he were deprived of his legs. He would then also be deprived of all possibility of self-realization.

The ascent toward the sefirah Yesod, described in the next chapter, will shed further light on this topic.

CHAPTER 9

Yesod, Sexuality, and Circumcision

YESOD, THE NINTH DIVINE SEFIRAH, IS THE "BASE," THE "FOUNDA-tion." It symbolizes a "divine accomplishment"—if one may separate this expression from the paradox of "movement/nonmovement."

It receives the energies of the first eight sefirot, focuses them and distributes them, causing them to blossom in the manifold yet unified profusion of Malkhut.

Yesod seems to be to Malkhut what the Ain Sof is to Keter: the Great Darkness in relation to manifestation.

According to kabbalistic tradition, it is as if Yesod were the ver-milion stone described by Ezekiel: a kind of prism through which the One-without-second turns himself into the Second-and-multiple in the splendor of Creation, perpetually emanating from his Glory (Hod, the seventh sefirah) and forever returning to it.

The level of Yesod seems to be a kind of center for the divine breath: "Thou sendest forth thy spirit [breath, word], they are created: and thou renewest the face of the earth" (Psalm 104:30). With his in-breath God withdraws into his essence, and this is the *shabbat* (Sabbath). This is the principle of rhythm.

Everything is respiration, and Yesod is its dwelling place. From here everything rushes into the splendor of the worlds, and from here every-thing returns to complete the One who is already complete, to bring to perfection him who is already perfect. Yesod is the Foundation of the worlds, an eternally creative act, and the sixth sefirah of Creation. It corresponds to the sixth day of Genesis, the day when man was created. By his word, in the image of the Divine Word, he is also a creator.

With the Fall, man turned his back on this power.

Let us attempt to see what happens from the perspective of his reascent, compromised as it is.

In the axis of the Middle Column, each sefirah is an icon of Ain (אין), the unknowable divine archetype, making itself known in the Name, *ha-Shem* (יהוה). Each of our names, participating in the Name, is registered on this column at different levels of realization, which correspond to the sefirot.

In Malkhut, one's personality is sculpted by one's given name. It embodies אין within the "I," the "self," in Hebrew *ani* (אני), made up of the same three letter-energies as its archetype, Ain.

But during childhood, this "I" remains somewhat undifferentiated from the archetype itself, which permeated it during its fetal period as well as for about the first three years after birth. Nor is it well-differentiated from those who gradually come to stand in for the archetype: parents or an authority of similar kind.

In Yesod, יסוד, "Foundation," which may also be translated as "secret (s*od*, דו) of the *yod* (י)"—"secret of the Name"—the adolescent begins to enter into resonance with his secret Name. Along indirect paths, he senses his connection with his future adult structures. He then begins to discover his personality, the first known expression of his person, which leads him to call into question and even sometimes to reject parental support.

The breath of the *yod* makes adolescents aspire to surpassing excellence. It is the period of the greatest mystical elation, invested in all kinds of areas—religious, patriotic, political, artistic, amorous, etc.—all of them fundamentally erotic.

It is the birth of eros at this level.

At this time a danger threatens the adolescent: that of reidentifying himself with the object of his exaltation, which he deifies because he unconsciously projects onto it *ha-Shem*, the Name, יהוה. This gives rise to different masks, behind which the adolescent hides himself from himself, forming and solidifying a false self. Or he may confuse his ordinary, nonexalted "self," אני, which is soon trivialized, with יהוה, which then becomes inflated and completely sterile.

Man is then no longer capable of becoming the cosmic creative Word by reaching Tiferet and then Keter. Instead he recreates himself again and again, reproducing his infantile "I"'s one after the other.

Generally, almost all of man's energies gathered in Yesod are invested in his descendants, his little kingdom (Malkhut) on earth, of which he is the self-proclaimed king. Man's becoming is reduced to the level of the ordinary.

It is essential to observe that this contact with the self—participating in the *Shem* (the Name)—partakes in depth of the same reality as the dawn of sexuality, the eros of this level. This is why most of the time man remains fixated at this level. Either he represses this vital force, associating it with condemnation and forbidden fruit, or he is submerged in the tidal wave of its quasi-deification.

Any sefirah on the Middle Path—where the *mi* joins with the *ma*—expresses the balance and harmony gained through working with these existential oppositions.

In this sense, *Yesod* is also called *tsedeq*, "Justice." *Yesod* must be experienced with justice.

Melchizedek, described in Genesis 14:18 as "king of peace [of *Salem*]," and whose name means "king of justice," levies a tithe upon Abraham. A tithe, the tenth part of his goods, is a symbol of the *yod*, which thus reveals its profound claim: part of the energies from this level must be devoted to the very construction of the Name. It involves self-discipline and concealment of the two erotic aspects of man's reality within Yesod: his "self" and his sexuality.

The ritual of circumcision, examined later, sheds light on this theme.

Any form of crushing self-discipline is wrong; any refusal of self-discipline is equally wrong. Acquiring freedom is not a matter of license, which is alien to all archetypes, but of justice, which is the image of the archetype.

Sod, the "secret" (from the Latin *secernere*, "to divide off") which partakes of the "sacred," is also an image of the archetype. Yesod gives birth to the first vertebrae of the spinal column, which are called "sacral." Any function pertaining to this level is sacred. Sexuality today has lost its sacredness in the illusory prospect of man's self-realization. This outcome is logical, in view of the sole end attributed to it by the religious imperatives of the last few centuries: procreation.

In the light of the diagram, let us try to discern the deeper sense of bodily union.

Mirroring Keter above, which introduces man to his ultimate marriage, Yesod, below, is the entrance to the nuptial chamber, the sanctuary where the secret marriage of man and woman is accomplished. During the first centuries of the Christian church, weddings were celebrated at midnight. Similarly, man, in the dead of night, in the heart of his inner winter, unites with himself in the depths of Tiferet. In the darkness of the abyss, he will unite with God in Keter.

On its different levels, the entire Middle Column brings into focus the mystery of the encounter of two becoming one.

Delight presides over this universal in-breath, in its varied degrees of participation in the ultimate delight known to man as he begins the process of deification. This delight remains long after the exhaustion of the body, which ends in death.

Any death that does not make of man a partaker of this divine union forces him—by the inexorable law of repetition in the commonplace—to start over. It forces man back to the Gate of Men, where the inhabitants of Thebes are devoured by the Sphinx, and where Edom (the Red Man) is engulfed in the Red Sea, which parts its waters, allowing Jacob, who has become Israel, to cross over. He is then on the way to the promised land, to the conquest of the Upper Triangle, to the realization of the Green Man.

In this context, physical delight on the level of Yesod, accompanied by rejoicing of the heart, is in itself good and just, and an image of heaven on earth.

Furthermore, this delight in Yesod, a reflection of the delight held within Keter, is also a means of reaching that ultimate delight.

Throughout many generations, willy-nilly, Western Christianity has been moralistic. Thus it is hardly ready for this experience. But it could at least become aware that delight and pleasure are authentic. Doing without them for the sake of being moralistic is as wrong as misusing them through ignorance and turns out to be destructive and childish.

Union of Man and Woman. Mirroring Keter (above), which introduces man to his ultimate marriage, Yesod (below) is the entrance to the nuptial chamber, where the union of man and woman takes place in secret. (Pen-and-ink drawing by Michel Mille.)

For eight centuries, Western Christianity has tended to identify itself with morality. In order to justify the "work of the flesh," whose deeper meaning it did not understand, it made children the aim of marriage and imposed this purpose upon married couples. This is the source of many false problems on which much energy is wasted today. This is where the wounded foot starts to grow.

The child, or the one born of two, is the image here below on earth of the spouses' *becoming*, reaching toward unity above. In this sense, the child is sacred. But he is not the couple's aim. Giving an image absolute value means mistaking the ordinary for something else. Sometimes the child is deified; he can then only remain the fruit of Having. Once he is an adult, he will unite with another adult, become "two" in order to acquire another "one," who will repeat the process. Procreated humanity multiplies without becoming fruitful and makes no progress toward Being.

In a different field, when a thesis and its antithesis give rise to a synthesis, which itself becomes the thesis of a new antithesis, and so on, we end up with a sequence of trite repetitions and are trapped in an infernal and wearisome round. If one of the terms is set up as an absolute, it generates a heap of destructive passions. To see this, we need only to look at ideologies enforced by religion or party politics.

So, how do we get off the roundabout?

How do we introduce the only real third term, which brings unity above, not below?

By conquering the Sphinx, or any guardian of the threshold relating to the Gate of Men, by crossing the Red Sea with the Hebrews, or by entering the ark with Noah. These are what our myths suggest.

All these themes imply a surpassing of one's self. This third term to be conquered transcends the physical and psychological worlds; its apprehension transcends our ordinary mental categories. Only a symbol can describe it, only myth can bring it to light. Getting to the heart of the message is the first step to be taken, to enter into knowledge of our destiny and embark on the path to realization.

Of course using myth is not the only way to enter into the experience of this Strait Gate. But it throws light on it, and those who in one way or another are confronted by the Sphinx may be helped by considering it.

As long as humanity remained childlike and irresponsible, very few men were aware of this passage. Today, as humanity is throwing away its crutches, as, like Oedipus, it leaves its adoptive father and sets out to discover the secret of its birth, it stands en masse before this gate, drowned in a flood of ignorance. Far from setting it free, academic knowledge often submerges it yet further by creating a technical, dehumanized world. All humanity is gripped by a latent anxiety, sensing the implacable jaws of a monster slowly closing upon them.

Who will set it free?

The Judeo-Christian tradition offers the children of Israel as the prototype of humanity. Their journey should enlighten us.

Circumcision

Out of Israel, the Word, the Logos, the Savior, is born. Abraham, the first patriarch of Israel, is its "Foundation," Yesod. He is the seed of a new humanity. The promise "I will make of thee a great nation" is the fulfillment of the command given in Genesis 1:28: "Be fruitful, and multiply."

This multiplication is not quantitative, which would imply the proliferation of children, or the "reign of quantity" denounced by René Guénon, but qualitative. One must first *mature* (be fruitful), which is to say attain the summit of the Tree, the true head, where the sap brings forth fruit. Only on this level will humanity experience the multiplication of the fruits of its Being rather than of its Having, a multiplication that is inseparable from the unity achieved.

It then becomes significant that this promise of fruit is given to Abraham at the conclusion of a covenant that God makes with him requiring that every male child born of his loins or of his posterity be circumcised (Genesis 17:11–12).

Circumcision does not come under Mosaic law. It does not come under the jurisdiction of a code made necessary because the people were immature or childish. It belongs ontologically to the people born of Abraham, whose calling is to bring to birth the Savior, the Messiah, the Word.

Israel, called to the Divine Likeness, must become Word.

When Israel brought to birth him in whom Christians have recognized the Word, a first council brought together the heads of the founding church to resolve the question that divided them: should Christians be circumcised or not? The decision was that there were no longer any grounds to practice circumcision (Acts 15): humanity had given birth to the Word.

Yet Paul was to insist that circumcision should take place on the level of the heart, then of the ears (Romans 2:29). The apostle renews the order of יהוה given in the words of the prophet Jeremiah: "Circumcise yourselves to יהוי, and take away the foreskins of your heart" (Jeremiah 4:4). These are other stages of the ascent to be considered later.

For the sap does indeed rise to the very top of the Tree, making it fruitful. "Be fruitful" or "be fertile" is the same word in Hebrew, *peru* (פרו), containing the root פר, *par*, as we have seen in chapter 8 (pages 103–4). It is found on all the rungs of the Tree, as if to mark out the rise of the sap. However, this sap will never reach the summit if it is absorbed into the lower branches.

This is why, when cultivating trees, the law of pruning governs the rising of the sap. Pruning is for the tree to bear fruit. This set expression for pruning shows how it is justified on all levels. The depth of its meaning can be seen at the level of interest to us here.

Cutting off the shoots, the low branches, removes the causes of bleeding. It seals off the wound, so that each man in particular—along with the whole of humanity—may bear fruit and "multiply" in his fruits.

Man's power then shifts from the procreative organ to the creative word. And paraphrasing the Greek fathers of the first centuries, whose summary of the Christian mystery was "God became man so that man may become God," we can reformulate the prologue from St. John's Gospel: "The Word was made flesh, so that flesh might become Word."

To make flesh into Word is man's creative calling. Circumcision, which is pruning the flesh on the level of Yesod in order for it to bear fruit, is the law governing this calling. (See the "flesh," chapter 11, page 165, and chapter 12, page 202.)

The ceremony *brit milah* (ברית מילה), or "covenant of circumcision," takes place in three stages.

In the first stage, called *orlah* (עורלה), the foreskin is cut. *Or* (עור; see chapter 3, page 21) is the coat of skin. *Orlah*, cutting the skin, is awakening to light. For the whole ceremony aims at uncovering the glans, which symbolizes the Light and Word. The skin—foreskin—is then thrown into the "dust" in order that Light may appear.

During the second stage, called *priah* (פריה), the flesh is pushed apart, divided, in order to uncover בשר, *basar*, the original "flesh" (Genesis 2:21), which is the principle of life. *Priah* (פריה) is the word meaning "fruitfulness, fertility, fecundity"—פרי (*p'ri*) is the "fruit." *Priah* is made up of the root פר (*par*), which symbolizes fecundity, and of the two sacred letters *yah* (יה) at the beginning of the holy Tetragrammaton.

Laying bare the original flesh is a return to man's ontological norms, to the power of his fertility, which in this case does not concern procreation, but the act of giving birth to יה, *Yah*, the Divine Child, who reveals the Name of which the actual child is the symbol.

Procreation is linked with the Fall and with time, in which we have to perpetuate the species; it is a secondary function with this aim in view.

In the third stage, called *mtsitsah* (מציצה, "sucking"), the *moel* (the circumciser) sucks the blood in order to uncover the *nefesh*, the living soul linked with the blood. The child becomes a living soul again. This touches on the mystery of blood, to which we shall return in chapter 12.

The *milah* is the final blood sacrifice, which is brought to an end by Christ the Word making himself the circumcision of the world.

In the word *mtsitsah* (מציצה), the Divine Name י‍ה, *Yah*, is at the heart of the verb *motsets*, "to suck." In a deep sense, the *moel* draws י‍ה. He spits out every veil separating the child from his profoundest soul, in order to return him to his Name.

Traditionally, a chair intended for Elijah is prepared for this ceremony, over which the prophet presides invisibly.

The law is never separated from prophecy, without which it would be sterile. Tradition says that Elijah's role is to prevent the light from being covered by a new and satanic darkness. To this end Elijah himself invisibly covers the light with a veil, to be uncovered only at the coming of the Messiah.

We see here how far the Christian mysteries are entwined with the Jewish. John the Baptist is "Elias [Elijah], which was for to come" (Matthew 11:14). Identifying himself with the veil and speaking of Christ, he says: "He must increase, but I must decrease" (John 3:30). If the veil is to diminish, this means light has come into the world, the Messiah has come.

As with the foreskin, John the Baptist, the man in a coat of skin (he is clothed in camel's hair), is put aside, so that the Word may appear.

When the *moel* sucks the blood in order for the soul to become a living soul (*nefesh-hayah*), he is an image of the Father, who draws up the blood of the Son so that the Spirit may descend into the world.

Milah (מילה, circumcision) is also the מלה, "Word of (י) the *yod*." Another word for circumcision is מול, *moul*, which is a face-to-face encounter.

After the successive circumcisions required by Jeremiah and Paul, man starts being face-to-face with himself until he reaches a complete face-to-face, discovering his true Self, his Name.

This aspect of circumcision lays emphasis on the Name, the true and mysterious "person" that each one of us is. Circumcision in this case is rather that of the self. To circumcise the self, the ego, is to take into account the "other," without whom one cannot reach the genuine אני, *ani*, the Name.

Initially, the "other" is oneself—the nonaccomplished *ra* (רע) aspect of oneself.

The "other" then becomes every being outside oneself, whom one may only approach in love, because he is the outer pole corresponding to one of one's inner energies partaking in רע, *ra*, and which we have to bring to light and make טוב, *tov*. Even the most wicked, even the enemy, is a reflection of the person we are.

Pronounced *réa* (רע), this same word becomes "friend," "neighbor"; you might say the only one with whom we can *realize* ourselves.

To circumcise the self is to begin plowing the inner earth, for which we are more responsible than we can imagine. Christ says about one who does not do this work: "From him that hath not, even that he hath shall be taken away from him." (Luke 19:26). Even his potential will be taken away.

Circumcision is the basis for all acquisition.

The tree must be pruned for it to bear fruit.

Procreation versus Creation

Women experience bleeding every month, and this is linked to a lunar rhythm. (Cosmologically, as we have seen, the moon corresponds to Yesod.) This phenomenon obeys the law of the Fall according to which humanity, on this level, loses its blood.

Eve—who is humanity—is wounded in Yesod. Through this wound, she loses her creative energy. This is why in all traditions women are deemed impure during the time of menstruation. *Impure* meaning still in the unaccomplished.

Moreover, women are regarded as impure during procreation and remain outside the Temple, doing penance for forty days after childbirth.

This penance ought to include an awareness of exactly what external motherhood involves in relation to the motherhood that man has to take on ontologically.

This essential motherhood is preset within the name of Adam. *Adam* (אדם) is built round the letter *dalet* (ד), the 4, which means "halt." Around this *dalet* is the word אם, *em*, "mother." Another contradiction! Where there is motherhood, there is begetting, movement, and life. Adam, having to bring to birth the god he is, must go through times of apparent standstill that are ontological gestations. Essentially, Adam mothers himself to become himself, to travel the whole way to himself through a series of "doors" (*dalet*, the full form of the letter ד).

In spite of the Fall, which entails losing the path toward likeness, Adam's vocation remains inextricably part of him, but now is to be accomplished in sorrow: "I will greatly multiply thy sorrow and thy conception; in sorrow shalt thou bring forth children" (Genesis 3:16).

We can also read the name *Adam* (אדם) as אד, *ed*, and דם, *dam*, respectively meaning "vapor" (Genesis 2:6; see chapter 6 of my book *La lettre: chemin de vie*) and "blood," that is, *water* (unaccomplished), which must be accomplished in *blood*, itself unaccomplished in relation to the totally accomplished Spirit.

The water vapor, אד, laden with energies destined to be accomplished, is waiting to be called up from the depths by man's desire for God. When it is linked with a desire for external possessions, blood flows outwardly.

This is what happens in menstruation and what happens too when blood is being spilled. People driven by a hunger for power rise up one against another in fratricidal wars and periodically lose their blood and their souls, remaining stuck in lunar rhythms unbroken by any dawn or any begetting.

When will humanity reach the age of fifty?

For woman is freed from this bleeding when she moves from her forties to the great jubilee of the number fifty (see *La lettre: chemin de vie*, chapter 16). She is freed from procreation, and if she has passed through the Gate of Men, she should enter into the springtime of her ontological *becoming*, which is truly creative. Outwardly she ages, but inwardly she enters into the joy of bringing herself to birth. It is the same for men at this time.

In Hebrew, the word *gil* (גִּיל) means both "age" and "joy."

Most women, reaching that age, put on the mask of a counterfeit spring. Humanity as a whole resembles them; it has not yet passed through the Gate of Men. It loses its energies, its blood, and its soul. Impure indeed, since it is completely identified with the nonaccomplished energies and thus remains unaccomplished.

Purification is accomplishment.

Outward motherhood may remain in nonaccomplished categories, when women make it an end in itself. Or it can be a pathway toward accomplishment, in which case it is one of the finest paths.

The child then is no longer a "golden calf" but an image of the Divine Child, and outward motherhood finds its resonance within the woman who now invests her energies in inner gestation. Men—and those women who cannot become mothers—do not have this experience, though they have many other means of experiencing inward motherhood.

Jacob parting from his brother Esau is the prototype of every being who, distancing himself from himself, proceeds toward inner marriage and inner motherhood.

On the path to this marriage Jacob has the dream of the ladder, mentioned earlier (chapter 6, page 59). The ladder is set upon the earth in a place called לוּז, *Luz*.

Luz, in relation to this cosmic ladder, corresponds to the base of the spinal column, that is fundamentally to the sefirah Yesod. *Luz* is the "almond tree." But it is also linked with the verb *laluz*, "to detach oneself," "to separate oneself." We can only bring to blossom the almond tree whose base is in Yesod when we have left behind whatever does not belong with the conquest of the *yod*, of eternity.

The almond—symbol of eternity—is the fruit of light hidden in the shell of time. The shell may be seen as "skins," or again as the foreskin. Jacob mobilizes *luz* and takes it with him to make it blossom, to shift from the symbol to the archetype, from image to likeness. Jacob therefore gives another name to the land on which the ladder is set. *Luz* is to climb the ladder with him.

According to one tradition, we possess a little bone at the base of the spine, which is incorruptible and cannot be destroyed, even by fire. It is our seed of eternity (see chapter 21).

CHAPTER 10

The Hod-Netsaḥ-Yesod Triangle,
or the Urogenital Plexus

THIS TRIANGLE IS THE REFLECTION OF THE UPPER TRIAD, WHICH calls to it and is a container for Man's first gestation on his way to becoming Word.

The urogenital grouping has the same pattern and fundamental structure as the audiovocal grouping at the level of the head, which was also an embryological unit.

A differentiation occurs in the third week of intrauterine life: the perception of sound becomes distinct from the vocal organs; the renal function becomes distinct from the genital function.

Each of these two units follows a fundamental respiration, a "breath," symbolized by the Hebrew letter ה (*heh*). The early form of this letter represents a man stretching his lungs, his arms, and his hands vertically. (Each side makes up the letter ה of the Divine Archetype הוה.)

Archaic Heh

In time, the shape of the letter evolved, becoming restricted to the upper part of the body. This image ⊔⊔, as it turned away from the sky above and moved more and more toward the horizontal, is the origin of our letter "E."

This is a consequence of the Fall and seems to have been taken yet further, with the breath becoming horizontal, so to speak, rather than vertical as before. The lower part of the body is fashioned by this

123

reversal. One of the traditional images of man is indeed that of the two ה inverted. The sex and the word then become mirror images one of the other.

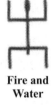

Fire and Water

The figure opposite emphasizes this double function of the "breath." The higher function, linked with fire, empowers the creative Word, which is inseparable from listening, and the lower function, linked with water, ensures procreation, the goal of which is to bring our generations to fulfillment. Procreation is inseparable from the function of the kidney, the "ear" on this floor (see next chapter).

The sefirotic triangle Yesod-Hod-Netsaḥ, which we are now looking at, corresponds to this lower *heh* (ה). Here the "genital respiration" is linked with the making of the actual child as well as with the formation of the inner child, the one being the symbol of the other. A child will grow better when his or her parents allow their own inner child to grow.

The letter ה is the "seed of life." God names us with his breath. We are "created," then "made" around the sacred Name within each of us. These two verbs, *bara* (to create) and *asah* (to make), are clearly distinguished in Genesis.

Nine months are needed to bring the baby to completion, but it takes a lifetime to complete the inner child and bring him from his embryonic condition (image), to the condition of the creative Word to which he is called (likeness).

Fundamentally, this Lower Triangle (and the other two) corresponds to areas of transformation well known to the Chinese as the Cinnabar Fields. "According to Taoists their awakening contributes to the search for immortality."[1]

The "search for eternity" might be the actual Chinese expression, for such is man's ontology according to the Hebrews.

The Cinnabar Field in the thorax governs fusion with oneself. And the Cinnabar Field in the cranium governs fusion with the universal in an encounter with the unique. This admirable message confirms that of the Hebrews.

The first area of interest is the place of sexual fusion with the "other," the pelvic Cinnabar Field—our Lower Triangle. Its concrete fruit will be the fetus, the future child. But rarely does motherhood or fatherhood correspond to an "awakening" of this center.

When the Taoist tradition speaks of an awakening, it speaks—like the Hebrew tradition—of a new kind of listening, for inner information rather than outer, which opens in the direction of a new field of consciousness.

On this level another dimension of the adolescent's sexuality comes into play: his encounter with his environment, his culture, everything that contributes to shaping him but more often than not maintains him in the commonplace. He is then either sterilized for a while within his profound "Self," his *yod*, or savagely tested by a world that cannot tolerate his "difference."

This environment is humanity as a whole, which we may take as obeying the same law of growth as man does. However, humanity has not yet come out of this first matrix, or passed through the Gate of Men, and it cannot enable one of its own to go through it. Its institutions, schools, universities, social groups, political parties of all stripes, and communities with religious pretensions reduce their members' aspirations to their own safe framework, because they conform to the logic of its first field of consciousness.

The person who is to be born to the Gate of Men takes charge of his evolution despite humanity and very often against it.

He experiences a distressing loneliness on this level. One is always alone during birth or death. But the loneliness experienced on the other levels, however great, is not tainted with the kind of despair endured by one who at the outset knows nothing of the path.

On this level, the adolescent becomes conscious of the bondage that ties him down—his fears, the fears and the bondage of the world, and the absurd spiral in which both he and the world are turning. He suffers, is prey to sickness, and sees his approaching death.

He is torn between the infinity that he senses within himself and what the world reduces him to. The question is whether he will have the strength to persevere and discover meaning in all this.

To uncover meaning is an awakening.

The energies weaving the tissue of this first field require some investigation in the light of the Divine Body. When we know them, we can attempt to gather them together, in order to mobilize the *yod* with "justice" and thus solidly form the embryo of the inner child.

At puberty, the adolescent entering this first triangle receives the energies of the three sefirot Hod-Netsaḥ-Yesod, which adumbrate the qualities of what are to become the fruit of the human Tree. This fruit is described for us in the book of Genesis: it is "good for food . . . pleasant to the eyes, and desirable² for success" (Genesis 3:6).

These three elements are those of our ontological structures:

1. Man is called to enjoy the knowledge of God. This *enjoyment* is linked with the sefirahYesod.
2. He is called to acquire knowledge. This *possession* is linked with the sefirah Hod, the divine Glory that pervades all things (see the Sefrotic Tree on page 27).
3. Finally, he is called to exercise power over all creation, in the invincible might granted him by the knowledge of God. This *power* is linked with the sefirah Netsaḥ.

In an archetypal sense, "glory, honor and power" (Revelation 4:11) are God's. It behooves man to partake of his gifts. They fashion man from adolescence onward, through the time of his interior gestation, obliging him to make his way painfully through the mysteries of life and the labyrinth of experiences, toward the Strait Gate of his true birth.

The same energies work on adolescent humanity, which has not yet solved its problems with enjoyment in spite of Freud, with power in spite of Adler, or with possession in spite of Marx.

These three great heralds of today's social sciences are unconsciously inspired by the archetypes of these three qualities of energy. But they bring them down to the level of this first triangle, instead of inviting humanity to consciously experience these energies in order to attain their respective archetypes. But it is only by opening ourselves to archetypal Reality that we will manage to solve the huge problems that are tearing the world and ourselves apart.

Great surges of generosity have chanted hymns to such triads as Liberty-Equality-Fraternity. These may not be foreign to our objective, but when reduced to the jejune forms in which they are usually experienced, they only move the problems about without solving them and bring no evolution.

What we have to do is climb Jacob's ladder, symbolized by our spinal column. We must build up the first ten vertebrae—five sacral, five lumbar—through the kind of work for which we desperately seek a master.

The master is within.

Any outside master is only genuine insofar as he stimulates the essential dimension within ourselves. And one way to stimulate it is to follow the strides of the heroes of our myths, those great builders of inner kingdoms.

To tread in their footsteps, place our hearts in theirs, and bring our understanding down into our hearts is indeed a path. It is the path set out by the amazing riches of our sacred texts—and secular texts too, for in the legacy of the collective unconscious, what appears to be secular is merely what secular eyes see, in the same way as a dream may appear silly to one who cannot decipher its divine language.

All myths have something to say about the three fundamental energies of Enjoyment-Possession-Power, whose tentacles cling fearfully and tenaciously to the world of Having. They also speak of their redirection toward the level of Being. Yet some myths emphasize a particular aspect of this triad.

Let us first look at the story of the Flood, which is common to all traditions. We can head with Noah for the acquisition of *enjoyment*, to which are opposed the anarchical and the absurd, which lead to disenchantment.

Then we will journey with the Hebrews into Egypt, where this people experienced for 430 years the bitterest servitude in a foreign land. We shall undergo the ten contractions of a birth induced by Moses in order to experience the Passover, the "crossing," and follow the divine guide in the conquest, the *possession* of the Promised Land.

Finally, we shall reread the story of the labyrinth. The Greek myth of Theseus seems the most enlightening of all labyrinth stories, although in a negative way, since the hero's ignorance leads him toward a lamentable illusion of *power.*

After that we shall return to Jacob and share his combat for an entire night—the night of our gestation—in order to be born to the light. The wound on his hip will be the fundamental language of this stage. Then, with Christ, we will sink into the waters of baptism in order to emerge from the waters, so that we may go with him toward the baptism of fire at the level of the heart.

Thus we shall accomplish the first part of our inner voyage, a voyage to the center of our first inner earth.

The Flood

The Flood is the image of the chaos and anarchy of the world.

An-archē (etymologically, "without archetype") means that the waters below (*ma*) are cut off from the waters they came from (the waters above, *mi*) and to which they are ontologically linked by the *shamaim*, the "heavens," on the second day of Genesis.

For man, the heavens are the different fields of consciousness or energy of which he is formed. When symbolized by the "waters," they are still unaccomplished. The energies composing them are within us ("The kingdom of God is within you," Luke 17:21), but they no longer have any meaning when they have been severed from the divine. They are the subject matter of our passions and our psychological life. They are devoured, as previously seen, by the Satan (chapter 8, page 103).

The Flood is a compelling description of each of us in our state of total unconsciousness. What we call "conscience" is part of this, and it is all the more dangerous when confused with an awakening to consciousness. It is also a compelling description of the present state of humanity.

During Noah's time (Genesis 6–8), "men began to multiply on the face of the earth and daughters were born unto them." The situation is revealed with startling conciseness. In regard to the divine command "be fruitful, and multiply," men forgot to grow and be fruitful, and they multiplied in the outside world, in "the reign of quantity."[3] That they gave birth to daughters means no one—man or woman—was inwardly male. In other words no one "remembered" their inner heavens, their energies; no one remembered their spouse, *ishah*, whom they must conquer in order to accomplish themselves.

In Hebrew the word "male" and the word "to remember" share the same root (זכר, *zakhar*). The "feminine"—נקבה, *neqevah*—is a "hole" containing the secret of the Name. Yet unless the male work is done, it is an empty hole. And the human being identifies completely with this vacuum, which he fills up with all sorts of outward activity: essentially, he eats, drinks, sleeps, breeds, and works, overcome by the fear of losing his consumer products, which saps his strength. He suffers, feeds the Satan, and dies exhausted.

And here is *Noah* (נח), a name whose root is linked with the notions of "leading" and "rest, consolation, repentance."

His father, Lamech, brings him into the world, saying: "This same will comfort us concerning our work and toil of our hands, because of the *adamah* which יהוה hath cursed" (Genesis 5:29).

Noah's calling is inscribed in his name: he repents and leads to the rest that is the state of likeness—the state of marriage between God and man.

Noah foreshadows the Messiah who was yet to come, says St. Hilary of Poitiers. In *Traité des mystères*, he speaks of Lamech's prophecy, saying "that it cannot apply fully to the Noah we speak of, but to him who said: come unto me, all ye who labor and are heavy laden, and I will give you rest. . . . For my yoke is easy, and my burden is light."[4]

יהוה sees the corruption of man. He repented that he had *made* him (not *created*, which is the work of Elohim). "Making" is man's interior work, under the governance of יהוה and his requirement for growth. This is not about God's repentance, but about man repenting inasmuch as he is a potential יהוה.

יהוה says to Noah: "My spirit shall not rule within man for him to remain intact" (Genesis 6:3).

Man's calling is essentially a marriage with himself in order to give birth to יהוה, who he potentially is, and to enter the divine wedding.

"For that this one (the Adam) also is flesh," says יהוה. And the word "flesh"—בשר, *basar*—is the primordial earth-flesh, containing in its center the letter ש—the kernel, the *shem*, the place of the ultimate wedding (see chapter 9, page 117, and chapter 12, page 202).

"A hundred and twenty years" are given him to achieve it. "יהוה begins working on the heart of man." He warns Noah of what is about to happen. Then Elohim himself intervenes and says to Noah: "The accomplishment [the end] of all flesh is coming" (Genesis 6:13).

This Hebrew word קץ (*qets*), which I translate as "accomplishment" rather than "end," has nothing to do with a punitive, annihilating ending but with the ending of a period of sleep in order to enter a period of realization. Its letters have a numerical value of 900 + 100 = 1000.

קיץ (*qayits*) is the "summer," the fruiting season, whose essential fruit is the *yod*. With this in view, Elohim commands Noah to construct an ark. The imminent events are to take hold of every living soul and compel it to transform according to its state of evolution.

The ark, the תבה (*tebah*) in Hebrew, is a word of great importance, as it joins the two letters ב and ת, which form the word בת (*bat*), the "daughter," virgin of Israel. Between these two are all the letters of the Hebrew alphabet except the *alef* (א). They constitute, symbolically, all the created energies.

In asking him to construct his *tebah*, Elohim invites Noah to "grasp"—to become aware of—all his energies, that is, to become aware of himself as being *ishah*, the reservoir of energies he must penetrate, in order to marry it.

Noah gathers together all his energies: the animals, the living beings (חית, *hayot*, in Hebrew). These "animals" are the energy fields of the different earths Noah will have to marry within his ark, meaning within himself.

We could say that Elohim causes Noah to pass through the Gate of Men by leading him into the ark. Elohim leads Noah toward the Gate of the Gods, inviting him to do the work that we have already approached through Oedipus's great adventure. (I will say more about this later.)

Noah's ark is our inner *being*.

יהוה now confirms Elohim's command.

Let us pause. This stage of the story admirably describes the operative process of our work within the Lower Triangle:

At first—through the intervention of יהוה—Noah awakens to consciousness. יהוה speaks and seizes man in his demand for the absolute. Most of the time this demand is invested in false mystical dead ends, because man in its grip is immediately allured by worldly voices sounding louder than that of יהוה—the voices of all the surrogate ideologies that are invested in Possession-Enjoyment-Power and follow their own agenda, instead of leading back to Elohim.

When יהוה speaks, if we are patient and attentive, sooner or later God—Elohim—himself will show the way. Between the voice of יהוה

and that of Elohim, a long, tortuous, and painful journey unwinds, made up of worldly enticements to which we respond, unconsciously giving them the value of absolutes ("golden calves"). The result is failures, disappointments, bitterness, loneliness, absurdity, and death.

Death can then also take hold of the physical body. It is the death experienced by all human beings drowning in the waters of the Flood without having gone through the Gate of Men.

They "expire," ויגוע (*vayugva*; Genesis 7:21).

But death can be initiatory. It can place man on the path of Elohim and prepare him to hear his voice. Such is the death experienced by those who are mindful of the divine breath within them.

They transform or "mutate," מתו (*metu*, Genesis 7:22).

Again, death may take hold of man who has heard the voice of Elohim, who has already partly come out of the waters, and who continues the work. This man has entered into the process of successive deaths and resurrections. He has emerged from the Lower Triangle and passed through the Gate of Men. He is then "blotted out," meaning "made subtle" ("you shall separate the subtle from the dense") in order to gain some weight in the heights (טוב) of his inner earths, before going back down into the רע, meaning, in this case, the waters.

This man is "subtilized," וימח (*vayimaḥ*, Genesis 7:23).

Only Noah "remains," וישאר (*vayisha'er*), for he is totally accomplished and becomes the "leaven," שאר, of humanity (Genesis 7:24).

For Noah has not heeded any external solicitations. He has kept his energies intact, and we rediscover them as a triad within him, symbolized by his three sons:

Shem (שם), the Name, linked with *enjoyment.*

Ḥam (חם), the hot one, linked with *power.*

Yafet (יפת), connoting "openness," "expanse," and "beauty," linked with *possession.*

Noah is 500 years old (500 is the cosmic seed) when his energies are born—when יהוה speaks. They are not vainly squandered as soon as they spring up. They are to enter into the ark with Noah, intact. Each of them is accompanied by their as-yet-unaccomplished sides, symbolized by the three sons' wives, who go into the ark with Noah's wife, representing the whole unaccomplished side of Noah.

So it is in full consciousness, followed as it were by himself, and being within himself, that Noah enters the ark. He is now 600 years old (the cosmic number of inner conjunction and inner fruitfulness).

This absolute consciousness is expressed by the confirmation יהוה gives to Elohim's command. The command Noah receives from יהוה has a still keener edge than that of Elohim. Obedience is not blind. It is lit by an additional light (compare Genesis 6:18–22 with Genesis 7:1–6). How great is man, having God within him to bring personal light and information to the divine will!

Nothing is said of what happens inside the ark during the forty days and forty nights of the earth's destruction by water. Nothing, but in some sense everything.

Noah sends out two birds that go back and forth to report on the weather outside and gauge the level of the waters.

Now the weather and events outside are external reflections of the events happening inside the ark.

Within his inner temple, Noah is accomplishing his successive inner marriages in order to be born from himself to himself.

The flight of the raven—the alchemical sign of the nigredo or "the black phase of the Work"—shows us that Noah is tearing himself away from a land that he has already conquered in order to descend into the depths of his unaccomplished self and marry some of the "animals" who are there. They will then make up a new land.

The flight of the dove—the alchemical sign of the albedo or "white phase of the Work"—shows us that Noah, enriched by a new marriage deep within himself, is growing toward the light and finding strength in it.

The raven takes over again, tearing Noah away from the land he has realized and making him descend once more toward a new field of consciousness, an inner *sea* (or *mother*),[5] still deeper than the previous one:

to marry the energies from which he is to make the next land, emerging toward an even greater light.

Gradually, everything outside is drying up. The raven and the dove fly out each in their turn to tell us in their way the story of this Great Work.

After 150 days, everything is dry (15 is the sacred number of יה, *Yah*). The raven and the dove no longer return.

Inside, all is accomplished.

Noah comes out of the ark with his wife. His three sons come out in turn, each with his own wife. When they entered, the sexes were separated; the marriages have been celebrated inside the ark.

When Noah comes out of the ark, he is completely realized. He can now eat the fruit of the Tree of Knowledge, because he has *become* it: he has achieved unity. Coming out of the ark is in effect passing through the Gate of the Gods. Beyond this gate, man harvests the sefirah Daat (דעת), knowledge. (More about this when we study the thyroid gland, known as the "Adam's apple," in chapter 15, page 306).

Noah. Noah sends a raven and a dove one after the other out of the ark, which means he is descending into his inner waters, then rising toward the light. (Monreale Cathedral, Sicily.)

Noah plants a vineyard, drinks its wine, becomes intoxicated, and sheds his clothes inside his tent.

The vineyard, the wine, and Noah's nakedness symbolize the intoxication of knowledge and the complete unveiling of mysteries, as well as the entire accomplishment of the coat of skin (עור), which has become light (אור).

Noah experiences total *enjoyment* and total *possession* of his Name. The names of his three sons are the threefold element of a unity beyond words.

Only Ham—linked with *power*—does not act rightly. His youngest son, Canaan, is to become enslaved to his brothers. Any power acquired through magic (the unveiling of the mysteries outside of the Name) derives from the Satan and amounts to an indiscretion: a man glances at the mystery he has not inwardly become and reveals it outside.

The scribes accuse Christ of healing the sick and casting out demons through the power of Beelzebub (Mark 3:22).

Noah prophesies, saying about his other two sons: "Blessed be יהוה, God of Shem; . . . may God enlarge Japheth's possessions, and may he dwell in the tents of Shem" (Genesis 9:26).

The mountain on which the ark rests symbolizes Noah's exaltation, but its name shows how Lamech's prophecy has been fulfilled. *Ararat* (אררט) is made up of אָרָר, *aror*, which is the "curse," plus the letter ט, equal to 9 (in arithmetic nine leads back to zero), which means that a cycle has been completed.

Ararat is the removal of the curse.

That is why the Flood is immediately followed by the establishing of a new covenant between God and his Creation. "The bow in the cloud" is its sign. The cloud here refers especially to inner darkness.

The Fall had destroyed the bridge between God and the inner lands of man. The rainbow is the bridge rebuilt. And this "bridge," the bow, is קשת (*qeshet*).

This bridge is יהוה himself, contained in the *shin* (ש), at the center of the word. Its first letter, *qof* (ק, numerical value 100), is the uncreated divine pole, and the last letter, *tav* (ת, 400), is the created human pole.

The sons of Noah now have a mission to accomplish the Name, *ha-Shem*, in the world. In a Christian perspective, יהוה is the Christ accomplished by the Hebrew people in the tree of Jesse. Coextensively, the whole of humanity's calling is to enter into the Name—"into the tents of Shem"—and to reach that dimension. The present study seeks to shed a little light on this royal road.

The description of the Flood in the Babylonian tradition confirms that of the Hebrew Torah. The hero Gilgamesh sets out to conquer immortality by meeting up in the hereafter with his ancestor Utnapishtim, who, he knows, has recovered this immortal state (we would say, his dimension of eternity).

In many ways, the story of Utnapishtim is similar to Noah's: Ea, the water god, warns Utnapishtim of the impending Flood:

"Demolish your house, build a boat . . .
Bring into the boat the living seed of every species."
The hero obeys, then enters into the boat, and closes the latch.
The rains came, the waters rose high, and brought about the
    destruction of man. . . .
The wind blew for six days and six nights, flood and tempest
    prevailed
over the land. On the seventh day, all was calm.

Then Utnapishtim, like Noah, sent out first a dove, which came back, then a swallow, which also came back, and finally a raven, which did not. The boat grounded, and Utnapishtim offered a sacrifice to the gods. Ea blessed him and said: "Hitherto Utnapishtim was no more than a man, but now let Utnapishtim and his wife be as gods like us. Let Utnapishtim depart far hence and inhabit a place at the river's mouth."

Like Noah coming out of the ark with his wife, Utnapishtim comes out of his boat with the one he has married. Both heroes have achieved unity. The river's mouth, which amounts to a return to primordial unity, confirms this.

In a Greek myth Deucalion and Pyrrha are saved from the Flood. They are the accomplished couple and repopulate the earth by throwing stones over their shoulders. "Stone"—אבן, *even*, in Hebrew, a word made up of אב, *av*, the "father," and בן, *ben*, the "son"—is the symbol of man in whom consciousness has awakened.

He participates in the life of the "cornerstone," who is the archetypal person of the Son, the Messiah יהוה. The awakened man, son of the Father, knows the path toward the unity to be recovered.

He whose consciousness has come to birth is a living stone.

The stones thrown over the shoulders of the heroes of the Greek Flood myth are the progeny of these heroes who took part in the experience of the Gate of the Gods. Their offspring are now able to remember.

The Flood, מבול (*mabul*) in Hebrew, is a word that in demotic French (*maboul*) has come to designate a person whose thoughts are anarchic, whose reasoning is false (we might say a crackpot).

One can read this word as מ-בול (*ma-bul*) and translate it then as "matrix for fruit," or again as ב-מול (*be-mul*), and translate it as "in the circumcision" or "in the face-to-face."

The fruit is indeed to be found in a complete face-to-face encounter with ourselves. The Flood is a trial, an ordeal that obliges us to go down into this face-to-face encounter and follow it through, whatever the level it surprises us at. And this "following through" consists of all our successive circumcisions, our deaths and resurrections, from ourselves to ourselves, in order to bring forth our "fruit," our Name.

The Flood is a cosmic circumcision, the pruning of the human Tree, so that it may bear fruit.

The Hebrews' Sojourn in Egypt

The conquest of the Upper Triangle in the Hebrew tradition is that of the Promised Land, the land promised to Abraham and his posterity according to the terms of the covenant between God and the patriarch, a land linked on the one hand with fertility and on the other with circumcision.

The Holy Grail, the Golden Fleece, immortality, Paradise Lost, or the New Jerusalem—different names in myth show how the whole world is expectant, in an indefatigable and painful quest, for what it knows to be its only happiness, its only freedom.

All ideologies born of an unconscious that is severed from this higher information are but distant—although real—projections of such a quest: from the "Great Night" to the bright millennium, humanity projects onto a happier future the realization of the Truth it carries within.

"In sorrow shalt thou bring forth children." By successive gestations, from matrix to matrix, by bringing itself to birth on ever more sophisticated levels of being, by slow and steep climbs, humanity will make its way back up its tree and make this conquest.

The Hebrews' sojourn in Egypt represents a major aspect of this evolution. Egypt is a crucial matrix. Yet the Hebrews refuse to emerge from this womb, much like our jejune humanity. They are frightened of the death that birth represents: "Let us alone, that we may serve the Egyptians," they say to Moses; "better for us to serve the Egyptians than that we should die in the wilderness" (Exodus 14:12).

In contradiction to its ontological quest, humanity deep down prefers enslavement to freedom.

Humanity is drawn upward but is seriously held back by the draining of its energies below. Humanity is frightened of being cured. Attached to its familiar festering sores, it dreads recovering a state of health it has forgotten. It would like to arrive at a certain stage of the race even before it has set off. This explains why it does not set off and chooses enslavement instead of freedom, ignorance instead of Knowledge.

Yet Knowledge is the very fabric of human ontology.

For this reason, it evokes in man an unceasing and insatiable need for conquest. If these are not conquests of the inner kingdom, they become conquests of time and space. Armed with the most admirable physical and psychological virtues, man sets out on the paths of his history without hesitation or fear of death.

What intelligence, what energy, what courage has man spent just in order to explore the boundaries of his prison! What a block he faces should he want to come out!

But, like this God "who repented of having made man," like Zeus engulfing Promethean humanity in a flood, like Ea guiding Utnapishtim into the dwelling place of the gods, the divine Tetragrammaton in man brings forth from amongst the Hebrews Moses, who fulfills the story of Noah.

Noah "brought men out from under the burden of the earth." Moses "will bring you [the children of Israel] out from under the burdens of the Egyptians and . . . will rid you of their bondage" (Exodus 6:6–9).

Who are the Egyptians? What does Egypt represent?

In Hebrew, Egypt is called מצרים, *Mitsrayim*. This word is composed of two letters, צר, *tsr*, surrounded by מים, *mayim*. *Mayim* are the primordial waters, the undifferentiated maternal waters carrying Heaven and Earth within them, at the genesis of all things, even before the *mi* was separated from the *ma*.

Like a fetus inside this matrix, the vibration ר, *tsr*, which tightens the throat, conveys what is narrowest, what is smallest. It also means "the oppressor, the enemy."

We encounter this root during the journey of Lot, Abraham's nephew, who lacks the strength to reach the mountain he is aiming to reach and asks for protection in a town called צער, *Tsoar*—meaning "the smallest" (Genesis 19:20)—"so that my soul shall live." This same root gives us צואר, *tsavar*, the "neck."

The prophet Micah announced the birth of Christ in the town of Bethlehem, "little among the towns of Judah" (Micah 5:2). "Little" is *tsayir* (צעיר), which here expresses contempt.

Finally, the word *tsor* (צר) brings us back to the necessity of circumcision, for it designates the "little stone" ritually employed to cut the foreskin (Exodus 4:25).

Egypt is a matrix. The children of Israel are carried in this womb, but they are enslaved to it and oppressed by the Egyptians. It becomes necessary for them to be born.

יהוה sets limits to the matrix of Egypt. The word for limit is *sof* (סוף), which occurs both in Joseph (*Yoseph*, יוסף) and the Red Sea (*Yam Sof*, ים סוף). Israel grows within this matrix. The root *yasof* means "to increase" (see chapter 6, page 63).

The Hebrews enter into Egypt with Joseph, eleventh son of Israel, the forerunner of all his brothers, who abandoned him and made him out to be dead, but were brought back to him a few years later.

Drought—and hence famine—is everywhere. Egypt is not exempt from the calamity, but divine wisdom has enabled Joseph to interpret Pharaoh's dreams and to avert the shortage: through seven prosperous years, he fills the country's granaries with food. Drawn by hunger, the other eleven sons of Israel come to dip into these reserves. They remain in Egypt 430 years (Genesis 39–40).

They emerge from it, as one is born from a womb, after ten painful contractions—the ten plagues of Egypt (Exodus 7–12).

The tenth plague governs the Passover. On that day, the waters from the Red Sea part to give birth to the people of God. The "Red Sea" is in fact, according to tradition, "the sea of bulrushes" or "the sea of the limit," *Yam Sof.*

After childhood, the departure for Egypt leads the twelve sons of Israel to leave the land of their parents, for it can no longer feed them. Famine here symbolizes the hunger of the soul: each one of us, impelled by יהוה, departs from the land of his childhood to make for the inner lands, the homeland, the Name. Kept in safety until then by his parents, man can only experience the freedom brought by absolute personal assurance once he has experienced the safety of enslavement.

Absolute assurance can only be based on inner values, not worldly values.

But man only becomes capable of cleaving with all his choices to these inner values when he has thoroughly seen how fragile the outer values are, although at first he took them for the only real ones.

Israel, to begin with, is led toward the experience of these outer values. Egypt symbolizes the world, and Pharaoh symbolizes the one holding power on whom immediate safety depends.

Subsequently, when passing through the wilderness after coming out of Egypt, Israel is to endure another famine. But this time there is no overbearing Pharaoh to provide safety. יהוה elicits the children of Israel's call upon him and asks them to measure up fully to inner values.

For Israel to gain access to the necessary strength, it must acquire some solidity of structure in Egypt. According to the law of opposition (*tov ve-ra*), consciousness comes to birth only through the hard experience of enslavement to worldly values. In Israel, it gives rise to Moses.

When יהוה invests Moses with divine power in order to confront Pharaoh (Exodus 3), he strengthens in Israel the consciousness of the Name. Moses, משה, *Mosheh* in Hebrew, is himself the Name השם, *ha-Shem* (the three letters reversed).

When the consciousness of a greater name is born, which no longer is the ego-personality experienced in Yesod, but the intimation of the person in the Name partaking of יהוה, man is led in the central column linking Malkhut with Keter.

Hitherto man has been buffeted about by the weary wanderings of the Lower Triangle. Suddenly he is rooted in something which, though he is not yet aware of it, is the land of his own depths, and in someone who he does not yet know is his Name, is *himself*.

Caught by his Name, he is now nourished, enlightened by it. Were he to enjoy complete consciousness, he would already experience complete security and freedom. But he is only at the beginning of the journey.

From the adolescent he once was, man must first be born to his manly dimension. He must pass through the Gate of Men and then make his way. This journey, as we shall see, builds up his twelve dorsal vertebrae. For the time being, the first ten vertebrae (five sacral, five lumbar) are adumbrated, which means they are anatomically present, but not yet "made."

The raising up of *Mosheh* in Israel corresponds to the Hebrews' foothold in the axis of their Name.

Just as the body of a baby, at birth, turns over in its mother's womb so that its head may be in line with the neck of the uterus, likewise man, who has taken root and is ready to be born, shifts from death to life and places himself in line for birth before this first gate. The contractions then begin.

These contractions, on a subtle level, are like the events of our lives becoming harder as we go on. They make up the rungs of the ladder that we are invited to climb. They force us to unearth new strengths in ourselves. They are no longer the self-willed strengths that for a time could camouflage our wandering under the guise of some ideological, moral, or ethical stance in the outside world. Rather they are ontological strengths, those of our inner lands; breathed in, they give both energy and information linked with this new field of consciousness. They also open out into a new understanding.

The birth contractions of Israel are the ten plagues of Egypt. Each in turn fashions the first ten vertebrae of God's chosen people. Each is indicative of an inner transmutation, indispensable for survival in each new land of birth—so indispensable that at the end of each trial, when Pharaoh might be ready to let Israel go, "then יהוה hardened the heart of Pharaoh" (Exodus 7–10).

יהוה and Pharaoh are the two poles, one positive, one negative, of the energy of the Name proceeding toward realization.

Pharaoh (פרעה) carries in his vocation not only the רע, *ra*, of "darkness," but also the פר, *par*, of "fruitfulness," and the עפר, *afar*, of "dust." He is identified with the Satan, the prince of this world who holds it in bondage and feeds on the slaves of dust who are unable to grow.

But let the Name *Mosheh*-יהוה appear, and from the dust is born the consciousness of enslavement, the desire for deliverance, and the impulse of the potential for fruitfulness.

It seems that this consciousness can only arise from an intense experience of the adversary, which amounts to an experience of death. When Moses saw an Egyptian smite a Hebrew, he killed the Egyptian, initially under the sway of a reactive response. Yet the blood that was spilled brought him to reflect: he entered a new field of consciousness and experienced the divine (Exodus 2:11–16).

At the outset, we are almost entirely identified with the reign of Pharaoh, and we unconsciously serve ourselves up to him. We blame others for our suffering instead of discovering its source within ourselves.

When consciousness is born, we take the problem within.

Mosheh and Pharaoh are within us.

We shall approach this mystery again in the book of Job, where *Mosheh* and Pharaoh become יהוה and Satan respectively (see chapter 13, page 245).

In these trials, some are without hope, without understanding, and they die. Others "enter into the event." They penetrate it, become "male," and "remember" the wife awaiting her spouse at all levels of being—which is merely foreshadowed by the event here.

The children of Israel, led by the *Mosheh*-consciousness, enter into the ten contractions (events), of which the tenth leads to the breaking of the waters. The Red Sea divides and engulfs the Egyptians, who are the Red Man, the old man within us, the oppressor, while those who are to become the Green Man pass through.

This is *Pesah* (פסח), the Passover, the way out of the "trap," פח, *pah*, pierced by the letter ס, *samekh*. *Samekh* is one of the symbols of the Tree of Life.[6] The Hebrew, עבר, *ever*, etymologically is "the one who passes over." Every "gate"—פתח, *petah*—is the way out of the trap, פח. This way out is realized by the letter ת, *tav*, which is the cross.

The Christian Passover, Easter, is to come later, at the Gate of the Gods.

From one end of this ascent to the other, we will have to enter into an understanding of the mystery of God, who stands in man's way, so that man can become god.

The Labyrinth at Knossos

Modern science has brought to light the fundamental fact that energy is inseparable from information. The word "information" is to be understood on two levels:

1. On the ordinary level, where we understand that a piece of information imparts knowledge;
2. On a more subtle level, where we discover, by the knowledge imparted, that information has an inner, formative role.

Knowledge fashions us from the inside, because it is energy. And for the same reason, it fashions the object that is known.

The Western world is plagued by an incapacitating illness by which we imprison our knowledge (information) in the intellect and use it only to make our prison walls ever thicker, in order to nestle inside in an illusory sense of security.

We have seen (chapter 1, page 5) that this need not be and that true knowledge is the act of giving birth to ourselves in ever deeper lands, each one made up of an informing sum of energy, until we reach the ultimate birth in the utmost depths—בשר, *basar*—translated as "flesh," which carries our Name.[7] When we finally reach and open this kernel of our *shem*, it frees the יהוה energy, at which point man-energy is totally informed.

Our secret Name contains all information.

The diagram of this path revealed in the Hebrew Torah is simple, but the path itself and its goal are infinitely difficult.

Apparently flight from this difficulty is the very subject of the myth of the Fall: man plucks the fruit from the tree before he has made it grow.

Ḥam, witnessing the mysteries of the fruit that his father has become, and "unveiling them on the outside" (chapter 10, page 135), perpetuates the transgression.

This transgression has been repeated by man since time immemorial. He uses his intelligence to acquire the power of the fruit without taking the trouble to make his Tree grow or to become his Name.

Each inner land yet to be conquered is linked with a period of time. Modern science has also discovered this unity of space-time, which weaves the fabric of each plane of consciousness.

Since this state of Fall, time is painful. The poet laments its "thorns," which tear at us.

Time's "cycles" make up the root דור, *dur*, in Hebrew, a root that is forever repeated after the Fall and symbolically captured in the word *dardar* (דרדר, "thorn bush"), which the unwed earth "will henceforward bring forth to the Adam" (Genesis 3:18).

Unconscious man feeds on it for his exhausting race toward outward lands and renown, rather than inner lands and the Name.

Double-quick,[8] through illusory paradises, man hastens toward death. To speed up time, to be rid of it even, is the unconscious leitmotif of wayward and errant humanity.

We have seen how the inner guide of Israel, יהוה himself, does not spare his elect by shortening time. Nine times "he hardened the heart of Pharaoh" (see chapter 10, page 142) to delay the hour of the Passover for which the people were not yet ready.

Ten vertebrae have to be forged. The body of an adult cannot stand with only three or four. It will only acquire the basis for complete uprightness with the full formation of the first ten levels of its structures.

But man is impatient.

In Athens, the Greek hero Theseus was impatient.

Following a conflict between Cretans and Athenians, Minos, king of Crete, exacts a tribute from the Athenians. Every year for ten years, seven young men and seven young maids are to be sacrificed to the Minotaur.

The Minotaur is a monster with a man's body and a bull's head who was the offspring of Pasiphae, wife of King Minos, and Poseidon, god of the underwater kingdoms, who appeared before the queen in the shape of a luminous bull. Minos, son of Zeus, wanting to hide this monster from the people of Crete, ordered Daedalus, the royal architect, to build a deep and inescapable labyrinth in order to hide the Minotaur at its center.

Daedalus built the labyrinth, which harbored the monster. For ten years Athens had to sacrifice to this monster and pay the heavy tribute drawn from the living strength of her land.

After three years, a hero stands among them: Theseus, son of Aegeus, king of Athens, courageously decides to confront the Minotaur, kill it, and put an end to this sacrifice.

Theseus was a son born to King Aegeus by a princess during one of his far-flung battles. He remained throughout his childhood with his mother. Through her lineage, he was a son of Poseidon, and hence no stranger to the Minotaur.

He grew up in his mother's country and acquired athletic stature and royal demeanor. From a young age he liked to confront the severest hardships, so he did not wait for his mother's approval to lift a huge rock under which were buried the golden sword and sandals. These were royal attributes placed there by his father and concealed until Theseus should be of an age to wear them. His mother alone knew the secret place, and she was supposed to reveal it only when she judged her son mature enough.

With the golden sword and sandals in hand, Theseus questioned his mother, who disclosed the secret of his birth before the right time.

The young lad then decided to go and join the king, his father. Still brave and strong, he overcame a host of difficulties and vanquished every pitfall on the way. One is noteworthy: the giant named Periphetes, armed with a huge leather club, used to knock unfortunate passers-by senseless in the foot of the deserted valley where he hid. Theseus confronted this giant, killed him, and carried off the leather club as a trophy.

Armed with the leather club and the golden sword, the son of the king of Athens arrived at his father's house. At first he kept his identity hidden, and the king and his wife, the sorceress Medea, were captivated by the youth's good looks. Theseus was invited to the royal court, where Medea used all her charms to seduce him. He rejected her, and in vengeful scorn Medea told the king that Theseus had tried to seduce her, thus accusing him of her own misdeed. They both decided to poison him.

When Theseus lifted his glass in honor of his hosts, unaware of its poisonous contents, he exposed his side. The king saw and recognized the golden sword. Snatching the glass from his son's hands, Aegeus broke it and embraced Theseus, who became his associate in ruling the kingdom.

Learning of the deadly penalty paid by his subjects to the king of Crete, Theseus decided to ignore his father's advice—he had seen the young man's immaturity and perhaps too the deep meaning of the need for ten years of sacrifice—and to go and present himself as an offering if he did not succeed in killing the monster.

His father let him go, but with a heavy heart. He made Theseus promise to raise a white sail on the boat bringing him back from Crete so that he might rejoice in his victory from afar. In the event of the opposite, a black sail was to be hoisted.

Theseus the brave, drunk with his own youthful strength, arrived at the court of King Minos and told him of his noble mission. He had to find out for himself how to meet the monster, but the king's daughter, the delightful Ariadne, was touched by compassion. Moved by what she believed was pure love for this valiant hero, she who knew the path gave away its secret to the one she loved. Unwinding from the entrance to the center of the labyrinth the ball of thread Ariadne gave him, Theseus succeeded in coming face to face with the awesome guardian of the threshold.

In one interpretation of the myth the Minotaur is the guardian of the Gate of Men. With a name composed of Minos (the king) and the bull (the god Poseidon), he is the completed brother of Theseus, who is not yet completed and who must confront him in order to become so.

The god of the underwater worlds is embodied in the first set of man's energies. It is symbolized by the bull (cf. the Sphinx). Only one who is aware of his ontological royalty and has begun to divest himself of the "coat of skin" side of his nature may confront him. Here this means one who has integrated the bull.

Now Theseus confronts the guardian armed with the golden sword, but also with the leather club—two weapons that belong to each nature respectively.

Aegeus, the Father-King, knew that the young man had not yet rejected the leather club and was as yet unable to wield the golden sword.

Theseus turns a deaf ear to the voice of the Word, the divine voice within him, symbolized outwardly by the golden sword. He obeys his unconscious virtues. These possess the rich potential of his future gifts, but taken on ahead of time, they are mere psychological virtues, energies unchecked by the knowledge of ontological laws. Courage, willpower, even heroism follow the drives of the man in a coat of skin, and these drives have not been sufficiently purified. Instead of being engaged in a conscious quest for the Name that the Minotaur holds, he is vainglorious, seeking after fame and power.

These drives can only be managed at the Tree's first level, that of power relationships, not of relationships of love and knowledge.

When Theseus kills the Minotaur with his leather club, he kills his own *yod*.

He reached the Minotaur thanks to Ariadne's thread. Ariadne represents his emotional feminine side brought back down to the first level. Wrapped in the deceptive aura of love, Theseus is completely identified with his feminine side and loves only his ego—a narcissistic love. The resulting momentum allows him to gain knowledge, but it is learned from the outside and does not originate within him.

When knowledge is placed too early in the hands of one who has not yet purified his heart, it enters into the service of vanity and turns against the one who thinks he has mastered it. He is a mere sorcerer's apprentice.

When Theseus retraces his steps—for the Gate has not opened—he continues wandering in the labyrinth par excellence. He takes Ariadne with him, but he is incapable of marrying her. He forgets her at the first port of call on the return journey. At his deepest level, Theseus is incapable of love. And the myth says that Theseus, proceeding back to Athens, "mistakenly" hoists the black sail.

Theseus is not mistaken.

He has killed his *yod.* He has died a deeper death than any physical death. For the Father, symbolized by King Aegeus, dies too. In Hebrew terms we could say that יהוה and Elohim die within the consciousness of the psychological hero.

The ten years of sacrifice correspond to the sacred number of the *yod*, which governs the formation of the first ten vertebrae, that is, the completed gestation of the first triangle.

To "make sacred" is to build up the *yod*, to nourish the divine kernel within oneself by devoting to it energies that have been drawn away from vanities. These energies are symbolized by the seven young men and seven young maidens. These young Athenians are the living strength of the royal land of Theseus, his land of the depths. In the biblical myth, they correspond to the tithe paid by Abraham to Melchizedek (see chapter 9, page 111).

In the eyes of the world, this amounts to a loss of energy.

In the eyes of God, there is a building up of the god in man.

"The foolishness of God is wiser than men" (1 Corinthians 1:25).

Only the eye that knows with love may see these values. Theseus is in a state of confusion.

Theseus is also like Daedalus, for he builds his own labyrinth and shuts himself up in it. He is each one of us. We are forever reinforcing our prison walls so long as we are not devoting any time to the search for deliverance.

As for trials, we painfully look for ways out of them, but we only investigate the possibilities within the space of the prison (a field of consciousness). But trials belong in fact to a different space and urge us to penetrate it, for there order will be restored.

The trials are guardians of the threshold. They devour those who refuse to come out of prison and those who are scared, but they build up those who are prepared to let go of their deceptively secure grip and become the man and the god they are in potential.

In this labyrinthine prison—the field of consciousness—that we navigate during the first part of our lives, we yield our power to the external forces of this world, among them the most insidious of golden calves—the god Chance!

Those who shut themselves up in the labyrinth also hold their children captive, as Daedalus does Icarus. Those we bring up can only partake of the level we ourselves have attained. For the education we give them consists of providing our own boundaries as structure and passing on things that relate to these boundaries as key values. These values are necessary for a time, but they become alienating when set up as absolutes.

Icarus symbolizes not only our biological children but all the productions to which we "give birth," in whatever field, artistic, creative, or technical.

Today many of our works are labyrinthine. Architecturally, the Pompidou Center, with its intestines in plain sight, is a masterpiece of labyrinthine construction. And our machines, designed to free us, on the contrary enslave us more and more day by day. On this level, the use of reason can only shift problems about without solving them.

The pattern of the labyrinth is a form of wisdom. It imposes a kind of journeying that respects the time needed for ripening. It also

The Labyrinth in Chartres Cathedral. Whoever reaches the center of the labyrinth reaches his own inner core.

requires a search for meaning that can only find its correct bearings in the archetypal triangle hidden in the *yod* (although it does provide some information in advance). The intestinelike convolutions are like those of a brain. They govern the digestion of information received in order to produce new substances.

On the level of Being, the labyrinth is experienced more consciously and becomes a mandala, a basis for meditation (see chapter 5, page 31). It is symbolized by the matrix of fire, which corresponds to the thoracic Cinnabar Field in the Chinese tradition.

When the labyrinth, on the first level, is not perceived as a matrix accomplishing the waters, but is seen as a shelter that does not lead to birth, it becomes a tomb, a place of aimless wandering.

The adolescent—as well as adolescent humanity today—has yet to realize that he who does not plant roots in his Name, his *yod*, does not plant them in the earth either. However much of a materialist he becomes, he is not yet genuinely incarnate.

This is one reason theories of reincarnation are so common: a person who is not genuinely incarnate unconsciously projects his "reincarnation" into another time, outside of himself, in a different body that he sees as no more than a "vehicle" estranged from his Name.

Barely incarnate, the adolescent—or the man who thinks he is an adult—flees still further from his true Self, his *yod*, by trying to escape the labyrinth, which feels so unsatisfactory. Nevertheless, even very late in man's life, the labyrinth that holds the path to his Name can still open up to one who is humble enough to discover himself in it and see his alienation.

Daedalus and Icarus have artificial wings brought from the outside by Queen Pasiphae. They are unable to leave the labyrinth by the Gate of Men, the gate of genuine incarnation, and draw the means of deliverance from unconscious values (Pasiphae and the mother archetype that is not realized in them). So Pasiphae, representing this unaccomplished mother archetype, gives them artificial wings, which they stick onto each other's backs with wax. These wings are to enable them to jump over the rectangle of incarnation and fly up to the heights of Wisdom and Understanding, even to the heights of the Crown.

This is merely a repetition of the sin Adam committed in Eden.

"Do not fly too high," the wise Daedalus then warns his son, "for the sun's heat will burn your wings; do not fly too low, for the vapors of the sea will draw you down."

What sublime mediocrity there is in this wisdom!

Understanding on the point of touching fire is formidable. Nothing can halt the desire for conquest inherent in man's very being: Icarus soars to such heights that he is brutally thrown down into the sea. Daedalus crashes down to earth.

"For . . . I will destroy the wisdom of the wise, and will bring to nothing the understanding of the prudent," says יהוה (Isaiah 29:14; 1 Corinthians 1:19).

The greatest knowledge, the highest technical skills, are mere illusions of liberation when they are not accompanied by work in the rectangle of the Tree, the only real laboratory.

Artificial wings replace the wings man acquires in becoming an Eagle (see chapter 14, pages 275–82). Beeswax replaces the wax secreted by man when he undertakes solar work.

The wisdom in most worldly philosophies rearranges the level of the labyrinth, but does not lead man out of it. It places the mask of wisdom on the countenance of folly.

Divine Wisdom strips off all masks, yet it is folly in the eyes of men. The apostle Paul says: "The Lord knoweth the thoughts of the wise, that they are vain. . . . Let no man deceive himself. If any man among you seemeth to be wise in this world, let him become a fool that he may be wise. For the wisdom of this world is foolishness with God" (1 Corinthians 3:18–20).

The Greek myth already prefigures the great Judeo-Christian revelation: Daedalus and Icarus are stripped of their illusion. Divine protection is operative here as in Eden. Wherever we look, the sin committed in Eden turns out to be a refusal of incarnation.

"Wisdom and understanding according to this world" belong to Prometheus or to Cain. (Once again, both myths cover the same ground, and we shall return to them; see chapter 12, page 208). They create ever more sophisticated civilizations built on values that cannot withstand the guardian of the threshold of the first Gate.

Religions enclosed in the wisdom of morality, or in the more subtle wisdom of discarnate mysticism; philosophies that inexorably reduce man to his animal condition, as well as those that deny it; sciences that use the play of his intellect to lead him to construct an external world that provides illusory happiness—all these are destined thus to be brought to nothing.

Theseus hoisted the black sail; his father, the king, died. His supposedly royal career ended tragically.

CHAPTER 11

Going through the Gate of Men

EMERGING FROM THE ARK, NOAH WAS TO EAT THE FRUIT OF THE Tree and be intoxicated with *enjoyment.*

The Hebrew people left the land of slavery behind and went toward the *possession* of the Promised Land.

He who can wield the golden sword will acquire true *power.*

These three energies make up the fruit man ripens with the growth of his inner tree; they will become clearer as we study the Tree of Jesse, the lineage of Christ starting from Jesse, David's father. It is an experience of the messianic lineage from Jacob—the root of the tree—to Christ, its fruit.

Jacob's Struggle with the Angel

Jacob obtained his birthright—the right to administer his inheritance— from his brother Esau and left his family for many years, while his brother remained with his mother and father.

Esau, the "man in a coat of skin," cannot let go of his crutches. Jacob, man become conscious, no longer identifies with this "brother." He sets out to master a strength that will enable him to return in order to "make" his brother (the name *Esau* is the verb "to make," עשה in

155

Hebrew). The strength needed for this can only be gained by marrying the first fields of feminine energy.

Jacob marries two sisters, daughters of his uncle Laban. With their handmaidens, they bear him eleven sons. Benjamin, the twelfth son of Israel, was born later.

Jacob also amasses many possessions while staying with his father-in-law, Laban. With his external wealth and the interior energies he has assimilated, Jacob leaves Laban. *Laban* means "white," but it is also a name for the moon.

On a deeper level, we understand that Jacob gathers all his energies and leaves the lunar level symbolized by Yesod. He moves out of the first triangle, governed by this sefirah, because his *yod* is about to be born.

For he departs at the behest of יהוה "unto the land of thy fathers, and to thy kindred." יהוה promises, "I will be with thee" (Genesis 31:3) as Jacob returns to his origins, where he will have to face—not without qualms—his "brother in a coat of skin," Esau, his other side, who had jealously sought to have him killed.

Three times Jacob sends presents to Esau in an attempt to appease him. Even though Jacob has acquired the birthright, he still trembles slavishly before his brother, who originally held it.

Jacob learns of his brother's approach with 400 men (this figure symbolizes the incarnation for which such an encounter is essential). Before meeting this formidable brother, Jacob must acquire a new stature, die to his fears, enter into a new understanding of the words spoken by יהוה, and come to know his true place in relation to his brother.

One night, with his womenfolk, his children, and his possessions, Jacob "passed over the ford at Jabbok." In this text (Genesis 32:22–23), the word *ever* (עבר), the name of the Hebrew people (passers-over), is repeated twice.

Not only does Jacob, a Hebrew, fulfill his name here, but the name of the river Jabbok is related to Jacob! In addition, both יבק (Jabbok) and יעקב (Jacob) play with the verb "to wrestle"—יאבק, *yeaveq*—which is to follow (Genesis 32:35). The root of this verb, אבק, means "embrace" but also "grind to dust."

Jacob undoubtedly opens an important energy center necessary for his encounter with the brother. He must now confront this force in order to become it.

It is night, the night of the soul. Jacob remains alone. And until daybreak a man "wrestles" with him: the Hebrew verb says this man "clasps" him, to the point of "reducing him to dust."

"And when he saw that he prevailed not against him, he touched the hollow of his thigh; and the hollow of Jacob's thigh was out of joint, as he wrestled with him" (Genesis 32:25).

Who is this man?

Ish, איש, says the Hebrew text, a "man" in the sense of "spouse," is portrayed by the oral tradition as an angel. In depth, Jacob enters into a marriage with himself at a higher level of his potential, encountering and "marrying" his brother Esau, the crude, animal, and unaccomplished Red Man, through whom Jacob is to become fully incarnate.

It is the dance of man with himself in that his very life is a dance—the dance of the encounter with God. The nocturnal dance of his depths, painful because of the separations it requires, leaves him lame!

Lame! He had forgotten that he had been lame since birth!

Lame, because he had not yet married the whole of himself. But now that this great work has begun, he remembers! He is lame. Henceforth he treads the path toward uprightness.

When Adam speaks to God after the Fall of the woman (his inward feminine side), he calls her "the woman whom thou gavest to be with me." This verse can also be translated as "the one you gave me that I might become upright" (Genesis 3:12).

Only through marrying the potential for energy sealed in his feminine side can man gradually attain uprightness. Adam knows this only too well, for at the moment of the Fall he returns to childishness on all fours. We have not yet emerged from this state, however upright and grand we think we are with our artificial wings.

Jacob takes the true path toward uprightness. Crossing at Jabbok geographically corresponds to the hollow of the thigh anatomically. Its opening releases the power of the *yod* on that level.

Jacob senses the identity of the man, *ish*, for he asks for his blessing. Yet when he asks for his name, the man replies "Wherefore is it that thou dost ask after my name?" But in truth the man had already revealed it.

Jacob fought with Israel in order to become Israel.

"Thy name shall not be called any more Jacob, but Israel shall be thy name: for thou hast wrestled (*saro*) with God (*El*) and with men (*ish*), and thou wast able" (Genesis 35:10).

Revelation of the Name, that is, revelation of the new energy released by the Name יהוה.

The transformation from Jacob to Israel took place with the verb "to wrestle," from תיאבק, "reduce to dust," to שרית (whose root, שר, *sar*, is the "prince"), that is, "wrestling" until the principle is reached.

Jacob-Israel can now meet with his brother Esau. Before, he was afraid of Esau, afraid of his animal strength, of his hatred. Now vested with divine power, he is no longer afraid; he has reversed the situation. The encounter is no longer to take place through a power struggle.

"And Esau ran to meet him, and embraced him" (Genesis 33:4).

In the labyrinth, unaware, we perceive others, or events, as adverse energies and then rise up against them. This savage and dramatic confrontation drains our strength and leads to deadly exhaustion.

Failure to recognize the *yod* found in the Sword-Tetragrammaton, הוה, means the two *hehs* (ה) develop as enemies and destroy each other, tearing the *vav* (ו) apart in the process.

When the *vav* "remembers" the *yod*, is pregnant with the *yod*, and becomes united in it, man becomes conscious, and each of the ה (*hehs*) reverts to its true place. The situation is reversed, and the foe becomes friend.

Rea (רע) is the same word in Hebrew for the two opposites, friend and foe. Its root, רע, *ra*, is a reserve of energy, waiting in darkness to be wed, to be revealed, and brought into the light.

For Israel there was a new dawn. Israel (ישראל) could then say—because his name contains it—לי-ראש, word for word: "for me the head": Israel is the one who has found the path of the *yod* and who wears a new head on his shoulders. "The sun rose upon him" (Genesis 32:31).

From the child that was Jacob, a man has been born. He starts out toward the Gate of the Gods and the process of bringing the Messiah—יהוה—to birth. The children of Israel born of him were to experience the same passage—Passover—coming out of Egypt. In this sense, Jacob's experience in Laban's service is equivalent to the Hebrews' experience in Egypt.

It is also equivalent to what humanity is experiencing in its present-day lack of awareness. For contemporary anxiety, as for all the major problems of our childish world with its artificial wings, the only solution lies in such a "passage."

Encountering the "other" within ourselves, in order to encounter the other as a friend in the outside world, reversing our hate in order to reverse his or her hate, is the only path for us to take, the only way for the "plagues of Egypt" in the contemporary world to cease.

We shall then become aware that far from having eagles' wings, our humanity is crippled.

For old people, spontaneous fracture of the neck of the thighbone seems a last reminder of their lameness before death catches them unawares on this side of the Gate.

In an instant, just enough time for an inner reversal, they may start becoming upright.

For there is a real question about the fate awaiting those taken by death before crossing the Gate.

Later in this chapter I shall attempt to clarify this question in the light of tradition. For now, let us turn our attention to the Son of Man as he accomplishes this same passage.

Christ's Baptism, or Reversing the Energies

Christ is clothed in humanity's coat of skin and is subject to the conditioning resulting from the Fall, but he heeds the conditions necessary for it to be restored. He undertakes the crossing of the triangle by accepting the baptism of water in the river Jordan from the hand of the Forerunner, John the Baptist.

In the language of myth, the labyrinth of ignorance is a variant of the Flood. The Lower Triangle, deprived of its vital reference, is stripped of meaning and abandons the physical and psychic world of the *ma* to anarchy. The "waters below" no longer reflect the "waters above" (*mi*); they lose their meaning and flow toward death.

The waters of the Jordan flow into the Dead Sea.

When Christ goes down into the Jordan, it is said, he sends the waters back to their source. The psalmist prophesied it a thousand years before the historical event took place:

> What ailed thee, thou sea, that thou fleddest? Thou Jordan, that thou
>   wast driven back?
> Ye mountains that ye skipped like rams; and ye little hills, like lambs?
>   (Psalm 114:5–6)

This cosmic jubilation means that the world has recovered its image, that the *ma* once again reflects the *mi* and rejoices to kiss in the mirror the face that gives it its beauty, its raison d'être.

Henceforth the Jordan is to flow into the Primordial Ocean, source of all life, *mayim*, in which the *ma* and the *mi* are intertwined like two brothers in an exquisite reconciliation.

And what is true for the world is true for each of us: our spinal column, like the Jordan, sweeps along energies that are doomed to die the instant they are born, gushing out unprofitably. But if the Divine Seed should wake up within us, the wound closes up, the flow of the current is gradually reversed, and our entire being, sharing in the rhythm of the universe, dances with the joy of a world transfigured.

By going down into the waters of the Jordan, Christ descends into all that is unaccomplished in humanity.

This immersion, טובל, *tovel* in Hebrew, is a setting in motion (ל) of the pole טוב, *tov*, of the Tree of Knowledge. This pole of "accomplished light" can only be mobilized by seizing that which is unaccomplished in us, symbolized by the waters. John the Baptist is literally "he who immerses."

The name of the river, Jordan (ירדן), can be read ירד-ן, *yared-nun*: "go-down-fish." Christ becomes a fish in order to go down into the depths of the unaccomplished.

The river Jordan can also be read as ר-דין, *resh-din*, "principle of rigor." The rigor of the path makes this hard descent necessary. However, divine mercy is present, and the voice of the Father is heard, naming the one who undertakes this path "my beloved Son."

Immersed, Christ treads again the path of Adam, entering the darkness of the "deep sleep" (Genesis 2:21), where he becomes conscious of his shadow side, conscious of the feminine within, which he must marry in order to recover her energies and open their kernel.

Christ takes charge of what Adam, halted by the serpent, could not accomplish.

Christ, the second Adam, is the *vav* (ו) of the archetype הוה and joins together the two ה in the marriage of darkness and light. As the cosmic *vav*, he joins the entire cosmos to the *yod*, the created to the uncreated. This is confirmed by the theophany of the Father and the Holy Spirit (in the form of a dove), naming the Son.

Named by the Father in the world of the *mi*, Christ is also named by humanity in the world of the *ma*. John the Baptist points him out: "Behold the Lamb of God" (John 1:29) and elsewhere, "I baptize you with water, he will salt you with fire"; "he must increase but I must decrease."

Man in his coat of skin—the prepuce of the Word, as it were—fades out and Christ, who is Light, appears.

The circumcision of humanity in Adam is accomplished.

The feast day of John the Baptist is celebrated in the Christian church on the day of the summer solstice. When the outer sun is at its highest elevation and begins to decline, Christ, the inner sun, begins to rise.

As the guardian of the Gate of Men, John is beheaded.

John the evangelist, the Green Man, guards the Gate of the Gods. His feast day is celebrated at the winter solstice.

The moment when man enters the rectangle on the diagram is when he genuinely enters the twelve months of the earthly year. Only then does he begin to be incarnate. Infancy, that outward sun, was but a prelude.

Christ's Temptation in the Desert: Going through the Gate for Each of Us

A prelude . . . and yet how crucial that it should be fully lived! If life's prelude has not been perfectly integrated, it seems that the ensuing melody will be out of tune, or even nonexistent, because its deeper structures are not in place.

This prelude was played, so to speak, leaning on the two crutches of duality. If these crutches had not been informed by the Upper Triangle, and thus were not projections of the essential structures (for instance, if the parents themselves were infantile, the moral codes devoid of spirituality, logic exclusively confined to rationalism, etc.), they could not supply the child with the food necessary for growing up. An adolescent thus "raised" stands little chance of being awakened. His consciousness, fast asleep, is dying in the depths of monstrous parental labyrinths.

The prelude is, then, a substitute for the entire melody, rather like a dawn continuing with no sun, lifeless, uncertain, and deceptive, attempting to play at day with fake light while dreading the night, a death with no morrow.

At this level, energies that have paid no tithes to King Melchizedek (see chapter 9, page 111) are wholly invested in values that have been falsely set up as absolutes. Their momentum is lost in disappointments of the cruelest kind. The upright course of the sap is deflected into the labyrinthine branches of conformity or vanity.

The more the crutches of duality are influenced by the Upper Triangle, the better they are at developing the child in the direction of his or her own ontological values. These then make themselves felt so strongly during adolescence that other values quickly appear to be relative. Yet consciousness is born in the crucible of the painful experiences that result. The Lower Triangle becomes a seedbed.

This consciousness of being is the *yod*. The *yod* has its demands, it seeks to be brought to light, and to that end secretly teaches each one of us the path to the Name.

The language of the body is one aspect of this teaching. The *yod* is the blueprint of the Divine Name יהוה—the fruit of the Tree of Knowledge guarded by the Cherubim at the east of the garden of Eden (Genesis 3:24).

East of Eden is the Gate of the Gods. Eden itself, through its western gate, is the Gate of Men, symbolized by every temple entrance.

Eden is the pathway to the Name, the axis of the Name in which man is taken up and "whirled round" in order to dance and become this Name.

This return to Eden means that we go through Adam's ordeal again, the ordeal Christ—the new Adam—goes through immediately after his baptism: "Then was Jesus led up of the spirit into the wilderness to be tempted of the devil" (Matthew 4:1).

Here the Devil replicates the serpent of the Garden of Eden, just as the three temptations he puts to Christ replicate the fruit of the Tree of Knowledge.

We have seen (chapter 10, page 126) that the virtues of this fruit make up the *yod*, which, as the kernel of Creation, determines the constituents of man's energy from the outset.

In their divine dimension, *enjoyment*, *possession*, and *power* can only be integrated by one who has become the *yod*. Adam ate the fruit without having become it.

Christ emerging from the baptismal waters as Son of Man has not yet become it. He only stands at the western gate for the time being. "If thou be the Son of God, command that these stones be made bread," says Satan.

The Father of Lies does not just make any random proposition. What he asks is charged with meaning—the reverse of anarchy. Anarchy is illustrated by the myth of the Flood and represents non-sense: the elements of the world are severed from their respective archetypes (see chapter 10, page 128, and chapter 12, page 194).

When man recovers his archetypal breath and takes his place within it (see chapter 12, pages 206–09), he begins a process of transmutation in which, Isaiah says, "Stone becomes iron, then silver, and wood becomes brass, then gold" (Isaiah 60:17).

The symbolism of iron (chapter 12, page 206), is closely linked with bread and flesh, and we shall see that to change stones into bread outwardly is to be oneself in an inner process of transmutation.

Christ begins that process only in the power of the Holy Spirit, not that of Satan, whom he must first send away.

Bread, as a staple food, is linked with *enjoyment*. This is the first energy Satan tempts Christ with.

Enjoyment of the Name

It is the all-embracing encounter, the encounter of marriage between God and man.

When Noah ate the fruit, he was intoxicated with enjoyment and experienced the opposite pole to anarchy, to separation.

Those who break down the wall of separation enter into the resonance of the Name. They heed the order, the meaning, the resonance of each element of the world with the world of *mi*, from which they proceed and toward which they are returning. Man, entering the resonance of the Name in Eden, emerges from the absurd, in its etymological sense: "*ab-surdus*," "coming from deafness."

They are then called to follow in Noah's footsteps, enter the ark, and gather all the "animals" from their land so as to marry their energies in the secret of the ark.

Their power is *basar*, the "flesh" sealed by God in the depths of the feminine on the day when this shadow side of Adam is presented to him (Genesis 2:21). The "depth"—תחתנה, *taḥtenah*—is a construct form of חתנה, *ḥatunah*, which means "wedding."

The "flesh" is what is ontologically sealed in our depths for our ultimate marriage (symbolized by the veil—the hymen—in woman's intimate parts).

The flesh is the seal of the Name in the last, ultimate, primeval earth. It is the principle of the most formidable and energizing force, that of eros, which leads us to the Divine Spouse and unites us to him.

The drama of the Fall has turned us away from the Divine Spouse. Where does the dread power of eros go now? What kind of weddings take up its energies? To what feast is our flesh now promised?

The flesh whose fruit has been opened and eaten becomes energy gone astray, deflected from the path toward likeness. It becomes food for the Satan, through the life of our passions and psyche. It builds the grandest and most terrifying outward civilizations.

Eros is terrifying in our passions, but no less so in the humdrum daily round of our psychological life. It gradually draws away our strengths from their true purpose, and it does so all the more treach-erously because we do not see it or think it does not matter. This eros rushes us toward death.

But the Divine Spouse loves his bride, even in its most abject form of prostitution. Faithful to the faithless, he gives fallen eros the nature of a symbol and power to return us to him. He makes human love into an image of the ultimate encounter.

Our dress in bondage, the coat of skin woven with our corrupted flesh, can become our wedding garment. When human love sees this, when our human undertakings are thus directed, they open the way to this fulfillment. They become the carriers of the power of the reintegration of the flesh to its ontological reality and its divine vocation.

"The accomplishment of all flesh is come before me" (Genesis 6:13), says God to Noah, ordering him to gather all his energies inside the ark.

We will soon see the great role that the pancreas plays in this Great Work of reintegration and realization.

Man entering the ark with his "animals" leaves behind the situation of flood, anarchy, and disorder. He gradually leaves behind the constraints of those organizations that before stood in place of order—worldly laws instead of ontological laws. He abandons those crutches that were necessary for a time but that soon become a prison and a tomb if one does not pass through the Gate. The moral and religious laws of a first level then fade away.

Does not Christ "work" on the day of *shabbat*? And did he not address the man who was cultivating his field on that day, saying: "Man, if you know what you are doing, you are blessed by my Father; but if you know not, you have transgressed the law, and you are cursed by my Father."[1]

At this stage the only force of law is the rightness of inner knowledge, knowledge of the will of the Father.

How can one find out what the will of the Father is?

It is the voice of conscience verified, that is to say, the language of the *yod* scrutinized to make sure it is not the voice of our unconscious desires or our repressions. This verification comes to us in concrete events: conscience speaks in the deep world of the *mi*, and its message is confirmed in the world of *ma*.

The *mi* and the *ma* always correspond when the axis, the path to the Name, is recovered.

Speaking of the *anima*, Jung, in his own terminology, describes consciousness: "She lives," he says, "beyond all categories"; and further on: "Although she may be the chaotic urge to life, something strangely meaningful clings to her, a secret knowledge, or hidden wisdom."[2]

Jung's words seem to describe the archetypes Binah and Hokhmah, Understanding and Wisdom, which now inform man's consciousness of being.

New understanding and new wisdom—at this level all values are turned upside down. The Tree of Knowledge of Good and Evil is henceforth to be experienced in its true meaning—light and non-light—and sheds its delusive fruit: good and evil. The real fruits no longer taste like this. What was perceived as "good" on the mundane level can become "bad," or vice versa.

The criterion is no longer the good, but what fits with the necessities of accomplishment. The apostle Paul confides: "All things are lawful for me, but all things are not expedient" (1 Corinthians 10:23).

Prohibitions no longer make sense. Laws attempting to order the disorderly world of the Fall prove to be relative, fragile, and ineffective.

Order will only be regained by emerging from the fallen world. This is why psychological laws linked with our fleshly nature must give way to ontological laws.

Once a friend asked me to join him in a specific course of action for a woman friend we had in common. I firmly refused because I was convinced that it was a huge psychological mistake, and I put my case methodically. I was sure I was right!

The following night, I dreamed that I was taking this same friend to collect a child at a day care center. We were passing a palace that was on our left. As my friend was on my right, I was blocking his view of what was taking place inside the palace. A wide, cyclopean entrance door lay open, and inside a banquet was being given. It could only have been the mystic banquet, so dazzling was its beauty, so indescribable its light. Men arrayed in gold, women in silver, all sparkling, turned around a huge oval table, decked in light.

As I watched this, I said to my friend: "I hope you don't mind me making you miss this banquet?"

When I woke, the situation was clear; I was right psychologically, but wrong spiritually. I was after a childish satisfaction. I went back to my friend's suggestion and accepted it. It was very difficult to live through, because it required constant spiritual discernment. Above all it required constant vigilance on both our parts in order to live it at the spiritual level in spite of the traps regularly set by our psyches.

Yet by compelling us to live on the ontological level, that decision was a source of blessing that also had something to do with the production of this book.

Psychological laws that do not give way in due course to ontological laws are mere childishness.

Discerning how long this "due course" should be requires great skill in *listening.* Only listening enables us to emerge from the absurd, from our deafness, and to advance toward the dimension of the Word.

Someone who has been born to this ontological level is a disciple of Christ, "in the world, but not of the world." Even if his situation in this world links him to civic and social constraints, or any other constraints perceived as unjust, he is able to live through these in freedom.

Insofar as they crucify him, these constraints bring him through a series of deaths and resurrections until he reaches complete inner freedom; they are his ascesis or training. Frequently inner freedom is known to be present when outer freedom, which is its result, can be seen. Events come up that the unaware attribute to "chance," and they transform the life of one who is "tuned in," so to speak. Constraints then disappear.

For there is no comparison between freedom on this level and the usual kind of freedom, which masks all our alienations.

Freedom means being freed successively from everything that separates us from the Name.

Possession of the Name

Only the possession of the Name frees us from all enslavement. All our worldly acquisitions give us a sense of security, but unconsciously they are compensations for the only royal conquest—the conquest of freedom, whose path is so hard to set out on!

"The Son of man hath not where to lay his head" (Matthew 8:20). Men, however, have roofs over their heads. Those who come to ask Christ how best to follow him are invited to completely lose their sense of security.

The path to the Name often obliges us to leave the shelter of our homes and our loved ones—yet there are still more subtle shelters: the hidden caverns of our knowledge and thoughts. Accumulating knowledge and using thoughts as sources of satisfaction root us to the spot. The path then becomes an impasse.

"All these things [the kingdoms of the world] will I give thee, if thou wilt fall down and worship me," says Satan to Jesus (Matthew 4:9). Outer kingdoms can never replace the inner kingdom, which can only be conquered by dying at every inner level of acquired consciousness.

Outward learning, acquired in an ever more injurious spirit of competitiveness, kills the *yod*. Nowadays it can even kill the body. I am struck by the number of serious, or even fatal, illnesses that suddenly cut down top graduates from institutions of higher learning in France.

Knowledge obtained from esoteric investigations or the integration of real-life experiences, but kept at, or brought down to the level of Having, may become more subtly sterile. We shall subsequently discover the need to strip away all inner wealth in order to become completely transparent to the infinite riches of the divine. For all truth on one level is untruth on the level above. We cannot possess truth. We can only allow ourselves to be grasped by it.

But at this stage of our work, we must simply be careful not to confuse Having with Being.

We need not dwell on all the material acquisitions claimed by a population who insist on *having* more because they are aware of not *being* enough. The civilizations of the world are out of breath.

Is man on the eve of understanding that the Gospel is the "Good

News"? "Seek ye first the kingdom . . . all these things shall be added unto you" (Matthew 6:33; Luke 12:31).

There is something "crazy" about receiving from the Father, the Spouse, all that we need in our outer as well as our inner life when we penetrate into the inner kingdom. But experience shows it to be true.

Freeing ourselves from one crutch, but not noticing another more subtle one sneaking in to replace it is dangerous. Only by avoiding this danger can we really strengthen our spine and make it grow, for that is when the Kingdom opens up.

Jung has this to say: "Only when all props and crutches are broken, and no cover from the rear offers even the slightest hope of security, does it become possible for us to experience an archetype that up to then had lain hidden behind the meaningful nonsense played out by the anima."[3]

When the Kingdom opens up, we are no longer afraid of shortages. All our needs are supplied . . . up to and including the Name.

"Cast thyself down," continues Satan to Jesus, whom he has led to a pinnacle of the Temple of Jerusalem. "He shall give his angels charge concerning thee: and in their hands they shall bear thee up, lest at any time thou dash thy foot against a stone" (Matthew 4:6).

Power

The power to go beyond the laws governing the distorted relationship between humanity and the cosmos only belongs to the man who has recovered his ontological norms.

Adam then returns to his spouse and mother, the *adamah*. "In the sweat of thy nostrils shalt thou eat bread, till thou return to the *adamah*, for out of her wast thou taken" (Genesis 3:19).

I shall have occasion to return to this vast subject when studying the blood. I will show the magical connections man attempts to establish in order to conquer cosmic power.

"In the principle," the Adam (spouse of the inner *adamah*) was also called to become the spouse of the outer cosmos, which was to obey him and give him its fruits. Since he no longer espouses his inner earth—the *adamah*—which the Fall caused him to forget, the outer earth becomes hostile. The only desire he feels is for possession, so he subjugates it. The relationship is no longer one of love but of a power struggle.

Thus seen, the psychological virtues that make the conquest possible belong to the categories of willpower, courage, or even heroism. Theseus died, as we saw, in pointless heroism. Fear is indeed defeated, but with such tension that our energies are not accomplished but drain away. This only makes the "wound in the foot" worse day by day.

Returning to the ontological plane means relinquishing Theseus's leather club, taking up the golden Sword of the Name like a true hero, and deriving strength by entering into its straightness.

If the martyrs in the Roman arena were not devoured by the wild beasts, this meant they had "married" the inner energies corresponding to those animals, which then sensed the presence of these energies in man (see chapter 18, page 343). The wolf accompanied St. Francis of Assisi, and the tigress St. Isaac, because these men had integrated their inner wolves and tigers in order to turn their devouring energies around and bring them back to their function of Light. Such power requires complete letting go, absolute love leading to complete accomplishment.

There are no miracles. There is only a return and an obedience to ontological laws.

Every technique used by man merely modifies the fallen world, the world of man, a wild beast among beasts.

Religions experienced outwardly do not reintroduce man to his ontological norms but lock him into moral categories that even exalt false heroism. They are compromises with the fallen world.

The evangelist Luke mentions a striking parable that ends with these words from Christ: "So likewise, ye, when ye shall have done all those things which are commanded you, say, we are unprofitable servants: we have done that which was our duty to do" (Luke 17:10).

All the treasure I have received from Christianity I owe to Bishop

Jean de Saint-Denys (Eugraph Kovalevsky), who taught me theology and was also my spiritual master.[4]

One day he sought to illustrate the sharp divide between psychology and ontology: "When I was fourteen, there was a family reunion in our house, and my uncle, who was an archimandrite, took me by the arm and walked me around our estate. In the portrait gallery, he asked me to respectfully consider pictures of our ancestors, many of whom had been heroes: 'Look well at them, my lad; every one of them had a sense of honor.' Then he took me to the chapel. There, before each icon, a little lamp was burning. The saints were watching. 'Look well at them,' said my uncle, 'they had no sense of honor.'"

I did not really grasp then what he meant by "had no sense of honor." Through my family and lineage, I felt that such values were no laughing matter. I have gradually learned to let go of these virtues and to make room for the inner information that brings about right action, even at the risk of being misunderstood by those around me and of being thought treacherous, cowardly, or even crazy.

Jung expresses this by saying that he who obeys his anima "can manage without insults and without praise" (praise being no less a trap!).

Man then finds his own authority within him, in the etymological sense of the term (from the Latin *augere*: to bring growth). Only the *yod* brings growth. Outward authority exercised on others, or received from others, is mere power. An adult—one who has relinquished his crutches —is the author of his actions. He alone is responsible for them. Responsibility involves an espousal (*sponsa*) with oneself.

This is why, on the level of the rectangle, there is no law resulting from power. The only laws having "authority" are those dictated by our fundamental structures, the cosmic order. And these laws can only be revealed to the irrational part of our being. Once given expression, they appear paradoxical. For example, a state can only aim for peace once its laws arise from a fact that is recognized as axiomatic by the collective consciousness: equal value must be given to a single person and to the whole of society. Political ideals that grant preeminence to one pole or the other, person or community, are in the wrong and impose power, which sooner or later becomes a source of conflict.

This anthropological reality is in the image of its divine archetype, revealed by the theological mystery. Christian "dogmas" express two apparently opposite realities:

— The coexistence of two natures, divine and human, in the unique Person of Christ;
— The divine Oneness in three Persons, each containing the fullness of divinity.

Far from being "dogmatic," in the restrictive sense of the word adopted in the West, these two realities are a source of freedom for those who experience and live by them.

When the term "dogmatic" designates objectified truths, or an alienating authority, it is inadequate. The Greek root *dogma* is linked to the root *doxa*: "that which seems just."

Even physical and mathematical sciences are underpinned by axioms that amount to authoritative "dogmas." Because they are the basis for growth, they are liberating.

These sciences remained for a long time on the first level, gradually discovering the immediate laws of nature. By laying down his principle of relativity (in today's language the principle of "the Absolute veiled by appearances"; chapter 3, page 20) Einstein propelled physical and mathematical sciences through the Gate of Men.

Now they are bringing to light fundamental, "metalogical" laws, whose reality can only be expressed by contradictory assertions: light is at one and the same time composed of particles and waves; knowledge on this level is at once subjective and objective; energy is spirit and matter, etc.

Human sciences are still trapped in childish forms of dualism because our psychological structures put up massive resistance when they are asked to evolve. These sciences have not yet gone through the Gate of Men. Hence the formidable gap that has recently opened up between man and his work, between his being and the productions of his brain, which he cannot control. This is one of the deepest roots of our modern angst.

Which is why, however paradoxical it may seem, present-day physical sciences are forcing us to go through the Gate of Men. They are giving us the impetus to discover our true dimension. If we do not, they will destroy us.

It is important then to insist on this transition from psychological to spiritual or ontological virtues. Let me share another experience:

Bishop Jean had died. One night, I dreamt that he had come to see me and his other disciples. He had come to teach us once more. But there came a point when he gave us to understand that he had to return to where he came from, for he was no longer of this world. He kissed everyone except me and walked away toward the door. I was dismayed, could not understand, and suffered greatly.

Suddenly, he turned and came toward me. I found myself kneeling in front of him, his stole was on my head, as during the rite of penance, and he said: "You, Annick, be total love." Then he left.

This dream left an indelible mark on my life. It revealed something profound: I was not to be encouraged, or to receive praises or emotional warmth from the master, but to live out the baptism of fire. My companions, encouraged by the master's embrace, were my energies, not yet accomplished, fragile, still nourishing the psychological plane within me and which had to be purified with fire.

This dream also enabled me to understand an aspect of the myth of Cain and Abel. More than any other, this myth illustrates the split between the psychological plane, belonging to the Fall, and the ontological plane to which the Gate of Men gives renewed access and where the baptism of fire has to be experienced.

Qain (קין) can be read as "nest, קן, of the *yod* י." Within this pair of brothers, he is the ontological man.

Abel (הבל) is the name of "vanity," of that which is illusory and has no intrinsic reality. In the fourth chapter of Genesis Abel's name is only given together with the phrase "his brother," and this gives him such reality as he has. He is the "man in a coat of skin" who is only "added on" to Cain. The Hebrew text expresses this by saying that he is the "keeper of sheep," whereas Cain is "a tiller of the *adamah*."

"At the ending of the days" or "of the waters" (Genesis 4:3)—the words "day" and "water" have a common plural, יָמִים, *yamim*, which is to say "at the accomplishment of a first sum of unaccomplished energies"—Cain and Abel bring an offering to the Lord יהוה. Abel's offering (the firstborn of his flock) is "looked upon,"[5] Cain's offering (the first fruits of the *adamah*) is not looked upon.

At the first level, we don't understand!

Nor does Cain. "It burns up within him; he makes his countenance fall," says the text: his field of consciousness is scarcely the one his *yod* is proposing! This is said in so many words by יהוה, who spells out these levels fundamentally: "Why doth the fire of wrath rise within thee? And why doth thy level drop? If thou art within the *tov* (the pole of light) there is order; if thou art not within the *tov*, sin lieth at the door; And unto thee shall be his desire, and thou shalt rule over him" (Genesis 4:6–7).

Falling into another field of consciousness is identifying with man in his coat of skin, giving oneself as food to the Satan (who desires this feast!), and entering, through Abel, into a struggle with Satan, in order to rule over him.

Being *tov* is changing the level of consciousness, entering into the light of the event, understanding its meaning.

There is no doubt that יהוה, at the heart of Cain's name ("nest of the *yod*"), demands that the nest be built and puts Cain to the test of love.

Abel is man in the coat of skin, in his weakness, and his understanding is enslaved by his animal drives. Abel needs to be encouraged, to be "saved."[6]

Raising one's consciousness and entering into the divine understanding of an event means acknowledging that we cannot understand it

when it happens, agreeing not to use our understanding in a male manner, but allowing it to be gradually penetrated by Divine Wisdom. This
wisdom is ontologically male, whereas our ontological understanding
is female.

Raising one's consciousness therefore means abandoning the idea
of understanding the event on a level to which it does not belong. It
means "letting go" and placing oneself on the axis of *tov*, which is what
the term שאת, *se'eth*, expresses in Genesis 4:7. I translate this word
as "order" and not, as is usual, "worthy" (being accepted) because this
latter term brings in the idea of a psychological virtue. "Worthy" is only
correct to the extent that it connotes that which is appropriate to the archetypal, a concept that is better translated as "order." The word *se'eth*
can be read *shet* (שת, base) of *alef* (א).

With such an attitude, emotion—in this case anger and jealousy—
does not even arise in man. There is no loss of energy. Everything is
tov! But if man lowers his field of consciousness, there is an upsurge of
emotion. Who will rule over it, man or Satan lying in wait to devour it?
This is where the struggle starts.

Psychologically, this struggle is exhausting.

Now the myth points to Cain and Abel "in the same field of being,"
which means in the same field of consciousness. So Cain has lowered
himself to a psychological level! He is not even struggling there. His
yod, his Word, is immediately turned against Abel. He kills his brother.
He kills with his Word. Whatever the instrument of death—the sword,
the knife, the sophisticated weapon, or the most treacherous one, the
tongue—it is always in its latent essence our Word.

"What hast thou made voice?" God asks Cain insofar as he is Word.

He who does not bring to birth the *yod* fundamentally destroys himself and destroys everything around him.

The double-edged Sword brings life or death.

It brings life to the one who is going through the Gate of Men, and
death to the other.

Yet in the light of what the Sefirotic Tree shows us, it is still possible to turn the energies around, and shift from the psychological to the on-tological plane.

Let us revisit the diagram for the study of right and left (see chapter 6, page 56).

After the Fall, the feminine crosses over to the right, the masculine to the left. Only the head, representing the Earlier Heaven, is not in-volved in this crossing.

This "crossing of the lights" is inscribed in the body at the level of the medulla oblongata. But in truth the "posterior body," in its coat of skin and with its psychology, has not forgotten the archetypal body, which obeys the Earlier Heaven. Superimposing the two levels is enlightening.

We have seen that the feminine crosses over to the right after the

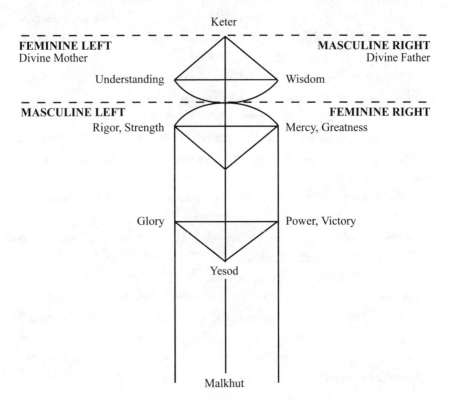

The Feminine and the Masculine on the Sefirotic Tree

Fall and essentially "feminizes" ontological wisdom, which turns into ethics, philosophy, religious wisdom, moral codes—all of them "foolishness" in the face of Divine Wisdom, say Isaiah (29:14) and St. Paul (1 Corinthians 3:19).

In this view, the god of the philosophers becomes a demiurge relegated to a transcendent and inaccessible heaven, an uncreated being unmixed with creation. Paradoxically, however, this demiurge is set up as judge of humankind, with whom he has nothing in common and for whom his grace intervenes only when he sees fit.

Similarly, Grace or Mercy, the sefirah Hesed, is feminized and diluted into emotional sentimentality, which is then transferred, by projection, onto the transcendent god. It makes humanity female and mobilizes well-meaning consciences around personal, social, and international organizations, all seeking to repair the inevitable mistakes made by others. These "charitable ladies" from all walks of life alleviate hardships, at whose true causes society refuses to take a hard look.

Nations resemble doctors who only treat symptoms. They alleviate ills without ever calling themselves into question.

Like the Danaids, we continually pour water into leaking vessels.

Then this sefirah (also called Gedulah, Greatness) may become the kind of greatness that belongs to those who believe they are magnanimous merely because they are attached to a self-image of generosity.

Feminized "Victory" becomes a conquest marked by vanity and serves outward glory.

Giving back to the right side its ontological dimension means giving it back its male power. Wisdom is called "Divine Father."

Divine Wisdom goes well beyond all ethics and beyond "the Law and the prophets." It is such folly compared to anything we could conceive of that even if someone could experience it directly, he would be at a loss to explain it. And—like Ham, the son of Noah, who "told without" the mysteries he had seen within—anyone who attempted to formulate it would be burned up.

However, considering the human folly our "masculine" understanding has put us in, it is urgent to turn toward this Wisdom. We must approach it "backward," as Noah's other two sons did, putting back the veil over what one cannot endure.

Going toward that Wisdom means becoming "male," that is, "remembering" what we are in order to follow the path of our inner lands, which is Understanding. The path is as fine as the blade of the Sword, and as we tread it we have the law on one side and prophecy on the other:

— The Law, which makes for stability and builds on one level of earth, but whose danger is stagnation;

— Prophecy, which tears us away from this earth in the direction of a new and deeper understanding, but which can also lead to madness in human terms.

The right side of our brain, hitherto silent, must awaken so that we may break through to that uprightness that is obedience to the need for penetration.

On this path, men and women are equal, but their respective talents and functions are different.

Ontologically, they are equal. Biologically, they are different and complementary: their gifts and their functions are not the same in outward life. The right masculine side requires that both men and women become aware that the accomplishment of one stage still leaves much left to be accomplished. This is the mark of true humility.

Ontologically, the masculine is humility and mercy. Biologically, man is called to rule over the outer cosmos. Physical strength is given him for that purpose, but if he does not put it at the disposal of feminine Understanding and of the Rigor linked with the information this Understanding offers him, he will become a false ruler.

Man is a builder who must seek information in a loving penetration of his inner cosmos as well as of the outer cosmos. He must be aware that his Wisdom is relative and not enclose it within a system.

After the Fall, the masculine energy crosses over to the left and essentially masculinizes understanding, which then takes the form of a penetrating force instead of a penetrated mystery. Understanding is then totally committed to discovering the outer world and domesticating it. When it approaches the inner world it is no longer open to a living experience but only to making intellectual patterns.

Understanding dominated by the masculine is intellectual.

The civilization we live in develops this understanding to its extreme. The left side of the brain develops in the greatest ignorance of the right.

Strength, which is also made masculine, becomes outward, physical, psychological, or intellectual. It is competitive, overwhelming or overwhelmed, conquering with a view to enslavement, or conquered in order to serve.

Masculine Rigor means sectarianism and closing down.

"Glory" is no longer the glory of the Name, but of fame.

Giving back to the left side of the brain its ontological dimension means giving it back its true feminine face. Understanding is the Divine Mother.

Understanding—בינה, Binah—is linked with information, acquired by man on the way to fulfillment, for every inner terrain that is penetrated will ripen its fruit. The last fruit is the *yod*. It gives birth to man, who, being totally informed, enters then into sonship (*ben*, בן, is the son).

This is why I said in chapter 6 (page 55) that ontologically, Understanding is a loving openness to the penetration of Wisdom. It makes up each of our inner lands. Once fertilized, each of these distributes the fruit of the *yod*, the strength, the energy-information latent until then. In the final land, it reveals the Name in its wholeness, the sum total of energy and information.

The left side of the brain, restored to its ontological function, is the yin side, I might even say the "belly," yin containing the Son (yang) in its depths. We are to give it back its feminine calling: to receive the Spouse who is Wisdom and give birth to the "self" by successive stages, in the Rigor—דין, *din*—of each stage, until the Son (*ben*) is born.

Understanding is parturition. Men, like women, are called upon to give birth, and we must be aware that that is a painful process. But woman has this in her makeup as an outward vocation as well, which means that by nature she is a mystery that will only blossom and reveal itself through love.

This mystery, once revealed, can give the world a new type of information because it is ontologically linked with the understanding of the world. Man's function is to build; woman's function is more invention and creation.

Without Wisdom, Understanding can give birth to monsters.

Without Mercy, Rigor and Strength can be devastating.

Ontologically, once they have left behind confusion, the masculine and the feminine are called, in successive marriages of each of us within ourselves, to "make the flesh one," meaning to restore to flesh its divine calling (Genesis 2:25; see also chapter 12, page 230) and to bring it to fulfillment with the Divine Spouse.

Marriage in the world is a symbol of this dynamic and hence a path toward it.

What I have said here may provide a starting point for the kind of reflection necessary in order to go through the Gate of Men. "Growing up," in that much-used phrase, is not a matter of sorting oneself out on the level of psychological energies, but restoring these to their ontological dimension, in relation to the Divine Body.

Only this will make men of us.

Posture and the Gate of Men

It will come more naturally for man to be inwardly upright if his body is itself upright and harmonious (see chapter 11, pages 157–58).

The spinal column is not a straight axis—if it were, it would be very fragile—but is made up of a succession of curves completing and

counterbalancing each other, giving it a remarkable
solidity and suppleness.

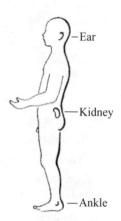

The Three Seeds

The ideal straight line running down these
curves joins ankles, kidneys, and ears.

Thus the three "seeds," foot, kidney, and ear,
continue one another and remain in correspondence
in the growth of the Tree. This axis needs to be correctly taken up in the cross-section of the *hara.*

Hara is a Japanese word meaning "belly"; in
Chinese it is *dantien.* It is a precise point found in
the center of an imaginary transverse section of the
body passing between the navel and the pubis.

The *hara* posture is when an exact relationship is established between this transverse section and the axis of the spinal column. This
means that man standing has his feet parallel to each other, separated by
approximately a foot. His knees are unlocked, ready to bend, ready to
move with the ankles and hips, for his mobile balance to be constantly
maintained.

Stable in movement, dancing as it were on his roots, man in his *hara*
is centered in himself. Neither leaning forward nor arching backward,
he is precisely anchored in the *hara* so that the belly is always free.

The head is free of the shoulders, which slope naturally downward,
letting go of tension. The cervical vertebrae unfold upward, extending
the spinal column and causing the chin to recede slightly, so that the
body is all ear, as we shall see, and man may become the Word.

In the West, equestrian terminology describes a skilled rider as one
who "sits his horse well." One who cannot "sit well," who is unable to
align his center of gravity with that of his mount, is liable to be thrown
off, because the horse, not feeling mastered, takes over the reins and
gallops away.

To "sit well" is the posture of the *hara.*

Man can be seated in his *hara* provided the belly is free. He does not
slump, nor is he rigid, but he is perfectly relaxed and therefore available,

receptive, and altogether attentive. All his energies are awake. His strength, centered on the *hara*, is radiant and keeps others at a respectful distance.

In a frightened man, strength is gathered up in the shoulders and is threatening. Tension is extreme.

Stability and Receptivity

In the integrity of the *hara*, neither stiff nor slack, man experiences a peculiar alertness, and his senses become keener. These are the first-fruits of a sensitivity that will open his heart and his understanding to another level of reality. The energies—the Chinese say the "breaths"—circulate with precision and optimal economy through the awakened body. And as the Temple of the Spirit, the awakened body can invite the king to enter his palace.

The Mystery of Death before and after Going through the Gate of Men

Death can intervene at any moment during the growth of the Tree. It is a mystery in itself, but so is the unknown moment when it may come. It belongs with all the deaths and resurrections that mark out our growth, but its nature is different, for now we have to leave our body behind and partake of a reality that completely escapes us.

Completely? Perhaps less absolutely than we think.

All doorways we have gone through to other levels of consciousness have been deaths and resurrections; insofar as death belonged with these, it is fundamentally mutation.

"Mutate" comes from the same root as the Hebrew word *mot* (מת), which means "death." It is built with the same two letters, the same energies, as the word *tom* (תם), meaning "perfection."

When a perfection is reached, when a field of light (*tov*) has been conquered, the law is that a break occurs, so that the conquest of a new field may begin (see chapter 3, page 19). We might think, then, that there is nothing to prevent this law from being applied to the total accomplishment of our being, even if physical death appears to interrupt it. This is precisely what tradition confirms.

Then why is our experience on earth so painful?

Only the myth of the Fall can provide an answer. If we heed it, we come to understand that *our experience on earth is necessary for us to regain the preeminence of our first nature.*

Going through the Gate of Men is the beginning of this process of recovery. After this passage, the death of our human body, in its coat of skin, seems a light matter.

But what of death before this passage?

The most complete answer is to be found at the end of chapter 7 of Genesis, in the light of the myth of the Flood (see chapter 10, page 128). When the waters are at their highest, all life is transformed. God had announced this at the very beginning of the cataclysm: "The accomplishment of all flesh is come" (Genesis 6:13).

This accomplishment, which is also a mutation, is then described on four levels. The last two concern the fate of those who have passed through the Gate of Men.

Among these, on the one hand there is Noah, who remains alone—*vayishaer* (וישאר). He is "the leaven" (*sor*, שאר) of future humanity, for he accomplished himself inside the ark (his "rectangle"). He was to mutate at the end of his life (Genesis 25:8).

On the other hand is humanity, which is "subtilized"—*vayimah* (וימח)—in the sense given by Hermetic law: "You will separate the subtle from the gross."

This is the portion of humanity "that held its head above the waters," meaning those who emerged from the unconscious and went through the Gate of Men without passing the Gate of the Gods. This humanity has faith and is tuned in to prophecy. It is, as it were, a flower in blossom, plucked by God before it has yielded its fruit. It goes on to join the mystic bouquet of humanity on the way to accomplishment in fields of reality of which we cannot speak but whose benefits we can appreciate because we receive their effects. Perhaps this humanity continues its mutations as Adam might have accomplished them before the Fall.

The other two categories of men who experience death during the Flood have not passed through the Gate of Men.

Those most developed have within them "in their nostrils the breath of God's Spirit," making them living souls (Genesis 2:7). They are within the tradition. On their level, tradition is law. They are men who obey the religious laws drawn up for this stage. They are not sufficiently adult and conscious to hear the Voice giving them life in the singularity of their person, or to live by the prophetic Word. However, caught up in the breath of tradition, they "mutate"—*metu* (מתו).

Imagine Noah before entering the ark, or Job before his trials. Both of them are *just*, according to the justness of law (*tsedeq*—"justness"— is the sefirah Yesod, situated in the Middle Path). If Noah or Job had died on this way of law, not yet accomplished in relation to it, would they not then have belonged in this category?

They are said to be *nishmot ruah hayim*—"breath of life within their names" (an almost untranslatable expression)—only in relation to the next category, for those whose evolution we have described have already let themselves be seized by the Divine Spirit and are taken further on within the "whorl" of their Name.

But those who mutate are already within the resonance of the *yod*. They are described as moving on "dryness," but this dry land is the word חרבה, *haravah*, which is חרב, *herev*, the Sword! They are seized by the Sword in the axis of their Name.

The other portion of humanity, which does not seem to have passed the Gate of Men, is that in which men's energies crawl and swarm on dryness, but this earthly dryness has just been completely covered by water.

Such men, I think, are wholly identified with their energies. They "expire"—*vayigva* (ויגוע)—but the text does not say they mutate.

What fate awaits those whose death is so described? The verb גוע,

gavoa, can be read as: man at the heart of the root גע, *ga*, which conjures up a very archaic state (being "gaga" may be related to this!).

Gao (גָעָה) is "to low," "to bellow," animal cries that are at the opposite extreme from the Word to which man is called.

If we examine this word גּוּע, *gavoa*, "to die," in different biblical
contexts, it seems to express a regression to the state that was Adam's
before he became a "living soul."

"Abraham *gives up the ghost* and mutates, full of days in a good old
age" (Genesis 25:8).

Job undergoes excessive suffering whose meaning he is at a loss to
understand, and he regrets not having "expired" when his mother bore
him (Job 3:2).

Giving up the Spirit, expiring, breathing one's last—these expressions render the idea of returning to an archaic condition as a necessary
preliminary to change (Abraham gives up the ghost *and* mutates).

But what happens to those whose state of regression brings no mutation because they have never experienced their "living soul"? Perhaps
they experience this negative phase, which is part of the evolutionary
process, but without the following mutational phase. They would then
remain imprisoned in a dramatic regression (that of hell), about which
we can know nothing except through a parable in the Gospel.

This parable relates the experience of a rich, hardhearted man who
after death suffers a thousand torments. He sees Lazarus, the poor man,
to whom he had always refused any help, blissfully lying in Abraham's
bosom. He asks Abraham for a little water to cool his parched tongue,
but Abraham can do nothing for him. Abraham answers: "Between us
and you there is a great gulf fixed" that cannot be passed at will (Luke
16:26).

The rich man then begs for Lazarus to go and warn his family of the
great torment in store for them if they end up in the place where he is.
Abraham answers: "They have Moses and the prophets" (Luke 16:29).

Abraham refers to the Law, which allows for a first mutation of the
most elementary kind. However, the man who experiences this must

subsequently undergo the ordeal of the "second death," of the "lake of fire" (Revelation 20:21), whose negative aspect is doubtless this rich man's ordeal.

On the other hand, Abraham refers to the prophets, those "who see the heavens open" and who hear the Word because they have lived through the baptism of fire in the rectangle of the Tree. Those who experience this go through a mutation such that they need not undergo this second death. It was experienced in their body during this earthly life. We shall consider this fire when we study the Cinnabar Field of the thoracic region.

It is clear that one who dies before having passed through the Gate of Men has not recovered the preeminence of his first nature. Identified with his unaccomplished animal nature, he can mutate if he has obeyed the law governing this stage. His soul remains alive, but he will undergo the second death.

If he has not obeyed the law, he is in the waters, unliberated. No longer possessing the body as an instrument for freeing himself, he is dependent on those who do have one. We may be subject to considerable interference from beings such as these. They are in great need of our help, and if we do not help them spiritually through prayer, they are probably able to sap our psychological, or even physical, energies.

It is plausible that many illnesses and incidents arise from this situation. Make no mistake: we must deliver our dead before we deliver ourselves, or at any rate while delivering ourselves.

Isn't this what the book of Exodus means when God, speaking through it, says: "I am a jealous God, visiting the iniquity of the fathers upon the children unto the third and fourth generation of them that abandon [hate] me" (Exodus 20:5)? But the generation that goes toward God and accomplishes itself emerges from the waters and helps its own to emerge.

A biblical proverb says: "The fathers have eaten sour grapes, and the children's teeth are set on edge." The sour grapes are the fruit of the Tree of Knowledge, eaten before man has become that fruit, and any error in our lives, ultimately, is a participation in this (seen from the angle of possession, enjoyment, or power). The symbolism of teeth set on edge (see chapter 17, page 338) shows how burdened we are with the faults of our fathers!

But if the fathers have done their work of liberation and therefore die after having gone through the Gate, "then," says Jeremiah in a prophecy about human evolution, "they shall say no more, the fathers have eaten a sour grape, and the children's teeth are set on edge. But every one shall die for his own iniquity: every man that eateth the sour grape, his teeth shall be set on edge" (Jeremiah 31:29–30). Each person will be responsible for himself alone.

Today's humanity, with very few exceptions, has not emerged from the waters, either in this life or in the next, and this creates a painful burden for us. However, the saintliness of the few exceptions is the leaven of the world.

If only for our descendants we have to go through the Gate and become men, gods even.

Those who have gone before and whom we may liberate will have to go through the second death on the other side.

I fear that those who are seized by death before reaching the Gate of Men and who have not obeyed the law suffer a painful fate on the other side. Until a time of which we know nothing, they cannot mutate.

Nevertheless, Christ descended into hell and saved them too.

But the time of suffering seems immense.

This fear of hell has made a large part of humanity march according to a simplistic morality, yet this morality was unable to bring it through the Gate of Men. All fear belongs to the unaccomplished, to the impure.

Love alone, and the desire for God, can correctly guide us toward the kernel, toward the Name, יהוה-Christ, in our complete realization.

Although supported by tradition, this meditation on death is mine, and my own responsibility. I describe it with all the Rigor of my vision, but I am bound to add that divine Mercy is infinitely greater than all our visions, eases our sorrows, dresses our wounds, and heals all things for anyone who calls upon it, from earth or from hell.

CHAPTER 12

After the Passage through the Gate of Men: The Life of the Body in the Rectangle Formed by Din-Ḥesed-Hod-Netsaḥ

VICTORIOUS OVER HIMSELF, PARTAKING OF DIVINE GLORY, HE who becomes a man and "walks on his two feet" (see chapter 7, page 88), has in so doing become conscious of the god he potentially is.

Hod (Glory) and Netsaḥ (Victory) have opened up, and their energy springs forth. These two sefirot are also called Majesty and Power.

"יהוה reigneth, he is clothed with Majesty, יהוה is clothed with strength, wherewith he hath girded himself" sings the psalmist (Psalm 93:1).

In the Tetragrammaton, the blade of the Sword rejoins the pommel, the *vav* is grafted back onto the *yod* and receives from it the nourishment with which it informs the two *hehs*.

The separation between God and man is abolished. In this great divine and human body that recovers its integrity and dresses its wound, circulation is set going again, the blood flows, the heart leaps, life sweeps in to color the features, and their deadly pallor retreats as the universal rhythm makes its way in.

The dialogue between God and man is renewed: "Gird up now thy loins like a man; for I will demand of thee, and answer thou me" (Job 38:3).

Thus begins the astonishing conversation between Job and his Lord. This mysterious character in the biblical myth is devoid of meaning if not situated on this level of Being.

But this stage can only be experienced if the kidneys (reins, loins) have become the source of all strength.

The Kidneys

They are the "feet" of the second level of the body, the level of Being. Like the feet, they are shaped like a seed.

The perfection reached through the first triangle or Cinnabar Field implied a death and a new consciousness that turns previous values upside down. The person discovers that the strength he has acquired is but weakness compared to the strength he has yet to conquer.

Perfection on one level is the seed of the next level.

The kidneys are a symbol both of strength and weakness. They are the pivotal point between the first triangle of water and the new level of fire, into which are dovetailed the organs of speech and hearing. The loins have their part in genital life and are at the root of man's realization, through his successive begettings of himself, until he becomes Word.

The ears are not distinct from the organs of speech during the first few weeks of intrauterine life; likewise the kidneys only become distinct from the sexual organs after a similar period of time (see chapter 10, page 123).

But the kidneys "remember" the organs of procreation in the same way as the voice continues to remember the ear and the entire fetus remembers its placenta. I will come back to this.

There is an identical pattern in these three examples. Throughout Creation the same fundamental structure reappears: the world of *ma* initially was one with the world of *mi* and, now that it is separate, nostalgically seeks its presence.

The essential role of the renal system is to filter the blood, extract from it any excess water, mineral salts, glucose, etc., and to give back to the blood the purified elements it needs.

It remembers the genital system in the sense that the suprarenal glands secrete sexual hormones.

These same glands produce adrenaline, which influences the sympathetic nervous system in its vasoconstrictive and tonic role. They govern the metabolism of salt. This seems to be the formal aspect of a far more complex and subtle function, which I shall attempt to describe.

The kidney, essentially a filter for the blood, corresponds to the foot, which filters information from the earth and also to the fetus in the womb, filtering information transmitted by the amniotic fluid.

Likewise it corresponds to the ear, which filters sounds from the air. Such "listening" is as much a function of the foot as it is of the kidney.

The entire body, whose intrauterine shape in the fetal state is that of a seed or a big ear, is called to become an ear once again, so that man can become the Word; thus the theme of his future uprightness is imprinted from the beginning in the first cell of the fetus (see chapter 16, page 317). The kidney may then be a relay station for this "listening."

Its Greek name, *nephrós*, whose root is found in all words relating to the kidney, is an anagram of the word *phrénos*, which is cognate with the French word for "kidney," "*rein*," and the English "reins." Now *phronéō* is the verb "to think," *phrónis* is "common sense," and *phrónēsis* is "thought" or even "wisdom."

The kidney, listening and hearing, is the seat of thought, wisdom even, throughout antiquity. God knows, for he "is a witness of his [man's] reins and a true beholder of his heart" (Wisdom of Solomon 1:6). The kidney must have an important role to play in intuitive listening and psychic understanding (see chapter 20, page 368).

The phrenic nerve is probably not foreign to the kidney. We know that it has its root in the fourth cervical vertebra and that it governs the diaphragm.

The diaphragm is the most important muscle of our body in terms of its surface area, yet it is sadly neglected. It should be our essential tool for breathing. It separates the thorax from the abdomen, and its job is to push the intestinal tubes far enough down so that the lungs—at every breath taken—may fill and blossom above.

But we breathe no better than we live.

We survive independently of the diaphragm by taking in just enough oxygen with the aid of the intercostal muscles.

With awareness of breathing, the diaphragm would massage the intestinal tubes in a constant and gentle wave motion and at the least allow activation of the digestive and excretory functions. Above all it would make for constant readjustment of the vagosympathetic system, whose correct balance is the foundation for the awakening of consciousness.

The diaphragm separates the thorax from the abdomen and resembles the border between the two ה that I described earlier with a diagram representing the structures of the human body (see chapter 10, page 122).

It is reduced to two "respirations": a pulmonary respiration above and a genital respiration below.

In light of this structure, *phrénos* and *nephrós* are the mirror image of each other, one (*phrénos*) above, governing pulmonary respiration, the other (*nephrós*) below, governing genital respiration.

The kidneys, then, in relation to the genital level of sexuality, play the part described in the oldest texts from ancient China, which say "the kidneys are the husband, and sexuality is the bride." They are "the minister who makes for robustness and vital strength; they lay up treasures of decision and understanding."

These texts also say that "the kidneys blossom in the hair."

It is no surprise to find the symbolism of strength linked with hair (see chapter 20, page 367). The opposite of strength is fear. When man is in a state of fear, his hair stands on end, and his kidneys, suddenly constricted (because the *phrénos* is blocked), make him urinate.

Hair, because it corresponds to horns, symbolizes the "crown," meaning fulfilled sexuality.

Sexuality, expressed on a purely genital level, is at the root of each person's tree, but it is called to rise like the sap to all other levels of being.

The loins give their strength to sexuality and to all subsequent levels of growth until sexuality bears fruit in the function of the Word.

And this is where their job as a barrier, purifying and filtering out elements of information between water and blood, plays a vital part on a more subtle level. We know how essential this role is physiologically. But more is at stake: the accomplishment of the human being, the possibility of his successive acts of inner begetting, and his births to new fields of consciousness. Failing this, man will enter into the humdrum existence that results from the death of the *yod.* All this depends on whether or not the kidneys perform their role on higher levels.

The kidneys govern both the passage from water to blood on the way to becoming Spirit and the passage from salt to fire on the way to light.

From his birth, the adolescent is blood physiologically, but he is still only water essentially. He is unaccomplished and unaware of being unaccomplished.

From the name *Adam* (אדם), he has only experienced the first part, אד, *ed,* which is water, "vapor" of desire, with which he is kneaded ontologically in the primal clay.[1] This desire, the basis of eros, links him ontologically with the Divine Spouse, but has been turned away from him in the episode we call the Fall.

Here lies the deep cause of suffering.

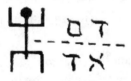

Water and Blood

Only when desire is redirected toward the Divine Spouse and seeks his response does man, rooted again in his ontology from heaven, recover his roots on earth. Water, enriched by the response, then becomes blood.

With a play on words, the word "response" is an "espousal."[2] The adolescent now crosses from אד, *ed* (water), to דם, *dam* (blood), and becomes אדם, Adam, man.

Entering the ark, Noah left behind the world of water (the Flood) to penetrate the world of blood. Obeying a divine order, he girded "about his loins" the animals (energies) of his created being in order to espouse them and become them. He becomes rich with their blood (see below, page 204).

Jacob, crossing the water of the river Jabbok and wrestling with the angel, became the blood of the divine-human body, expressed by his new name, Israel.

Moses, halted by "יהוה, who sought to kill him" on the road to Egypt, became blood. His wife said, "Surely a bloody husband art thou to me" (Exodus 4:25). He then became able to fulfill the mission received from יהוה, to go and free his people.

To go through the Gate of Men is to go from water to blood and become Adam.

After Christ's three temptations in the wilderness, his "public life," his life as a man, begins with the changing of water into wine at Cana—Qanah—in Galilee.

A wedding feast is being celebrated at Qanah, a wedding in the world, belonging with the first Cinnabar Field (marriage with the "other"). Such marriages are only authentic insofar as they are in keeping with the dynamics of two further weddings in the other Cinnabar Fields (the other triangles on the Tree) that are their laboratory: marriage with oneself and marriage with the universal (see chapter 10, page 124).

The name Qanah means "to acquire."[3] At Qanah, through this wedding, there begins the complete acquisition of all energies that have not yet been accomplished, whose symbol here is the married woman.

Qanah (קנה) is the counterpart of the murder committed by Qain (קין) when he kills his brother Abel and sheds his blood on the earth. In depth, Cain sheds all his potential of energy—his "animals," which Abel symbolizes—and their power is given to the earth, the outside world. At Qanah, in the outside world, wine runs out. It is needed for rejoicing, which symbolizes *enjoyment* in the acquisition of the Name.

"Woman, my hour is not yet come" (John 2:4), says Christ to his mother, Mary, who asks him to intervene when she sees the incident. His hour was to come in the matrix of the tomb, when Christ celebrated the universal marriage feast, the Son of Man opened his kernel, and the New Adam, spilling *water* and *blood* from the wound in his side, brought the name of Adam to complete fulfillment and became יהוה, who he is and whom he fully reveals at that moment.

Meanwhile, as a first step Christ changes water into blood with the symbol of wine. The second step is to be taken on the eve of his death, when at the Last Supper he changes the wine into his blood (Mark 14:24–25). By shedding his own blood onto the earth, Christ makes Abel's blood—which cried out from the ground—flow again in man's body.

After his temptation in the wilderness, the first sign Christ accomplished was the changing of water into wine. The first time he preached to His disciples he told them: "Ye are the salt of the earth. . . . Ye are the light of the world" (Matthew 5:13–14). The water in the first triangle is not without savor.

The waters in which the child is steeped in its mother's belly, the water of blood serum and seawater, are all of similar composition and represent in depth the same water of nonaccomplishment; they have savor. They bear within themselves the seed of the accomplished. The *ma* carries the seed of the *mi* in its bosom.

Salt is the living creature that enables food to bring out the best of its savor and glorifies it. It is the image of the seed of the *mi* in the *ma*, the image of the waters above in the waters below. They would have no savor were they not bearing the Divine Seed, just as the world would have no savor were it not carrying the promise of the Kingdom.

Melaḥ (מלח), "salt" in Hebrew, is made up of the same three letters—the same essential energy—as "bread," לחם, *leḥem*. We see in bread and salt the archetypes of the divine flesh, as Christ shows by changing bread into his body and wine into his blood.

Melaḥ (מלח) is the setting in motion, ל, of מח, *moaḥ* (the marrow), of what is most precious at the heart of the bone (see below, page 203), of what is to be "subtilized"—מחה, *maḥo* (see chapter 11, page 184)—because it will have been accomplished.

Salt is the driving force of accomplishment.

The metabolism of salt governed by the kidneys plays a decisive part in the equilibrium and subsequently in the accomplishment of every cell in the body.

Each cell is in the image of the primordial tree, *tov ve-ra* (טוב ורע). Each, roughly speaking, consists of a *tov* part, programmed to recreate the same cell (a skin cell for the skin, a liver cell for the liver, etc.) and a *ra* part, capable of recreating the whole body. Hence the recipe for cloning.

This structure is one of the essential aspects of the Trinitarian archetype applied to Creation: each element of the body is potentially the whole body. Interfering with a cell is interfering with the whole body, and what is done to one man is done to the whole of humanity.

In this perspective, when I speak of the kidneys, as of any other part of the body, what I say concerns not only the kidneys or the other organs themselves but the principle of each organ as present in each cell of the body, and of course in a particular way in the organ itself.

To return to the *ra* (רע) part of the cell, it is an immense reserve of energy that seems to be there needlessly and that is inhibited from invading the *tov* (טוב) part by biochemical repressors.

If such an invasion occurred, it would be pathological either because of an unusual thrust of energy on the *ra* part; or because the repressors were themselves inhibited; or through a collapse of the *tov* part.

These repressors are somewhat like the *vav* (ו), linking the *tov* and the *ra* (טוב ורע) and playing the part man plays at the heart of the archetypal Tree, הוה: coordination within an essentially dynamic equilibrium.

If there is a dynamic link between the role of salt, its metabolism, and the role of the biochemical repressors, we might understand better the words spoken by Christ to man to bring to light one of his deepest realities: "Ye are the salt of the earth" (Matthew 5:13).

The salt of the earth might also be translated as the "salt of the dry," because the earth, *erets*, is also the "dry" in relation to the "wet," in other words, the accomplished in relation to the as yet unaccomplished.

The salt of the accomplished, of *tov*, may then play a far greater part at the level of the cell. The energy reserve that is *ra*, a kind of "darkness" in the cell, which seems, as I said above, to be there needlessly, now appears on the contrary to be fundamental to the complete destiny of the cell, which is *tov*.

After telling his disciples: "Ye are the salt of the earth," Christ added: "Ye are the light of the world." Within the cell, salt may therefore govern the espousals of light with darkness, until all darkness is accomplished and becomes light.

When man begins work on this new level of his being, we shall see in subsequent chapters that he bears the fruit of his labor at the heart of every tiny cell in his body.

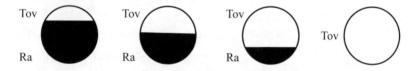

The Evolution of the Cell

The skin of man, once he is accomplished, bears no relation to that of the ordinary man he previously was, nor is any other organ the same. Ultimately, man becomes wholly light (see chapter 18, page 343).

The salt, bearer of the *mi*, functions as a repressor throughout the first part of man's life, like a moral code that prevents unconscious energies from overwhelming the whole man like a tidal wave. Its fundamental function, however, is to fertilize the *ra* part of the cell, to draw from it a portion that will be transmuted into light (*tov*), and then to maintain a new border between *tov* and *ra* until a new fertilization takes place. This process continues throughout the inner marriages, until the whole cell becomes *tov*—light!

Christ states the law of this work when he says: "For every one shall be salted with fire" (Mark 9:49).

Salt bears the *mi*; it is like an umbilical cord linking the *ma* with the *mi* and fertilizing it. It has the same calling as the Hebrew letter *qof* (ק), which is a symbol of wisdom.[4] Salt is a symbol of wisdom.

During the destruction of Sodom and Gomorrah by fire, this great purification, which is a passage from darkness to light, Lot's wife is changed into a pillar of salt. She is then the divine barrier that God lays down at the limit *tov* and *ra* of the cell called Israel.

Tov is experienced by the couple Abram-Sarai, which has just been made active and fertile.

Ra is experienced by Lot, whose name signifies "the veiled one," and his mysterious, unnamed wife.

Abram and Lot left Ur in Chaldea. Genesis (13 and 19) portrays them as returning from Egypt. They arrived in the Negev. There, acknowledging each other as brothers, they separated and the boundaries of their territories passed through Sodom.

God then asked Abram to look upon the whole of the surrounding territory: "To thee will I give it." The whole of the land was to become the property of Abram-*tov*. The work of purification, *ra* gradually becoming *tov*, then began. Sodom and Gomorrah, two cities of iniquity, were destroyed by fire.

Lot was saved and asked to escape to the mountain, symbol of *tov*, light; but he was weak and could not go far. His wife, changed into a pillar of salt (the ordinary translation, which has Lot's wife looking back, is highly questionable), symbolizes the new limit between *tov* and *ra*, between Abram and Lot. She represents Divine Wisdom from the depths of the unaccomplished in the cell that is Israel; she becomes manifest at this level to act as repressor and to fecundate the unaccomplished. Lot escaped to a small city; Abraham became the father of a great nation.

The limits marking each successive stage of purification will be like the new kidneys of each evolving cell. The salt of Wisdom governs this work.

Salt, then, with its physical properties, plays a considerable part in the process of man's becoming light and also in the opposite case—if he stays and grows old in the humdrum and his cells no longer have access to the realm of Divine Wisdom.

No outward medicine can cure sickness belonging to this high alchemy of being. I do not think cancer in particular will be cured by anything other than a forward march toward universal consciousness.

So it is in the kidneys that Divine Wisdom becomes manifest. Salt is its sign. It governs the equilibrium of cells, because Divine Wisdom governs the calling of man toward deification.

The description of the Son of Man in the vision of Ezekiel is centered on the kidneys (loins): "And above the firmament that was over their heads was the likeness of a throne, as the appearance of a sapphire stone: and upon the likeness of the throne was the likeness as the appearance of a man above upon it. And I saw as the color of amber, as the appearance of fire round about within it, from the appearance of his loins even upward, and from the appearance of his loins even downward, I saw as it were the appearance of fire, and it had brightness round about. . . . This was the appearance of the brightness of the glory of יהוה" (Ezekiel 1:26–27).

The word "loins" is *matnayim* (מתנים), whose root is that of the verb for "to give." Thus the kidneys, like any seed, contain all gifts. The above description concerns the "accomplished loins," the Glory of יהוה corresponding to the sefirah Hod and resplendent with the radiance of all its gifts.

The two first letters, מת, signify "death" and remind us that there is no accomplishment of gifts without the acceptance of deaths (mutations), which are also rebirths.

This is why, on the day of the Passover, the Hebrews are ordered to be ready for departure. They are to eat standing, with their staffs in their hand, their feet shod with sandals, and their "loins girded" (Exodus 12:11).

All gifts are brought together where the two halves of the body join, as they already are in the sandal containing the foot. This totality is expressed in the Hebrew word *kiliah* (כליה), which also describes the "loins," but here it is the Name itself, יהוה, which designates the gifts. For *Yah* (יה) is the sacred Name, יהוה. *Kol* (כל) expresses totality.

"For thou hast fashioned my reins; thou hast woven me in my mother's womb," sings the psalmist (Psalm 139:13).

For God weaves יהוה within man from the start and obliges him to become him: "He cleaveth my reins asunder and doth not spare; he poureth out my gall upon the ground," cries Job (16:13) in the pangs of bringing himself to birth.

In the same pangs, the psalmist repents of his "foolishness": "For my loins are filled with a loathsome disease: and there is no soundness in my flesh. . . . I am feeble and sore broken" (Psalm 38:7–8).

The word *kesalim* (כסלים), which here renders "loins," expresses this part of the body as the seat of thought, even of wisdom. Up to this point its thoughts have been nothing but foolishness; so hope is present in this word.

Finally, when God confirms Jacob in his new name, *Israel*, and promises him fruitfulness: "A nation and a company of nations shall be of thee, and kings shall come out of thy loins" (Genesis 35:11), the word "loins" in this case is *halatsayim* (חלצים), whose root *halets* is the verb "to deliver."

The royal, messianic dimension is in man's loins.

Bone and Blood

Becoming a man, becoming Adam, shifting from water to blood, also means consolidating one's "bone."

The work of marrying oneself, which begins genuinely on this level, is the work of marrying the feminine in each of us, earth after earth (mother by mother!), field of consciousness after field of consciousness, until the ultimate field is reached, the ultimate earth that conceals the secret of the Name. This work gradually makes one more and more upright (see chapter 11, page 157 and chapter 16, page 317), which also means consolidating the bone structure.

In Hebrew, the "bone" is the word *etsem* (עֶצֶם), built on the root *ets* (עֵץ), which is the "tree."

From the sefirah Yesod up to the passage through the Gate of Men, the adolescent has already begun constructing his Tree. The first ten vertebrae have been erected, yet how fragile they remain! The "sacrum"—*atseh* (עָצֶה)—is the "Tree (עֵץ) in its incipient state (ה)."

Note that whoever has gone through the Gate, although he no longer belongs to the level below, keeps one foot in it for quite a while! Closing the Gate definitively behind oneself is difficult. Sometimes man falls back painfully into the previous level and finds himself once more "crawling in the dust" and being devoured by the pseudospouse. The difference is that he is no longer completely identified with this level, so he can call upon inner resources and stand up again.

The spinal column will only become solid at its base through the gradual construction of the twelve dorsal vertebrae, marking each of our inner marriages.

Ḥulyah (חֻלְיָה) is a "vertebra" or the "link" in a chain, or a "jewel." The Name *Yah* (יָה) governs it, "dancing" (חֹל) within it. Climbing the Tree is the very dance of life. The *yod* is at its heart healing the "sick" (חֹלֶה) man.

The "self" can be strong only in the knowledge of its weakness; it can be healed only by knowing how sick it is.

"A chain is no stronger than its weakest link," says the proverb.

Man will be tested until he has a solid base. The first dorsal vertebrae cannot be built up without such testing. The *yod* will become stronger. The "self" discovered in Yesod and gradually affirmed has already undergone the necessary pruning (circumcisions), and there will be more, until the discovery of the true Self, the discovery of the Name.

Bone, the most solidified part of the body, carries awareness of the Self more than any other part. The word *etsem* (עֶצֶם), "bone," also means "substance" or "essence." When declined, it renders "myself, yourself, himself," which may be read as "my bone, your bone, his bone," in other words, what belongs most intimately to each of us.

It corresponds to the Greek *hypostasis*, the "person" in that the "person" is unique, a "divine image" created in the "sound" of the Word, in the resonance of his or her Name.

Led by God into his depths, Adam is placed face to face with himself, with his shadow side (chapter 3, page 20), in order to become aware of what is still unaccomplished in him and of the marriage he must now bring to fruition. Contemplating his feminine side, he exclaims: "This is now bone of my bones and flesh of my flesh" (Genesis 2:23). We might translate: "Here she is, the essence of my essence."

The "flesh"—*basar* (בשר)[5]—ontologically sealed in the deepest depth of the Adam, is his ultimate earth; once wed, it will reveal the secret of the *Shem*, the Name.

"Here she is, the essence of my essence; when unveiled, she will reveal the Name," says Adam.

After the Fall, flesh means something completely different. It is the source of the Name ontologically but becomes the source of *enjoyment-possession-power* turned outward. Man then invests his energies in relations with the outside world. So flesh becomes the focus of psychological life and the erotic power that governs relationships in the outside world (see chapter 11, page 165).

When the "Word was made flesh" (John 1:14), he came to make himself into the physical and the psychological life of man in order to seize his energies anew and to reinstate them in their vocation as Word, as Name.

The Word was made flesh, say the fathers of the church, in order to make the flesh into Word, to restore its ontological nature. Christ reinstates eros in its ontological vocation.

But let us return to bone, *etsem* (עצם). These three letters, inverted, form the verb מצע, *matso*, "to be in the middle" (the place of the *mi*).

Every bone in the body replicates the spinal column with variations in size. All our refusals to let go, our refusals to evolve, our refusals to love, are inscribed in it as blockages. By the same token, it is the place where our conflicts resolve themselves and our interior marriages, our liberations, are accomplished. In a word, if the *yod* is not suffocated, the *ma* goes up the length of this ladder to encounter the *mi*. This is why marrow at the heart of the bone is a sublime constituent of the body.

In the Chinese tradition, marrow is among the "curious (or marvelous) entrails," whose vocation is to ensure a long-lasting quality, a return to the One. For the Chinese, it is "the essence, the quintessence," linked with the brain,[6] in a shared function of "ordering principle, disseminated throughout the body and transmitted in particular by the marrow, whether bone marrow through the blood or the marrow of the spinal cord through the nerve impulses."[7]

In the heart of the bone marrow are formed the red cells of the blood, which are the noblest of its three constituents: red corpuscles, white corpuscles, and platelets.

Roughly speaking, the platelets ensure coagulation; white corpuscles, the defense of the organism; and red corpuscles, oxygenation.

The red cell in its function of oxygenation is linked with that of the entire body. It summarizes the name of *Adam* (אדם), which can also be read as: "*alef* (א) in the blood (דם, *dam*)." The letter א always indicates the divine name Elohim (אלהים).

Adam is Elohim in the blood.

This confirms the insistence of Scripture on the communion, the identification even, of "breath" and blood (Genesis 9:4; Leviticus 17:11; Deuteronomy 12:32).

His Name is breathed into man from the start (Genesis 2:7) so that he may endeavor to become this Name and return to Elohim, the Spouse.

Our life is basically a divine outbreath (א) as "created" and a human-divine inbreath, *yod* (י), as "made" (or "in the making"; see chapter 10, page 124).

Between these two moments of our history—one going from the
alef to the *yod*, the other from the *yod* to the *alef*—which mark out our
journey from the image to the likeness of God, all our breaths are written, on every level, this one being the archetype. And the red corpuscle
is the bearer of this mystery. Imbued with divine breath, the red blood
cell pulses energy.

Perhaps, with Rudolf Steiner,[8] we should overturn our usual view
and consider the blood as pulsing energy, which the heart then takes
up, purifying through air what the kidneys purified through water. In
the perspective of this work, the heart and the kidneys are closely connected. But what process on the level of the bone marrow gives the red
corpuscle its pulsating energy?

It seems to happen in a kind of suspension of respiration, an imper-
ceptible instant between Elohim's outbreath and man's inbreath. In this
instant, Elohim abandons the red cell formed in the secret essence of
being, in the deep, secret Self, his Name, so that *ha-Shem*—the Name
יהוה—can dwell there.

At the instant of this *shabbat,* the red cell loses its nucleus.

A nonnucleated cell is propelled into the bloodstream.

What becomes of this nucleus?

Nobody knows.

As a nucleus of energy, it is the א whose withdrawal allows the *yod*
to flow in the blood and man to become his Self.

The vocation of marrow (*moah,* מח) is to "erase" (מחה, *maho*), to
subtilize the most subtle, so that the other, unaccomplished, may come
to be.

The whole of anthropology is here in a nutshell.

On the day of the *shabbat,* Elohim withdraws so that his Creation,
now pregnant with his withdrawal in the Name יהוה, can embark on
life's great adventure in a different, more discreet, kind of Presence.
The life of Creation is called to become יהוה. Then, along with each
one of us, it will be wed by Elohim returning in Glory!

At the heart of the bone marrow, the greatest divine-human mystery is played out. The withdrawal of the nucleus, א, from the red corpuscle of the blood, דם, frees the energies of the *yod*, the energies of the Self. The withdrawal of *alef* and the pulsation of the *yod* make up the archetypal "pump," which determines the pumping of the heart. But God has "primed" it in the mystery of blood.

Love consists in withdrawing oneself so that the loved one may be.

Here blood finds the source of its pulsating force. Only because the א leaves can Adam (אדם) run the whole race to the *tav* (ת), the last letter of the alphabet, the last energy to be integrated (in Greek, from Alpha to Omega). To integrate the *tav* (ת) is to become *damot* (דמת), "likeness."

From the image that is Adam (אדם) to the likeness that is *damot* (דמת), his life is centered on the blood, *dam* (דם), in the rhythm that the *alef* (א) pulses, penetrating and withdrawing from him, and so imprinting the *yod*, the life.

The red cell loses its nucleus at the heart of the bone marrow in seven days, the time of a *shabbat*.

"In the human embryo, until the fourth week, only nucleated red cells are to be found, and then the non-nucleated cells gradually take over, so that by the third month the nucleated cells only represent a third or a quarter of the total amount. At birth, the blood no longer has any nucleated cells."[9]

A premature baby, albeit anatomically and physiologically "finished" at the end of the sixth month, is still, as it were, steeped in the Elohim and does not have the necessary pulsing energy to live outside the womb. Outside help on the physical level can enable him to find this energy—but what happens psychologically? Will the child not have to struggle to find his *yod*, his Self? Will he not find it difficult later to fit into the world, and even harder to realize himself?[10]

These questions may perhaps find their symbolic answer in the Visitation of Our Lady, that is, the day Mary visited Elizabeth, her cousin (Luke 1:36, 44).

Elizabeth, pregnant with John the Baptist, was in her sixth month of pregnancy when the Virgin Mary, in whom the divine fruit, the *yod*, had been deposited, visited her.

One day, I was present at this Christian feast at Ain-Karem in Israel, where the Visitation took place. There I had the sense that at the sixth month of our gestation—like John recognizing Christ inside his mother's womb—we thrill at the *yod*'s visit within us. This would confirm what the Tetragrammaton הוה reveals, namely, that between the *vav* (ו) and the *yod* (י)—between the 6 and the 10—is the story of our life, symbolized in the last three months of pregnancy (see chapter 3, page 16).

The child at birth is *Adam* (אדם), א in the blood, דם, *alef* then withdrawing so that יהוה may be. The child breathes because he is his Name.

The life of a red blood cell is 120 days. The life of man, says God to Noah, is 120 years (Genesis 6:3).

The number 12 is an essential part of Adam's becoming upright, and its theater is the twelve dorsal vertebrae. This is why the cosmic matrix surrounds man through the zodiac with its twelve gates.

I shall return to this. For now, we can note that the chemical element occupying the twelfth place in the periodic table of elements is magnesium. Its atomic weight is 24, twice 12. Its presence in the green chlorophyll of plants is structurally similar to the presence of iron in the red corpuscle of blood. The two pigments have the same composition except for magnesium in one and iron in the other.

These two chemical elements are complementary for the exchanges involved in respiration. Iron (atomic number 26) has 26 electrons circling around its nucleus. Twenty-six is the sacred number of the divine Tetragrammaton, יהוה!

Nature writes into its most concrete rhythms the divine mathematics of Creation.

The Red Man, made of iron, dances his Name in the hidden depths of his blood. As chlorophyll takes over, so to speak, he will become the Green Man and reach his kernel.

Sacred dances in our tradition were nothing more than the expression (as they still are in traditions that have kept them alive) of this demand-ing march of the Red Man toward the Green Man.

Like the dance of the planets around the sun, like the dance of the electrons around their nucleus in the iron atom, is the dance of man ripening his Name, celebrating his God, caught up in the universal rhythm.

Such is the man of tradition, who, entering Eden by the western gate, consciously dances his Name and allows it to carry him "where he did not think to go" (John 21:18).

When Jacob gave Esau—the Red Man—a "red pottage" in order to exchange this dish for his birthright, he was giving him iron.

This iron gave further strength to Esau as Red Man. He invested its energy in hunting and in seeking women, outward activities "which were a grief of mind unto Isaac and to Rebecca" (Genesis 26:35).

Nevertheless Jacob, by taking the inheritance, was gradually to re-cover all his brother's energies, enriched by iron. Seen in this light, Esau is the iron reserve in Jacob's blood. And Jacob was to draw again and again from this ore as his inner work moved forward. We shall see later the higher meaning of drawing from this deposit of iron.

But what about all the Jacobs who remain identified with Esau their whole life long, and whose reserves of iron are left untapped? What happens to the man who remains in the outer darkness, does not go through the Gate of Men, and does not forge his blood?

He is Cain killing Abel.

It is now time to dig deeper into this myth (see chapter 11, pages 174–76): Cain's murderous weapon is his *yod*, his word, his Name. He has not accomplished it inwardly and so turns it outward for the shed-ding of blood.

This murderous circumstance is the first time in the Bible that blood, *dam* (דם), is named. Earlier it was discreetly present in the name of Adam (אדם) and the word *damot* (דמת), "likeness," but the drama of the blood, the drama of this *dam* (דם), no longer caught between the א and the ת (the Hebrew Alpha and Omega, but in this case particularly heaven and earth) is part and parcel of the drama of man, who has left the path of his Name and his "likeness."

Qain (קִין), put to the test, could have reestablished himself in the axis of his Name and "made a nest of his *yod*," for such was his calling. But, refusing to hear the divine word, he turns his *yod*, his Word-Sword, against Abel and kills him.

Blood is spilled.

"The earth drinks the bloods of your brother" (Genesis 4:11: "the earth, which hath opened her mouth to receive thy brother's blood from thy hand"), says God to Cain. The cosmos then becomes invested with the power of the *yod*. Deified, the cosmos is worshipped and hated by man. Worshipped, because he wants to win it over, and to this end makes sacrifices on altars. Through it, Satan, the false spouse, is ever more insatiable for blood. Hated, because, all-powerful, it is an object of fear. Man struggles against it for power, putting all his understanding and his *iron* in the construction of an outer world that he exploits, enslaves, and conquers in rage.

And the false spouse, defeated, cunningly withdraws, but reappears elsewhere, again and again, in myriad ways, like a hydra athirst for blood, whose tentacles are severed, only to grow back in greater numbers.

And man loses his strength in this exhausting work, whose limits are apparent at the present time, although we have not begun to live.

Cain killing Abel sterilizes his *yod*; he invests its energies in excessive brainwork.

For seven generations, the descendants of Cain do not live: they have no age, no time, so no inner space. They represent our humanity, which has been "algebrized," as Marcel Jousse says,[11] solely occupied in building outer civilizations, proud civilizations, at whose heart blood continues to flow in wars, in crime, on the roads, and through the daily murders committed by our perverse tongues. Blood flows in procreation, it flows in the painful burden of our coat of skin! It will continue to flow until, emblematically coinciding with Cain's last generation,

Violence. This is what we are like: as long as our energies do not serve us on the path of accomplishment, we identify with them and kill. (British Museum, London.)

we confess to Abel's murder and replace the Sword in the sheath of our Name! Then—again quoting Marcel Jousse—we shall become "earthy" once more.

To Cain's last generation belongs Tubal-Cain, the smith. The smith works iron and bronze and other metals in fire.

Fire outside is a symbol of fire within us. Iron and bronze are symbols of metals within us that are called to become *silver and gold* in the forge.

For our body, on the level of the thoracic triangle where baptism by fire takes place, is essentially a forge.

To this unaccomplished inner work corresponds outwardly the iron and steel industry—man's unconscious compensation. The first piece of iron known to have been worked apparently goes back 3000–5000 years before our era. It was a meteoric iron from the sky.

The Greeks called iron *sidēros*, from the name of the sky.[12] It is as if this historical phenomenon meant that iron—which, according to Isaiah

(50:17), must be transmuted into silver, a symbol of intelligence—were connected to the world of the divine.

In Mesopotamia, where that iron seems to have been manufactured for the first time, the Sumerians called it *An-Bar* (fire from the sky). The Israelites were to go to that country in exile.

Leaving the path of the Name, Israel entered the land where iron was worked outwardly.

An-Bar has a common root with the Hebrew word for "iron," ברזל, *barzel*. The root *bar* forms the first two letters of the Torah, and Hebraic tradition says of them that they contain the Torah in its entirety. The essence of this vast subject is that *bar* is the "young son," the fire from heaven and from earth. When joined within him, they turn him into the accomplished son, *ben*.

Bar becomes *ben* when iron becomes silver. Here, too, sonship is linked with the quality of iron in the blood.

In antiquity, the work of the forge was inseparable from blood sacrifices. Normally a young boy was sacrificed. When *bar* does not die inwardly to transform his blood and become *ben*, he is sacrificed outwardly to nourish the god of the forge. And this was so strongly anchored in the collective unconscious that there were sacrifices for the founding of cities, and for the construction of temples and houses, in order to appease the spirits of the place.

Any appropriation of outward land demanded the price of blood. "Satan, your honor, in exchange for a little blood, I will take possession of this place . . . "

Magical rites in which the power of blood prevails latch themselves onto such forms. Magic is one aspect of the balance of power between man and the cosmos. It employs secret means requiring a repetition of Adam's action in opening his kernel before time. Magic is the daughter of Ham, the son of Noah who looked in at his father's intoxication and nudity, at the nuclear energy he had become, and then "told his two brethren without" this unveiled mystery (Genesis 9:22).

Far from releasing man from his coat of skin, magic imprisons him in it even more. It has nothing to do with the art of the magi, priests and men of science from antiquity who originally formed the sacerdotal caste of the Medes.

The magi come and bow before the Divine Child of Bethlehem, the child who will free humanity from its coat of skin. Their art bows with them before the Word.

The magicians, descendants of Ham, serve Pharaoh. When Moses—prefiguring the child of Bethlehem—rose up in Egypt to deliver his people, the magicians were in competition with him. Filled with the Divine Spirit, Moses listened to them. After the third plague of Egypt, the magicians declared themselves to be powerless. After the sixth, they are no longer present.

The Hebrew God then gradually gave his people awareness, not of a new reality, but of their ontological reality, the reality of the power of blood within man, the power of energies nourished by the Father-Spouse that enable man to become accomplished through his marriage with the divine.

To this end, God puts himself in the place of the false spouse. He slips himself, as it were, into the sacrificial rites and diverts them by artifice from Satan, so that the blood that sullies becomes blood that purifies.

The rites are complex and innumerable. They reach their climax on the great fast day, the Day of Atonement, the day when the chief sacrificer enters the Holy of Holies to sprinkle blood on the Mercy Seat. He offers, first, a calf for his own sins and those of his household; then, a ram for the sins of the people; and finally, a goat for the sins of the nation, while another goat, a scapegoat with the sins of the people laid upon it, is sent into the wilderness into oblivion.

Suddenly, God sets out the real situation. Through the voice of the prophets he says to his people: "I hate, I despise your feast days" (Amos 5:21–22).

So David sings in his psalms: "For thou desirest not sacrifice; else would I give it: thou delightest not in burned offering. The sacrifices of

God are a broken spirit: a broken and a contrite heart, O God, thou wilt
not despise" (Psalm 51:16–17).

And David, king of Israel, brings his people back to the need for
their inner death, the need to work the inner iron in one's blood. He is
the spiritual brother of Tubal-Cain's father, Lamech, who suddenly becomes aware of Cain's crime, speaks to his two wives (the awakening
feminine consciousness) and says, "I have slain a man to my wounding,
and a young one for my healing!" (Genesis 4:23).

Confessing his sin, he prophesies and says: "Cain shall stand straight
again sevenfold and Lamech, seventy and sevenfold" (Genesis 4:24).

Christ tells us to forgive seventy times seven times (Matthew 18:21).
Ceaselessly the wounded will be forgiven, healed, redeemed, with the
price of blood.

For as the forge gives birth to gold and silver, all birth comes at this
price:

Abraham, giving birth to Israel, is ready to sacrifice his son Isaac.

Moses, freeing his people from slavery in Egypt, leads them into the
fire of the Sinai wilderness and the fire of God's Word after the angel
has sacrificed the firstborn of the Egyptians.

The massacre of the holy innocents follows the birth of Christ.

And Christ himself, the last blood victim, redeems the Father's
Bride, that is the chosen people (cf. Hosea 1:19). He is her *goel* (גאל),
her savior; in Hebrew terms, the one who has the right to redeem the
betrothed. This is the price of blood.

To redeem the blood is to redeem the soul, because "the life thereof
. . . is the blood thereof" (Genesis 9:4–6), as so many biblical texts repeat (a mystery we begin to perceive in the light of what was said earlier
about the loss of the nucleus).

Redeeming the blood is redeeming the right to love, to be loved.

Redeeming the blood is reintroducing the living *yod* into man's
heart and returning the Sword to its sheath.

"And," says Genesis, bringing Lamech's confession to a close,
"Adam knew his *ishah* again and she bare a son, and called his name

Seth ["foundation"]. . . . Then began men to call upon the name of יהוה" (Genesis 4:25–26).

Genesis then spells out the names of the ten great patriarchs who, from Adam to Noah, take up the story of a humanity that has returned to the working of its inner iron. Noah symbolizes the man accomplished in his Name יהוה. All of them fit into definite periods. They are both inwardly and outwardly incarnate.

Today we might say that we belong to the race of Tubal-Cain the smith, for we sacrifice innocent blood on all sides while splitting the nucleus of the atom. For all that, we are still not genuinely incarnate.

What Lamech among us could rise up and exclaim: "I have slain a man to my wounding, a young one to my healing"?

The One begotten for the nations is sung of by the prophet Isaiah: "He is despised and rejected of men; a man of sorrows, and acquainted with grief: and we hid as it were our faces from him; he was despised, and we esteemed him not. . . . He was oppressed, and he was afflicted, yet he opened not his mouth: he is brought as a lamb to the slaughter, and as a sheep before her shearers he is dumb, so he openeth not his mouth. . . . He hath poured out his soul [breath] unto death" (Isaiah 53:3, 7, 12).

Yes, he gave his blood, for the breath is in the blood.

When Judas had sold Jesus and experienced remorse, he gave back the thirty pieces of silver to the chief priests and elders, who said: "It is not lawful for to put them into the treasury, because it is the price of blood. And they took counsel, and bought with them the potter's field, to bury strangers in. Wherefore that field was called, The field of blood [*sadeh ha-dam*], unto this day" (Matthew 27:6–8).

From the wedding in Cana of Galilee, where Christ, Man-God, changes water into wine, to the Last Supper, where he changes wine into his blood; and finally to the cross, where he undergoes the ultimate *shabbat*—"My God, my God, why hast thou forsaken me?" (Mark 16:34)—in order that man may reach his kernel and return to the Father, the mystery of blood is totally accomplished.

Christ gives back the Bride to the Father.

During the feast of Pentecost, the red Passover, the church cele-brates the Holy Spirit coming from the Father, poured out to fecundate the Bride. (For the symbolism of the white blood cell, see "Thirty Years On," pages 396–401).

The Navel and the Heart

From the Gate of Men to the Gate of the Gods, man symbolically climbs twelve successive spirals, each of them shaping a dorsal vertebra.

From one solstice to the next, on the sun's journey marked out by the twelve months of the year—inscribed in the twelve signs of the zodiac—man advances in the night of his history. Yet beyond the alter-nation of day and night, of summer and winter, he is aware on another plane of going through a protracted winter, a profound darkness. These are the cradle of the only spring and the matrix of the only sun that really gives life.

Will he find this sun and know this spring?

Man's body bears within it the promise of what he is to become: at the very heart of his being is the solar plexus. This assurance of the sun that he carries in his center has survived through the most agnostic ages, just as his "sacred" vertebrae have always assured him of the secret contained in Yesod.

In the Hindu tradition, the rise of kundalini at this level opens the chakra first of the navel and then of the heart. The first, blooming in ten petals, is the *omphalós*, the center, associated with the "Center of the World"[13] as one pole, the other being represented by the heart, whose chakra is described as a red lotus flower opening into twelve petals.

Here we shall distinguish, but not separate, join, but not confuse, these two centers. However, it is on the level of the heart that the twelve-petaled lotus opens out, and twelve is a number specifically linked with Being.

At the center of the lotus is its heart, the flower-cup, the thirteenth element toward which the first twelve converge. The twelve tribes of Israel strove to give birth to the God-Man, Sun of Righteousness. The twelve apostles surround this Sun of Righteousness, Christ himself.

At a later date, the Christian West, in the search for the Holy Grail, was to build one of its last myths on the Round Table, where King Arthur sat with his twelve knights.

In Greek mythology Hercules emerges victorious from the twelve labors Eurystheus imposed upon him in order finally to accomplish the thirteenth labor by marrying Omphale—which means identifying himself with the center of his being. This gives him access to the abode of the gods, where he is greeted by Hera, the goddess whose "seed" he carries within his name.

Whatever the quality of the "center" of the *omphalós*, of the heart of the flower, it is to this thirteenth element that the twelve petals, the twelve stages of the path, lead. And this thirteenth element, like the hub of a wheel, occupies the center. It is light in darkness, immobility in movement, the invariable at the heart of the variable, the principle in Genesis, and the calling-into-being of the many. There burns the fire that does not consume. There, love is awakened inside the "chambers of the king":

> Open to me, my sister, my love, my dove, my undefiled . . .
> Thou art beautiful, O my love, as Tirzah, comely as Jerusalem . . .
> I am black, but comely, O ye daughter of Jerusalem. Look not upon
>   me, because I am black, because the sun hath looked upon me . . .
> Stir not up, nor awake love, till she please.
>   (Song of Solomon 5:2; 6:4; 1:5–6; 2:7)

Darkness, sun, fire, love, beauty, perfection—everything points to the sefirah Tiferet on the Tree.

In the divine pattern, Tiferet is divine harmony at its fullest. It gathers together all colors, all sounds, all perfumes, all rhythms and elevates them in the perfect unity of their encounter. It is Measure, as well as

The Solar Center. The navel that once connected us to the placenta is a place symbolizing manifestations of God, a solar center with the lion as its guardian. (Ferrare Cathedral, Italy.)

Beauty. It is the divine Sun, the supreme Wheel, all the spokes of which gather together darkness and light and from whose formidable swirl break out all the possibilities of Divine Love.

Love is gift and also receptivity. An endless beaming forth, it is at once perfect emptiness and complete attraction. The center of all movement, the measure of all rhythm, it can only make itself known by veiling itself and limiting itself, being enclosed in the gems of all manifest life, which emanates from it and which it draws back to itself.

The man who attains this degree of experience is drawn into the tremendous whirl of the solar wheel. Sucked in by the centripetal force of its movement, he descends into the bowels of the earth—his inner earth—before being raised to the abode of the gods.

Marrying the divine, in Tiferet, means marrying contradictions—above and below, right and left, before and behind—marrying the Mother contained in Malkhut in order to be married by the Father hidden in the Ain.

Here we meet again the wanderings of Oedipus, the wandering heroes in myths, the wandering saints in history. This experience obeys the fundamental rhythm of all life: every winter, the sap from the tree descends into the depths of the earth before bursting upward in spring toward the sky to give its fruit.

The principal law of incarnation is to marry the earth in order to be married by heaven.

When the Adam weds *adamah*, the Mother Earth from which he is formed, he returns to his ontological norms. We have seen him overstepping his norms and marrying his own image. To tread the path of truth again means in the first place entering one's own depths, becoming dust again, and espousing the virgin earth, which will bear the Divine Child.

This is why, at the level of the solar plexus, the body asks us to experience the sacral chakra (at the level of the navel) before that of the heart chakra.

The navel is where the umbilical cord links the fetus with the placenta. It is where we experience our first actual wound, our first severance from the source of life in the mother. This nourishing cord joins the fetus with what might be considered its twin brother, since the placenta arises from the same egg as the fetus and is separated from it during the first few moments of life.

The placenta symbolizes the archetype of nourishing (chapter 7, page 72). It is the symbol of Elohim, the Father-Spouse, who nourishes Adam, the Daughter-Bride.

Since the Fall, humanity has been prostituted to Satan, the false spouse, and devoured by him. But ontologically it continues to receive from Elohim all the nourishment that constitutes its being and informs every instant of its life.

Symbolically, fetus and placenta are Daughter and Father, called to reunite with the archetypes and become Bride-Spouse.

The actual umbilical cord is only severed at birth to make way for the cord linking each being, in its ontological reality and its eschatological calling, with the nourishing Father-Spouse.

The actual placenta is—like the nucleus of the red blood cell—only eliminated to make way for the nourishing seed-placenta that is the Name יהוה inside the Name-Seed, the nucleus of each being.

In this sense, each one of us is also a twin brother of יהוה and is called, through a process that is at one and the same time evolutionary and regressive, to recreate with him the unique egg (see chapter 13, page 249). The significance of twinning is confirmed (see chapter 6, page 57, and chapter 7, page 86).

So the navel remains one of the key places of the body where God may manifest. This is why Hesychast monks (from the Greek *hēsukhía*, "rest") used to be called "navel gazers" by their detractors.

Derision is an easy means of defense for those who have been stirred at a subtle level of their being that they have not yet accessed. They reject and destroy whatever has stirred them.

The Hesychasts "feed" on the Name of Jesus-יהוה and allow themselves to be "carried in their middle" (the etymology of "meditate") on the cord joining them to the Holy Name.

Mount Sinai certainly remains one of the "navels" of the world—for the earth's body is analogous to our own and has its points where energy emerges.

Here, before setting out from the darkness of slavery on the great path of freedom, Moses experienced the burning bush (Exodus 3:2). He saw the Uncreated Light and heard his Name: "I AM" (Exodus 3:14). In the Hebrew text, "I AM," *Ehieh* (אהיה), is an imperfect, a verb form signifying what is not yet accomplished. In this holy place, Moses is invested with divine power before leaving in order to accomplish the Name of Israel, so that the Messiah may come.

When Moses went by Mount Sinai a second time, with the children of Israel brought out of Egypt, he went up to the mountain top, saw יהוה face to face (Exodus 33:11), and received from him the revelation of the ontological laws. When Moses came down from the mountain, the people saw him shining with an unendurable brightness. The quality of the law was to be similarly unendurable.

On Mount Tabor, in the Christian mysteries, Moses was to shine once more with this dazzling light—Moses, the man of Law, with Elijah the prophet, surrounding the transfigured יהוה—Christ.

Surpassing both law and the prophetic dimension, Christ is totally accomplished, the fruit ripened on the Tree of Knowledge, one and three.

Those who witnessed the Uncreated Light, the new burning bush at the summit of Mount Tabor, were Peter (the man of the Law), John (the man of prophecy), and James, *Yaaqov* (the root of the Tree).

Tabor (טבור) is the Hebrew word for "navel." It is also the "hub" of the wheel, that changeless place that is the source of all movement and transcends all opposites.

Tabor (טבור) means the principle ר, *resh*, of *tov* (טוב), the "good" of the Tree of Knowledge, or the "emergence of light."

The three disciples, overcome, overwhelmed by a light that they had not yet become, were granted the grace to see this Light.

And in this experience of Light, טוב, there is a great temptation to stay where they are: "Master, it is good for us to be here: and let us make three tabernacles" (Mark 9:5). The desire to settle, to halt, which ultimately means to die, is inscribed in the coat of skin!

Jesus then brings the three apostles down from the mountain and links this event with his imminent descent into hell: "He charged them that they should tell no man what things they had seen, till the Son of man were risen from the dead" (Mark 9:9).

The final access into Light goes through טוב ורע, *tov ve-ra*, the two poles of duality truly experienced on this level as a wedding, a relationship of love, and not of power.

Jesus also came down from the mountain, leaving this "navel" to take on the second pole, the heart. There he was to experience *ve-ra*.

Ra (רע) is not "evil" (see chapter 3, page 19, and chapter 9, page 119). In Hebrew, this word designates the enemy, the adversary. But with the ambiguity peculiar to the Hebrew language, רע, the "adversary," is also "the other, the friend, the neighbor" and ultimately "the brother."

Here is confirmation of what we saw with the crossing of Egypt, namely that Pharaoh (פרעה), the enemy, is in depth the friend, Moses's brother. The one and the other are the two poles of an essential unity.

Nevertheless, within the cognizable fabric of history, Pharaoh appeared as an adversary to the Hebrew people as they crossed their first level, and Satan himself is now to appear in the same context at the center of the rectangle, in the heart chakra.

The rectangle is based on the number 4 and represents a halt, a trial, or a prison. It may be experienced as a tomb, or it may take on the quality of a matrix. The number 5 is then identified with the seed of life, which is inscribed in the matrix in order to be brought to the fullness of its development.

The number 12 governs the structures of the second level. It corresponds to 3 x 4, that is, to the 4 entering into a dynamic of conquest. So the number 13, corresponding to 5 on this new plane, is a completion as well as a seed. This is why the number 13 implies death in order for there to be resurrection.

Christ as cosmic Seed is identified with the fish. He is to die and descend into hell, encounter Satan, and return to rise again.

"Except a corn of wheat fall into the ground and die. . . ." (John 12:24). From Tabor to the depths of hell, between these two poles *tov* and *ve-ra*, is the royal path of all men living their incarnation to the full, aiming at the final resurrection.

The heart chakra, which from the point of view of the Great Work is inseparable from the sacral chakra, is fire. Essentially it is the tip of the triangle Ḥesed-Din-Tiferet in the sefirah Tiferet (Beauty), which is an image of Keter (Crown).

In the secret of this thoracic triangle—this Cinnabar Field, a new matrix of immortality, according to the Chinese—man encounters himself through successive marriages, deep into his feminine, until he marries the ultimate land that harbors the kernel, his Name.

This part of our body, the matrix of fire, is described in myths by the symbol of the forge.

In Greece, the master of the forge is Hephaestus, or Vulcan, god of fire. He is lame and labors in the depths of the earth before becoming the heavenly smith. He chisels the crowns of the elect. He also shapes the cups for ambrosia and fashions the breastplates of heroes.

These symbols show that Hephaestus works in the depths beneath the earth on behalf of the highest levels of evolution. His helpers are the Cyclopes, giants whose single eye sees—like the eye of Shiva in India—all that must be destroyed in order that life may come forth from death, beauty out of decay, light out of darkness (see chapter 6, page 66).

The first smith presented by biblical myth is Tubal-Cain (Genesis 4:22), son of Lamech and Adam's descendant of the seventh generation through Cain. The number 7 (*sheva* in Hebrew, recalling the name of the Hindu god Shiva) symbolizes a change of cycle, a death for resurrection.

Tubal-Cain, the blacksmith, has a sister called Naamah, whose name means "Beauty" and is thus synonymous with Tiferet. Naamah is as intimately linked with her brother as are the trials in Tiferet relating to fire and Beauty.

He alone will awaken to Beauty, to the splendor of Divine Light, who as dust (עָפָר) has undergone trial by fire and become ashes (אֵפֶר). He will have transformed *ayin* (ע) into *alef* (א), the seven into one. Dead and risen again, he will enter eternal splendor.

Our body on this level is a forge.

The Forge

The Stomach

The stomach is the furnace of the forge, which must be fed healthy fuel.

To eat is to incorporate.

Ontologically, to eat is to incorporate the Divine Energies that are the nourishment of the Adam in Genesis (1:29). They are symbolized by herb and fruit, the forerunners of bread and wine.

Okhel (אכל), "to eat," is א, Elohim, giving himself totally (כל, "all") to the Adam. With man, it is also "to seize" (כ, to take in hand) Elohim (אל).

Ontologically, then, one must eat God, for the Father-Spouse nourishes his bride, who is progressively enriched by his energies and grows toward marriage. At the end of her growth, she is wed by God and enters into archetypal *enjoyment.*

Ontologically, food has the same nature as marriage: it is *enjoyment.* After the Fall, man is separated from the Father-Spouse and offers himself to Satan, the false spouse, who eats him. Man then becomes Satan's enjoyment.

Devoured in his inner cosmos, man feeds on the outward cosmos, which he depletes. There can no longer be marriage.

This single ontological function, nourishment-marriage, suffers division, and man seeks enjoyment in sexuality and in food. We know from psychology how closely linked these are.

The stomach will only return to its ontological function if man, by gradually counteracting the disorder of the Fall, restores this organ to the cosmic order and turns it into a receptacle for the divine.

Singing the Divine Glory is nourishment.

Praying is nourishment.

Loving is nourishment.

Living by beauty is nourishment.

Hate and ugliness nourish the Satan and destroy. Certain ritual meals can be diabolical. The ritual meal, rightly used, leads toward a return to the ontological norms.

The Christian Eucharist is such a return.

Man who can experience *enjoyment* at this level can gradually eliminate sexual life and psychological food.

Psychological food is emotion; it requires "having guts." It keeps alive in us the man in a coat of skin, man identified with the animal, making up the jungle that is still our world.

Food for the body is necessary in our present state. It should be chosen rightly in order not to burden the laboratory of the Great Work, for ontologically man is hungry for God.

This hunger is translated existentially into a hunger for happiness, which good food and an affective sexual life, as well as those ideologies that promise paradise, attempt to fulfill. All of these may be acceptable insofar as they are part of a human approach toward conquest of the divine.

If, however, they take the place of the divine, sooner or later they destroy man. Here I am merely confirming what the sefirah Yesod reveals of its divine secret.

For the Chinese, "the stomach is the sea of liquids and cereals which it takes in, cooks, and digests."[14] On every level it is where things are matured and worked through. Because the stomach is the furnace of the laboratory, we can see the implications of the fire that will be discussed in relation to the gall bladder.

The Fire

Fire—esh (אש)—is at the center of the covenant that in its principle unites the uncreated with the created.

Bereshit (בראשית), the first word of Genesis, which according to Hebraic tradition contains the entire Torah, can be read as brit-esh (ברית-אש), "covenant of fire."

This fire is manifest at all levels of the union and, in a special way, at the heart of the forge. It is life itself.

It is the breath of the creative Word, the breath of the Name, reaching down to the level of the body according to the energetic combination of each organ.

In the function that concerns us here, the Chinese call it the Triple Heater.

It is the threefold organ of the one Divine Fire. It has no material reality, for it is the mystery in the now, the Trinity becoming the Divine Smith, or, one might say, "Divine Cook."

The *heater above the navel* transforms and develops the energies. It separates the pure from the impure ("the subtle from the gross," says the book of Hermes in the Egyptian tradition).

The *heater below the navel* essentially eliminates waste and preserves what must be purified anew.

The *upper or thoracic heater* distributes the purified energies and blows the air needed to the two other heaters.

Before being summoned for trial by fire, these energies seem to be reserved in the cellar, by which I mean that earth in the depths, which is the pancreas. When they are purified and accomplished they are stored in the liver.

The Liver

The Hebrew word for "liver"—*kaved* (כבד)—also means "heaviness, weightiness, wealth, power." It essentially expresses the seat of divine power, the seat of God's Glory. This Glory is so intense that, in biblical times, when it filled the tent of the congregation of the Hebrews in Sinai, no man could enter the tent (Exodus 40:34–35).

The liver is the place where the light of the accomplished is stored. (See the myth of Prometheus in chapter 14.)

And when "all is accomplished" (John 19:30), the liver becomes dense with the richness of יהוה. This is the resurrection, the passage through the Gate of the Gods.

The numerical value of the word *kaved* (כבד) is 20 + 2 + 4 = 26, which is the same as the sacred number of יהוה. The liver has the same value and power as the Name and is called to be enriched by the Name, to acquire the totality of its energies.

When the liver is not given this wealth, we weigh it down with physical or psychological food, which are hindrances to its accomplishment.

Emotions—anger, fear, jealousy, etc.—make us eat away our liver by fretting (French: *se ronger le foie*, "to gnaw on one's liver").

Let us fast and pray, and divine Glory will enter in. Fasting, whether from physical food or devouring thoughts, must of necessity go along with prayer, or else—while all is not yet accomplished and the Satan is still prince of this world—it can open up the liver to spiritual forces of a diabolical kind.

"And the last state of that man is worse than the first" (Luke 11:25–26).

Burdening the psyche with worries and troubles—or even joys—and letting them take the weight that should be given to the Divine Light, means closing the door on this Light and withdrawing any possibility of transmutation from the energies in play.

"For my yoke is easy, and my burden is light" (Matthew 11:30), says Christ, because with a view to this coming transformation the hardest of trials carries within itself its weight of accomplishment.

Every sickness bears within it its seed of recovery.

Sickness is first a *perversion* of energy, which requires *conversion* into light. Western medicine looks for healing only on the outside of man.

Medicines following tradition, of which Chinese acupuncture is one, reharmonize the discordant energies. Not only do they seek healing from within man, but they also bring him to ask questions about the language his sickness is using to communicate with him.

Only the sick person himself, cooperating with the Divine Smith in this work of accomplishment, can act wholly correctly and effectively.

To this end he must descend into the unaccomplished, that obscure part of himself that carries his symbolic reality down into the pancreas and the spleen.

I want now to underline the "luminous" aspect of the liver's vocation. Storing up the accomplished, the energies turned toward the *tov*-light pole (טוב) of the Tree of Knowledge, the liver partakes of knowledge; it has power of vision. It becomes the seat of a new Understanding about events, of a new Wisdom about decisions to make. This power was known in antiquity, when the livers of animals were used to read the future.

The liver, whose etymology in French (*le foie*) is from the Latin *ficus*, the fig tree, has analogies with this Tree. The fig tree often appears in biblical texts. Three examples will throw light on the subject.

1. In Genesis, after the Fall, Adam and Eve "sewed fig leaves together and made themselves girdles" (Genesis 3:7). This verse may also be read: "They stir up a growing desire, and they do it for themselves (i.e., they work for themselves and no longer for God) outside themselves," for the same Hebrew word, *teenah* (תאנה), means both "fig tree" and "desire," and the word עלה, *aleh*, means both the "leaf" and the "rising."

The word "girdles," *ḥagorot* (חגרת), is in apposition to "themselves," Adam and Eve, and qualifies the about-turn man experiences after the Fall, which we have spoken of in relation to the "flesh"—בשׂר, *basar*. Man becomes a "stranger" to himself, from the root גר, *ger*, in the middle of the word "girdle."

2. In the Gospels Christ "was hungry. And seeing a fig tree afar off having leaves, he came, if haply he might find anything thereon: and when he came to it, he found nothing but leaves; for the time of figs was not yet. And Jesus answered and said unto it, No man eat fruit of thee hereafter for ever. And in the morning, as they passed by, they saw the fig tree dried up from the roots" (Mark 11:12, 20).

The fig tree symbolizes desire, and its leaves, the stirring of desire, so the fruit symbolizes its accomplishment. Whoever does not direct his desire toward God but toward the world obeys the law of the seasons. "While all the days (time) of the earth remain, seedtime and harvest, summer and winter shall not cease," says God to Noah (Genesis 8:22).

He who directs his desire toward God bears fruit in all seasons. God curses the world-related fig tree.

3. Finally, Christ compares the events of the end of time—or of days—to the development of the fig tree and all the trees: "When they now shoot forth, ye see and know of your own selves that summer is now nigh at hand. So likewise ye, when ye see these things come to pass, know ye that the kingdom of God is nigh at hand" (Luke 21:30–31).

What brings these three narratives together is the fig tree as ontolog-ically linked with man's desire for the Divine Spouse and hence for his accomplishment in the *yod*.

The symbolism of the liver, *ficus*, or fig tree, is here corroborated. It is the place where energies rise. If they are psychological energies, it is a "curse"; if they are ontological energies—desire, love of God—the liver then bears its fruit, *tov* (טוב), accomplishment. When all is accom-plished, the *yod* is born.

For the Chinese the liver is the "shield, or buckler, used for pro-tection."[15] In that sense, it is connected with the Hebrew letter *tet* (ט), whose design is that of a shield made from a serpent biting its tail. This letter symbolizes energies that have been accomplished or "girded."[16] It corresponds to 9, symbol of perfection, and governs the word *tov* (טוב). The ט, *tet*, 9, preceding the *yod*, 10, is the shield before the Sword הוה.

The Gall Bladder

The liver—"treasure organ" for the Chinese—transmits its power of "light" to its workshop organ, the gall bladder, which according to tra-dition is the seat of discernment.

Seen in the context of what the Chinese call the six "curious en-trails" (see above, page 203), the gall bladder is paired with the uterus. In the Lower Triangle, the uterus is a "sheath of water," whereas the gall bladder—in the Upper Triangle (the forge)—is a "sheath of fire." It contains the Divine Fire.

When Christ was in the baptismal waters, the divine fire came down: "The heaven was opened. And the Holy Ghost descended in a bodily shape like a dove upon him, and a voice came from heaven, which said, Thou art my beloved Son; in thee I am well pleased" (Luke 3:21–22). The divine Trinity reveals Itself, designating him who will henceforth baptize, no longer with water, but with fire.

The gall bladder is the matrix of this level. Essentially it is the seat of baptism by fire.

"Pure and impure" here mean what is "accomplished and unaccomplished" of the energies out of which we are woven.

The Chinese call the gall bladder the "straightness of the middle." It functions as umpire. It decides and judges. All other functions obey it; it takes on responsibility for them. It is the path of the Golden Mean, in the land of the "Middle Empire."

In the Hebrew Tradition, Tobias heals his father's eyes with the gall and the liver of the fish from the deep (see the story of Tobit, chapter 19, page 347).

Most illnesses of the liver or of the gall bladder surely come from a refusal to see clearly, a refusal of discernment and of straightness at a deep level. This refusal is no longer a matter of moral virtue, but concerns seeking out the path of the *mi*, for which baptism by fire is necessary. Such a refusal can only lead to the blocking of right decisions and makes situations more difficult than necessary.

Clearly, to be able to see the light, one must first descend into the depths of the earth, which harbors its energies. This is made possible by an experience of the "principle of light" at the level of the navel, which is Tabor.

The *spleen* appears to be the earth organ, and the *pancreas*, the organ where energies have been deposited, waiting to be accomplished.

The Pancreas

The word "pancreas" has always been puzzling to me. Its Greek roots, *pán* and *kréas*, mean "all flesh" and no doubt reveals its purpose. What might this be?

The word "flesh" is confusing. Sometimes it designates the body—"sins of the flesh" are often mistaken for the cause of the Fall—sometimes the psychological soul (the language of St. Paul is difficult), but it is always opposed to the spirit, or the spiritual side of the soul.

Flesh linked with matter then becomes equivalent to the evil that must be fled, while spirit (in this context it is conveniently forgotten

that the spirit may be diabolical) is the good to be sought. Obviously, this meaning of the word "flesh" is false. But what does it really
mean?

If we examine its Greek etymology, *kréas*, we note that its root is
the same as for *kreíōn*, "sovereign chief"; *kreíssōn*, "better," "stronger";
krátos, "strength"; and *kréousa*, "queen."

Bearing in mind that the feminine column of the sefirotic Tree is
governed by Binah, Understanding, called the Divine Mother, and
that this column is also called the column of Rigor or the column of
Strength, we can say that from a Greek perspective "flesh" seems to be
linked with the feminine in the best, the strongest, and the most royal
senses.

The Hebrew tradition confirms this: *basar* (בשר) is the "flesh,"
a word that may also be read as ב-שר, "within the principality" (see
chapter 11, page 165). But here the letter *shin* (ש) especially, at the
heart of בשר, is the key; it is caught within the root *bar* (בר), the root
of the "covenant of fire" we have just mentioned: the word *bereshit*
(בראשי) may be read as an intertwining of the first two letters spelled
in full, *bet*, ב (בית), and *resh*, ר (ראש).

Basar is therefore the *shin* (ש) of *Bereshit*. The letter ש is a sacred
gem from the deep and holds the *shem*, the secret of the Name, the
Strength, and the Kingdom.

In the light of Hebraic tradition, "flesh"—*basar*—is the place of
man's ultimate wedding with himself when he has laid hold of his royalty, a wedding whose ultimate fruit is *ha-Shem*, the Name.

Hebraic tradition calls the husband of this inner marriage *ish* (איש),
and his bride, *ishah* (אשה).

Remember that when God reveals Adam's feminine side and when
he (יהוה-Elohim) "seals the flesh within the depths" (Genesis 2:21),
the word "depth"—*tahtenah* (תחתנה)— has essentially the same root,
hatunah (חתנה), as "wedding" (see chapter 11, page 165).

So the flesh sealed within the depths is the earth with which Adam
must realize the ultimate covenant, whose fruit is the *Shem* (שם).

Flesh is the seat of complete accomplishment, the place of the most intimate union with God.

So ontologically, flesh is the culmination of eros. After the Fall, this erotic potential goes awry, is shifted outside Adam and motivates all his relations—no longer with himself or with God within him—but with the world and the elements of the world.

Flesh, turned inside out, becomes the psychological, erotic, and passional life of man. In this sense it becomes the source of all evils, but it also bears within itself the seed of all healing, the power of redirection toward man's accomplishment.

Hence God's words in the time of Noah, when men's forgetfulness of their ontology is at a peak, but consciousness has grown in the line of the patriarchs before Noah. God says: "The end [accomplishment] of all flesh is come before my face" (Genesis 6:13). "Before my face" signifies the ontological level. "All flesh"—*kol basar* (כל בשר) in Hebrew—is the Greek *pan-kréas*!

Thus "all flesh" is mobilized by God to embark upon its accomplishment.

In this cosmic body, which is that of the Adam, that of humanity, all that has life is put to the test. We might say the Adamic pancreas is mobilized in order that its energies may be accomplished.

In each of us, every trial strikes the pancreas so that it may release an amount of energy that is necessary for the proposed accomplishment. Our erotic quality—in the true sense of the word, inseparable from love—will either ensure accomplishment or determine its contrary, sickness.

The most joyful confirmation of what is revealed in the word "flesh"—*basar* (בשר)—is brought by the other word that shares the same root: *basorah* (בשרה), the Good News, "the Gospel."

The Good News is truly the certainty that the accomplishment of the flesh, in its totality, is made possible and that every sickness is cured.

When John the Baptist was in prison on the eve of his beheading, he came to the gate of his ultimate earth and experienced complete unknowing; יהוה-Christ then sent him word that "the blind see, the lame walk, the lepers are cleansed, the deaf hear, the dead are raised, to the poor the 'Good News' is preached" (Luke 7:22).

John the Baptist was then in the depths of darkness of the ultimate earth, the ultimate flesh, symbolically at the heart of his pancreas, an organ that opens up to deliver the Good News, his interior Christ.

The pancreas secretes the gastric juices that are indispensable for digestion, that is, for the work of the forge. It produces insulin, the fundamental agent for metabolizing sugars. Sugars appear to be symbols of the energies passing from the unaccomplished state in the pancreas to the accomplished state in the liver, whose glycogenic function concretizes its more subtle role.

The Spleen

The pancreas is inseparable from the *spleen*, an organ whose French name, *rate*, is an etymological enigma. It might conceivably be the French word for "female rat," which symbolizes Understanding for the Hindus, while Ganesha, the elephant on top of the rat, is the symbol of Wisdom. It may also symbolize the unconscious, that is, "all flesh" not yet accomplished.

These two energies, Understanding and Wisdom, the highest on the Sefirotic Tree, lead to Keter (the Crown) and form the base of the Upper Triangle; they determine the quality of each new head that man is called symbolically to put on his shoulders. For as *ish* gradually descends toward *ishah* in his depths, new fields of consciousness open up within man.

Understanding and Wisdom, placed in the light (accomplished), entail the release of the energies that correspond to them in darkness (not yet accomplished) and their purification by fire.

Within these feminine depths, holding both strength and royalty sealed with the Name, the link uniting the spleen to Understanding invites us to unite the pancreas and Wisdom (the elephant).

In Judeo-Christian symbolism, the "all flesh," or the totality of energies, is symbolized by the Serpent (Wisdom), which Christ identifies with the Tree of the Cross, the Tree of duality, becoming through his death and resurrection the Tree of Life.

Thus, *spleen* and *pancreas* are organs found in the depths of the earth. Alchemical language speaks of them when it says: *Visita interiora terrae; rectificando invenies occultum lapidem*: "Visit the interior of the earth; by rectifying you will find the hidden stone," [the sentence in Latin being an acronym spelling V.I.T.R.I.OL.—*Ed.*]

Vitriol, linked with sulfur, is the body of the depths of hell or the underworld.

The English word "spleen"—*splēn* in Greek—used to mean a deeply depressed psychological state, the hypochondria of the ancients. Curiously, the Hebraic root *retet* (רתת), which means "terror," is also one of the names for the pancreas.

These two indissociable organs are linked with the necessary descent into the underworld, which harbors the terrifying energy of the Name.

Any being who experiences the descent into his depths and does not have Understanding and Wisdom about what is happening is in a state that can lead to terror (like that of Job), even death.

Certain bodily techniques, or certain drugs, are "diabolical" in this sense: they separate the being instead of reuniting him or her. They renew Adam's error in the Garden of Eden by taking him to his kernel before he has conquered it.

If this pathological state is analyzed with psychological categories, and if the understanding brought to it is not referred to ontological values, the problem presented cannot be resolved. Thus, present-day psychiatric medicine, which remains agnostic, can only make use of drug therapy to elude the problem. Antipsychiatry seems to have reached a new understanding, although it has not yet pushed open the door of ontology (see chapter 13, pages 267–70).

The spleen is only linked with psychological states because it is linked with the ontological. And it is linked with the ontological through the mystery of blood.

The spleen is where red blood cells come to rest. It amounts to a veritable iron deposit and takes this metal to a state of purification and transmutation into silver, which means a new understanding of the transmuted "self." The white blood cells that it also produces contribute to this transformation.

Finally, the making of bile from broken-down blood cells enters into the dance of the new "self" and its new vision.

Might not the spleen, which is the seat of the transmutation of the "self," also be where the "self" is regulated? It holds back the red corpuscles that are too numerous inside the organism for redistribution when necessary.

A stitch in the side may not be unrelated to a swelling of the "self." The popular French expression *courir comme un dératé* ("to run flat out"—literally, "to run like someone with no spleen") expresses a state of excess, or the roaming of a being who is no longer "earthed."

Furthermore, the spleen is linked with the ontological through the mystery of blood and amounts to a cemetery for red corpuscles. It also complements the bone marrow, which as we have seen is the cradle of those red cells.

The marrow, we recall, "subtilizes" the א of אדם, *Adam*, so that the *yod* may be and the "self" may play the part that properly belongs to it (see above, page 203). One might think that the spleen, which in its turn obliges the "self" to undergo a death, contributes to reconquering the א.

The spleen is an organ of earth. It obliges one to return to earth, to new earths and ever deeper ones. It brings about some painful breaks.

The Chinese say, "It is the thunder, it is the earthquake." They also say that it is the "gong," which makes a link with the Hebraic word for cymbals, *tsiltsalim*, made up of the double root *tsal* (צל), "shadow."

The cymbals, like the gong, resound in the depths of "the shadow of the shadows,"[17] that is to say, they partake of the same quality of vibration and energy: the quality of the depths of Mother Earth that contain the Name.

This is why the spleen is closely related with the center of man, where the "self" becomes the *yod*.

The spleen transforms the "self" as it transforms on the way to the *yod* and transports the accomplished energies toward the liver. The liver is thereby revealed as the privileged site of nuptial preparations, those of man becoming יהוה from his encounter with Elohim. Perhaps then the liver is the place where the Spouse א returns in glory.

Kaved (כבד), "liver,"also means "glory."

The Heart

The center of the forge may be the *heart center* rather than the *heart organ*. The heart center is well known in Christian tradition, and the apostle John the Evangelist was in a position to listen to it.

The apostle of the "Good News"—*basorah*—whose feast is celebrated at the winter solstice, on the level of the Gate of the Gods, cannot but have heard the heartbeat of the Father.

On the evening of the Last Supper, while Christ was pointing out the one who was to hand him over, John had laid his head on the bosom of the One who was about to die through love. Judas and John are the shadow and the light. They carry out the Father's commands. They are the two sides of the heart: Judas, the right, shadow side; John, the left, light side.

The twelve apostles represent the entire circulatory apparatus. After they had been visited by the Holy Spirit, they were sent through all the earth to teach and baptize the nations; they are the renewed, oxygenated blood vitalized by the lungs, which will supply life throughout the body.

The heart center should no more be confused with the organ of the heart than the Father—source of all life in the mystery of the Christian Trinity—should be confused with the Christ, Son of the Father, surrounded by his twelve apostles. Among the latter, Christ is the thirteenth and the first. The letters forming *eḥad* (אחד), the number 1, correspond to 1 + 8 + 4 = 13, as do those of *ahavah* (אהבה), 1 + 5 + 2 + 5, which is "love."

At the heart of the twelve dorsal vertebrae, Tiferet (Beauty, Love) is the infinite unity of God, the dazzling magnificence of the Spouse coming to meet the bride in an ultimate orgasm, an ultimate death.

[She:]
My beloved spake and said unto me, Rise up, my love, my fair one,
    and come away. For, lo, the winter is past . . .

[He]:
I charge you, O ye daughters of Jerusalem, by the roes, and by the
    hinds of the field, that ye not stir up, nor awake my love, till she
    please. . . .
Behold thou art fair, my love; behold thou art fair; thou hast dove's
    eyes within thy locks.

[She]:
Awake, O north wind; and come, thou south;
Blow upon my garden, that the spices thereof may flow out.
Let my beloved come into his garden,
and eat his pleasant fruits!

[He]:
I am come into my garden, my sister, my spouse:
I have gathered up myrrh with my spice;
I have eaten my honeycomb with my honey;
I have drunk my wine with my milk:
Eat, O friends; drink, yea, drink abundantly, O beloved.

I raised thee up under the apple tree:
There thy mother brought thee forth;
There she brought thee forth that bare thee.

Set me as a seal upon thine heart,
As a seal upon thine arm:
for love is strong as death.

                            (Song of Solomon 3:5; 4:1, 16; 5:1; 8:5, 6)

Love penetrates to the origin of all things. Death shares the cradle of birth. Love that does not accept death is not love.

When Jeremiah calls for circumcision of the heart ("take away the foreskins of your heart" [4:4]), he recommends dying to emotional and sentimental love that has not been visited by divine Understanding. He calls for reawakening to Divine Love—Rigor and Mercy—which brings the person who has attained it to the stature of the Bride. She then becomes capable of comprehending "the breadth, and length, and depth, and height" (Ephesians 3:18) of the love of Christ, he who made himself death itself, because he is love itself. He descended into hell and took away the foreskins of humanity, so that humanity might be resurrected with him as Bride. He is יהוה, *ha-Shem*, the Name who came down to set free all our Names.

The invisible heart center, master and origin of all, is the א, image of the Father.

The cross-shaped heart organ, place of death and rebirth, is the י, *yod*, image of the Son.

The "cross"—*tselev* (צלב)—is the "harpoon" (צ) inside the "heart" (לב).

The heart seems to bear the same relation to the entire body as the red blood cell (whose nucleus disappears; see page 204) bears to the blood. The heart center is this nucleus (*alef*); the heart organ, the cell (*yod*). The א withdraws, the *yod* is; man becomes his Name and is harpooned by Elohim, the Father. Thus the heart of the world beats in the mystery of a unique and manifold *shabbat*.

The Chinese confirm this view when they say that the heart center is "the sovereign, the emperor, the master who holds authority. It is the source of life, source of light, the sun of man. The heart organ is his secretary of state, the ambassador who carries out his orders."

When the Divine Sun disappears, and its messenger no longer brings the Good News, the heart organ shines only with illusory joys, artificial rays, enjoyments whose sadness, as we know, has bitter aftertastes. The heart organ soon then gives way to the brambles and thorns of the spleen-*adamah*. It is bruised and dies a death without resurrection. The property of the divine heart-love is to bring about death, which is also resurrection.

The Lungs

For the Chinese, the heart organ is the secretary of state, who carries out the orders of the heart center–emperor. The lungs are the secretary of state, linking the state with the imperial order in the heavens. They are therefore the essential order of the heart center.

"The lung is the master of breath. For breathing is a continual to and fro between the order of the world, which is deposited at the center of each universe, of each being, and the multiplicity of its regions, structures, functions, and manifestations."[18]

So several millennia before Christianity, the divine Trinitarian structure was lived and breathed by the Chinese through their experience of the body.

The heart center is the image of the Father, Source of All.

The heart organ is the image of the Son eternally begotten by the Father, the express image of the Father, who carries out his orders (the secretary of state, who carries out the orders of the emperor).

Jesus says: "Wist ye not that I must be about my Father's business?" (Luke 2:49), and again: "For I have not spoken of myself; but the Father which sent me, he gave me a commandment, what I should say, and what I should speak" (John 12:49).

The lungs are the image of the Holy Spirit, who eternally proceeds from the Father alone and links with the Father. He is "the Lord and giver of life," and fills the entire universe.

Before dying, Christ says to his apostles: "I came forth from the Father, and I am come into the world: again, I leave the world, and go to the Father" (John 26:28). "But the Holy Spirit, which proceedeth from the Father, and whom the Father will send in my Name, he shall teach you all things" (John 14:26; cf. 15:26).

Mirroring the Trinitarian image, the entire Creation breathes, going from the one to the many and from the many to the one. And Creation itself, in the order presented by Genesis, is the divine outbreath, whose *shabbat* is the suspension of breathing before the accomplishment of Creation with an inbreath.

Bara-shit-bara, such are the first two words of Genesis: "Create, withdraw, create Elohim": Light-Darkness-Light. A rhythm of two beats is initiated: outbreath, inbreath, outbreath. Everything breathes with the divine archetypal respiration as its basis. This is revealed here, and it begets and gives rhythm to the breathing of the cosmos.

The Spirit of God, the *ruaḥ Elohim* (etymologically the "breath" of God) penetrates and fecundates the primeval waters, making them gush out into the multiplicity of created worlds, before he seizes them and makes them swirl back into primordial unity.

Expiration and inspiration: everything breathes.

And man, who brings together all these worlds, breathes. He breathes through all the pores of his skin. We have studied the kidneys as a center for his respiration, for they distribute part of the breath toward what I call his "genital breathing" (governing procreation and making children), and the other part toward the breathing of the forge (governing creation and leading man to his birth to the Word).

Adam, the Red Man (Red Tree), branches into a urogenital tree and a pulmonary tree. The latter is a preparatory stage for the Green Tree in the dance of the exchanges between *iron-magnesium* and *oxygen-carbon*.

The pulmonary tree bears the name *rea* (ראה) in Hebrew, a word which, pronounced *roe*, is the verb "to see." This word could be read as the "light" (אור) within the breath (ה).

Its archetype is the *ruaḥ Elohim*, breath of God (רוח), whose name is a diversification of the name of light. When the Divine Spirit takes on the form of the principle (ר), which guides man (ך) toward the trial barrier (ה), and man goes through it, the Spirit becomes the principle that makes man (ו) partake of Elohim: this is the word אור, "light." I am tempted to say: if our kidneys can hear (see above, page 191), our lungs can see.

When he came out of Eden, man heard but no longer saw (Genesis 3:10). He had severed the connection with the archetypal respiration, which is symbolized by the "to-and-fro of יהוה-Elohim in the garden." Soon even hearing was to become impossible.

Reentering Eden, in the resonance of the Name, man begins to hear, then to see.

The first part of life, linked with urogenital respiration, is centered on listening.

The second part, linked with the pulmonary tree, is centered on vision.

We have seen how the organs that make up this level work toward acquiring vision.

However, they do not forget the progressive acquisition of a more finely tuned capacity to listen, for at a given moment, in the discovery of the Name, listening and seeing are to join together.

The pulmonary tree is also connected with the utterance of sound. One might call it the tree of the Word, of Speech, which cannot be accomplished without listening (see chapter 16, page 315). That is why breathing has its roots in the kidneys and deep within the pelvis, for it does not cease to undertake its listening function with a view to its total realization in light.

What do these kidney-lungs hear and see, if not *ha-Shem*, the Name הוה, whose two ה (the two "breaths") on the level of the body are the two kidneys and the two lungs, of which the hands are an extension?

The *shabbat*, the suspension at the end of the divine outbreath, is the very essence of the act of creation by which Elohim withdraws so that יהוה may be (above, page 204). In the depths of the *shabbat*, Adam is breathed into his Name יהוה, and each of us is breathed, kneaded, fashioned by the divine hands, and attuned by his chant, in the secret Name that is our own: *nishmot hayim* (Genesis 2:7). It is this Name-Seed that makes us into breathers and speakers.

Nishmot, essentially made up of the root *shem*, the Name, also contains the verb *nashom* (נשם), "to breathe"! Breathing is the very life of the Name שם; through it the Name must pass from its seed state (symbolized by the letter *nun*, נ) to its accomplished state.

Immediately after God has breathed Adam in his Name, "He plants a garden in Eden; and there he places the man he has formed" (Genesis 2:8). The words "there," *sham* (שם), and "place," *yasem* (ישם), are both made from the root *shem*, which is the Name.

The Garden of Eden is the state of Adam placed within his Name, launched along the axis of his Name, nourished, propelled by it—guided, one might say, as by a true conductor of souls.

After the drama of the Fall, man has lost direction, is ousted from his Name, and only breathes from his kidneys.

Tradition then begs him to "Hear, O Israel, hear! יהוה our God, יהוה One." In Christianity, rooted in Israel, the Word issues forth.

From listening to the Word, countless breaths are articulated. They join with the prayers linked with breath found in every nation, psalmody, mantras, the prayer of the Christian Hesychasts, the Muslim *dikr*, and chant.

Breathing then becomes a rhythmic-melodic memorization following a precise rocking motion of the body. It is a memorization because rocking is the most archaic motion connecting with the original outbreath and inbreath through a primordial binary rhythm. It brings strength and vigor to the primitive brain called the *rhinencephalon*, which carries man back to a quasi-vegetable state, to "wood," and hence to his essence.

It is also a memorization because man, returned to his essence, at the heart of his feminine side, which seals the Name, begins his "male work," a work of marriage that implies that he "remembers" what he is.

The root *zakhor* (זכר) means both "male" and "to remember" (see chapter 3, page 20).

To marry the feminine means descending into the depths of the unaccomplished, in order to rise to the heights of the accomplished. The purpose of all breathing is to prepare and accompany this two-way movement.

The ultimate outbreath will see the birth of the Name.

The ultimate inbreath will see the crowning of the divine-human marriage.

The ultimate breath will reestablish man within the archetypal divine breath in the Father's bosom, Ain, from which everything proceeds and toward which everything returns.

CHAPTER 13

The Great Work: Wedding Mother Earth, or the Nigredo

The Story of Job

This story takes place in the land of *Uts*.

Because man has distorted his ontological norms, he fails to experience his marriage with the earth that bears him. Nonetheless, the link that unites him with this earth belongs to the level of essence. Therefore the human being who lives according to these norms makes a marriage with the earth, which is a prelude to his alchemical wedding. The name *Uts* bears this message within it.

Job, who was "upright, and . . . feared God," has realized the first level of his being. He dwells in a land whose name is closely linked with his evolution. *Uts*, in Hebrew (עוּץ), is made up of the name of the "tree"—*ets* (עץ)—with the *vav* (ו), man, in the middle. The story of Job is the story of "man within the tree," incorporated in his Tree, committed to his *Shem*. His story therefore unfolds inside the rectangle, in the forge. Man is called to enter the matrix of fire in order to become his Name.

Job had acquired everything he was to acquire. The biblical text lists his children, his livestock, and his servants. This was past and completed; the level of Having had been established. He served God and did good; he was happy with his family, respected by his peers, honored by all, wise counselor to all men. Whenever he appeared, the elders stood up, and the young trembled. He describes himself thus—a man of good conscience who praised the Lord.

A mysterious dialogue then developed between יהוה and Satan (שטן), and its subject was Job.

These three names—יהוה, Satan, and Job—refer us to another dialogue, one that arose at the heart of the myth of the Fall, between יהוה-Elohim and the serpent-Satan: "I will place an enmity between you and *ishah*, and between your seed and her seed," says God to Satan. "It [her seed] shall wound you, as you being the head, and you shall wound *ishah*, as she being the heel" (Genesis 3:15).

The word "enmity"—*aiyov* (איוב)—is Job's name in Hebrew.

The story of Job is the story of the "enmity placed" by God in *ishah*'s relationship with the serpent, in the relationship of their "seeds," that is, their "principles," which are respectively יהוה, the Name sealed at the heart of the feminine, *ishah*, and Satan, principle of the serpent.

Job is the very enmity between יהוה and Satan.

It is apparent in this myth that the hero of the drama in which divine destiny is played out is man himself. And the drama is played out now on the level of man's Being.

In the Yesod-Hod-Netsaḥ triangle, we have already encountered situations that are symbolical of this one. Moses's relation to Pharaoh was the same as the relation between יהוה and Satan, but in the eyes of the children of Israel still enslaved to Pharaoh (man still imprisoned on the level of Having), they were both men.

On the level of the heart, at the center of Being, we encounter not men but the divine principles themselves, the "seeds" in created duality: man-יהוה, the as-yet-unaccomplished one of God, is confronted with the "Adversary" (the translation of "Satan") in order to accomplish Elohim, even though God is already completely accomplished.

Only by going beyond the two poles of this paradox will the divine mystery offer itself for contemplation. Only within the "hollow of his unaccomplished pole" lies the pole of Creation—the pole of man!

Moses and Job—contemporaries in the eyes of historical criticism—
follow each other in messianic accomplishment. Both foreshadow
Christ, יהוה made flesh, Christ, who was to bring together these two
levels of accomplishment and lead man to his complete deification.

יהוה-seed, a germ of consciousness within the Adam of the garden
of Eden, is weak, so weak as to be dismissed altogether in the serpent's
speech without *ishah* noticing: "Yea, hath Elohim said, Ye shall not eat
of every tree of the garden?" (Genesis 3:1), although the order had been
positively given by יהוה-Elohim (Genesis 2:16).

But now Adam has grown, his consciousness has been strengthened
despite the drama of the Fall, for "enmity has been placed." And Job
experiences his Passover; in him, יהוה brings Adam out of the land
of slavery. This is expressed by the first trial, which afflicts Job on the
level of Having: he loses all his property.

"Doth Job fear Elohim for nought?" Satan asks יהוה. "But put forth
thine hand now and touch all that he hath, and he will curse thee to thy
face."

"Behold," says יהוה, "All that he hath is in thy power; only upon
himself put not forth thine hand" (Job 1:9–12).

Here is the distinction between Job's Having and his Being.

So in this first stage, Satan destroys all that Job has, even his children: seven sons and three daughters.

The description of his Having may be read on several levels. We
shall see at the end of the myth that the three daughters who are to be
restored to him are linked with his own person, with the mystery of his
Name. Here at the beginning, Job's three daughters are to be linked with
what constitutes his personality, structured by the energy triad of *enjoyment-possession-power* (see chapter 10, page 126, and chapter 11, page
164), acting, on this level, within psychological categories.

Job is afflicted in his psychological being and in his material goods.
But his consciousness is being strengthened.

יהוה leads man to secret knowledge. Confronted by the trial, Job professes: "Naked came I out of my mother's womb, and naked shall I return thither: יהוה gave, and יהוה hath taken away; blessed be the name of יהוה" (Job 1:21).

He intuitively knows that man must become a little child again, become "seed" in order to enter the Kingdom, Malkhut: he knows the great mysteries of Israel. He is broken, but he knows and accepts.

In this, Job is already undergoing an accomplishment, because anger—which is contrary to the power of accomplishment—does not arise in his heart (see chapter 11, page 176, and chapter,12, page 224).

Satan then decides to go further.

"Skin for skin," he says to יהוה. "Yea, all that a man hath he will give for his life, but put forth thine hand now, and touch his bone and flesh, and he will curse thee to thy face."

"Behold he is in thine hand," says יהוה to Satan, "but save his life (breath)" (Job 2:5–6).

יהוה allows the bell to toll, the earth to tremble, the "earthquake" to take hold of Job, and man to be shaken within his deeper earths, symbolized by the organs of the spleen and the pancreas. The Great Work of baptism by fire thus begins. It is summed up in the program Satan draws up: "skin for skin," which translates literally as "skin to the very end of skin"—*aor beod aor* (עור בוד עור).

From skin to ever deeper layers of skin: Job is to delve into himself until the end of his inner earths, that is, from fields of consciousness to ever renewed fields of consciousness.

Aor (עור), the "skin" with which Adam is clothed after the Fall, is the darkening of his consciousness reduced to an unaccomplished mass, mingled with a feminine whose very memory he has lost. The word "skin"—*aor*—if pronounced *iver*, means "blind" in Hebrew (see chapter 3, page 21). Adam is reduced to what he was, not only before God revealed his feminine to him, but even before he was able to name his energies—the animals—in his first inner earth.

The Great Work is in the first place an effort to "remember," mobilizing Job's "male" power (see the Hebraic root of these two words, *zakhar*, chapter 3, page 20), so that by remembering he may marry his feminine side and recover the light it hides.

The final "skin" (עוֹר) is to be *aor*, this time spelled (אוֹר), the "light." God calls the light *tov* (טוֹב) from the first day of Genesis, but it will only become wholly *tov* when it integrates the whole of *ru* (רע), in this case the whole עוֹר, "skin."

Job's feminine, his depth, is clearly intimated in Satan's speech by the words "his bone and his flesh." We recall that before the Fall, Adam identified his feminine side with these words: "This is now bone of my bones, and flesh of my flesh" (Genesis 2:23), meaning: "Here is she who is essence of my essence and secret of my kernel" (see chapter 12, page 202).

Job's feminine side is mobilized: his unconscious is touched. Suddenly the perfect man, with such control, no longer recognizes himself. Under the symbol of "his wife" he is in a state of revolt: "Dost thou still retain thine integrity? Curse God, and die" (Job 2:9).

In our contradictions when faced with a trial we have similar reactions: part of us (consciousness, what is accomplished in us and participates in יהוה) knows there is a meaning, a rightness in this trial, and that it is pregnant with potential for fertilization and growth. This part of us, though broken, is love.

Yet another part of us is frightened, trembles in our old "skin," and refuses to shed it, feeling safe in old habits. This part is tempted to curse, and rebels.

However, Job silences this dimension of himself: "Thou speakest as one of the foolish women speaketh" (Job 2:10).

He plows this part of his inner earth. And the work continues. The whole of the following speech focuses on the search for meaning, the opening of higher levels, that is, the two sefirot Wisdom and Understanding.

Job is to place on his shoulders a series of new heads that will oblige him to die and rise again many times.

The three friends who visit him are three aspects of himself in the births for which he enters into travail. They represent three "heads," becoming more and more knowledgeable as he continues to marry himself. These marriages are penetrations of his darkness, of his inner earths, his feminine, his mother-bride.

Like Oedipus, he begins his great journey into the night. But with Job the language is more alchemical. Smitten "with sore boils from the sole of his foot unto his crown," Job, on his bed of sorrows, undergoes the phase of the Great Work called "putrefaction." "My flesh is clothed with worms and clods of dust; my skin is broken, and become loathsome" (Job 7:5).

"Teach me," he asks his friends, "and cause me to understand wherein I have erred. . . . my righteousness is in this matter" (Job 6:24–29).

At first he looks for the cause only within the punitive categories of a primary field of consciousness. But he knows no fault in himself. Might God see with different eyes?

> Hast thou eyes of flesh? Or seest thou as man seeth?
> Thine hands have made me and fashioned me together round about,
>   yet thou dost destroy me.
>   Remember, I beseech thee, that thou hast made me as the clay; and
>   wilt thou bring me into dust again?
>   Hast thou not poured me out as milk, and curdled me like cheese?
> Thou hast clothed me with skin and flesh, and hast fenced me with
>   bones and sinews. . . . and these things hast thou hid in thine heart!
>   (Job 10:4, 8–10, 13)

His trials are those of the nigredo, the black phase of the Work. At times they involve the aridity of the fires of hell: "When I waited for light, there came darkness. My bowels boiled and rested not; I went mourning without the sun: . . . I am a brother to jackals, and a companion to ostriches. My skin is black upon me, and my bones are burned with heat" (Job 30:26–30).

At other times the trials involve the wet of the abyss: "Am I a sea, or a whale, that thou settest a watch over me? When I say, My bed shall comfort me, my couch shall ease my complaint; then thou scarest me with dreams, and terrifiest me through visions: So that my soul chooseth strangling, and death rather than my life" (Job 7:12–15).

Job is indeed strangled. Seized by the throat at the Gate of the Gods, he shifts to another level of consciousness: "I was at ease, but he hath broken me asunder: he hath also taken me by my neck, and shaken me to pieces. . . . He cleaveth my reins asunder, and doth not spare; he poureth out my gall upon the ground. He breaketh me with breach upon breach" (Job 16:12–14).

And again we meet the vital organs of the forge, which are all affected by this trial.

Job continues his terrifying voyage. I say "terrifying," because of its alchemical connotation, the two phases of the Work often being expressed by the formula: "Heaven terrified, matter quintessenced."

And "fixing the volatile" is the biggest test. Christ himself implores the Father to let "this cup pass from me." Job, too, cries out.

Job is an image of the Christ to come and has the strength to continue. No longer in ignorance of the unconscious, but consciously, in the night that contains light, he carries on with his painful journey. On this new level of the labyrinth, the darkness deepens until it becomes the counterpart of the Ain, the "No thing" of abyssal depths.

Such is the "descent into hell": a headlong drop to the level of the feet, a return to the seed containing all promises, the archetypes "from above" and their images "below," the *mi* and the *ma*, the *maim* of the primordial chaos when the earth was "without form, and void."

The experience undergone at this moment of the human adventure by one seeking God seems to be—in an apparent regression (see chapter 12, page 218)—a return to what was "without form, and void" in his own coming into being so as to experience his essential vocation. If not in the course of his life on earth, perhaps his death will amount to the same thing (see chapter 11, page 183).

Job dies here and now. He beseeches his friends: "I cannot find one

wise man among you?" (Job 17:10). The depth of his suffering is greater than the height of their wisdom:

> Able are you, and wisdom shall die with you. . . .
> But ye are forgers of lies, ye are all physicians of no value. O that ye
> would altogether hold your peace! And it should be your wisdom.
>
> (Job 12:2; 13:4–5)

They speak within Job, and Job sends them away again: "I have
heard many such things: miserable comforters are ye all" (Job 16:2),
and further on: "How long will ye vex my soul, and break me in pieces
with words?" (19:2).

Finally, he sends his friends away for good. He cuts off, as it were,
his last head:

> How hast thou helped him who is without power, how savest thou the
> arm that hath no strength?
> How hast thou counselled him that hath no wisdom? And how hast
> thou plentifully declared the thing as it is? (Job 26:2–3)

Job now goes much further. His approach is that of negative theology. He finds and does not find meaning; his taste for God always leaves
him unsatisfied, because the answer lies in an ineffable experience beyond all conceptualization.

Every change of skin is a change in consciousness, an emergence
into a field of new understanding and wisdom.

With his friends, he has taken away the last skins of his heart and
his ear. All circumcisions are accomplished; he reaches the last of his
inner earths:

> Surely there is a vein for the silver, and a place for gold where they
> fine it.
> Iron is taken out of the earth, and brass is molten out of the stone.
> Man setteth an end to darkness, and searcheth in the depths of the
> abyss the stone hid in the darkness, and the shadow of death.
>
> (Job 28:1–3)

In approaching this hidden stone, he approaches the source of the two sefirot: "But where shall wisdom be found? and where is the place of understanding?" (Job 28:12).

Then, like Elijah presiding over all circumcisions, like John the Baptist presiding over the final one and preparing the paths of יהוה, a fourth friend comes forward and sends away the other three. His name is *Eliahu* (Elihu).

אליהו is the very name of יהוה, whose last ה is replaced by אל. In this sense he is Job, a part of whom (one ה) is not yet in Elohim. He prepares Job for total light. Already the spirit of Elohim is within him: "The spirit within me constraineth me. Behold, my belly is as wine which hath no vent; it is ready to burst like new bottles" (Job 32:18–19).

The Holy Spirit is within him and folly is with him, for Divine Wisdom is folly in the eyes of men, while Job's wisdom, in his three friends, was folly in the eyes of God.

> Suffer me a little, and I will show thee that I have yet to speak on God's behalf. . . . [God] delivereth the poor in his affliction, and openeth their ears in oppression. . . . Hearken unto this, O Job: stand still, and consider the wondrous works of God. (Job 36:2, 15–16; 37:14)

With these words Eliahu is preparing Job to go to where the ore of Understanding is deposited, to the springs of Wisdom, in his final earth, "where there is gold, and the gold of that land is *tov* (טוב)" (Genesis 2:12): טוב, or light wholly conquered.

This verse describes the first of man's four inner lands or earths, which are fertilized by the single river coming out of Eden. The number four symbolizes the structures of the inner man, but it does not account for the actual reality. Another image, the ladder, puts forward thirty-three steps, each of which can be considered as an earth waiting to be constructed.

Whatever the image, the first land described in Genesis is the one man conquers last, in his ultimate depths. Eliahu is the guide who leads to the gates of this earth. The three other friends led Job to the first three levels of energy, that is, the first three earths named in Genesis in descending order, till he reaches the one watered by the Phrat, or Euphrates (Genesis 2:14). Starting from the latter, Job began his growth.

In his case it was called *uts* (עוץ), the man-*vav* ו (ו = 6) inside the Tree (עץ). Now man reaches the 9, as in the ninth month of his gestation. He will only be born to the 10, the *yod*, when guided by יהוה himself, the Name, who alone can open the kernel.

This is why Eliahu withdraws in his turn. Like John the Baptist, who was to say, "He must increase, but I must decrease," Eliahu removes the last skin and disappears.

All circumcisions of Wisdom-Understanding have been completed except one, which only יהוה can accomplish with man.

> Then יהוה answered Job out of the whirlwind, and said,
> Who is this that darkeneth counsel by words without knowledge?
> Gird up now thy loins like a man; for I will demand of thee, and
>   answer thou me.
> Where wast thou when I laid the *foundations* of the earth?
> Declare, if thou knowest *understanding.*
>
> (Job 38:1–4; emphasis added)

From Foundation (Yesod) to Understanding (Binah), the sefirot are brought together in a cosmic intertwining, and יהוה calls Job to wholly remember.

Here Understanding becomes completely feminine again: "I will demand of thee," says יהוה-Wisdom, that is, the male strength in Job, "and declare if thou knowest Understanding," that is, the feminine strength, which is called to open up and bring forth its fruit. The whirlwind is the ultimate upheaval operating within Job, the ultimate "thunderclap" of the spleen-pancreas, for we are reaching the final earth.

To begin with, we witness a climbing down "to the springs of the sea . . . in search of the depth . . . to the gates of death . . . where light dwelleth . . . in the place of darkness" so that Job may remember his origin: "Knowest thou it, because thou wast then born? Or because the number of thy days is great?" says יהוה (Job 38:16–21).

This is where man comes to a revelation of his eternity. Created from all eternity, beyond time, he may remember his seed and go right to his kernel. God leads the way there.

At this point, יהוה, singing a cosmic hymn, shapes Job's final head, the one that the Hebrew tradition symbolizes by the first archetypal triangle, the one the Chinese call "the upper Cinnabar Field, where man's marriage with the universal takes place."

God delivers Job to the ultimate light of Wisdom and Understanding.

"Who hath put wisdom in the reins? Or who hath given understanding to the heart?" (Job 38:36) יהוה asks, before ending his cosmic song with the description of the ten energies, from lion to eagle, now integrated.

From lion to eagle, Job has taken on all his successive skins.

Job become eagle has flown across Eden and appears before the Gate of the Gods. But between the Gate of the Gods and the east of Eden lies the abyss, symbolized by the passage between the two triangles on the

Judgment. A strange creature made up of parts of the hippopotamus, the lion, and the crocodile has open jaws to receive those hearts that were found wanting when weighed in the scales of justice. (From the tomb of the pharaoh Seti I, nineteenth dynasty.)

Sefirotic Tree and the neck on the level of the body. Genesis tells us that the East, the Orient, is guarded by "Cherubims, and a flaming sword which turns every way" (Genesis 3:24).

"Gird up thy loins now, like a man: I will demand of thee, and declare thou unto me," says יהוה again (Job 40:7), insisting still more authoritatively on this order, for Job is now called upon to gather up his last energies, to go yet further and cross the abyss.

Two lords of the depths are its guardians. Their skins are the final two fields of Job's consciousness. Penetrating them is impossible without becoming them.

"Behold now Behemoth. . . . He is the chief of the ways of God: he that made him can make his sword to approach unto him" (Job 40:15, 19). Behemoth is the guardian of the eastern gate and guides man on the path of the Sword, the path of his Name.

Behemoth (בהמות) is a plural. This plural entity might be the Cherubim, who approach the Name in the final mutation. They are close to the Name because the "Cherub" (karov, כרב), is the one who is "close" (qarov, קרב), the kaf (כ) on a cosmic plane referring back to the qof (ק).

They compel the final mutation, because Behemoth (בהמות) can be read as "in (ב), the (ה), death (מות)." As a feminine plural, the Behemoth are symbols of strength and Understanding.

The Cherubim uphold the throne of God.

In the strength of יהוה, Job crosses the angelic barrier of the Cherubim.

In the strength of יהוה, he confronts the final lord of the deep: Leviathan.

Who is Leviathan?

יהוה celebrates his beauty, the impenetrability of his skin, which is a breastplate, the beauty of his jaws, which are shields joined one to the other. Terror surrounds his mouth:

> Out of his mouth go burning lamps, and sparks of fire leap out.
> Out of his nostrils goeth smoke, as out of a seething pot or
>   caldron. . . .

He maketh the sea like a pot of ointment.

He maketh a path to shine after him; one would think the deep to be
hoary. . . .

He is a king over all the children of pride. (Job 41:19–34)

A great mystery surrounds this last monster. As a monster from this side of the abyss, might he not be a Seraph, a "fiery one"? The Seraphim with the Cherubim and the Thrones form the last triad of the nine angelic hierarchies.

"His heart is as firm as a stone; yea, as hard as a piece of the nether millstone" (Job 41:24). The last phrase may also be read: "melted like the sacred childbirth of the depths."

The heart of Leviathan is the kernel of being, sealed in place from the beginning, when יהוה-Elohim "sealed the flesh of Adam in his depths" (Genesis 2:21).

We have seen that the "depths" (*taḥtenah*, תחתנה) also contain *ḥatunah* (חתנה), "marriage" (see chapter 12, page 229).

Leviathan is the final earth Job has to penetrate, the object of the final marriage, which he must celebrate within himself. Leviathan is deep within Job's underworld and is the dragon he is to embrace in order to open its heart, to be cast, to be melted with "stone," the cornerstone, the heart of the edifice, in the ultimate work of the forge, to give birth to the divine.

Job becomes his Name.

"I have heard of thee by the hearing of the ear: but now mine eye seeth thee" (Job 42:5: one might also read, "mine origin seeth thee").

"Blessed are the pure in heart," Christ says, "for they shall see God."

In Tiferet, Job is wholly purified; he becomes light. He eats the fruit of the Tree of duality that he was, the fruit of the unity he has become, now that he has conquered his Name.

Unity is inseparable from multiplicity; both here are in apparent contradiction, because they belong to the Reality that goes beyond all realities experienced in duality until this final experience.

This multiplicity is no longer what was experienced in the beginning under the symbol of "dust" (see chapter 8, page 103). In Tiferet (תפרתר), dust (עפר), *afar*, has become "ashes" (אפר), *efer*, in the fire of the forge, obeying the order of growth (פר), whose root governs the whole of the Great Work.

"Be fruitful, and multiply, and replenish the earth, and subdue it" (Genesis 1:28).

Job has taken on the *ayin* (ע), his "source" or his "eye" of the beginning; through fire he has become *alef* (א), the "horned" head that is now "crowned" (see chapter 5, page 38, and chapter 20, page 365).

Job's breaking out into universality is symbolized by the manifold goods that are restored to him, by the abundance of his new livestock, and by the ten children crowning him, ten being the *yod*. Among his ten children, three daughters reveal their names. They are Job's name under the symbol of the triad of energies accomplished.

Yamimah (ימימה) is the fullness of space and time, now the possession of Job.

Qetsiah (קציע) is the "summer"—*qaits* (קיץ)—at its root (ע), the season where one "cuts" (*qatsoa*, קצע) the fruit. In the past, this fruit was potentially in the tree עוץ, *Uts*, the land of Job. Now it is the *yod* at the top of this Tree, עיץ. This fruit gives out a fragrance. *Qetsiah* is an aromatic plant, the cassia. The fruit's perfume and flavor are the enjoyment attained by Job, like the intoxication experienced by Noah.

Qeren hapukh (קרן הפוך), "the crowning of the contraries," "the transcending of contradictions," is the pommel of the "turning Sword" guarding the east of Eden. The word "turning" is *hapukh*, qualifying the two edges of the Sword יהוה. *Qeren* (קרן), the "horn," corresponds to 100 + 200 + 700 = 1000. It is domination, power wholly conquered: unity.

Hindus call it Advaita.

Now that Job is the fruit of the Tree of Knowledge which has been accomplished, he can go and pluck the fruit of the Tree of Life.

Jonah

We cannot leave Job without looking at the prophet Jonah in the same tradition, for his experience inside the "great fish" belongs with the same journey.

Jonah, out of communion with the understanding of יהוה, had disobeyed the divine command to travel to Nineveh and preach repentance to that great, corrupted city.

Instead, he fled this fate and embarked on the first outward-bound ship. But a mighty tempest soon rocked the boat and threatened to wreck it. The fearful mariners drew lots to find out who among them was responsible for this distress. The lot fell upon Jonah.

But Jonah had taken refuge in the hold and, further still, in deep sleep.

Jonah, apparently, was far from being accomplished and was brought back to harsh reality by the mariners, who "cast him forth into the sea," that is, into the heart of his "unaccomplished."

Swallowed up by the sea monster, which the oral tradition calls a whale, Jonah seems far from recovering the light. But from deep in the belly of the great fish, he remembers יהוה, calls upon him, and is answered:

> For thou hadst cast me into the deep, in the midst of the seas; and the
> floods compassed me about: all thy billows and thy waves passed
> over me. . . .
> The waters compassed me about, even to the soul: the depth closed
> me round about, the weeds were wrapped about my head.
> I went down to the bottoms of the mountains; the earth with her bars
> was about me for ever: yet hast thou brought up my life from
> corruption. (Jonah 2:3–6)

יהוה spoke to the great fish, and it vomited Jonah onto dry land. Clothed with power drawn from his depths, Jonah was now able to confront Nineveh and enter into understanding of divine mercy toward the city.

He experienced transcendence.

"It is to this Transcendence that we give currently the name of God," says Sri Aurobindo.[1] But in the first instance man attains this level of cosmic consciousness, which transcends our ordinary level of consciousness, by becoming a seed once again, by becoming a fish, by going down "to the bottoms of the mountains," to the ontological roots, to the archetypes of creation.

A recent embryological theory suggests that the seed inside the maternal womb possesses cosmic memory. It *knows*.

The respiratory trauma of birth may push this memory, back into the depths of the unconscious. It seems that someone who consciously and voluntarily becomes a seed once again (and breathing techniques may help such attempts) "espouses the mother," penetrates the darkness of the unconscious, breaks open the vault of memory, and recovers Knowledge. Having reached the heart of himself, the knower is at the heart of all that is alive.

"Mine is the sun, mine is the moon, mine are the stars, mine is the mother of God, mine are all creatures! What more do you ask for and what more are you looking for, O my soul! All is yours and all is for you!" exclaims St. John of the Cross, the poet par excellence of this experience, after his voyage in the darkest of nights.

Emerging from the same night, and bearing in his body the stigmata of his Master's wounds, St. Francis of Assisi praises the Lord, in whom he now apprehends the entire universe: he is born in the bosom of a new family, each element of which is intimately "his": they are "Brother Sun, Sister Moon and Stars, Brother Wind, Brother Fire, and Sister our Mother Earth!"

Psychoanalytical criticism is not appropriate for such poems, which are the fruit of a mystical experience.

The Hebrew name for Jonah, *Yona* (יונה), contains the Tetragram, the *nun* (נ), whose numerical value is 50, replacing one of the *hehs* (ה),

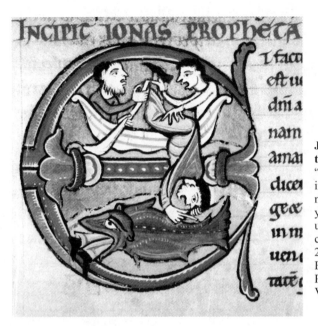

Jonah Thrown into the Heart of the Sea. "Thou hadst cast me in the deep, in the midst of the seas . . . yet hast thou brought up my life from corruption." (Jonah 2:3, 6; "St. Bernard's Bible" in Troyes. Photo by Michel Vuillemin.)

whose value is 5. Jonah is this *nun*. The Arabs call him *Dhûn-Nun*. *Nun*, a letter corresponding to 50 in Arabic as in Hebrew, means "fish" in both languages; it is the male fish. The whale plays the same part as the ark in Noah's story, that of the female fish, holder of the energy-information.[2]

Whether whale, dolphin, crocodile, or Makara, these fish living in Malkhut, on the land and in the water, whose heart is of diamantine fire, are identified with the divine dark mother of the deep. She is Kali, Shiva's bride for the Hindus, Isis for the Egyptians, Cybele for the Cretans, Dana for the Celts, Persephone for the Greeks. The one and only Lady of the Night, whom Apuleius praises with these words:

> I am nature, mother of all things, mistress of all the elements, the origin
> of the centuries, the supreme divinity, queen of the shades, the first of
> the inhabitants of heaven, the exemplar of the gods and goddesses. I am
> she whose will governs the luminous arches of the sky, the salubrious
> winds of the oceans, the gloomy silence of hell. (*Metamorphoses*, 11.4)

The Descent into the Underworld
in Greek Myths

Becoming a seed again: this operation holds such a central place in our evolution that all traditions describe it by identifying it with the experience called ורע, *ve-ra*, the experience of non-light.

We find it in *The Book of the Nocturnal Voyage* by Ibn Arabi, in *The Tibetan Book of the Dead* (*Bardo Thödol*), *The Egyptian Book of the Dead*, the descent into the underworld in Greek myth, and Dante's *Inferno*. Finally, the blindness of many heroes in our legends conveys this same descent into darkness, also following a labyrinthine path but fitting into the framework of the first inverted triangle.

In this first triangle, we are no longer dealing with the darkness of ignorance. The subject has already experienced *tov* (טוב), the good, the light. He is living through great darkness, but is already conscious of the light it carries. The light will only burst forth when its rays encounter the matter that can receive them, a matter they can penetrate.

This is the wedding.

Matter is the "dark mother of the deep," namely the lower archetypes into which Jonah and Job were precipitated, those that Oedipus married in Jocasta.

This is why no one can come back up from hell who has not first tapped into the essential light of his being, after beginning to "separate the subtle from the gross."

Neither can anyone take on this new labyrinthine path, nor find the way out, without a guide.

יהוה was a guide for Jonah and Job, Antigone for Oedipus; Ariadne offered her guidance to Theseus. Hermes accompanied Hercules; the Sibyl of Cumae guided Aeneas. The seven-stringed lyre given by Apollo to Orpheus is the voice of the god guiding the "orphan." The hero's lyre is the dawning of his word, the song of the god he potentially is, and it enchants the depths of the underworld to release Eurydice, his divine being, plucked from the depths of Tiferet. Orpheus confronts the sefirah Din (Justice). Will he pass through the Gate of the Gods? Standing before it, he looks back. He wants to see Eurydice, to capture her with his eyes, to possess her.

But "to look back" is to fall back into ordinary consciousness, recovering eyes of flesh, stopping life. The vision vanishes.

A man who is seized by Divine Love experiences the divine and seeks to conceptualize it, enclose it in a vision from which he is not yet free, and shatters it.

The pain is inexpressible and as powerful as the experience of love. It enfolds the one who was ready to see the light in a night darker than that of the underworld. Orpheus dies of pain.

How dangerous, when there is a transcendent experience, to seek to bring it back to the categories of ordinary consciousness and enclose it in our conceptual frameworks!

And if this journey into hell is experienced in the context of modern analytical techniques, how many guides are real masters, able to discern experiences of alternative levels of consciousness in what comes up from the depths?

According to a fundamental law experienced on the level of Being, "when the disciple is ready, the master appears": Raphael appeared at Tobit's gate, ready to go and accompany the young Tobias on his journey (see chapter 19, pages 347–48). The true master appears for one who seeks his true head, his Father.

Aeneas, an orphan too, addresses this single prayer to the Sibyl when he decides to go in search of his father: "Make me descend into the underworld and see his dear face again. . . . Show me the underground path that will enable me to find him whom I carried on my shoulders."

Whom did Aeneas carry on his shoulders? Was it not his true head, his own "dear face"—in other words his divine face—which had been removed and replaced by a mask, as with every man whose consciousness has become cluttered up?

Who is this Father but the pommel of the Sword, the *yod*, the god?

It is remarkable that Aeneas, though seeking the divine, does not ask the Sibyl to transport him into the heights of a heaven that is inaccessible, but into the depths of the abyss, of his abyss.

God is not to be sought on high, but within ourselves, in this "lower" pole whose integration alone provides the "key" to the divine, the recovery of the true head upon the shoulders.

Once he had recovered his Father, his true face, Aeneas came back up to earth, with the strength to found the city of Rome with her seven hills, a mission entrusted to him by the gods.

Aeneas, guided by the Sibyl, is equipped with a golden branch, which he must offer to the queen of the underworld (the Mother). This ray of light is the symbol of the restoration of his divine sonship, which alone allows him to enter the infernal abyss. It is the key whose importance I have already underlined. He who is not armed with it, and is unaware of the divine dimension of the experience, encounters only the monster of death below and cannot return.

Theseus had inherited the golden Sword from his Father, and yet . . .

Hercules had just stolen the golden apples from the Garden of the Hesperides from Atlas, the bearer of the celestial arch, when he was ordered by Eurystheus to descend into the underworld and bring back Cerberus, the monster who guards its depths.

Empowered by the previous adventure, Hercules could go down. Nourished by these golden apples, he possessed the key to the underworld and knew how to use it. It was not the first time he had tackled such a task. He had already confronted Geryon, a colossal giant with three bodies joined together at the waist, whose underwater home was guarded by a three-headed dog, foreshadowing Cerberus.

Dante and his guide Virgil, crossing the eighth circle of hell, at the foot of the Malebolge chasm, descended on the shoulders of this same Geryon. They crossed the ninth circle borne in the arms of the giant Antaeus, whom Hercules had also encountered and had crushed against his chest. Remarkably, the poet undergoes the same experience as the Greek hero. Both were able to confront hell only after vanquishing the lion.

The lion was the first animal described by God to Job, the last being the eagle. The lion and the eagle are central to the Tetramorph.

"In this operation, the eagle devours the lion," the alchemist Salmon writes in the preface to the *Bibliothèque des Philosophes*.[3] The eagle heralds elevation and sublimation.

What does this sublimation involve? What has been integrated at the expense of the lion? What part of the Work is accomplished by our heroes when they approach hell and confront the lion?

The lion symbolizes psychological energy experienced at the level of the heart before it has become, on the level of Being, Divine Love in the heart. Symbolically, the lion is thus linked with passion, with ardor, with courage leading to heroism, with anger too—so many psychological virtues that have to be transmuted into ontological ones.

When the apostle Paul preaches circumcision of the heart, he agrees with the alchemist: "The eagle must devour the lion."

The lion is of royal lineage; he must not die, but be identified with a higher royalty. The royal eagle, devouring him, takes in his solar energy and transmutes his qualities into Love-Knowledge.

The man who has defeated the lion in himself, and who puts on its skin—as Hercules did, has overcome the psychological nature of his impulses and has put on the beginnings of his garment of light. He has thus taken his first steps on the royal path. But the road is long and hard; other labors have to be accomplished in order to level it. At the end of the path, in Dante as in the Greek myth, Cerberus guards the gate.

Cerberus—*Kérberos* in Greek—is an enigmatic word. It seems to result from the contraction of *kéras* and *barús* and would then mean "powerful horn." This would confirm my intuition: because of his trinitarian structure and the power of his horns, Cerberus seems to be the dark face, the negative polarity of the dragon, with whom man is preparing to unite and who is a brother of the Hebraic Leviathan.

Another etymology would make the monster a "devourer of flesh" (*kréas*, "flesh"; *boráō*, "devour"). His role would then be the same as that of Satan, who, as long as we do not return to the Divine Spouse, is a "devourer of dust."

A third possible etymology is drawn from Sanskrit. According to this, Cerberus would be the very name of the night, Savari.[4] This would be connected with the dog accompanying Artemis, the moon goddess, born a day before her brother Apollo, the sun god.

Whichever origin we adopt, Cerberus bears the same relation to the becoming of the man who confronts him before entering upon deification. That is the relation of night to day, moon to sun, evening to morning in Genesis: one reality in its dual polarity.

Cerberus's head is that of a dog. I have often been surprised to see dog-headed men in Christian iconography, mainly on the right of the head of the glorified Christ (on the tympanum in the narthex of the basilica of Vézelay, for example).

St. Christopher with a Dog's Head.
Christophoros, who visibly is the "bearer of Christ," is invisibly borne by him. Tradition says this of the old man called Simeon (Luke 2:28). Only the one carried by Christ can walk through all of his inner hells (symbolized by the dog). (Cynocephalic St. Christopher, Musée Byzantin, seventeenth century.)

Why is the name of the Dog given to the constellation found near the sun at the highest point of its course?

Common language calls the very hot days during July and early August the "dog days." The symbolic correspondence between the anatomy of the physical sky and that of earth leads us to think that the dog is close to the god with whom man recovers his totality.

In Hebrew, "dog" is pronounced *keleb* (כלב) and carries the root *kol*, "totality." Reversing two letters, we have *kebel* (כבל), meaning "link," "chain." The dog Cerberus, or Satan, chains man, who has chosen him for master (the myth of the Fall) to his "nonbecoming light" (*ve-ra*, ורע, has thus become "evil"), to this single pole of the Tree of duality symbolized by the darkness of the underworld.

With Cerberus, man experiences the enemy, the adversary to his pole of light. Everything points to this being the character we encountered with Job, the "adversary" of יהוה.

But no one can "embrace his Satan" (see below, page 273) unless he has expelled from himself the cohort of demons whose name is "Legion" (Mark 5:9). They are parasites of creation and "devour the flesh."

The Underworld of *The Tibetan Book of the Dead*

We encounter these demons called "thought-forms" in the *Bardo Thödol*, or *The Tibetan Book of the Dead*. The *bardo* is precisely that intermediary state between a death and a birth, a state indicated by Dante when he describes himself as "outside of life and of death."

This after-death state, described by the *Bardo Thödol* and by *The Egyptian Book of the Dead* as well as by different mythic accounts of the descent into the underworld, does not necessarily imply a physical death, except when the latter accompanies the mutation in question. This mutation opens the way to another level of consciousness, which each and every one of us must go through before being born to the Gate of the Gods. The *Bardo Thödol* says:

O noble son, what they call death has now come! You are leaving this world, but are not alone, death comes to everyone. Do not stay attached to this life through weakness. Even if, through weakness, you were to remain attached, you have no power to dwell here. All you will obtain is to wander in the Samsara. Do not be attached, do not be weak; remember the precious Trinity.

O noble son! Whatever the fright or terror assailing you in the Chönyid Bardo [the encounter with the Mother of Reality] do not forget these words, and by keeping their meaning in your heart, go forward, because in them is found the vital secret of Knowledge.

Alas! When the Experience of Reality shines upon me, and all thought of fear, of terror, all dread of appearances has been rejected, may I recognize that all appearance is but a reflection of my own consciousness, may I recognize them as being the nature of the appearances of the Bardo.

At the decisive moment of accomplishing a mighty end, may I not dread the hordes of peaceful and wrathful divinities who are my own thought-forms.

O noble son! If you do not recognize your own thought-forms despite your meditations or devotions in the human world—if you have not taken in this present teaching—flickers of light will subjugate you, sounds will fill you with dread, rays will terrify you.

If you do not know this absolute key to all teaching—not being capable of recognizing sounds, light, and rays—you will have to wander in the Samsara.

The subject then experiences sounds, lights, and rays, all of which are thought-forms, our demons.

Man undergoing this experience of darkness loses his self. But if, during the preceding experience of light, he has acquired the structures necessary for containing this divine breakthrough, then the thought-forms die with the self, and man begins to participate in the great Divine Name contained in his kernel, his heart.

If he has not acquired them, the structures of the self blow apart, are not replaced by others, and man is a prey to his demons, to his thought-forms, who eat his flesh and drink his blood. He becomes a demon. This is why Christ offers his own flesh as nourishment and his blood as drink, so that man, nourished by God, may become god.

The Schizophrenic's Hell

I was a happy little girl living in the family house where I had been born five years earlier. Suddenly "the bell tolled."

One spring morning, we left in a rush. I left behind the land, the house, my dear ones. I guessed that some drama was unfolding but was told nothing about it. I was a cumbersome object, deemed incapable of understanding or even sensing the situation, and was placed in a convent in Paris by myself.

The sole familiar element was my big sister, two years older, placed in the same convent, but from whom I was separated all day long.

A few months went by—one death. At last I was reunited with those I loved, in a drab little Paris flat whose entire furniture was soon to be removed by the bailiffs. We had nothing left to eat. Everyone was crying—another death.

A child, in order to survive, must resort to herself, to unsuspected depths in herself, where she discovers a sacred reality that enabled the little girl I then was to be solidly grounded. I gave this solid ground a name by saying: "Only the heavenly Father is reliable." And I no longer expected anything from anybody.

Here splitting begins.

The breath is split on the level of the *phrēnos*, between "genital respiration" and "respiration of the Word" (see chapter 12, page 192).

In order to survive when the earth quakes and the bell tolls, the child, gripped in the jaws of the deep, at the Gate of its Name, is blown upward into the heights. The child is put in touch with its monsters and saved by the heavenly Father.

Grace in abundance meant that splitting did not tear apart the little girl of yesterday.

In the refectory of the convent, she devoured the salt on all the tables. Doubtless, like Lot's wife after the purification by fire of Sodom and Gomorrah, the placing of limits around a new inner land required such salting! But the woman I am today can understand the hell of the schizophrenic.

The psychiatrist Friedrich Husemann quotes some remarkable case histories on this subject, one of which is a man recounting his own experience:

> Gigantic beings were crumpling me up like a piece of paper. I felt I was in great danger of losing my Self, and I realized this would mean madness. After a while, one of my demons left me after a violent attack, but came back in another shape. It often seemed to me that I resembled him, but this was only a feeling. . . .
>
> People around me thought these scenes were only imaginary ideas. But I could see no relationship between ideas and such sensations; even today, I do not see any. When I form an idea, it is not in space, it remains colorless, in my head or behind my eyes, whereas with these sensations I could see a world coming towards me from outside, a world that was nevertheless not the world of the senses. What it contained was reality for me; its forms were full of life.

After all these attacks admirably described by the subject himself, he relates the visit

> of a being whose appearance had something agreeable about it and who spoke winning words. . . . I felt myself drawn to this outpouring of the universal consciousness which I had formerly known. I was allowing myself to be won over, and, after ten to thirty minutes, the scene changed completely. I felt myself swallowed up into a funnel and once more the whole series unfolded: the din of quarrelling was let loose. . . . At length enormous monsters would assail me—demons would rise from the abyss like guardians, like a horde of Cerberuses. I determined

to fight the decisive battle. . . . At that moment the illumination came. I saw into the true nature of the tempters, and I abstained from their food. They were both the guardians and the enchanters of my dear personal self. Yet this self appeared to me now as illusory and nonexistent as they themselves. And when the light of a bigger and broader Self began to dawn, the demons vanished and died.[5]

He who reaches the dragon of the deep also reaches the Father on high, who gives the power to turn around.

Seen in this perspective, can schizophrenia be called a sickness? It is first and foremost that stage in the underworld that it is necessary to pass through to reach the Gates. Failing to understand the nature of this stage, agnostic medicine calls it pathological.

If it is treated as a sickness, and the one who is undergoing this trial is isolated within some kind of straitjacket, he is thereby maintained at a stage of the process that is split off from its context, so that development is sterilized and turns into a pathological collapse.

Now "instead of being a collapse, it can become a breakthrough" to the Name.[6]

Dr. Daviller, psychiatrist and author of this last remark, continues:

One could say with the antipsychiatrists that the sole function left to madness nowadays is a sacrificial function:

An individual scapegoat is chosen by the group, which thus gets rid of its own contradictions.

There is a transference of the group onto the symptom-individual.

The group becomes unified on the basis of the rejection of the symptom-individual.

Psychiatry exists to provide authority for this sleight of hand, which turns collective problems into individual ones.

We have studied the principle of the scapegoat in Jewish ritual. In the new perspective sketched out here, the scapegoat is the principle of a universal knowledge going back to the most archaic times. According to it, a man—who is also the whole of humanity—can take upon himself the burden of the group's perverted energies, in order to convert them or take upon himself the burden of impurity—that of the unaccomplished—transferred onto him by the group, so that it may be accomplished.

If the group or a member of the group becomes conscious, he can then work toward healing the sick person-scapegoat by undertaking his own purification and his own descent into hell. Approaching his kernel in turn, he has the power to convert the energies for himself and to heal the other.

More often than we think, the sickness of a member of a family or group is the unconscious discharge upon the sick person of the collective burden of perverted or unaccomplished energies. At a deep level the sick person is healed when a conscious member of the family or group, working toward his own kernel, turns everything around with the help of God through the divine contact he experiences at that moment.

Great saints have taken on the sickness of the group.

Christ took on the sickness of humanity.

Suffering

When the shock of great suffering touches a so-called adult, like Job at the beginning of his trial, he argues, rebels, and calls on his sense of justice. In a word, he interposes his intellect between the event and its profound and creative meaning.

This creative power of suffering will only become effective if man becomes a little child again.

"Except ye be converted, and become as little children, ye shall not enter into the kingdom of heaven" (Mark 10:15; Matthew 18:3; Luke 18:17; John 3:3).

The four evangelists quote this fundamental dictum of Christ. The true adult is the one who can become a little child again, who can switch off mental activity and let himself be carried by the event toward the new earth of his being, while accepting that he does not understand. There, on that new earth, he will be given understanding. He blames no one, but calls himself into question, so that the light may penetrate further within him, and so that "the works of God should be made manifest in him" (John 9:3).

Abraham went up the mountain in order to sacrifice his son in obedience. While climbing the mountain, he was precipitated into the greatest drama of his depths. There he touched his divine kernel. God halted the arm that was about to sacrifice Isaac and put a ram in place of the young child.

The man who came down the mountain was not the same as the one who went up. The works of God had been made manifest in him: as the root of the Tree of Israel, he brought forth his messianic fruit: Christ, the new Isaac, the ram of the burned offering on a cosmic scale.

Ail (אַיִל) means the "ram": God (אֵל), who carries in his womb the yod (י), divine kernel of humanity.

Christ's Descent into Hell

And it was about the sixth hour, and there was a darkness over all the earth until the ninth hour.

And the sun was darkened, and the veil of the temple was rent in the midst.

And when Jesus had cried with a loud voice, he said, Father, into thy hands I commend my spirit: and having said thus, he gave up the ghost.

(Luke 23:44–46)

The veil of the Temple separates the holy place (the nave for Christians) from the Holy of Holies (the sanctuary). Christ, returning to the Father, rends this veil of separation to give back humanity its true head.

Shortly before, John the Baptist, the man in a coat of skin, had been beheaded. John the Evangelist becomes the prototype of humanity in its becoming.

The death of Christ is the last circumcision of humanity, the last blood sacrifice, and leads the New Adam to his last earth, the final matrix containing the kernel and symbolized by the tomb.

The "darkness over all the earth" is the outward sign of the darkness of hell.

The ninth hour is the hour of accomplishment and of birth.

The shift from 6 to 9 began at Cana, where Christ, turning himself as it were into the seventh water vessel, changed the water of the world into life-giving wine. On the day of the crucifixion, the wine became bitter. Christ, who was thirsty—thirsty for the Holy Spirit—was given a sponge soaked in vinegar by the soldiers (John 19:29). Having drunk it, Christ cries out, "All is accomplished." Wine became blood, blood was spilled, the Spirit came. It was the ninth hour, "and Christ bowed his head, and gave up the ghost (Spirit)."

The "barriers" of the adversary had been destroyed one after the other, through a series of necessary deaths or mutations symbolized by the eighth hour.

The Tree of Knowledge of the accomplished and of the not-yet-accomplished brings forth its fruit. "In the day that thou eatest thereof," said God to Adam, "death, thou shalt die!" (Genesis 2:17).

Adam, doing away with death even though he had not borne it, became sterile. Mutation became impossible for him. The New Adam, destroying death after having taken it on himself, also destroys Adam's sterility. He vivifies humanity and restores its initial fecundity.

Breathing between man and God starts anew. Blood begins to flow again, and man's body receives the breath of life.

"And I will lay sinews upon you, and will bring up flesh upon you, and cover you with skin, and put breath in you, and ye shall live; and ye shall know that I am יהוה!" prophesied Ezekiel (37:5–6).

Nothing is said about Christ during the three days and three nights in the darkness of the tomb, the matrix of light. Tradition however offers for our meditation the image of Christ in hell.

About it Karlfried Graf von Dürckheim, speaking at an international interreligious conference organized by Pir Vilayat Inayat Khan in March 1969, had this to say:

> A long time ago, near Paris, I encountered an extraordinary man, Father Gregory, a hermit who painted icons. Among these icons, one represented Christ full of love leaning towards Adam in hell. I asked Father Gregory: "Father, tell me what this represents for you." He answered: "If man encounters himself in his deepest and most wicked depths and finds himself face to face with the dragon that he is deep within himself, if then he is capable of embracing that dragon, of uniting with him, the divine breaks out, and it is the resurrection!"

Nor is anything said about Mary, the mother of Christ, carrying these same three days and nights in her inner tomb:

> Shall I go with you or wait for you?
> Say something, O Word,
> Do not pass by in silence!

are Mary's words in a liturgical hymn for the morning of the Passion.

Every mother resonates intimately with the hell of her child and with its journey toward the marriage with its inner dragons. Receiving a human seed in one's womb, bringing a child into the world, means agreeing in advance to accompany him or her, without expectations, on their inner path. It means dying with them in silence and unknowing.

"Say something, O Word!"

But the Word is silent for Mary, as the Father is silent for Christ.

Accepting that nothing can be known anymore, nothing wanted . . .

Then the unbridgeable chasm is bridged. With her son, Mary crosses the abyss; she shows us that the impossible is possible.

Mary is suffering humanity, accomplishing itself through deaths and maternities conjoined.

She is the silence that becomes Word.

CHAPTER 14

Passing through the Gate of the Gods:
The Albedo

The Eagle: Hands, Shoulders, Collarbones

So who guards the Gate of the Gods?

The last animal named by יהוה in Job among the first ten lords of the earth and air, the eagle.

The eagle, guardian of the Gate of the Gods, snatches from death anyone who has just integrated the black phase of the Work.

God said to Job: "Where the slain are, there is she [the eagle]" (Job 39:30). Christ uses the same words to speak about his own death: "For wheresoever the carcase is, there will the eagles be gathered together" (Matthew 24:28).

But Christ here identifies the eagles—in the plural, though the carcase, unlike in the Job text, is in the singular—with those of his disciples who are to carry his message throughout the world and release fallen humanity from death. Fallen humanity is a slave to Satan or fights against him only through pious moralizing, while being incapable of embracing his Black Dragon.

The royal eagle par excellence is the apostle John the Evangelist, the "apostle with a divine secret" who assumed Tiferet with Christ (see chapter 12, page 215).

The "secret of *yod*" had been touched in Yesod; it is accomplished by the apostle who goes through the Gate of the Gods.

The feast of St. John the Evangelist is celebrated at the winter solstice. Christmas then breaks forth in the liturgical cycle: earth germinates the divine.

The eagle guards the Gate of the Gods, which in the diagram of the body corresponds to the level of the throat guarded by the two collarbones extending into the two arms and two hands.

Its Hebrew name is *nesher* (נשר: 50 + 300 + 200 = 550). It is constructed in such a way that the two 5s (that is, the two hands), imaging the two ה, *hehs*, of the Tetragrammaton, are the arithmological translation of the two wings of the eagle. Through their complementarity they already indicate unity reconquered (5 + 5 = 10).

The hand, in Hebrew *yad* (יד: 10 + 4, making 5 by adding the digits), is simply the letter *yod* (י) of the Tetragrammaton. It is linked with knowledge: *yada* (ידע), "know," also means "love." It is not an intellectual quality, it is an experiential knowledge, the carnal knowledge man has of woman, the knowledge every man grasps of every element of creation, every element of the *ma*, by penetrating the depths of its mystery, that is to say, what is hidden within it because it belongs also to the world of *mi*.

This knowledge is a wedding. It is love.

Its "concreteness" requires a new kind of receptivity. This receptivity is a bodily phenomenon and concerns our senses, opened out and attentive to the Real.

Reality acts on an infinitely large panel of wavelengths. A very narrow band of these touches our immediate senses, but the senses of the man who "climbs his Tree" open onto ever-widening bands of Reality.

However abstract this Reality may appear to the ordinary man, it is concrete for men and women whose senses allow them to touch the heart of things, of beings, of the world. Our sensations are not linked solely with the immediate tangibility of matter. Divine Glory is palpable too. But one contains the other; and, when matter is cultivated, questioned, and loved, it makes itself known, opens up, and glorifies its creator.

The Eagle-Man. The eagle-man plucks from the vine the fruit of the Tree of Knowledge, which he has carefully brought to fruition. (Assyrian art, Kalash, ninth century BC; from the Louvre.)

If we repeat a word, the power of repetition opens it up. If we consider a flower, it will open its heart to us. Let us listen, touch, and learn to feel. Everything that may be an object of meditation is there, "at hand," provided the hand is an extension of the heart, Tiferet, itself informed by Keter.

For behind our immediate sensations lurk all our psychological stirrings: irritation, pleasure, hate, and love. If uncontrolled, they are an insurmountable wall. But the touch of the Divine Glory, which is sealed at the heart of beings and things, demands the quality of love that is reached only through death and resurrection in Tiferet.

The different levels of receptivity are best shown in a passage of the Gospels (John 20:24–30) where Thomas, who was absent when the other apostles met the Risen Christ, is invited by him to place his finger, then his hand, in his wounds. This concrete touch opens the door to spiritual touch, the door to Knowledge.

In the breaking of bread, a concrete symbol of flesh, the disciples at Emmaus, supping with a man they encountered on the road, recognize in him the Risen Christ.

"And their eyes were opened" (Luke 24:31).

The eagle's eyes "behold afar off" (Job 39:29).

The Hebrew word *yada* (ידע), "to know," is built on the root *yad*—the hand—to which the letter *ayin* (ע), meaning "eye," is added. We could say that the hand is gifted with vision, and the eye with a quality of touch.

Vision and touch lead to Knowledge that frees.

Christian iconography never depicts the Person of the Father in the Holy Trinity, for he is the Unknowable, but indicates his presence with a hand—the extent to which the Unknowable makes himself known.

"Out of the abyss, my beloved put forth his hand, and by breaking down, his power was upon me," sings the Shulamite (Song of Solomon 5:4). In her encounter with God she links divine power with the hand or the *yod* breaking down the most secret barriers of the soul's garden. "Breaking down" is the word *ai* (עי), which can be read as "the hand (or the *yod*) at the source."

Only at the source of being may one experience the *yod*, the Name, which puts us in the Father's "hands." If the *yod* were fully written in the word *ai* (עי), we would have the word ידע, "to know, to love."

This "breaking down" in the Song of Solomon is the breach through which the Divine Spouse penetrates his Bride.

Christian iconography also represents Christ in glory with disproportionately long hands (the Christ in the basilica of Autun, for example). This means the man of Knowledge. The hand of man is all-knowing insofar as it is an image of the hand of the Father and receives his energies.

Christian tradition, on the framework of Judaism (the Psalms), speaks of the two hands of the Father acting in the world:

The hand of the Son, the Word who gives form,

The hand of the Holy Spirit, who gives life.

In this image, both hands of the knowing man give form and life. And depending on whether man takes his part on a mundane level or in an increasingly profound experience, the hands form, shape, fashion, give rhythm, and then give life to these different levels. The one is nothing without the other.

It is the "withered" right hand that Christ heals (Luke 6:6) on the day of the *shabbat*, showing that the rigor of law without life is sterile.

By the laying on of hands, all power is given to the one who is consecrated, anointed, or instituted according to the rituals of different initiations: bishop, priest, knight, or king. By the laying on of hands, life springs up again. The physician—when he was still a priest—knew this.

The number 10 is linked with the *yod*, which is *yad* (the hand), and symbolizes the unity man is supposed to attain on the level of the head. Two hands with their ten fingers joined recreate this unity. Each hand is a tool working in the knowledge implied by the conquest of this unity and in the power it gives. Thus a scepter often has a hand where one might expect a head.

There is a beautiful Christian image representing a spinal column whose energies criss-cross in a design similar to that of the caduceus. They blossom at the top, not into a head, but into a hand haloed with the mandorla of the saints. We see here an almost total identification between the head and the hand, between the *yod* of the Sword הוה, the archetypal head, and each of the two ה, "breaths" forming each of the two hands: each hand contains the other, and both form the head.

The two cerebral hemispheres are inseparable from the two hands, like the two lungs, of which they are an extension. And the Hebrew language tells us that the "lungs can see." There is a sense, then, in which the hands can see.

When knowing (ידע) is just a cerebral matter, it is no longer love. If knowledge is also love, the hands become the creative breath.

Through its five fingers the hand is linked with precise organs of the body.

The thumb (finger of Venus) is linked with the head. The Romans, who put their thumbs down to signify a death sentence, knew this. And the story of Tom Thumb is a marvel: every detail is meaningful and relates the evolution of man from his alienating relationship with his parents to his total freedom beyond the conditioning of time and space, which is symbolized by the seven-league boots.

The index finger (finger of Jupiter) is linked with the gall bladder.

The middle finger (finger of Saturn) is linked with the spleen and pancreas.

The ring finger (finger of the Sun) is linked with the liver.

The little finger (finger of Mercury, formerly called "ear finger" in English) is linked with the heart, as confirmed by the collective unconscious, which surfaces in nursery rhymes: "his little finger tells him everything."

Every finger has its secret and its power. The gestures of the hand and fingers performed by yogis and sacred dancers mobilize energies that link man more specifically with a given aspect of his divine potentiality. The yoga of fingers in India is called mudra; each mudra is significant, and each movement of the hand, or of both hands joined, is charged with power.

The Hand at the Top of the Caduceus. The hand, *yad*, is already the head, *yod*, of the divine Tetragrammaton. It represents the power of knowledge. (Photo: Belzeaux-Zodiaque.)

A Western yoga must have existed, as the work of the Kabbalist Abraham Abulafia indicates. And the position of the priest's hands during the celebration of the Holy Christian Mysteries might be a remnant of this yoga. Western priests, no longer understanding the symbols, have cleared them away and the mysteries with them.

For the Jewish people, the hand has retained great importance. "The children," states a *Bulletin de l'alliance universelle israëlite*, "carry a small golden or silver hand. The first present offered to a fiancée is a golden hand. Hands are drawn on the walls next to the house where a wedding is being celebrated."[1] We meet the same symbol of protective power with the Hand of Fatima worn by Muslims.

In our Western civilization, all popular expressions concerning the hand, such as: to lay hands on, to ask for a young woman's hand, to hand over, etc., are applications in daily life of the life force contained by the hand, whose archetypal source I have tried to explicate.

It is essential to highlight that both hands, in the deepest sense, are one. They express the two faces of unity, the sole power, the sole knowledge that is manifest in duality by the number 5. This number is a symbol of the seed and the promise of the totality that both hands, joined together, realize by reconstituting the 10.

The two hands coupled in unity thus symbolize "force," in Hebrew *koah* (כה) (20 + 8, making 10 by adding the digits). We are on the path of Justice-Rigor, which is also traditionally the path of Force (Gevurah, the divine force).

The Eagle therefore means Force and Knowledge.

He grasps in his powerful talons the many messengers sent to men by the gods:

A white goose (*Odyssey*, 15.160);

A dove (ibid., 15.525),

A fawn (*Iliad*, 8), etc.

And the eagle snatches from the earth what belongs to the gods (the myths of Ganymede and of Prometheus).

The myth of Prometheus will clarify the symbolism of the eagle and its precise relationship with the human body.

The eagle brings about sublime elevation in the Greek myth, but let us not forget the part this lord of the heavens plays in the story of Job. Job can undertake his last descent into hell with Behemoth and Leviathan only after incorporating the energies of the eagle.

For it is obviously as wrong to pursue the albedo (the white phase of the Work) while refusing the nigredo (the black phase of the Work) as it is to pursue the nigredo before one has been nourished by the albedo, which makes its accomplishment possible.

The myth of Jason and the Argonauts shows this first error. We have already seen Daedalus and Icarus plummet down to earth, because to complete the white phase of the Work they mimicked the eagle by putting on false wings. Glue butterfly wings onto a caterpillar and it won't get far! The myth of the labyrinth is thus shown to be accurate.

Through the Rigor of the Work, we are able to experience Grace and Mercy. Rigor and Grace, Din and Ḥesed, are the two "hands" springing forth from Tiferet.

How far we are from the dualism of grace versus free will, which has kept the Christian West bogged down in a pseudoproblem.

Man goes up, then down, God comes down and then lifts up. Man is free within his God-man dimension, within the illumination of the encounter. Any other kind of freedom is only apparent, reduced to the possibility of choice that Knowledge alone makes effective.

Knowledge alone makes free.

"Forsake the foolish (ignorance), and live" (Proverbs 9:6).

The Hebrew name for "eagle," *nesher* (נשר), contains the Trinitarian letter par excellence, the *shin* (ש). It is set within the word *ner* (נר), meaning "lamp," the light. So the eagle is the bird bearing in its heart the Trinitarian Light. This word, *ner*, is formed with the two letters *nun* (נ, 50) and *resh* (ר, 200), of which one is the fish and the other the head. The letter *shin* (ש), uniting them and symbolizing the cosmic expansion from the heart of the foundations, joins the feet to the head (see chapter 7, pages 77–78).

The root *sar* (שר), also found in the name of the eagle, is "lord, prince." Breath, Knowledge, Force, Power, Lordship, and Light: such are the qualities of the Master of the Heights, the one who draws man out of the darkness to introduce him into the light with which he is potentially woven.

The Din-Ḥesed path (Rigor-Mercy), which is also Gevurah-Gedulah (Force-Greatness), is built on the shoulders of man.

In Hebrew, the word *shekhem* (שכם), "shoulder," also means "term," "goal." It is also the name of Shechem, a town in the land of Canaan, the Promised Land, containing the *shem* (שם), the Name, Knowledge of which is the only goal. שכם is also the biblical verb "to rise early in the morning." The shoulders represent a new dawn.

The collarbones (clavicles: etymologically, "little keys") close the path in the Middle Column. They are the "keys" of the Gate of the Gods. The Hebrew word for "clavicle," *briaḥ* (בריח), does not mean "key," but "bolt," and also "runaway, fugitive."

Who is man but a runaway from Eden, now "bolted" by the "Cherubims and a flaming sword which turned every way" (Genesis 3:24) guarding its entrance?

Heracles (Hercules), whose name means "key of Hera," is victorious from birth over two snakes put in his cradle by the goddess Hera, who seeks his death.

The hero's birth here is the birth undertaken at the Gate of Men, on whose level each man becomes conscious of his seed (for Heracles, Hera), of the opposing energies offered by her (the two snakes), and of the unity toward which he must bring them (strangling them).

The death appointed for the hero is indeed the one his seed requires of him, driving him toward Tiferet. The goddess's keys are again these two snakes, which, on the level of the Gate of the Gods (the two clavicles), are transcended in the eagle.

The physician's caduceus represents this symbolism, for the doctor to begin with was a priest, an image of Christ, priest and doctor of humanity. He had the power of the keys. Today he is no longer a priest, but a kind of magician with power, who acts more like a mandarin than any other professional. He treats the body like an object and practices medicine by transferring the burden of sickness onto the enemy microbe, the scapegoat. The sick man too is then made into an object.

Many doctors are very competent and devoted on this level of knowledge. They are nonetheless the creators of new illnesses because they have only treated the symptom and not the profound cause of the harm, and also because, by refusing to seek the cause in the way the subject manages his or her energies, they encourage man to be irresponsible. This becomes a source of new ailments.

No measure taken within the limits of such unconsciousness can resolve the pseudoproblem of the welfare state, itself a symptom of our collective mental illness. The root of the illness, namely, our infantile and murderous unconsciousness, is what needs treatment.

The true physician helps man rediscover the harmonious balance of the energies he embodies in their program of accomplishment (see chapter 12, page 225). This is why he is also a priest, a priest according to the order of Melchizedek (see chapter 9, page 111), who "performs the sacred" and therefore knows the way of such acts and their laws.

In the Christian tradition, the one who has received the power of the keys is the apostle Peter. His Hebrew name, *Petros* (פטרוס), means "he who opens."

Whoever enters the energy of this name can open or close the Gate of the Gods. What a responsibility for one who describes himself as the successor of this apostle but who no longer sees the oneness of the twelve, a small human cell constituted in the image of the divine Trinity, in which each person contains the whole of divinity and none is greater than the other!

All the apostles receive this power through Peter, just as each of them specifically receives a power belonging to all: John, at the foot of the cross, becomes the "son" of Mary.

Is he the only one?

Each apostle is a symbol of the gift received but cannot be identified with it.

The exercise of power without knowledge means authoritarianism and hence the trap of power games. Anyone who operates thus belongs in the labyrinth of the first level and imprisons those kept there under his authority.

He becomes one who closes, no longer one who opens.

The keys are the accomplished snakes, which have become the eagle.

On the path to Knowledge, the eagle guards the eastern gate of the Garden of Eden.

Dante's Paradise

"On your knees, on your knees! Behold the angel of the Lord! . . . Closer and closer to our shore he came, brighter and brighter shone the bird of God."[2]

The celestial bird brings to the shore a group of spirits chanting "In exitu Israël de Egypto . . . " These spirits emerge from the sea, in a boat guided by the angel rowing from the air. Their song celebrates the Hebrews coming out of Egypt. In their physical death they have just passed through a gate corresponding to the Gate of Men. Again we encounter the bulrushes of the Red Sea, from which Virgil makes a belt for the poet, as if to mark the nature of the crossing on the traveler's body.

"Bulrush," in Hebrew, *sof* (סוף), also means "threshold" or "limit." It is clear that Dante goes through a gate when he comes back up from out of hell, for Virgil continues to accompany his disciple to the summit of a mountain and leaves him only there.

It is then that Dante sees "a lady under her green cloak" (symbolism of the Green Tree). Beatrice, Dante's spiritual soul, is there to console him on Virgil's departure: "Dante, though Virgil leaves you, do not weep, not yet, that is, for you shall have to weep from yet another wound . . . " Dante sheds tears of purification in pathos and penitence. He must dress the wound. "She had led me into the stream up to my neck; now drawing me along she glided light, and with a shuttle's ease, across the stream."

Then follow the thirty-three cantos of the *Paradiso*, in which Dante and Beatrice gradually penetrate into the first nine celestial spheres. At the gate of the eighth sphere, Beatrice in turn withdraws to let St. Bernard guide the traveler. Dante, whose "gaze newly empowered, penetrated still further into the ray of light, where all is Truth" cannot express in words the splendors he contemplates. Later, writing down these cantos from Paradise, the poet recalls: "I think I well preserved the universal form of this knot in my mind which joins so many diverse substances."

In this divine "knot," this Divine Unity, Dante seeks to know how the union of the two natures is realized. "But to understand such a mystery, my strength was not sufficient."

And Dante's vision seems to meet up with the vision of another poet, Oscar Vladislas de Lubicz Milosz, who savored illumination and confessed:

> All I understood,
> the Annunciation and the Word made flesh
> Yes, in a lightning flash of thought
> I understood, I felt, I saw
> —HOW IT HAD ALL HAPPENED—
> Now the three years of renunciation following the forty years of
>   waiting are coming to an end. I understand. I feel at last that I
>   know . . . that I have always known, and that right here there is
>   here a certain way of knowing all.
>
> (*La confession de Lemuel*, 1922)

With Dante and with Milosz, we join with John of the Cross and Francis of Assisi in the experience of cosmic Knowledge regained, about which we have already spoken (see chapter 13, page 258).

The Myth of Prometheus

An eagle released Job from the jaws of death and led him to royalty; "the angel of God, the celestial bird" guided Dante to Paradise, where the poet seems to have been carried on its wings from heaven to heaven; and the eagle, again, introduced Prometheus to the Elysian fields. But first the Greek hero confronted the White Dragon, who here governs both the black and the white phases of the Work.

Prometheus belonged to the race of the Titans. These giants joined with their brother Cronus in rebellion against Uranus, the Father, whom they dethroned. They were all confounded by Zeus and hurled down into Tartarus, the river of the underworld.

Prometheus could only beget serfs of time, men tied to the wheel of eternal beginnings, cut off from their divine roots. Creator of these "fallen men," who are deprived of divine fire, he modeled them from the silt of the earth, which he moistened with his tears.

Linked with earth and water, deprived of fire, of any source of light, this humanity in exile (on the level of Having) feeds on fruits that, symbolically, were ripened by no sun and which no fire could cook.

These men were hungry and cold. Prometheus, their father, took pity on them. Doubtless he was also jealous of the gods, whose lineage was full of light. He decided to go to Hephaestus's forge and seek a spark of divine fire to bring back to men on earth.

Our earlier studies allow us to appreciate the greatness of this myth. Prometheus's name—the "foreseeing one"—contains a certain ambivalence (foresee/provide): he who is provident, like a father for his children, naturally seeks to avoid want and brings back what they need. In this sense Prometheus, going and stealing the fire from heaven, is a good father, although we cannot say that he is provident in begetting, with his own limited seed, beings who are destined for Tartarus, for death.

But which of us thinks of such things before bringing children into the world? We imagine that the warmth of our affections and the kindling of the fire of their intellect will suffice for their life.

He who "foresees" must also know that divine fire can only descend into this place of exile if humanity endeavors to make its way out, and sets off to win the fire in Hephaestus's forge (Tiferet).

Of course, the path is long and hard and appears to be yet more impossible when envisaged less for oneself than for one's children.

Prometheus was impatient and could not envisage this route. He wanted to gratify his children instantly with a heaven that knew no hell, with a life that did not evolve through the cross.

Here we find an almost exact replica of the biblical myth of the Fall. Through impatience man and woman bit into the apple, the fruit of knowledge of duality, which they were not yet ready to take in. The woman appears in the Greek myth as Pandora, whose name means "all giving."

Born at the hands of Hephaestus by order of Zeus, Pandora carried the potential divine fire in the famous box she was given and was not allowed to open. As a divine gift, these fire energies become elements of life if man can use them, of death if he does not know their powers and has not won mastery at the same time as Knowledge.

Pandora's box, with the receptivity to "all gifts" contained in it, reminds us of the feet. The opening of the box seems to correspond to the wounding of the foot, through which human energies leak away in vain. A deplorable hemorrhage, unleashing passions, feverish agitation, and all kinds of activism.

Prometheus is incapable of recognizing in Pandora the fruit of divine mercy sending him, through woman, the seed of fire he desires and of which he has dispossessed humanity. Seeking solutions only in the physical and psychological powers belonging to a pseudomasculinity, he does not discern the divine gift.

Prometheus is typical of the human being who has not gone through the Gate of Men, whose thought, albeit foreseeing, crawls along at the level of Having, and whose sleeping consciousness cannot discern the gift of life he carries within.

Prometheus should have married Pandora, his *ishah*, held on to the sealed box, and taken up the difficult path of the forge with her by going through the narrow gate. Pandora's "gifts" would have then been properly released.

They had neither the patience nor the obedience asked of ignorant children. Alas! While Prometheus went to steal the fire from the forge, Pandora married Epimetheus, and they opened the forbidden box.

Epimetheus is to Prometheus what Esau is to Jacob: he is the Red Man, the man stuck in the mundane, who marries in Pandora the fire of earthly passions.

In depth, the stolen fire and the gifts pouring out of the unsealed box are the same: the reality of their investment in the level only of Having, in a craze for power of which man unpurified has no mastery.

Prometheus became aware of this folly. He resolved to take up the path of the forge again, to win, rightly this time, the fire of life. He left Epimetheus.

This is the about-turn, the *teshuvah* or "penitence." He went through the Gate of Men and stood before Hephaestus.

Where penitence is concerned, our Western psyche—imprisoned in a legalistic framework—has great difficulty in getting rid of the notions of judgment and punishment. Spiritual vision, in contrast, reveals the liberating purpose of the potential of energy that is set in motion.

Prometheus, chained by the divine smith to a rock in the Caucasus mountains, suffers only the ordeals that every being at this stage of the way must confront. We are dealing here with the law of evolution, involving a necessary regressive phase, which is not in essence punitive.

This myth places on high what others have us endure in the depths. But it is the same fundamental process. Here the alternation of descent into darkness and ascent into light is symbolized by the agonizing succession of night and day suffered by the hero:

"Parched by the scorching rays of the sun, you shall witness the flower of your body wither away. Too late, to your liking, will the night come and shield the day under its coat of stars," says Hephaestus, who does not hide the fact that Prometheus will also be frozen during the night.

Something must be said about the symbolism of the rock to which Prometheus is chained, for the stone is none other than man insofar as he is alive and conscious.

Prometheus is a prisoner of himself, until, dying and being born incessantly over many nights and days, he experiences total liberation.

Prometheus's stone therefore follows the alchemical process. The hero submits to the ordeal. Every morning an eagle visits him and feeds on his liver, which grows whole again every night.

As the White Dragon, guardian of the threshold of the Gate of the Gods, the eagle appears, on this side of the gate, in the guise of a devouring monster.

The liver is the organ that integrates accomplished energies (see chapter 12, page 224).

By devouring Prometheus's liver, the eagle compels man to go down into the night of the unaccomplished ra (רע) in order to celebrate his wedding with Mother Earth, symbolized by the spleen and pancreas. Every morning the hero offers the eagle the "honey" of the elaborated tov (טוב). This, throughout a thousand years.

After a thousand years—the number corresponding to unity regained—Prometheus is released. He is introduced by Zeus into the abode of the gods.

However, the myth does not end here. The crowning of Prometheus does not take place without the death of the centaur Chiron, whose end confirms the healing of humanity.

Chiron, *Kheírōn*, means "the inferior" in Greek. Half man, half horse, a hybrid of man and animal, he was renowned for his wisdom and his understanding, but also for the incurable wound on his foot. Seeking a cure, he became a doctor and taught the art of medicine as well as other sciences.

He educated Achilles, teaching him the virtue of a balm with which the hero dressed the wounds of his warriors, without, however, being able to cure the one he himself received on the foot, and from which he died.

The centaur teaches according to an understanding and a wisdom inherent in the lower labyrinthine triangle. He suffers cruelly from the ontological wound, which no existential wisdom or understanding will enable him to heal. Weary of such ills, Chiron craves death from Zeus in exchange for Prometheus's release.

Chiron, the man-animal in the Greek myth, appears to be completely identified with the wound on humanity's foot. His death means the healing of that wound.

We discover yet again the fundamental unity linking all myths and all traditions. Its light today seems to be dawning once more in our otherwise heavy sky.

"For the wisdom of their wise men shall perish, and the understanding of their prudent men shall be hid" (Isaiah 39:14; 1 Corinthians 3:19).

This "perishing" seems to correspond to the death of the centaur. Love, the divine fire, crucified in Tiferet, transforms and recreates.

Love alone heals.

Love alone can free us from the centaurs who still lead the world today.

After Chiron's death and Prometheus's release, the world suffered a Flood similar to the one described in the Bible.

Humanity, linked with Epimetheus-Chiron, was purified by water (cosmic circumcision; see chapter 10, page 137). The couple formed by Deucalion and Pyrrha, who survived the Flood, repopulated the earth by throwing stones over their shoulders. As Divine Seeds on this level, these stones represent future humanity in whom the divine can grow, now that its prototype, in a correct ascent, has won back the fire of which "his children" had been dispossessed and which he had gone on to steal.

Thus the Greek Prometheus seems to announce the Christian Messiah. Perhaps then the etymology of his name may be linked with promise rather than foresight.

The Counterfeit Albedo, or the Conquest of the Golden Fleece

There is also, unfortunately, a counterfeit white phase of the Work, which is illustrated in the myth of the Golden Fleece.

Phrixus and Helle, children of King Athamas, were threatened by their stepmother, Ino, and escaped from the palace on a ram with a Golden Fleece. The ram could move in the air as well as on land. It was also endowed with speech.

During the journey, Helle was frightened and fell into the sea. Phrixus reached the land of Colchis by himself. He sacrificed the ram to Zeus and made a gift of its fleece to the king of the land, who hung the shining mantle on a tree guarded by a dragon.

Such is the origin of the Golden Fleece. Its symbolism is clear.

Born from unity (Athamas means "the indivisible," "the nonmultiple"), Phrixus and Helle are the duality that childishness (Ino means "child") tears away from their original unity. But Ino—Athamas's feminine—may also be his unaccomplished, which Phrixus and Helle have a duty to accomplish.

The bright ram is a gift from Mercury that they ride. It represents their primary nature, which makes them partake of earth and air. Phrixus is linked with fire, and Helle with water. The animal is gifted with speech. Phrixus and Helle, children of god, are ontologically word.

When their unity is broken, their separation becomes inevitable, and

The Golden Fleece. The myth of the Golden Fleece was one of many ancient myths that fed the alchemists. They thought to find within it the secret of the Great Work, here depicted with a set of the principal alchemical symbols. (Print in Maurice Bessy's *Histoire en 1000 images de la magie*, Pont Royal, 1962.)

the two part. Helle "experiences fear," meaning she transfers the power that only the father had over her onto the cosmos, which was meant to serve her. Severed from his source, man reverses the currents. The current that stirred "fear and trembling" before the divine is focused onto the created world, which then instills fear.

The fall of Helle into the sea means she abandons her divine nature in favor of a new nature, self-created, before the manifest world she is about to experience. In biblical language, we would say that Helle is clothed in her coat of skin. In biological language, she becomes a seed in the maternal waters.

Helladic songs lamented the lost paradise of the paternal palace and sought the light-fire of the ram left behind.

A Green Tree now holds the Golden Fleece, the tunic of light, and inherits the gift of speech from the ram.

Phrixus, the brother, seems to become the adversary.

To recover speech, "to make the flesh into Word," to win back the garment of light—such is humanity's fundamental quest.

Let us now follow the about-turn undertaken by Helle, who, according to one version, became Diomedes in a sequel to the myth. As the man in a coat of skin, he was born into a family that was royal but dethroned, a symbol of his lost ontology that he decides to win back.

In Iolcus, Pelias had seized the throne from his brother Aeson and reigned over Thessaly. Diomedes, Aeson's son, decided to recapture the throne. Pelias learned of this plot by an oracle and sought to have his nephew killed. Aeson published the news of the child's death, whereas in reality he had entrusted him to the centaur Chiron to remove him from harm. Diomedes was initiated by Chiron, the physician, into his arts and received from him the name Jason.

Jason's name is linked with the notion of cure. But is it not just a common cure after the manner of ordinary medicine? The myth will reveal whether Jason is the divine physician humanity awaits.

Pelias organized a feast in honor of Poseidon. He invited Jason, unaware of the young man's true identity. Pelias knew only what the oracle had told him: his illegitimate reign would come to an end. He would be dethroned by an adolescent who would appear with a "foot unshod." On his way to the royal palace, Jason crossed a ford, took off his sandals, and dropped one into the river. Jason appeared before Pelias, lame, with one foot unshod. Unfortunately, our hero was very like his master! So there was every reason to fear that the conquest of the Golden Fleece, to which Pelias compelled his young rival, would be carried out by means incommensurate with the greatness of the task. Unless Jason passed through the Gate of Men and raised himself, in the rigor of the Royal Art, up all the steps that separated him from the garment of light, the Golden Fleece would not be won, or would be won fraudulently.

What did Jason do? He immediately showed that he was powerless to take up the challenge by himself. He gathered round him valiant heroes: Castor and Polydeuces, Hercules, Theseus, Orpheus, etc. They were fifty-two, bearing the name Argonauts after the ship Argo, in which they sailed.

The number 52 is clearly symbolical. The 2, duality, linked with the number 50, indicating the totality of latent possibilities, gives the idea that this noble crew carries within it both the duality of the manifest world, which is its point of departure, and the potential to reconquer the divine, the One, which is its goal.

The whole of Olympus looks kindly upon the Argo. Olympus, in Greek, is the equivalent of the Hebrew world of *mi* (see chapter 1); and the *mi*, the world above (מי = 40 + 10), corresponds to 50, as does the word *kol* (כל = 20 + 30), which means "all." The letter *nun* (נ), also linked with the number 50, is the "fish," the "seed" (on the feet containing the "all," see chapter 7, page 71.) At the beginning, the fifty-two Argonauts below have found favor with the entire heavens above.

The Argo (from the Greek root for "shining"), sailing toward the Golden Fleece, represents the color silver on its way to becoming gold, or the lunar stage before the conquest of the sun. The moon, symbolized by Argo and the sea that carries it, are symbols of the Lower Triangle of the Tree, belonging psychologically to the domain of Having. Will these young conquerors pass through the Gate of Men?

Formidable trials could be foreseen. Thanks to Hercules's admonitions, Jason tears himself away from the delights of the attractive queen of the islands of Lemnos. Again thanks to Hercules and his strength, the ship manages to make its way through the barricade built by six-handed giants at the entrance to the port that sheltered it. But soon Hercules leaves his companions, and his defection is to be followed by others. The early unity is shattered, the wound reopened, and blood let. The diminished crew of Argonauts approaches a narrow pass, guarded by two moving rocks that keep driving together, crushing between their dreadful jaws any boat unfortunate enough to venture there.

There the Argo confronts an important gate guarded by a devouring monster. With the help of a soothsayer, it manages to pass through, though not without serious damage, for the rudder at the back is crushed by the closing of the jaws. If the thinking head, symbolized by the rudder, is devoured, can it be said that there was a victory over the trial?

Without a rudder, in other words without Knowledge, the Argo hugs the coasts of Asia, like a blind man groping his way along a wall, in order finally to reach Colchis. But the ship's little company has not lifted itself up to the level of consciousness. Its blind body may be in Colchis, but the qualities of its soul have been left behind. The arrival of Jason at the palace of King Aeëtes is much like the arrival of Theseus at the palace of Minos.

There, for love's sake, Ariadne the pure invited the hero to the search for Knowledge.

Here, in the fire of passion, Medea, the sorceress, becomes Jason's accomplice.

Magic is put in the place of Knowledge.

Medea is to use all her powers to overcome the obstacles set up by the furious Aeëtes between the young man and the fleece he lays claim to. Medea is not "divine thought." On the level to which Jason regresses, he is only able to encounter "pure thought" (albeit unpurified!), that is to say, cerebral thought, or thought perverted by magic.

"I will let you take away the Golden Fleece," says Aeëtes to Jason, "only if you succeed in the following task: I have a pair of brazen-footed, fire-breathing bulls. These you must tame, and yoke, and with a single steel share you are then to plow four plowgates in the barren wilderness. Then you shall sow, not corn, but the teeth I shall give you. They will straightway grow into giants. As soon as they have come out of the ground, attack and kill them all. If you finish this task in a single day, you may carry off the ram's fleece."

Courageously, Jason accepts. Yet we know that courage belongs on the psychological plane and offers no solution. Only the art of the Great Work provides the genuine solution, but for this divine science Medea substitutes magic. The sorceress has some connection with Chiron, the ordinary doctor. Chiron dresses wounds with the balm of the intellect. Medea makes the hero invulnerable with the balm of magic. Anointed with this magical balm, Jason is empowered with colossal strength and brings off the harsh trial successfully.

Yet Jason's trials are not over. We recall that a dragon guards the tree on which the fleece hangs. It cannot be taken without confronting the monster. The stages of the nigredo are avoided. Incapable of undertaking them, Jason allows Medea to lead the way. By concentrating her "powers of thought," she puts the monster to sleep. So it is easy for Jason to kill it and steal the Fleece.

In sum, it is nothing but a theft. By means of the kind of magic called black—for it is negative and stands in lieu of the positive black phase of the Work—man embezzles powers that soon turn against him. The garment of light can but burn one who has not become the light.

That is the essence of the myth, which continues with further dramatic adventures. Jason flees from Colchis, abandoning Medea. As a wedding gift to the lady who is to marry Jason, Medea sends a poisoned tunic, which burns the hapless woman as soon as she puts it on. She dies, consumed by fire, while her spouse continues to use his magical powers to usurp his father's throne without having won it back. In turn he himself is dethroned, leads a lamentable life, and ends up committing suicide.

Such is the counterfeit white phase of the Work.

The grand temptation of power, one of the three tentacles of the hydra Satan, is an inexhaustible subject of meditation. It is a work of darkness through the refusal of the black phase of the Work.

Many black arts appear white. The Golden Fleece, whatever happens, remains the Golden Fleece. But when the black phase of the Work is avoided, sooner or later the tunic burns the one who has stolen it.

This is the pitfall of all techniques claiming to lead to the white phase of the Work, when not taught by Masters who can awaken in their disciples awareness of the Work as a whole.

The West is tempted by this "counterfeit white," because for centuries it has been imprisoned in an uninspiring moralism. It has tried to make up for this with excessive intellectual activity, leading to our present impasse.

In reaction against this dryness, the West is running the risk of falling into the "wet" trap of mysticism at any price. This has already begun to happen with indiscriminate experiments of all kinds, from techniques that look wise to the most eccentric of artificial journeys.

The dry way and the wet way are both sought in compensation for a tradition that is rejected because it is perceived as childish and wholly inadequate for what humanity facing the devouring monster of the Gate of Men now requires.

Man must recover tradition and find in it another dimension of its message. When he lives according to this message, tradition will reveal the rest of its treasures, and man will begin to live out his true incarnation.

Christ's Resurrection: The Body Glorious

"I said, Ye are gods" (Psalm 82:6), exclaims the Holy Spirit through the psalmist.

Christ reminds the Jews of this when they gather stones to throw at him because he claims divine sonship (John 10:34). Further on, he adds: "Verily, verily, I say unto you, he that believeth on me, the works that I do shall he do also; and greater works than these shall he do; because I go unto my Father" (John 14:12–13).

Is there a greater work than to become "god"? To complete the Great Work by transforming this body of flesh; "sown in corruption; it is raised in incorruption: it is sown in dishonor; it is raised in glory: it is sown in weakness; it is raised in power: it is sown a natural body; it is raised a spiritual body" (1 Corinthians 15:42–44).

Christ's resurrection, the first fruits of the universal transmutation, takes us into the reality of this becoming.

This is the Good News, *basorah* (בשרה), in which "flesh," *basar* (בשר), sealed at the heart of Adam's unaccomplished, is today totally accomplished.

Forgive me here for mentioning mysteries that should not be spoken about by those who have not experienced them. I do so because the life of the church traditionally has us partake in them day and night, in a daily life that already knows something of the first fruits of the universal resurrection. And also because these mysteries are inscribed in man's flesh, and the sole aim of this book is to restore to him his rightful place, his calling, his greatness.

This chapter concerns the passage through the Gate of the Gods, but at the end I am placing an event that radically transcends it.

The east of Eden is situated well beyond the Gate of the Gods (see chapter 13, page 253–54).

The appropriate place for Job's encounter with Behemoth and Leviathan was not in the work of the thoracic triangle, which gives access only to the light of the eagle.

After Christ's entry into Jerusalem—corresponding to the crossing of the Gate of the Gods—his death and his descent into hell were not in their appropriate place either.

These last two experiences belong in the Upper Triangle. So does the mystery of Christ's resurrection.

This form of presentation was meant to preserve the coherence of the stories. But I am conscious of the risk of confusing levels of experience.

I hope the reader's inner light will enable him or her to clearly follow passages that my inadequacies have rendered obscure. This light can only come from participating in the messianic dimension, without which, like Job, one cannot go to the far end of the experience of hell and hence to the experience of light that opens from it.

The great traditional mystical currents of humanity can bring us to the point where we listen to the Name. Only the Christ-Messiah, once heard, can make us enter into the Name and become his Light.

On the level of the Upper Triangle, all traditions become accomplished in the unity of his Person, inseparable from the Holy Trinity.

Christ is in the night of the tomb. His body is covered with a shroud. First thing in the morning, Mary Magdalene, one of the women bearing myrrh, approaches the sepulchre. It is open; she thinks the body has been stolen. Doubtful at first, the apostles go and enter the sepulchre. The shroud lies on the ground. The veil that covered the head is neatly folded aside. At the entrance of the sepulchre, Mary Magdalene weeps. Two angels dressed in white ask why: "Why seek ye the living among the dead? He is not here, but is risen!" (Luke 24:5).

Suddenly a man approaches. Supposing him to be the gardener, Mary Magdalene begs him, "Sir, if thou have borne him hence, tell me where thou hast laid him." Jesus answers "Mary"; she recognizes his voice and cries out: "Rabboni" (Master); (John 20:15–16).

The two disciples on their way to Emmaus do not recognize the Risen Christ any more than Mary Magdalene does. Even his voice instructing them on the road does not reveal his identity. Only "when he took the bread and blessed it, and brake, and gave to them" did they know him (Luke 24:30).

The apostle Thomas, absent on the day of the resurrection, cannot believe the astounding news: "Except I shall see in his hands the print of the nails, and put my finger into the print of the nails, and thrust my hand into his side, I will not believe" (John 20:25).

"Blessed Thomas!" as Monsignor Jean de Saint-Denys once said. "It is he who brings us the proof that Christ's risen body is none other than his material, physical, perishable body which has become spiritual, imperishable, and glorious."

This body can pass through walls. It comes into the closed upper room where the apostles are met. It vanishes from the sight of the two disciples at Emmaus, without opening the door.

This body does not feed on material elements. It belongs to the Upper Triangle and feeds on the divine. If Christ then eats bread or fish with his apostles, it is by freely participating in their bodily condition, to which his own bodily state has access, just as he enables those to whom he gives the eucharistic bread to rise to that state.

The exchange takes place at the level of that state and underlines man's fundamental unity. His qualities are integrated one after the other starting from the flesh and ending with its most subtle elaboration as it becomes deified.

In the words of René Schwaller de Lubicz, "There are not two worlds, one small, the other large. There exists but one world, and on the royal path of accomplishment, man risen represents the totality of this world."

Neither are there two bodies, for the tomb is empty. The risen body is the same as the one that lay dead in the tomb.

What happened?

An event took place that goes beyond what words can describe and beyond what our understanding can grasp. Only modern science, with its negative approach, can approach the inexpressible reality.

By laying down the principle of "the absolute hidden by appearances" (see chapter 3, page 20, and chapter 11, page 173), Einstein gave to investigation of the outer world a power that man is incapable of applying inwardly. Einstein lifted the veil of appearances.

The fruit of the Tree of Knowledge has been plucked, the atom's nucleus has been split, and the energy released—outwardly.

In the tomb, Christ became this fruit, opened its kernel. He became his Name. The energy released took hold of the matter of the body in its entirety and transfigured it. Created energy was completely turned round toward its pole of light, ready to enrich the Uncreated.

Rather than an explosion that would have destroyed more than the earth, there is an implosion, which leaves the veil of appearances intact. It hardly even disrupted the environment of the Risen Christ: it rolled away the stone sealing the tomb and seems to have left an imprint of the body on the shroud before this was laid down onto the ground (Luke 24:12; John 20:5–7).

Inwardly, in the secret of creation, in the silence of the Name of each of us, this implosive work continues. It is the work of the Holy Spirit putting the world out of joint in order to accomplish it.

The lapse of time separating the resurrection from the ascension could well not have been. Christ could have ascended to the Father without the event being visible to our eyes of flesh.

Personally, I sense those fifty days as the grace of the most resplendent testimony of the whole human adventure:

Testimony of the glorious body each one of us is called to become in his own body;

Testimony of the Holy Spirit's implosive work, which God's Word heralds through the words of Christ: "And, behold, I send the promise of my Father upon you" (Luke 24:49).

"The Spirit of Truth, which proceedeth from the Father" (John 15:26), and which today makes man grow into his dimension of Truth.

In Christ, on the day of the resurrection, earth goes up to heaven, as on Christmas day heaven had come down into the depths of earth. From that time on, in silence, earth had germinated its God.

> People, let us today shine with joy, it is the Passover of the Lord. From death to life, from the earth to the heavens, God in Christ has led us. Let us sing the hymn of victory. Come, let us drink the new drink, not the spring which a miracle brought forth from the rock, but Christ, the incorruptible Source, springing forth from the tomb and giving us his power.
>
> All is drenched in light, the sky, the earth, and hell. Let all creatures celebrate the resurrection of Christ, in him they are strengthened!

These are the words sung in the Orthodox liturgy on Easter morning.

The Jewish Passover (see chapter 10, pages 137–44) enabled the children of Israel to go through the Gate of Men. The Christian Passover enables all to pass through the Gate of the Gods.

In Christ, man becomes upright in the fullness of the gifts from Eden. And in the words of a Eucharistic prayer he sings: "You have wonderfully created man's dignity, but even more wonderfully, you have restored it, regenerated it, resurrected it" (from the offertory in the Roman liturgy).

This is "Christian triumphalism," false if it is expressed on the psychological level, correct if it exults on the spiritual level.

When he descended into hell, Christ espoused his mother of the depths, Adam espoused *adamah*. The Beloved no longer "brings forth thorns and thistles" (Genesis 3:18), but gives out the fragrance of her seeds. The curse of the Fall has been undone. The laws governing the relationship between man and earth are overthrown. Death has been vanquished, pain done away with. Malkhut, the Queen, has received the King's visit. She has been raised with him into the heights and receives the Crown: Keter.

The ascension of Christ is an extension of his resurrection and brings it to completion.

The apostle Paul on the road to Damascus knew the firstfruits of this experience. He links the two moments that make it up: "Now that he ascended, what is it but that he also descended first into the lower parts of the earth? He that descended is the same also that ascended up far above all heavens, that he might fill all things" (Ephesians 4:9–10).

CHAPTER 15

Access to the Upper Triangle: Keter-Hokhmah-Binah; the Neck; the Seven Cervical Vertebrae and the Nine Angelic Hierarchies; the Thyroid; the Medulla Oblongata

THE NAME OF THE NECK, *TSAVAR* (צואר), BEGINS WITH THE LET-ter *tsadi* (צ), a divine fishhook, seizing man to bring him to the light, *aor* (אור).

The same ideography is present in *oref* (עורף), the word for the nape of the neck, literally, release (ף) from the coat of skin, *aor* (עור).

The man with a "stiff neck" resists being seized by the divine *tsadi* and so refuses to flow back to his source, *ayin* (ע), in order to be healed, *raf* (רף). Consequently his wings (*of*, עוף = "bird") cannot be stretched.

"My soul chooseth strangling, and death rather than my life," said Job (7:15), harpooned and thrashing about, before becoming a little child again. The strangling may be read in the root *tsar* (צר) of the word *tsavar* (צואר), for here is where, archetypically, the *alef* (א), Elohim, withdraws to leave room for יהוה condensed in the *yod* ('), the Seed, which is also the pommel of the Sword, the Alpha and Omega of Creation.

In this primary *shabbat*, the Father deposits the seed of the divine Son (') as the principle of Creation. This is why the *yod* and not the *alef* forms the pommel of the Sword, הוה, head and principle of man.

Whatever head we place on our shoulders as we evolve, it continues to retain the image of the sky it symbolizes, partaking in the *alef* (א), whose primitive ideogram is the head of a horned animal.

When man places his final head on his shoulders by giving birth to the Seed, *yod*, he has ripened, he suffers this strangling to return to the Father, א, Elohim.

We recall (see chapter 4, page 25) that the first three sefirot, Keter-Hokhmah-Binah, forming the Tree's Upper Triangle, refer to divine transcendence, even though they have emerged from the *ain* (אין), the Great Darkness of the divine. They are called the Greater Countenance, are only revealed in divine immanence under a veil, and unfold into the seven other sefirot, called the "sefirot of construction" or Lesser Countenance.

We may imagine a kind of prism between the Greater and the Lesser Countenance; through it the Divine Triunity unfurls in a sevenfold rhythm with its boundless creative potential. The seven colors, the seven sounds, the seven days that structure our visible world proceed from it. This prism, acting as a relay station between Divine Thought and its sevenfold execution, appears, then, to contain the One and the sevenfold and to be defined as one and sevenfold itself.

The seven-stringed lyre given to Orpheus by Apollo symbolized the gift of God, the unknowable Word, making himself known in seven modes of vibration, which also correspond to the seven traditional heavens and are symbolized by our seven cervical vertebrae.

Above the seven cervical vertebrae is the thyroid gland. From the Greek *thuroídos*, "door-shaped," the thyroid seems to be the gate from the One to the sevenfold and the gate of the return from the sevenfold to the One. Curiously, this gland secretes iodine, in which I can hear the word *yod* (French: *iode*).

Called the Adam's apple, it is the pommel of the Sword, the *yod*, the Word. Anatomically, it is the base of the tongue and hence symbolizes the Logos, the Word. Physiologically, it acts directly on growth.

Adam, as seed within the secret of the *yod*, was commanded by

Elohim to grow: "be fruitful and multiply, and replenish the earth." Symbolically, this is the place of the sefirah Daat.

Daat (דעת) is not found in the body of the ten sefirot. It means Knowledge and is a kind of eleventh sefirah, situated by tradition on the way between the Gate of the Gods to Keter.

It is the seed and the fruit of the Tree of Knowledge.

He who becomes this fruit and plucks it becomes Word and opens the "path to the Tree of Life," guarded by the Sword and the Cherubim after the Fall.

So the body here registers "above" what is played out in the depths of the underworld.

Seven heavens open up before man, like so many steps he has to climb before the sublime union. They are described in the Hebrew tradition by the word *hekhalot*, the "palaces."[1] The "man above," Elohim, wraps himself in these *hekhalot* as in a mantle. Each twist, each palace, is like the rung of a ladder, whose form is beyond human imagination but is symbolically represented by our "bulb" (of spinal marrow), or in French, *bulbe rachidien*, "the bulb of the spinal column," the term used for the medulla oblongata).

Bolbós, in Greek, means "onion." Like an onion wrapping robes around its center, the seven heavens are wrapped around Divine Light, whose brightness they pass on hierarchically through successive veils until it reaches the Gate of the Gods.

During his return journey through the Gate of the Gods, man goes through these palaces wherein he is clothed with successive robes. These are symbols of the divine mantles of light and enable him progressively to reach the Splendor of Splendors: he has given birth to the Divine Child and passes from the dimension of the Mother to that of the Bride.

The Virgin and Mother become Bride and Queen.

The final robe is the wedding garment.

This royal apparel adorns the bride, who is introduced into the king's chamber, Keter.

These palaces correspond to the angelic dwelling places.

The most complete treatise on angelology we possess, the *Celestial Hierarchies*, was written by Dionysius the Areopagite, also called Pseudo-Dionysius. He seems to have entered the mystery and experienced it firsthand before attempting to express it. In this sense at least, he is authentic. He reveals that these heavenly hosts—divine, created energies—transmit the Divine Light through successive degrees. Each degree is structured, ordered, illuminated, and unified by one of the hierarchies.

There are three triads within these angelic hierarchies.

The first surrounds the heavenly Throne. Made up of Seraphim, Cherubim, and Thrones, it partakes of divine transcendence and corresponds to the Tree's Upper Triangle.

The second triad consists of Virtues, Dominions, and Powers. It receives light from the first and corresponds to the first inverted triangle. It brings order to the worlds and arrays them in beauty.

The third consists of Principalities, Archangels, and Angels. This triad is the agent of divine economy in relation to man. It guides and controls him, fashions his destiny, works according to the law of numbers, and corresponds to the second inverted triangle.

And Dionysius might have said about the celestial hierarchies what he said about the ecclesiastical hierarchy, which reflects them: "Know that our hierarchy communicates a science, an inspiration, and a perfection whose nature, whose principle, and whose results are truly divine."

Through the angelic worlds, the Divine Light emerges from its hiding place and shares itself out in a grand harmony of sounds, colors, smells, and all of what Creation can taste to draw life. It then returns to its secret place, enriched by Creation, albeit perfectly rich already.

If someone knows how to enter into these divine vibrations and let himself be carried along by this movement of return to the heart of the secret, he must know the reversal in the experience of putting on the nine angelic "bodies."

The body concretely inscribes the principle of this reversal (see chapter 5, pages 51–52). For the medulla oblongata is where the fibers coming from the right hemisphere of the brain and going to the left side of the body cross with those coming from the left hemisphere and going to the right side of the body.

More subtly, on the energy plane, three important meridians cross at this same level.[2]

This passage from right to left and vice versa also corresponds to the passage from the Later Heaven to the Earlier Heaven (see chapter 6, page 57). But the Earlier Heaven thus recovered, which before the Fall was burdened with the unaccomplished, is now completely accomplished. It was then the west of Eden; now it is the east. The Cherubim and Seraphim encountered in the depths of hell are met in the light. They open the gates to the path of the Tree of Life, Keter, the path of the Ain Sof . . . Ain . . . "Nothing."

Christian liturgy celebrates each of the nine hierarchies during the nine days separating Ascension from Pentecost. Symbolically, this time marks the nine steps that the Son of Man ascends in his return to the Father, יהוה returning to Elohim.

"Touch me not: for I am not yet ascended to my Father" (John 20:17), says the Risen Christ appearing to Mary Magdalene.

Before his death, Christ had already spoken of this, but his disciples did not understand: "I came forth from the Father, and am come into the world: again, I leave the world, and go to the Father. . . . It is expedient for you that I go away: for if I go not away, the Comforter will not come unto you; but if I depart, I will send him unto you" (John 16:28–7).

Pentecost, the pouring forth of the Holy Spirit on the apostles, is the beginning of his pouring forth into the world.

The Holy Spirit introduces experience of the universal. We shall look at this by studying the Upper Triangle, or the cranial Cinnabar Field, which contains its secret.

CHAPTER 16

The Ear and the Tongue;
Listening and the Word;
the Red Phase of the Work

IN THE HEBREW TRADITION, MAN GOING THROUGH THE GATE OF the Gods goes through seven palaces and clothes himself with the light of nine angelic hierarchies, whereas in Dante, he accedes one after the other to ten celestial spheres.

In this context of Paradise, each sphere is the body of a planet. As Dante numbers them, we find the traditional construction of our solar system, based on the Tree with its ten sefirot—"sphere" and "sefirah" being the same word.

From within the first sphere, Malkhut, the Earth, man reaches the second sphere, the Moon (Yesod); then the third, Mercury (Hod); the fourth, Venus (Netsah); the fifth, the Sun (Tiferet); the sixth, Mars (Din); the seventh, Jupiter (Hesed); the eighth, Saturn (Binah); and finally the ninth sphere, the stars. Within the ninth sphere, he sees the Divine Essence manifested in the angelic choirs. Entering the tenth sphere, he is introduced to the Empyrean, here identified with the Ain Sof. This is the ultimate birth of the God-Man, the opening of the final chakra, the crown chakra (Keter: Crown).

In this celestial experience, Saturn, originally linked with Malkhut in man, has now reached the Upper Triangle: the feet have joined the head (see chapter 7, page 79). The crown in Keter reunites the small Saturnian crowns of the knees. Lead has turned into gold.

But before experiencing this "single crown," man puts on his shoulders the successive heads previously studied, particularly in the story of Job. They all symbolize different stages of the human being working toward his universal and divine dimension.

From childhood onward, the cranial Cinnabar Field, the Upper Triangle, is a symbol of the sky compared with the two other triangles. One, below, is a symbol of the earth. The other, at the level of the thorax, symbolizes man's encounter with himself on successive planes of communication.

In the diagram of the Temple of man, the nave, entered after purification by water, is the rectangle for the incarnate life and baptism by fire of the thoracic level.

The choir, where the mysteries are celebrated, corresponds to the head. The mysteries also have several stages. Lifting the veil on the final stage means gathering heaven and earth within man in an ineffable embrace.

From birth onward, the egg-shaped head, the shape of the face, and the cranial functions amount to a single, powerfully dynamic project, in view of this very embrace.

The face brings together, concentrates on a higher level, and repeats in a major mode everything the body has hitherto revealed. The ears correspond to the sefirah Malkhut and more particularly to the feet.

The angle of the lower jaw, where its two axes, vertical and horizontal, meet, corresponds to the knee; its vertical axis to the leg, its horizontal axis to the thigh. The latter axis opens into the mouth, itself corresponding to the sefirah Yesod (the "secret of the *yod*"). The nose

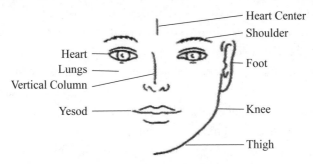

Facial Correspondences

is the middle path at this level. It corresponds to the spinal column. The cheeks recapitulate the lungs. The eyes correspond to the heart and the hands; the arch of the eyebrows corresponds to the shoulders.

But at the root of the nose, between both eyes, "the eye with three-fold vision" corresponds to Tiferet as the heart center. The entire skull is, as it were, the head of the head. Its forehead is the pelvis. The hair at this level corresponds to the kidneys and to our roots in heaven.

The face also represents the marriage of the masculine and feminine poles. The lower part of the face can be seen to be feminine, echoing the female genitals: the eustachian tubes connect each ear with the mouth, as the fallopian tubes connect each ovary with the uterus.

The upper part of the face echoes the male genitals, the nose corresponding to the penis, and the eyes to the testicles.

The ovaries and testicles develop near the kidneys. They are, as it were, their twins, and the kidneys continue to give them their procreative power.

The urogenital organs in men and women are undifferentiated in the first few weeks of fetal life.

The same goes for their counterpart, the audiovocal organs. Only from the fifth week in utero do the organs of hearing and speech become differentiated, at the same time as the urinary organs become distinct from the genitals.

The Ear

Symbolically similar to the feet and kidneys, the ears are shaped like a seed. They also recapitulate the entire body, which has given rise to auricular therapy or ear acupuncture.[1]

This medical technique, after the traditional method of acupuncture, brings together in the ear alone the points intended to invigorate a given part of the body. For according to the lines of harmonic correspondence linking the ear to the whole body, a given point on the ear, when stimulated, resonates with the precise part of the body with which it is linked.

The author of this therapeutic method says it may well have been used (empirically perhaps, but genuinely) from time immemorial: "In Egypt under the Pharaohs, women would pierce their ears for birth control; the Scythians cauterised the pinna of the ear in cases of impotence, and Valsalva [Italian doctor, 1666–1723] did the same to calm toothache. During the last century a large number of French doctors, good ones too, would still burn the root of the helix to cure sciatic pain."

Japanese acupuncture sees a similar correspondence between the feet and the rest of the body. This technique is based on the same principle as auricular therapy and makes use of the foot as a seed.

The feet "listen" to the earth in order to filter information—on several levels—so that they may stand on solid ground, and the kidneys filter water and blood (fire) in order to distribute energy above and below. Likewise the ears filter the air, which symbolizes the divine breath.

The ears bring together the functions of feet and kidneys in the cranial Cinnabar Field. Their fundamental vocation is to enable man to become fully upright, to bring him from the unaccomplished multiplicity of the function of speech toward the accomplished unity of his function as Word.

The creative Word has veiled his glory and hidden himself at the heart of Creation, in the depths of the matter he fashioned with his outbreath (see chapter 1, pages 3–4). Man the microcosm conceals the Word within him. Man's growth in all senses, including physical development, is but the formidable germinating force of the *theós*, the *yod*, returning to Divine Unity, the *alef*, through his inbreath. I am speaking of a complete growth, from which, as a result, physical development is inseparable.

The first manifestation of this *theós* is the cry of the child emerging into the air at birth. Man's cry, whenever uttered, is always a reassuring return to the *arkhós* ("leader," "chief"), the state nearest the Word and the most ontological. His entire life is a gradual elaboration of this cry, which becomes language, then song, and finally silence at the heart of which the *arkhé*, the Word, is reached. Man is born from the great Divine Silence and can only return to it when he is capable of perceiving it, for man only speaks insofar as he hears. His growth is limited by the range of what he hears. His speech expresses his evolution, and one confirms the other. Both depend on his capacity to listen.

The ear thus moves from perception through the amniotic fluid in the maternal womb to perception of the awesome Divine Silence. The vibrations received during this gradual evolution modulate and structure man in order progressively to adapt him for his new births.

Man, with the final head, the third level in the diagram of the body, becomes Word, structured by the silence he is able to perceive. He extracts the *theós* from the cosmic mass.

But he cannot receive and hear this silence without having previously perceived all the vibrations necessary for this final construction, which depends on earlier constructions.

What is acquired in utero is important (see chapter 7, page 81), because what was not received by hearing through the amniotic fluid is extremely difficult to recover later.

Dr. Alfred Tomatis recounts significant experiments with birds: "eggs of songbirds hatched by nonsinging birds give birth to nonsinging birds."[2] He has perfected a treatment for children who are mute but not deaf. It consists of an attempted recreation of the milieu of the mother's womb in order to bring such children to "remember" their fetal life. The child hears recordings of the mother's voice through liquid. Can it thus recover what its mother was unable to give at the proper time?

This eminent therapist describes spectacular recoveries. They confirm my conviction: the child who, as fetus, fails to receive the affective vibrations necessary for its psychological structuring runs the risk of psychological handicap for the rest of its life. And this remains true at all stages of its evolution.

Many current methods of psychotherapy are centered on the importance of expression, combined with the importance of communication. But actually I think that problems relating to utterance depend for the most part on a blockage at the reception stage. Whether because the "earth" was not cultivated or was not sowed, or whether it received poisoned seeds, it cannot express the wealth it potentially holds.

As long as the ear resonated in harmony with the sounds of nature, or with a music built to harmonize with man's inner structures, he was not engaged in self-destruction. The noisy frenzy of our towns, pseudo-music founded on a din amounting to the disintegration of sound, hymns that are childishly sentimental rather than authentically spiritual, all encourage the deadly plants of our being to proliferate.

The curse relating to the ground that shall bring forth "thorns also and thistles" (Genesis 3:18) concerns this earth from which Adam was

Ears Listening to Feet.
The fundamental vocation
of the ears open to
consciousness is to ensure
the uprightness of man so
that he can become Word.
(Chartres Cathedral.)

formed (Genesis 2:7). His "disobedience" deprived it of the Divine Seed.

Hence it is urgent for man's listening to become inward.

Hence also Israel's chief prayer, beginning with these words: "*Shema Israel*" ("Hear, O Israel"), repeated like a mantra. Now the first word שמע, *shema*, is made up of the root שם, *shem*, which is the Name, the Divine Name par excellence. The last letter, *ayin* (ע), has a numerical value of 70. According to Kabbalistic tradition, it expresses all 70 divine names, multiple and one!

The letter *ayin* (ע), meaning "source" or "eye," conveys above all that the Name can only be heard at the source of being. Listening is the "eye" of the Name.

In our listening, our secret Name, our participation in יהוה, can be discovered. How?

Returning to the notion of uprightness (see chapter 11, pages 157–58), we remember the crucial part played by the Adam's feminine in the work of becoming upright, to the extent that Adam designates *ishah* by that quality he knows she alone is capable of bestowing: "The woman whom thou gavest that I might stand straight" (Genesis 3:12). The ear, a feminine organ, receptive par excellence, is linked with this theme.

Quoting again from Tomatis: "The body straightens up so that the ears can attend and man, in order to become wholly ear, a kind of aerial tuned in to language, is endowed with a nervous system which answers to this function."[3]

In the mother's womb, the child is a large ear, receiving complete information from the world of archetypes that permeate it and sounds from the world of its mother. It hears and registers, but is not yet aware.

In Tomatis's view, both the child's development in utero, and its growth for the rest of its life, are secretly brought on by the demands of its speech function, which brings the adult man—and this is what being adult is about—to become that great ear in the cosmic matrix, capable of hearing the totality of information in order to become it, to become Speech-Word. Tomatis's scientific experiments confirm what tradition asserts: from conception, man's function as Word, his participation in the speech that is his Name, lead him on, as Adam is led forward from the origin (principle) of his creation by יהוה.

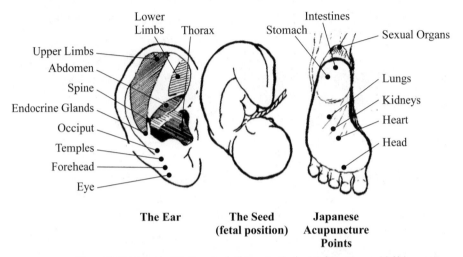

The Ear   **The Seed (fetal position)**   **Japanese Acupuncture Points**

(From P. Nogier, *Traité d'auriculothérapie*, Paris: Maisonneuve, 1969.)

"It is as though the ear was given precedence in the role of triggering the later amplification of the nervous system," says Tomatis; "the ear is given the nervous system in order to introduce the function of speech."[4] He thus overturns the classical notions of ontogenesis, which continue to give precedence to the nervous system and see sensory functions as subsequently added on to it.

This reversal means that the labyrinth becomes central. Everything else is organized around this primordial organ of the internal ear and its energy.

The secret at the heart of the labyrinth of the ear is a growth-inducing force with an inspiring purpose. This converges with the fundamental theme of many myths and with the theme of a universal mystical quest in which labyrinths and mandalas are symbolic objects for meditation. This secret—the Name—has its root within the first embryonic cell, which is programmed in view of this sole objective: speech.

Fundamentally man is nothing but Word. He is born to become his

Name. This is ingrained in the inmost texture of the embryonic labyrinth and organizes everything around itself, from the night of the womb
onward. Man, created by the Word of God, bears within him a hidden
vibration fashioning, sculpting, modulating, and singing him until he
becomes Word.

The Hindu tradition says that the primordial sound AUM is enclosed
in the conch, *shanka*, and that this conch has the same design as the
human ear.[5]

The cochlea within the internal ear is the *kokhlías*, which means
"conch" or "shell" in Greek. We are spontaneously aware of this when
listening to the sound of the sea in a shell.

The same Hindu tradition calls Creation *shruti*, which literally
means "what is heard." As René Guénon writes,"It is enclosed from the
beginning in the *shanka* conch containing the AUM."[6]

The conch in the ear is therefore the cochlea, which, with the labyrinth, forms part of the internal ear. It is the most archaic part of our
structure.

In India, as in Tibet, the monosyllable AUM is ritually intoned as
the primordial and imperishable sound, the Name of the Word made
manifest.

It is sounded on several levels within the cranium, so that the last vibration is distinctly nasal, thus stimulating the rhinencephalon, the most
archaic part of the brain. It thus nurtures the awakening of the Divine
Word in man (see chapter 20, page 363).

This last vibration is close to the one induced by the letter N, so
there is a close connection between the sound AUM and the sound that
resonates in the *amen* of the Hebrews. *Amen* (אמן) is an untranslatable
word, for no concept contains it. As with all Hebrew words, its very
body is alive and extends to the sharp edge of its spirit, which makes
the person intoning it correspond completely to the reality of the Divine
Mystery.

AUM, like *amen*, is centered on motherhood, אם, *em*, in Hebrew,
which obliges us to a series of deaths (to one earth) and resurrections (to
another) until we attain the dimension of the Word, with which the letter

N is linked. The final *nun* of the word אמן is the Leviathan, the ultimate fish of the deep, symbolizing our last mutation. It is also the final letter of the word *ben* (בן), "son," our ultimate reality.

The letter N of the word *amen* stresses with even greater precision than the AUM the successive incarnations to which our inner begettings lead, right up to the one that opens the kernel hidden within the assembly of the cochlea and labyrinth. Embryologically, this assembly was united with the rhinencephalon. Throughout life it continues to inform that olfactory part of the brain, which is the Alpha and Omega of the human adventure (see chapter 20, page 363).

Insofar as the ear is analogous to the entire body, this third part, known as the "internal ear," corresponds to the head and is in charge of balance and uprightness. Wisdom and Understanding govern it.

Balance and uprightness outside are symbols of the same qualities within, which this part of the ear essentially ensures.

The middle ear is made up of the cavity of the eardrum, in which the three auditory ossicles—the stirrup, the anvil, and the hammer—refer to the tools of the forge.

The work of accomplishment in the forge, on the second floor of the body, corresponds to the work of the middle ear, that is, to relay sounds and control pressure.

The outer ear is made up of the auditory canal and the pinna. In contrast with animals, the pinna of the human ear is not mobile, but is much more intricately chiseled.

The animal moving about solely in the outside world has no other means of defense than speed of movement, so it requires this capacity to sweep around for instant information.

The delicate complexity of the pinna in man is shaped by his understanding, which economizes on outward movement, and hence on the information it brings, in order to bring inner listening to bear. An adult who has begun to integrate his animal nature ought to move about in the outer world only in accordance with inner listening. All restlessness then disappears. The human ear thus appears as an organ of inner listening, attending entirely to the heart of the labyrinth, which, once heard, provides the key to the path of the Name and then the key to the Name itself. It opens out onto the universality of Creation.

The heart is only heard by those who, like John the apostle "in the divine secret," lay their ear upon it. For the heart of the labyrinth is also Christ, the Word, present in each one of us.

The heart of the labyrinth is only heard by the person who has become completely upright because he has fully wed himself in the sanctuary of the forge.

The fetus, a great ear, as it were, in the maternal womb, only emerges when its blood totally sustains its spirit, that is, its Name in embryonic form. Likewise when man, like a fetus accomplished inside the cosmic matrix, becomes the great ear hearing his Name, he is ready to be born.

Because he knows his Name, he becomes Word.

The upper part of the heart, image of the Word (see chapter 12, page 236), is made up of two "auricles" whose subtle function coincides with that of the ears.

The heart beats only in order to hear.

Hearing, it will see.

"Blessed are the pure in heart: for they shall see God" (Matthew 5:8).

Because he had not ears to hear the angel utter the name he was to give to his son, Zacharias lost the power of speech for nine months (Luke 1:20).

The Christian tradition speaks of the "Eucharist of the Word." Hindu mantras agree with this idea of Word as nourishment. This nourishment is received through the ear, etymologically connected with the notion of "opening." The mouth, which receives physical food, is also an "opening"—from its Latin root os, oris.

"Ephphatha, that is, Be opened," Christ says to the deaf man, brought to him by his disciples so that he may be cured (Mark 7:32–37), "And straightway his ears were opened, and the string of his tongue was loosed, and he spake plain."

And Mark, insisting on the close connection between ear and speech, tells of the admiration of the disciples who say about Jesus: "He maketh both the deaf to hear, and the dumb to speak."

In Hebrew, the ear, *ozen* (אֹזֶן), calls up the idea of obedience (a word whose root also means "opening"). When our present-day language, severed from its profound roots, makes "submit" and "obey" into synonyms, there is confusion. In reality submission is servitude, whereas obedience is liberation.

This same word *ozen* (אֹזֶן) is made up of the root *zan* (זַן), which means "species, sort." With this symbolism, the ear ensures the continuity and the growth of a species nourished by the א (*alef*), the divine power of Creation.

Thus seen, the ear receives—through the nourishing umbilical cord, which is subtly attached to the tragus—the heavenly manna that is the Name: "To him that overcometh will I give to eat of the hidden manna, and will give him a white stone, and in the stone a new Name written, which no man knoweth saving he that receiveth it" (Revelation 2:17–18).

The number 7, on which the Book of Revelation is constructed, like Genesis, to which it is a counterpoint, seems to be linked with the opening of the seven palaces. Each of the seven letters addressed to the seven churches ends with this admonition: "He that hath an ear, let him hear what the Spirit saith unto the churches."

When his last letter is written, John sees the Divine Throne in a vision.

Christian iconography does not represent Christ or the saints with big ears. It only emphasizes the egg-shaped chakra of the throat, where the energies of the Man-Word are released.

To my knowledge, there is only one example of men portrayed with long ears, which is the little characters situated at the extreme right of the lintel of the Vézelay tympanum. They have "heard"; they have become aware of their wounded feet and stagger toward uprightness and divine accomplishment.

These symbols are encountered especially in India, in the Vedantic tradition, first in the shape of the elephant with long ears and then in the Buddha.

Ganesha, son of Shiva, has an elephant's head and a man's body. He is mounted on a rat.

> His spiritual force is symbolized by the size of the head with its wide ears and its trunk, which together resemble AUM written in Sanskrit. AUM, we know, is the symbol of infinity, of supreme Reality in the form of a Sound-symbol. Imbued with Divine Light, Ganesha is weightless, as light as air. The rat beneath him is not crushed. It is a sagacious animal, clever and cunning, which can get into difficult and narrow places, and symbolizes understanding getting to the heart of the most arduous problems.[7]

The Buddha, the image of the realized man, is not only represented with elongated ears, but the lotus flower has opened out on the crown of his head.

Christian tradition rarely represents men with long ears, but it does venerate the donkey.

In the most ancient legends the donkey is connected to man's immortality and carries it in one shape or another—precious stone, flower, woman—on its back. When the donkey bears kings and popes on its back, it is because their function belongs in some way with the dimension of the eternal Adam.

An ass like Balaam's (Numbers 22:25) sees angels and hears their language. The donkey, with the ox, is present at the birth of Christ. The immortal who made himself mortal was carried first into Egypt to hide and later into Jerusalem to be exalted, on the back of a donkey.

When Christ mounted "a colt, the foal of an ass" and rode into the holy city on Palm Sunday, entering Jerusalem to die, he rode the animal "which hath ears to hear." Through this symbol he took on one aspect of our last coat of skin, the one that was now to die—as Christ was—in order to attain the garment of light and reach vision. We have

Men with Long Ears. With their long ears, these men have "heard." They have become aware of their wounded feet and are taking the road of healing. (Vézelay Basilica.)

already studied the shift from listening to vision, with Job foreshadowing Christ.

There is a play on words in Hebrew between the word the "ass's foal" and the "city," according to whether their single root (עִיר) is pronounced *air* or *ir*. The ass's foal, or the city, are the *yod* at the heart of the unaccomplished עד. Only listening to the Name enables us to enter into our last darkness, the holy ·city within us, which then becomes a city of light.

This passage can only be experienced in the inner Jerusalem. This is symbolized in the body by the final matrix: the first archetypal triangle, or cranial Cinnabar Field.

In Golgotha—the "skull" in Hebrew—Christ died on the cross. In the place where there was a garden, he was buried, and here too he rose again.

The ass's foal, our last coat of skin insofar as it means listening before reaching vision, used to be celebrated annually by a "donkey's feast." On this occasion, the donkey was ceremonially brought into church and walked around in magnificent attire, which symbolizes the coat of light hidden under the coat of skin. The folktale "Donkey Skin" recounts something similar.

The donkey is renowned for its silence, which is indissociable from its ability to listen.

In Greece, Midas, king of Phrygia, could not recognize that the sounds that the divine Apollo plucked from his cithara were finer than those of his rival. Midas was given ass's ears by Apollo.

The "donkey's bonnet" (dunce's cap) was originally given to the schoolboy or schoolgirl incapable of listening; not to shame them, but so that they should learn to understand.

Until recently Christian tradition kept alive the symbolism of the rabbit and hare. These long-eared animals used to appear on Easter cards. Easter ears and Easter eggs are part of the same symbolism of resurrection.

Similarly, the bull's ears are offered to the matador who has just given a magnificent show in a bullfight. The reward thus received is par excellence a homage to the accomplishment of the Great Work.

The origins of tauromachy go back to a sacred ritual linked with blood sacrifices. The matador, arrayed in his garment of light, pierces the heart of the black bull with his sword.

The Celts, according to Frédéric Lionel, offered to Ogmios, the god of eloquence, the ears of animals that were sacrificed by the Druids. Here ears and speech are again closely linked.

A very ancient icon of the Nativity represents the Virgin stretched out on her bed at the far end of a cave. She has just given birth to the Word. Everything is dark inside the cave—the darkness of the earth—except for a bright patch containing the Virgin, her bed, and, in the center, the God-Child.

This bright patch is shaped like an ear. A bright umbilical cord connects the Word, lying in the depths of this ear, to heaven, at the top of the cave.

Elijah, a prophet in Israel, whose Hebrew name is *Eliahu* (אליהו;
see chapter 13, page 251) "went. . . unto Horeb the mount of God" (1
Kings 19:8). He withdrew into a cave and listened. A great and strong
wind blew in front of the entrance of the cave. "The Lord was not in
the wind." And after the wind an earthquake. "The Lord was not in the
earthquake." Then a fire. "The Lord was not in the fire." And after the
fire "a still small [silent and subtle] voice."

"And it was so, when Elijah heard it, that he wrapped his face in his
mantle, and went out, and stood in the entering in of the cave."

The Hebrew word "silence," which paradoxically describes the divine Voice, is *dmamah* (דממה), containing the word *ma* (מה), "water,"
and *dam* (דם), blood. Let us enter this reality: the divine Voice cannot
be heard in the wind (air element), or in the earthquake (earth element),
or in the fire element, but only in silence, which partakes of water and
blood and hence of Spirit. "And there are three that bear witness in
earth, the Spirit, and the water and the blood: and these three agree in
one" (1 John 5:8).

It may be that silence reigns in the underwater depths, but the child's
cry marks its arrival on earth, birdsong sounds on high, and man in his
highest yearnings gives voice to song. Nevertheless, he can only recover silence by becoming seed again.

As the receptacle of the Divine Word, the ear is steeped in the waters
of a new genesis. Emerging from the matrix of the cave, Elijah is born
to a new dimension. In Adam he was created in God's image; now he
attains his likeness.

The word "silence," *dmamah* (דממה), carries within it the word
damah (דמה), "to be like." Elijah has traveled along the path leading
from image to likeness (see chapter 1, page 3, and chapter 5, page 33).
He is the Word, he is יהוה, he is the Sword. The name *Eliahu* (אליהו)
is none other than the Tetragrammaton, יהוה, in which one of the two
hehs (ה) has become אל, *El*, which means "God."

Elijah went up Mount Horeb (חרב), a word meaning "sword." Elijah climbed the mountain of the Sword because he himself became the

Sword. It sits within his throat and within his mouth.

In the first chapter of Revelation, St. John reveals that he was "as dead" before the vision of "one like unto the Son of man. . . . and his voice was as the sound of many waters. And he had in his right hand seven stars: and out of his mouth went a sharp two-edged sword: and his countenance was as the sun shineth in his strength" (Revelation 1:13–16).

The Divine Name, a two-edged Sword, is the Tree of Knowledge. The two edges, *fifiot* (פיפיות) in Hebrew, are the two "mouths" or the two breaths, the two *hehs* (ה) of the Tetragram, the two opposing manifestations of the *yod*: light and non-light. If man, who confronts the Sword, becomes light (the albedo) and non-light (the nigredo) and is killed by neither of the two edges, he has then entered the paradox and gone beyond all contradictions. He has become identified with the Sword and become his Name, in perfect likeness to God.

Only with this key can the hidden secrets of the episode in 1 Kings 18 be understood. The prophet of Israel exterminates the false prophets of Baal "by the sword." More precisely, he "cuts their throats." It is at the throat, the Gate of the Gods, that the false prophet is confronted with the Divine Name and annihilated. He has not become the Sword; his throat is cut by the Sword.

In fact, the bloody carnage described in the story is not the real subject. Underlying this is the theme of the annihilation suffered by any man whose coat of skin has not become a garment of light; when confronted with the Light-Word, he is struck down by It. Elijah, who had become Word, struck the false "Word" (false prophets); he had become the Sword and "cut the throats" of those who claimed to be the Sword.

We read in the Gospel (Luke 22:50–51; John 18:10–11) that when Christ was arrested on the Mount of Olives, "then Simon Peter having a sword drew it, and smote the high priest's servant, and cut off his right ear. The servant's name was Malchus."

Peter's sword foreshadows the Word he was to become. Psychologically it corresponds here to wordiness. Peter had not understood

the situation spiritually. He resembles us all here by "cutting," with too
hasty a judgment, into the heart of events whose deeper meaning we fail
to see, by speaking haphazardly, by using the Word to kill. A spiritual
approach would involve becoming dead to all judgment so as to discern
the works of God—often "scandalous" compared with our usual ways
of thinking.

The Hebrew word *ḥerev* (חרב), "sword," which also designates
Mount Horeb, contains formidable power. This homograph speaks of
an energy that destroys, devastates, withers, and exterminates. When
we switch the letters around, we discover the word *raḥab* (רחב), which
speaks of release, or freeing, and the root *rab* (רב), which means
growth-multiplication, the root of "be fruitful and multiply" of Genesis
1:28, concerning spiritual growth and fruit (see chapter 10, page 126).

The word *rab* (רב), meaning "multitude," connotes above all grandeur, lordship, principality. Mary Magdalene, recognizing the Risen
Christ, exclaims "Rabbi"—Master, Lord!

The word *ḥabor* (חבר), obtained by a new permutation of the letters,
means "to join, to link," or it may mean "friend." Whoever can grapple
with the power of these three letters, these three "live beings," in whatever order, without being annihilated, is "linked," joined up with the
divine (see chapter 3, page 14). And Christ says about such: "Henceforth I call you not servants . . . but . . . friends" (John 15:15).

The two letters at each end of the word, namely ח (*ḥet*) and ב (*bet*),
form a new word, *ḥob* (חב), meaning "secret, hidden." They surround
the letter *resh* (ר), which means "head." The Sword, then, appears to
carry the "head" in secret.

The head is the *yod* of the Sword-Tetragram. He who becomes identified with the Sword recovers his true head, his divine sonship. He is
"joined." Beheaded, like John the Baptist, he is regrafted onto his genuine head. Humanity recovers its true face.

We recall that Yesod (יסוד) is also the divine secret (see chapter 9,
page 111). Israel, circumcised in Yesod, gave birth to the Word. Any

man becoming Word accomplishes Yesod, the divine secret contained in the pommel of the Sword. He brings forth his real fruit on this level. Fruit springs forth and bursts like pomegranates.

This is the red phase of the Work (rubedo).

The Mouth

The tongue in the mouth is an image of the Sword and symbolizes the red phase of the Work. In Christian tradition, on the day of Pentecost, tongues of fire descended from Heaven setting the apostles ablaze, raising them to this experience. Whether it be tongues of fire, the fiery chariot taking Elijah up from the earth, or the intoxication of Noah, the red phase of the Work is undergone through fire, no longer destructive but liberating. Its symbol is the color red.

The Christian Pentecost (50 days), or "red Passover," is superimposed on the Jewish Shavuot (7 weeks = 49 days) or "harvest festival." Wheat and barley have ripened and bring forth their fruit. They are the symbol of man's fruit, the Word.

The apostles, gathered in Jerusalem with all the nations present for the feast on that day, received the tongues of fire and became drunk with the Holy Spirit. They then spoke a language understood by all, a language standing in for all languages, the one language from before Babel, whose unity was enriched by the diversity of people's tongues (the peoples being symbolized by the eleven apostles and Mary).

It was also during the feast of Shavuot, some 1200 years earlier, that Ruth had met Boaz, her *goel*. The *goel* can redeem or buy back (see chapter 12, page 212); he is the liberator. Ruth the Moabite symbolizes the nations foreign to the Hebrew people, or the nonaccomplished part in us, which is foreign to us and hence to the Name.

By entering the tent of her *goel* on the day of Shavuot, Ruth married Israel. She entered her accomplishment and freed herself, giving birth to her Name. Ruth and Boaz begot Obed, who begot Jesse, the father of David and forefather of Christ. Christ was to be the *goel* of humanity.

In Hebrew the root *gaol* (גאל) means "to free."

In heraldry the color red is called "gules," which seems to be from the French and medieval Latin word for "throat," perhaps by allusion to the open mouth of a heraldic beast.

Lined with red, the mouth opening on the final palace takes its French name (*bouche*) from the Latin *bucca*, whose etymology is the same as for "buckle" and "buckler."

The buckler or shield protects from the Sword יהוה. Its original form was a circle formed by a serpent biting its tail, which symbolizes an accomplished totality, a closed or "buckled" cycle. Once this buckle has been formed, man with his feet meeting his head appears before the Sword, his Name, symbolized by the tongue. The shield protecting him from it is symbolized by the teeth.

The dragon of the deep guarding the Name is famous for his terrifying jaws. And all guardians of the threshold inherit their role of devouring monster from him. He who loosens the jaws of Leviathan in the deep, and opens the mouth of the monster, becomes Word.

In the guise of the monster's mouth, the mouth is "liberation." It means winning the final skin and the ultimate freedom that the accomplishment of the Word is. Identified with the feminine, the mouth is *ishah*, who sealed in her depths—and now reveals—the secret of the Name; and with it, *basar* (בשר), the flesh, entirely restored to its Divine Spouse, and *basorah* (בשרה), the Good News proclaimed by the tongue that has become Logos.

In this Pentecostal feast, יהוה is returned to Elohim. No impulse of the heart, no rhythm of the lungs sustains Creation any longer. All is love and Fire.

The "covenant of Fire"—*brit esh* (ברית אש)—is consummated. Everything returns to the principle, בראשית, *bereshit*.

Saliva

Saliva seems to have great virtues. It plays an important part in the formation of the bolus and in its absorption; but its power to purify and help in scar formation is well known to those who instinctively suck wounds, uninfluenced by contemporary medical conditioning.

When we saw the gesture of the *moel*, the circumciser, sucking the wound left after the cutting of the foreskin (see chapter 9, page 118), I did not mention the part played by saliva in this ritual operation. Of course it purifies and heals the wound. But I am struck by the fact that it comes in when the *moel* makes the light shine forth with the glans of the child.

To give light back to the blind man, Christ, "when he had spit on his eyes . . . put his hands upon him" (Mark 8:23).

The word for "blind man," *iver* (עַוֵּר) in Hebrew, is the same word as the "coat of skin," which is pronounced *aor* (see chapter 3, page 21).

Christ practices a form of circumcision on the eyes of blind humanity, which is the "salt of the earth," called upon to become "light."

Saliva is perhaps linked with salt in relation to light.

If we indulge in a kind of phonetic Kabbalah, the name "saliva" contains *sal*, "salt," as well as *salva*, "salvation," the "savior."

In Hebrew, "to spit"—*yaroq* (ירק)—is the same word as *yereq*, "greenery." And green is the color of life, of eternity even (see chapter 7, page 61). Hence it is light.

To spit in someone's face—which is shame (Numbers 12:14)—is punished with leprosy, a skin disease. Spit changes into non-light for him who has spewed out his hate. But for one who is love, saliva, with speech, is light.

Saliva is indispensable to speech and closely linked with the desire for nourishment, with the desire to "eat God," to wed God.

CHAPTER 17

The Teeth

THE TEETH SEEM TO CROWN THE SWORD, OR PERHAPS THEY ARE the final bulwark encountered by man at the entrance of the final palace. Is this "circlet of fine pearls," in the poet's words, a crown? Or a portcullis?

In serried ranks behind the lips, the teeth resemble the ultimate guardian of the threshold, monster on one side of the door, Divine Reality on the other.

As stated earlier: the teeth placed before the tongue are the shield before the Sword.

Which myths confirm this image?

Teeth have the role of seeds in two Greek myths. In these tales, an army of warriors springs up from the teeth, and the hero must defeat them in a single day.

The first hero is Cadmus, the founder of Thebes.

The second is Jason.

In both cases, the teeth come from the dragon killed by Cadmus.

This monster is the guardian of the treasure par excellence. Its reptilian body is scaled with countless brazen rings, its fabulous wings are those of a bird, but its head has the golden shine of metal. Its mouth is armed with a triple row of teeth, its tongue is pointed with three sharp, quivering stings, and fire rolls in its eyes. This legendary beast guards the earth, the sky, and hell.

Cadmus defeated the monster by nailing it to an oak (the Green Tree, symbol of fecundity) by its gullet, the Gate of the Gods. "Tear out the dragon's teeth," said Pallas Athene, the soldier goddess who was born from Zeus's head wearing a golden helmet, "and sow the teeth in the earth, so that they may become the seed of a new people of renown."

From these seeds sprang up thousands of armed men. Cadmus, obeying the goddess's orders, tossed a stone into their midst. The warriors, thinking they were attacked from within, killed one another. Five valiant heroes emerged unscathed from the carnage. With Cadmus, they then became as it were the foundation stone of Thebes.

The building of Thebes, ordered by the Delphic oracle, is not unlike the building of the Holy City (the New Jerusalem of the Hebrews). We recall that the dolphin (linked to the Delphic oracle) was carrying out the orders of Neptune, the god of underwater depths, whose sceptre is the trident. In this emblem we again meet the symbol of Cerberus, a three-headed dog with a dragon's body guarding the entrance to the underworld.

Defeating Cerberus and defeating the dragon fundamentally correspond to the same truth: one must first defeat hell in order to enter the palaces and build the Holy City.

Once the monster is slain, Pallas Athene acts as guide. Since she came out of Zeus's head (the crown chakra), the virgin warrior is the only one to know this heavenly level: the "city above," of which the "city below" is an image. Thebes, like Jerusalem, only exists on earth as an image of what is in heaven.

At this point, the monster's teeth play a major role as "seeds" of the future inhabitants of the city. These inhabitants rise up as Pallas Athene did, armed and helmeted for a divine battle. What battle?

The drama unfolds around the stone thrown by the hero on the order of the goddess. Believing themselves to be attacked, the soldiers kill each other. In truth, they confront the stone. This is where stone and teeth reveal what they are.

We have frequently recalled the symbolism of stone. In Greek

Guardians of the Threshold. Devouring monsters, guardians of the threshold, are there to test those who go through the doors on the way to becoming the Word. Similarly, at the level of the body, the teeth guard the tongue. (Silk and leather embroidery, Tibet, nineteenth century, Newark Museum.)

mythology Deucalion and Pyrrha threw stones over their shoulders to repopulate the earth destroyed by the Flood. Again the stones were the seeds of a future race, born of a couple that had "emerged from the waters," that is to say, entered a process of spiritual development. Thrown over the shoulders, the stones were indeed a promise of spiritual fruit.

Each tooth of the defeated dragon plays the part of a small stone. But here we are on a higher level of the myth: the defeat of the dragon, the descent into hell, and the teeth sown in the ground in order to germinate and bear fruit all speak of the process of death and resurrection that each being becoming Word must undergo.

The warriors born fully armed and helmeted, like the goddess—who seems by her creative Word to take the part of father and mother in one—think they have been attacked by the stone thrown in their midst. They are to the stone what the elect in the Judeo-Christian tradition are to the Sword. They must confront it. Five of them survive. Five of them "reveal themselves as stone" and join Cadmus to found the Holy City.

The Sword or the stone, identified with the Word, find the fullness of their symbolic power in the Scriptures. Correspondences between the Old and the New Testaments corroborate each other on this subject: "The stone which the builders refused is become the head stone of the corner" (Psalm 118:22). The apostle Luke follows this with Christ's own words: "Whosoever shall fall upon that stone shall be broken; but on whomsoever it shall fall, it will grind him to powder" (Luke 20:18).

The apostle Paul, for his part, also refers to prophecy (Isaiah 8:14; 28:16) by saying: "Behold, I lay in Sion a stumblingstone and rock of offence: and whosoever believeth on him shall not be ashamed" (Romans 9:33).

The headstone of the corner is the foundation stone of the Temple. It is its principle and contains its completion. The first and the last, it is the Alpha and the Omega, and both are one. This is why the Holy City can only be built by those who become the foundation stone and confront the headstone of the corner.

Simon, one of the twelve, having just confessed Christ to be the Son of God, confronts the headstone of the corner, about which Christ says, "upon this rock I will build my church" (Matthew 16:18). Simon then becomes Peter (*pétra* = rock), one of the twelve foundation stones of the church.

The second Greek myth about the dragon's teeth is the myth of Jason usurping the Golden Fleece. The symbolism of the story repeats the one we have just seen, but instead of a goddess presiding over its dispositions, here Medea, the magician, manipulates the forces present with her infernal powers. None of the warriors born of the dragon's teeth survive the carnage. Satan rises against Satan, his kingdom is "brought to desolation" (Matthew 12:25).

On the other hand, the divine Kingdom, the Holy City, is built from stones, each one of which, after confronting the headstone of the corner, the Alpha and Omega of the building, has become a foundation stone.

The apostle John ends his book of Revelation with the vision of the heavenly Jerusalem. After "he that sat upon the throne said, Behold, I make all things new. . . . It is done. I am the Alpha and the Omega, the beginning and the end" (Revelation 21:5–6). John describes the city: "And the wall of the city had twelve foundations, and in them the names of the twelve apostles of the Lamb" (Revelation 21:14).

The surrounding wall of a city, its crown, once ritually marked out during the foundation ceremony, linked it with heaven more than it defended it from its enemies on earth. Its indented (toothlike) battlements have the same origin as *qeren* (קרן), "horn"—which also gives "crown."

The dental crown, the wall of the Holy City, surrounds and protects the tongue, the Sword, the Word.

Hebrew symbolism confirms this.

The "tooth" is the letter *shin* (ש), which has the shape of a trident and whose numerical value is 300. If we break it down, it is written שן and is equal to 300 + 700 = 1000 (like the horn, *qeren*, קרן, which corresponds to 100 + 200 + 700 = 1000).

We here come across the profound unity of the divine Trinitarian mystery presiding over the creation of the worlds, but especially in the symbolism of 1000 we experience unity rediscovered, reconquered, and embracing the whole of the accomplished worlds.

For the Hebrews, the letter *shin* is linked with the three patriarchs—Abraham, Isaac, and Jacob—the foundation stones of Israel supporting the twelve tribes from which the Word is born.

The tooth, *shin*, also means the "point of a rock." The truncated pyramid of Egypt is given its finishing touches. In Israel, Keter, the Crown, has been placed on the head of the crowned one. Keter (כתר) corresponds to 20 + 400 + 200 = 620.

The crowned head is he who "has made the above as the below," who has reunited the *mi* and the *ma* (see chapter 1, page 3). In Genesis, the "firmament" separating the *mi* from the *ma* (Genesis 1:6) is *raqiya* (רקיע), which corresponds to 200 +100 +10 + 70 = 380, which Keter (620) complements: 620 + 380 = 1000.

The number 380 is also found in the name of *Yeshua* (ישע), the Savior (10 + 300 + 70 = 380).

This firmament (*raqiya*) is named *shamayim* during the second day of Genesis, so the *mi* and the *ma* are indeed reunited around the letter *shin*.

Symbolically then, the tooth resembling the point of a rock is the crown and the crowned head at one and the same time. It is the completion of the Work.

The point of the "rock" (from *resh*, the head) is the crown of the head (see chapter 20, page 365).

After our study of the dog's head (see chapter 13, page 264), we may observe that the canine teeth occupy the same position in relation to the incisors as the constellation of the Dog occupies in relation to the sun at the summer solstice, or as the dog-headed characters occupy in relation to the glorified Christ in the wreath (crown) of the elect around the tympanum of the basilica in Vézelay.

Wisdom teeth, with their three roots, are related to Wisdom (Hokhmah joining Keter) and to the trident.

The trident, the scepter of Neptune, the Greek underwater god, and of Ganesha, the Hindu god of the unconscious, symbolizes the single power of the divine Tri-Unity.

The teeth are a "crown of fine pearls," but also "shields" in closed ranks before the Sword. The shields only open up when they have checked the credentials of the person entering into his dimension as Word.

The teeth are foundation stones and can only be of the same quality as the headstone of the corner, the Word.

When dream symbolism brings us images of damaged or falling teeth, we should always question our deep structures and the quality of our word. Our shields should never let an unjust word through.

"The fathers have eaten a sour grape, and the children's teeth are set on edge" (Jeremiah 31:29; see chapter 11, page 187).

Teeth, as structures, also have parental roots. We owe it to our children to give them sound ones, which requires our own holiness, or accomplishment.

CHAPTER 18

The Nose and Cheeks

THE SAP UNDERGOES THE BLACK PHASE OF THE WORK IN THE depths of the earth during winter, draws from this earth its vital juices, and incorporates them into its own being, which brings them up to the top of the tree. There, in the heat of the sun, matured by its warmth, lit by its rays, flowers blossom, then fruits appear.

The tree is characterized by its flowers and its fruits.

On this third level, the feet meet the head (see chapter 7, page 79), and the prophet exclaims: "How beautiful upon the mountains are the feet of him that bringeth good tidings, that publisheth peace" (Isaiah 52:7).

The fruits are peace.

"Peace" means going beyond struggles and contradictions and crowning duality through unity restored "upon the mountain," at the top of the Upper Triangle.

In Hebrew, "peace," *shalom* (שלם), is the same word as "accomplishment." It is also the *shem* (שם), the Name, reached at the tip of the goad (ל).

The fruits are therefore the Speech-Word and the seeds of new fruit to come. They are the many, inseparable from unity gained at the height of growth.

Fruits are characterized by their flavor: the fruits in Eden are "good for food," and the entire Tree is "pleasant to the sight" (Genesis 2:9).

The spinal column is born of Yesod, Foundation, and centered on Tiferet, Beauty. Its higher equivalent, the nose, expresses the flourishing of all the energies sublimated on this level: the flourishing of eros praised by the Song of Solomon: "Fair as the moon (Yesod), clear as the sun (Tiferet)" is the Shulamite glorified by her beloved (Song of Solomon 6:10).

"Thy nose," he sings, "is as the tower of Lebanon which looketh toward Damascus" (Song of Solomon 7:5). The tower, like the column, the ladder, or better still the tree, expresses well the symbolism of the spinal column.

In Hebrew, the "tower"—*migedal* (מגדל)—contains the root *meged* (מגד), which means "the best," what is exquisite and precious.

This tower is even more precious considing that Lebanon is a mountainous country famous for the beauty of its forests. The tower of Lebanon expresses fecundity, that is to say, the highest realization of the Green Tree.

The Hebrew word *laban* (לבן) means "white." After the black phase of the Work, and before the red phase, comes the white phase, the final sublimation, an upward climb with no descent to follow, up to the top of the tower of Lebanon.

The phrase "the one who looketh toward Damascus" (word for word: "the one who sees her face emerging toward Damascus") suggests that there is profusion, invasion, fabulous wealth, and overabundance in fecundity. In the heart of the forest, the tower is the point of emergence. It looks toward Damascus.

Damascus—*Damesheq* (דמשק) in Hebrew—is a word sparkling with countless facets. Two are essential here: it contains the word *dam* (דם), the blood, which brings life. And if we replace the last two letters, שק (300 + 100 = 400) by the letter *tav* (400), we obtain the three letters of the word "likeness" (*damot*). Man, created in the image of the divine, now emerges and looks towards his likeness, almost attaining it.

Finally, דמשק, *Damesheq*, contains the word שקד, *shoqed*, which designates the almond tree. Of all trees, the almond symbolizes man's likeness to God, man's deification. And when "the almond tree shall flourish" (Ecclesiastes 12:5) is indeed when man enters his eternity.

Permuting the letters *shoqed* (שקד)—the almond tree—gives the word קדש, *qadosh*, which means "holiness." And holiness is likeness. The name Damascus powerfully evokes all this. It was on the road to Damascus that the apostle Paul was "caught up to the third heaven . . . and heard unspeakable words, which it is not lawful for a man to utter" (2 Corinthians 12:1–6).

We have spoken of the fruits, but what of the flower, its beauty, its fragrance? Beauty! We are again in the inexhaustible wealth of Tiferet. On the level of the Upper Triangle, however, are not the features of a face harmonized around a well-proportioned nose? Does not cosmetic surgery attempt first to rebuild this "tower of Lebanon" when man has mismanaged the creator's work?

A grave responsibility is incurred by whoever takes the liberty of interfering with a nose. It is a more serious act than the actual operation implies, for through this organ the surgeon contacts much deeper elements of being. Once the scalpel has sundered them, they will not necessarily put themselves back together.

The correspondences between the nose and the spinal column ultimately concern the rising of sexuality through its different modes of expression. They are as important as those connecting the ear with the kidneys, the voice with the sexual organ.

An unshapely nose can be tolerated. The ugliest of women acquires beauty when she loves and is loved, and a different kind of beauty when she is expecting a baby. More marvelous still is the expression of the person who becomes refined on every level of his or her evolution, who "separates the subtle from the gross," who keeps chiseling away at the gross, to spiritualize it. How moving can be the beauty of a face that has experienced the depths of the underworld and already shines with the firstfruits of the encounter!

The beauty of the flower blossoming in fecundity! The word Tiferet (תפרת) contains *far* (פר), "fecundity," as we have seen (see chapter 8, page 103), but also פרת, *perot*, the "fruits" promised by the flower.

By its shape and whiteness the fleur-de-lis symbolizes the heart,

Tiferet, flooding out in both arms, Rigor and Mercy. Similarly, in the face, the flower of one's being blossoms at the root of the nose and exhales its fragrance.

"His cheeks are as a bed of spices," sings the Shulamite, "as sweet flowers" (Song of Solomon 5:13).

Here we come upon levels so rarely experienced that to speak of "the fragrance of one's being" seems a mere rhetorical device.

Yet no fragrance is more genuine than the flower of one's being, so unconsciously sought after. Man cannot give off this fragrance by himself, so he puts on perfume derived from the essences of flowers.

This is another instance of the law by which humanity puts on the outside what it is incapable of experiencing within, artificially obtaining what it is not ready to become.

In day-to-day sexuality, perfume is not the least of charms.

With a person born to his or her "becoming," however, smell is the fragrance emanating from the body that has been quintessenced in the accomplishment of the Great Work of alchemy. The body has then become the nuptial chamber of heaven and earth, and the heart beats with the rhythms of universal life.

To better understand this rarely observed reality, I strongly recommend Dr. Hubert Larcher's authoritative study.[1] Here I can do no more than quote a passage from an inspired author whose poetic language strangely illustrates the direction of my approach since the beginning of this study. The subject is Narayana, the hero in the novel by Makhali-Phal. He says:

> "In chastity I shall put forth my sap, and it shall grow like a tree, and it shall spread its branches out boundlessly, and it will rise from the testicles to the navel, and from the navel to the heart, and from the heart to the spirit, and there shall be the top of my tree, the tree of my virility, that grew upwards in chastity and around which the burden of the world will find a solid support."
>
> And, just as he said, this virility had grown in him like a tree, right up to his head . . . and one had only to see the light in his eyes to

feel permeated by the superhuman power of his virility. This virility in blossom gave out around Narayana the smell of the hero, which was probably the Adam's smell in the Earthly Paradise. This smell, which was instantly recognized and loved by a tigress, is what Christians would call the odor of man before sin.[2]

St. Isaac the Syrian mentions this "odor of Adam before sin," in his *Maxims* (84): "When a man of humility draws near to wild beasts, no sooner have they considered him than their ferocious nature is tamed: they approach him as their master, with heads low, licking his hands and feet, because they smell the same scent coming from him as the scent Adam gave out before the Fall."

Reinstated in the palaces, man recovers the state of Paradise. The fragrance exhaled by the sexuality of the human being who has reached this level of evolution bears witness to a state of supreme virility, beside which ordinary virility appears feeble and risible. Animals recognize it, and hence serve the person giving it out.

The wolf of Gubbio had this in common with Naryana's tigress: that it devoted itself to the person of St. Francis and served him. Wild beasts, supposed to devour martyrs, sometimes lay down at their feet.

"How many rishis, in India, walk unharmed through jungles popu-lated by wild animals and poisonous snakes?"[3]

There are many cases in Christian hagiography, as well as in other traditions, of people whose bodies exhaled sweet smells before or after their deaths. In the West, rationalism with its superior smile has rel-egated this subject to the realm of legend. This attitude falls short of scientific rigor. Let us at least be courageous enough, with Dr. Larcher, to investigate it. We shall then begin to understand that legend too be-longs with the Logos structuring the foundations of Creation, that is to say, its ontological laws.

The scent of flowers is but the symbolic reflection of the scent of man who has attained the highest expression of virility, of man deified and partaking of the bright, resonant, and fragrant vibrations of God.

CHAPTER 19

The Eyes

FOR THE HEBREWS, THE ESSENTIAL PURPOSE OF THE EYES IS TO see the Divine Vision.[1]

The original ideograph of the letter *ayin* (ע) in Hebrew is the shape of an eye—the meaning of the word. The "eye," *ayin* (עין), corresponds to 70 and implies the death necessary for resurrection. This 70 is linked with the black phase of the Work, which is the marriage with the mother, one of the two poles of the divine marriage, of which every actual wedding is a symbol. When this trial ends, the eyes of those who were "in darkness and the shadow of death" are opened to Divine Vision.

"I have heard of thee by the hearing of the ear: but now mine eye seeth thee," says Job to the Lord (Job 42:5).

When Noah came out of the ark, he was open to this same vision and shone with such fire that when his three sons approached him, the first two walked backward while the third looked within and told without what he had seen. He was called Ham, the hot one, and became a slave to his brothers.

The word *ayin*, "the eye," also means the "source" (wellspring), confirming that vision and vision of the depths are the same.

In addition, the letter *ayin* (ע), which corresponds to 70, is close to its sister letter, the *zayin* (ז), which corresponds to 7. The ideograph of *zayin* represents an arrow piercing an animal's skin. This arrow symbolizes the male power given to man so that he may undertake his inner marriages and reach the successive levels of consciousness from which our "layers of skin" separate us.

The eye can thus be identified with the arrow that pierces our coat of skin and brings with it the vision of a world transcending the one in which our fallen state imprisons us. The piercing of our animal skin symbolizes the piercing of our conditioning to the world cognizable by the senses. The eye then appears as the organ of vision for the transcendental world, the world of the divine.

Paul the apostle, caught up to the third heaven, became blind to the ordinary world (Acts 9:7–9; 2 Corinthians 12:2). Yet this experience— undergone by a man who said about Christ, "Now that he ascended, what is it but that he also descended first into the lower parts of the earth?" (Ephesians 4:9)—must have involved a descent into hell. And Paul's blindness following the white phase of the Work leaves open the question of the black phase of the Work, which he must have undertaken in the following three days, though he says nothing about it.

Some time after the Transfiguration, Christ was laid in the tomb (see chapter 13, page 272). He remained there three days, as Jonah before him remained in the darkness of the whale's belly.

Paul regained his sight only when Ananias, a disciple of the Lord, laid hands upon him.

Blindness is found in many myths. The example of St. Paul is all the more striking because it was actually experienced. Wherever found, blindness symbolizes the darkness of the labyrinth experienced no longer through childish ignorance, but by consciously returning to the archaic state of the knowing child.

Only when Isaac was blind did he bless his son Jacob. The latter had just usurped the birthright and had put on the Red Man's coat of skin, in order to accomplish the Green Man destiny of his race (see chapter 7, page 92). Isaac responded to this calling on the level of his being. The age at which he died, 180 years, "full of days" (Genesis 35:28–29), means that he had accomplished his destiny.

Because the second patriarch goes through his own nether labyrinth, symbolized by blindness, he fosters the rise of the divine for his race.

Beginning with Abraham and Isaac, the Tree continued to grow through Israel.

The grand myth of Oedipus (chapter 7, page 82), if read on the higher octave of Reality that this book hopes to open to the reader, is not a moral tale. Oedipus's blindness is linked with his marriage with the Mother, and the Widow, too, meaning the black phase of the Work, without any notion of punishment for disgrace.

Oedipus's daughter, Antigone, who guided her father, is one of many guides who have accompanied travelers into the Great Darkness. Only Christ, the Son of God, descended alone into hell. But the cosmic dimension of that ordeal goes beyond all norms.

Another myth throws a striking light on the close relationship between the eye and the solar plexus and, more specifically, between the eye and the heart. This is the biblical story of Tobit.

The Story of Tobit

The aged Tobit was virtuous. His patience is compared with that of Job. Like Job, he had a trial to undergo: struck with blindness, he did not cease to pray and praise God. Sarah, a virgin, was praying to God elsewhere at the same time. Seven men had married Sarah one after the other, and each had been killed by an evil spirit as soon as they entered the bridal chamber.

Tobit and Sarah prayed that they might hear no more reproach; and Sarah, that she might be "taken out of the earth." "So the prayers of them both were heard before the majesty of the great God. And Raphael was sent to heal them both" (Tobit 3:15–17).

In Hebrew, Raphael is the divine physician; רף, *raf*, is the "healer." With this root, we encounter again the two letters that, when inverted, govern the rising of fecundity: *far* (פר). *Raf* (רף) corresponds to 200 + 800 = 1000, namely: unity regained through healing.

This healing, which is the rubedo, or red, phase of the Work, also involves the other phases.

Tobit's blindness refers to the black phase of the Work. Tobit knew he was going to die. Thinking it to be the death of the body, he stated his last wishes and entrusted his son Tobias with the task of collecting a debt that a certain Gabael had contracted with him.

The journey undertaken by Tobit's son—his other self—on behalf of his father is an expression of wandering in the darkness of the labyrinth experienced on this level of Being.

As with all such travelers of quality, Tobias receives his guide in the person of Raphael, whose true identity is unknown. Coming out of his home, the text says, "he found a young man standing, full fair, and girded up as ready to go" (Tobit 5:5, Vulgate).

Here is a striking illustration of the fundamental law governing the development of every being: when the disciple is ready, the master appears. It is up to the disciple to recognize him.

Tobias does not recognize the guide's identity, but he does recognize his quality.

The journey begins.

Tobias's dog followed and often went before the travelers by night. The tale only recounts the nocturnal episodes of the journey. They are, then, the journey into darkness undergone by the elder Tobit within himself, which the myth projects onto the events undergone by the outer "son."

Tobias stopped by a river to wash his feet, when suddenly a huge fish leaped out of the water to devour him.

Here we find all the symbols studied in the black phase of the Work: the dog, night, water, purification of the feet, and finally this *dag ha-gadol*, this great fish, brother of the whale who swallowed Jonah, of Job's Leviathan, and of the Hindu Makara.

Frightened, Tobias obeyed Raphael's command, drew the fish out of the water, gutted it, and kept on one side the heart, the gall, and the liver. These major elements of the solar plexus "are necessary for useful remedies," says the guide. Raphael commanding Tobias to remove the heart from the big fish is like יהוה in his speech to Job (see chapter 13, pages 253–54) gouging the heart of Leviathan out of its magma. The two characters Job and Tobias seem to be caught up in the same experience of the deep.

Smoke rising from the heart burning on coals "through the power of God casts out all manner of evil spirits . . . the gall is good to anoint the eyes with for healing." There is some confusion between liver and heart. In some versions of the text both are used to drive out Sarah's demons; in others only the liver. Remembering that the liver (see chapter 12, page 224, and chapter 14, page 290) is the power of immortality and has a close relationship in Hebrew with the Divine Name, we penetrate at this level the mystery of the encounter of יהוה and the Adversary, the mystery of access to the divine dimension in man. This takes place in Tiferet.

The two wayfarers set off again, equipped with these remedies and accompanied by the dog. The second night, Tobias wondered where they were to stay. The angel revealed that Sarah lived nearby, that they were to spend the night at her parents' house, and that this young maid must become his wife. At the house they were greeted with joy by Sarah's parents, who recognized in Tobias the son of a dear cousin. Tobias then asked for the young woman's hand in marriage.

In this myth, as in nearly all those we have examined in connection with the black phase of the Work, marriage is the chief symbol of unity regained in the death of duality. Just as Noah came out of the Ark with his wife, and as Utnapishtim through the same ordeal achieved the divine dimension with his wife (see chapter 10, page 136), so Tobias emerged from the wedding chamber after confronting the Satan.

At the wedding feast at Cana, Christ alludes to his own imminent wedding, his death, his descent into hell (see chapter 13, page 271). Tobias, entering the wedding chamber, confronted the tomb. He obeyed his guide, took the fish's liver from his bag, and burned it on the live embers.

"Then the Angel Raphael took the evil spirit, and bound him in the desert of the utmost parts of Egypt" (Tobit 8:3).

During the night, Sarah's father, who had already buried his daughter's seven husbands, began digging a grave for Tobias. He could not believe the Angel who had assured him that the God-fearing Tobias was the man meant for his daughter. A maid was sent before daylight to the couple's chamber to see whether he was dead and "found them both in good health, and asleep in the same bed."

Sarah's father is Raguel, whose name means "foot" (see chapter 7, page 77). We recall that the foot, which is shaped like a seed and symbolizes the embryo, then the fetus in the womb, also symbolizes the seed that man becomes again, when, consciously "becoming as a little child," he experiences the descent "into the depth . . . the foundations of the earth . . . and the springs of the sea" (Job 38). God, who leads Job into hell, gives this place another name: "the doors of the shadow of death" (Job 38:17).

Tobias becomes "seed" again through Sarah, Raguel's daughter. He espouses his earth, which he frees from the Adversary. He espouses Malkhut; the path to Keter is free. He makes his way back toward his blind father. This is the last part of his journey—coming back up from hell. The dog is the first to emerge "above"! Tobias and his companion hasten after him.

"Then Tobias, taking the gall of the fish, smeared it on his father's eyes. After half an hour, a little white membrane, like that of an egg, began to come out of his eyes. Tobias took hold of this, drew it away and straightway his father recovered his sight" (Tobit 11:13–15, Vulgate).

Mention of the egg is no accident. Recovering sight in the sense of the myth—access to the Divine Vision—is like coming out of an egg, a birth to the divine.

Then their eyes recognized the angel Raphael. "Then they were both troubled, and fell upon their faces: for they feared." Every birth into an unknown world is marked by a cry, but in this case it is the awe and trembling of man before the sacred.

"Peace be with you," said the divine physician, "fear not," and they saw him no more.

Tobit, who had been blind for four years (symbolizing the rectangle), sings the marvels of the heavenly world he is at last able to contemplate. His soul is jubilant. Like Job, he rejoices in the riches with which he is blessed, the fruits of his tree now at the fullness of its virility.

Gall is the fire from the "matrix of fire" (see chapter 12, page 227), the gall bladder, into which man leads the energies released by the spleen-pancreas in order to accomplish them. These successive accomplishments open the doors, at each level, to a new understanding, a new vision. Gall is the sacred nectar of vision.

Up to this point I have not mentioned the recovery of the debt that Raphael undertakes by continuing the journey while the couple spend three days and three nights in the wedding chamber. In fact the completion of Raphael's journey and the final marriage of Sarah with Tobias signify the same underlying reality: the complete accomplishment of the energies contained in potential within the feminine side of Tobit, represented by Sarah. These energies are so many debts in relation to God.

Raphael binds the last demon, for the seven previous ones had been integrated through with Sarah's earlier weddings. In these weddings, Tobit died to himself, but in this final union he dies and rises again. So he recovers the light; he was blind, but now he sees. Gabael is released from his debt. *Gabol* (גבל) is the "limit." Gabael is Tobit in the final prison before his complete release, before his conquest of unity in perfect marriage, before attaining the vision of total Light.

Raphael, the divine physician, is יהוה-Christ, bringing the person who has paid his debt back to the wedding feast.

More directly than the myth of Noah or Job, the tale of Tobit emphasizes the marriage of man with his *ishah*, with his feminine, from which the Fall had turned him away, seemingly without hope of recovery.

However, the text of the Fall may be read less conventionally, so that it fits with this tale of accomplishment.

In what is commonly called the threefold curse (Genesis 3:19) cast on the three protagonists of the mythical tale, God says to Adam: "In the sweat of thy face shalt thou eat bread, till thou return unto the *adamah*; for out of it wast thou taken: for dust thou art, and unto dust shalt thou return" (Genesis 3:19).

The necessity of "returning" is twice emphasized.

In chapter 8, in which I discussed the knees, I pointed out that the man of dust was called, beyond his fallen state, to turn around and again become aware of the power of fecundity contained in his nature as dust, and to recover the integrity of his original calling.

Here I wish to underscore that the Adam has the power to restore his original norms, and this power is rooted at the very heart of his error, in the possibility he has of a loving about-turn in the direction of his inner earth, the *adamah*, which is an integral part of his *ishah*, his Spouse.

Tobias marrying Sara dies to himself seven times in order to rise in the dimension of "Son" and to "see" (see chapter 20, page 362).

Tobias's name, *tovihu* (טוביהו) in Hebrew, is יהו-טוב. *Yod-heh-vav*: just another *heh* is needed to form the Tetragrammaton.

This other *heh*, in Tobias's name, is replaced by the root *tov* (טוב), the pole of accomplished light in the tree of duality. Tobias's experience is written in his name: to attain complete light, the just man, who is already *tov*, must take on the last *heh*, the last רע, *ra*, the ultimate darkness and the ultimate marriage.

Tobias is obedient to the injunctions embodied in his name. There is his freedom, that is to say, his release. Tobias goes through the Gate of the Gods.

The Divine Vision he acquires is symbolized in many traditions by the eye in the forehead, called the "third eye."

The Eye in the Forehead: The Emerald

What is this third eye?

In the Judeo-Christian tradition we encountered it with Balaam, who prophesied, saying· "Balaam the son of Beor hath said, and the man whose eyes are open hath said: he hath said, which heard the words of God, which saw the vision of the Almighty, falling into a trance, but having his eyes open" (Numbers 24:3–4).

The opening of this mystical eye is linked with man's deification and hence is a symbol of the Tetragrammaton. Often seen in synagogues and occasionally in Christian churches, replacing the Divine Name at the center of an equilateral triangle, it is sometimes surrounded by three swords.

Psychologically, the eye is linked with guilt. Whoever feels guilty also has the sense of being looked at by this divine eye, which is his own judgment symbolized in the third eye.

In Greece we saw the Cyclopes—distinguished by their frontal eye—help Zeus dethrone Cronus and restore the kingdom to Uranus, god of the sky. This myth tells the same story, in a different form, as all myths dealing with an about-turn.

The most abundant literature dealing with the third eye is found in India. To begin with, at the heart of the Trimurti, the third eye is the chief attribute of Shiva, the god who destroys the succession of phenomena, time (Cronus), in order to construct lasting harmony, the transcendent (Uranus).

> His third eye, Trilochama, is a powerful flame that burns the god Kama (the god of carnal love), and the god of death. As the destroyer of Kama, his third eye is the symbol of the conversion from physical love to spiritual knowledge. As the destroyer of death, it is the symbol of his victory over death. . . . The third eye of Shiva is the symbol of knowledge and of illumination.

The Eagle. The eagle, the eye with threefold vision, is the guardian of the Gate of the Gods and brings man into his dimension of royalty. (Tomb of Queen Hatchepsout, Thebes, Egypt; photo by Roger Viollet.

Durga, the *shakti* of Shiva, meaning his feminine energy, is worshipped as Lakshmi, the goddess of beauty and harmony.

"At her feet, the owl, symbol and synonym of knowledge and of good omen, indicates that Lakshmi, in her perfection, is always accompanied by knowledge."[2]

The owl, which can see in the dark, is indeed essentially a symbol of knowledge, of vision going beyond the opposition of darkness and light. Vision beyond duality—such is the gift of the frontal eye, whose name, Trilochama, indicates "threefold vision," rather than just "third eye." Its middle position in the face means it belongs with the Middle Column of the Tree, the path of return to unity.

The frontal eye is related to the frontal stone, the emerald. Legend has it that the emerald adorned Lucifer's forehead, then Adam's in Paradise when Lucifer lost it. Adam fell in his turn, and the emerald fell away from him. The angels then received it, hollowed it out, and shaped from it the cup used by Christ during the Last Supper. Joseph of Arimathea kept this and collected in it the blood flowing from the side of Christ on the cross after the centurion had pierced him with his spear. This legend carries on through the myth of the Grail, the cup that was this same emerald brought to Britain by Joseph of Arimathea himself.

The emerald eye is to both eyes what the heart as center is to the heart as organ, a symbol of the Father.

The emerald filled with the precious blood is the image of the Father's hands receiving the life of the Son and giving it back through the breath of the Holy Spirit.

The emerald, with its green color, shows that the person who recovers it on his forehead, with the opening of the third eye, has integrated the Tree of Life.

The emerald—or the eye with threefold vision—is also linked with the unicorn.

Tears

A tear, *dimah* (דמעה), is the "blood" (דם) of the "eye" (ע), or "the blood at its source." It is also the "origin" (מ) of "knowledge" (דעה).

These are not emotional or sentimental tears, but tears that flow from spiritual vision.

For if someone sees and weeps over his mistakes as he goes down to his source, this source opens up and delivers the energy-information belonging to this stage—"a new heaven and a new earth" (Revelation 21:1).

Man then "straightens up"—עמד, *omed* (these are the same letters as in "tears"): man cannot become upright without tears (see chapter 11, page 158).

The gift of tears is a divine grace familiar to mystics. It brings joy.

CHAPTER 20

The Skull

The Brain

Looked at in profile, the brain has the shape of a seed, whose stalk is the brain stem.

The spinal cord expands into the brain, which is, as it were, its fulfillment after its rise up the spinal column; yet at the same time the brain is a germ, a beginning.

It is also the *yod* of the Sword-Tetragrammaton הוה, in which the *vav* has fully played its role as coordinator.

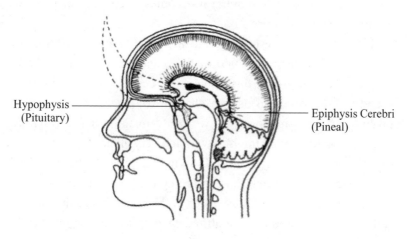

Hypophysis
(Pituitary)

Epiphysis Cerebri
(Pineal)

Profile of the Brain

All the heads successively placed on man's shoulders have represented an ever-increasing participation in the *yod*, their archetype. They have all been obedient to the structures of the Upper Triangle of the Sefirotic Tree.

On the level of the Divine Body, this triangle is called the Greater Countenance. It begets the seven other sefirot called the Lesser Countenance and brings them all together.

Likewise the head, the *yod* of הוה, is also the Tetragrammaton in its entirety. The *vav*, the spinal column of man's body, is here the final vertebra, which opens out at the top to form the cranium. This vertebra is in reality one and three: occipital, sphenoidal, and ethmoidal, forming a curve whose face is upward, thus determining man's necessary uprightness.

The *vav*, which is also the spinal marrow set inside the neural tube running the length of the upper body, becomes the brain itself at the level of the head. The brain arises embryologically from a triple swelling of the neural tube, the upper part of which forms:

The two cerebral hemispheres, the two *hehs* of the Tetragrammaton;
The head of the Tetragrammaton, the *yod*.

To begin with, the *yod* remains hidden, curved within the most archaic convolutions of the brain; it becomes a seed, the shape of which is called "Ammon's horn."

Unconsciously, we have given the name "Ammon's horn" to the hippocampal formation coiled in the most ancient part of the brain. Whatever the origin of this name, it is certain that the fundamental sound AUM—Amen to us (see chapter 16, page 319)—is laid down in this archaic formation. And we could imagine that a ritual developed around this sound might govern the very elaboration of this shape, called upon to uncoil and fulfill its loving function of "divine hand," the *yod*, grasping the *vav* and thus becoming the Sword's handle.

But for the moment let us return to the structures of the cranium itself. I have compared it to the ultimate vertebra opening out into a bony structure, both hard and supple, at the top of the spinal column.

Hard, because it is bone and, as bone, it is the most well-knit structure in the human body.

Supple, because it is like a puzzle whose pieces fit together without being fused, forming sutures to accommodate the motion, which is the life of the brain. These tighten and loosen to the rhythm of an autonomous "cranial respiration," the primary respiratory mechanism.

As bone, the cranium is part of the mystery linking all the bones in the body, by which this substance, *etsem* (עֶצֶם; see chapter 12, page 202), becomes the very substance of being, its divine inwardness. In this sense, the cranium is no more separable from the brain than the bone is from the marrow, or the vertebrae from the spinal cord.

For the Chinese, the bone marrow, linked with blood, and the spinal marrow, linked with nerve impulses, are indissociable and form with the bones and the first two Cinnabar Fields (matrix of water, the uterus; and matrix of fire, the gall bladder) the entrails known as "curious" or "marvelous," which ensure the perpetuation of the species.

This perpetuation means the continuation of the race in the matrix of water, but from this matrix of water perpetuation also means essentially creation, that is, the conquest of eternity by reintegration into unity (see chapter 10, page 124).

With the language peculiar to their tradition, the Chinese call the head the "cranial Cinnabar Field," the final place of gestation of the divine, where man becoming One weds the universal. "This being gives birth from the head," they say. "He is Tao."

To the Greeks, he is Zeus, giving birth to Pallas Athene.

To the Hebrews, he is יהוה.

Our own anatomical language points to this state of motherhood, by naming "mother" the three layers of membranes of the meninges:

The dura mater, the "hard mother," on the outside;

The pia mater, the "meek" or "dear mother" on the inside;

And, between the two, the fine-spun arachnoid. *Aráchnē* is the spider spinning its web and working from the "middle," like Ariadne inside the palace of Knossos, and like the smith in his sanctuary of fire.

The *yod* therefore grows in this last matrix. In the *vav*, the cerebro-spinal axis receives, at each level of the vertebrae, the sensory information gathered from inside or outside the organism and transmits it to the organs it governs in the form of commands that cross from right to left. Throughout this climb the marriage of the two *hehs* has been brought about.

In the brain, the two ה become the two cerebral hemispheres whose convolutions appear as a final labyrinth whose center can only be reached in the company of the divine guide (as witnessed with Job), when all fear of death has disappeared.

This final matrix is the Golgotha or the "place of the skull," *gulgolet* (גלגלת) in Hebrew. It is the "liberation (גל)" of "exile, *galut* (גלת)." It is also the cross, indicated by its last letter, *tav* (ת), caught up in the wheel, גלגל, *galgal*, of death and resurrection. The *tav* (ת), as the tree of the cross, then becomes the Tree of Life.

The Tree of Life has given its name to a section of the brain situated behind the medulla and called the cerebellum.

Our Chinese friends say of the brain that "placed on man's firmament, it is the sea of marrows." "A sea receding," we could add, with a play on the Hebrew word *moah* (מח), "marrow," whose root, we have seen, is "the withdrawal, the erasing" (see chapter 12, page 204).

A sea of which *alef* (א) is the ebb and *ha-Shem*, the *yod* (י), is the flow.

A sea whose respiration is rooted in the *shabbat* of the *alef* (א), attracting the *yod*.

Man, anchored in heaven, receives from the *alef* the descending flow of energy. In his immediate reality, it makes up both his coat of skin, intended to become a garment of light, and this most noble of fabrics, pearly white, fragile, and essential—the nervous fibers, the marrow, and the brain.

In its mediate reality, the bright substance of the *alef*, becoming *yod*, energizes the brain, which stores the very essence of being, brings it together, and disseminates it so long as man's desire is for the Divine

Spouse—in other words, as long as he is in conformity with his Name, his *yod*, and aspires to the *alef*, Spouse and Father, whence he comes.

The play on words linking the *alef* with the *yod* can be read in the word *ei* (אי), which is the interrogative pronoun "where?" This game of encounters and separations weaves the different inner spaces, fields of consciousness, in which the *vav* is, as it were, drawn upward, grasped by the Divine Hand.

The Cerebellum

When the cerebrospinal trunk of the *vav* enters the cranium, it gives rise to the six roots of the cerebellum, also called the Tree of Life, as we have just seen.

A sagittal section of the cerebellum reveals an astonishing shape, resembling an oak leaf. The oak is a sacred tree par excellence, and its sap rises according to the ordering of a structure that seems to compare with that of energy rising in man.

Each of the folia in the cerebellum represents a part of the body. The cerebellum too recapitulates the entire body in its specific vocation, involving the rising of sap and its coronal organization at the top of the Tree: the cranium-crown.

This is why the cerebellum coordinates all of man's posture, particularly his uprightness. It receives its information from the labyrinth of the ear and the proprioceptors in the joints and ligaments. Together they link listening and posture, the *shema* of "listening" (שמע) with the *maasah* of "action" (מעשה): listening and action are made up of the same letter-energies.

One can realize here the divine character of the action performed by one who is listening to the *yod*, a dance springing from music whose song is an image of the Name.

At the base of the cerebellum is the "vital knot," the respiratory center giving life to the entire being. In front of it is the hypophysis or the pituitary body, governing all the endocrine glands, particularly the sexual glands.

The hypophysis, through its influence on genital sexuality, links the cranial Cinnabar Field with the pelvic field, while the epiphysis or pineal gland, situated behind the vital knot, seems linked with the thoracic Cinnabar Field.

The function of the epiphysis is still unknown. I am inclined to say that it is unknown because the pineal gland, asleep, has not yet been stimulated to send its influx into this thoracic field, because humanity in its present state of unconsciousness has not yet experienced its matrix of fire.

The epiphysis may well be intended to represent for the Word function what the hypophysis is for the reproductive function. The name "pineal gland" comes from its shape like a pine cone, which is also a symbol of the Word.

The epiphysis is rich in melanin, the black pigment also present in the retina. Perceptions of light from the eyes, the eyelids, the cheeks, and especially from the forehead are analyzed here. A solar rhythm is worked out, regulating the duration of sleep and waking. The Egyptians called this gland "the sun inside the head."

The two thalami, or "nuptial layers," also called "optical layers," are found above the vital knot ending in the pineal gland. Vision is inscribed from the outset in the very purpose of marriage. The final union is celebrated on the level of the optical thalami, that of the two cerebral hemispheres, each opening out into white matter in a mass called the "radiant crown."

The Divine Father, Wisdom, the right hemisphere, has entirely wed the Divine Mother, Understanding, the left hemisphere. He has lovingly removed all her veils. Dazzled by the sight of her, he urges her to bring forth her fruit.

She carries this fruit in the very heart of her name, Binah (בינה). It is *Yah* (יה), the Son, *ben* (בן), יהוה.

Praise the Lord, and sing alleluia with all our organs dedicated to *Yah*!

For there they all are, summed up, portrayed, taken up into the "radiant crown." All the motor, sensory, cognitive, intellectual, and affective functions can be found there in their individual expressions and their most harmonious and subtle interactions.

The Forehead: The Horn

The forehead remains mysterious. It is specific to man and is the only part of the cranium not to be covered with hair. The frontal lobes seem of little use, which may suggest that the forehead is an important site of functions as yet unknown.

In Hebrew, it is *metsah* (מצח), an ultimate "marrow" (מח), within which the divine "harpoon"—צ—"erases, subtilizes" what is most subtle.

The forehead is the ultimate place where the "purest" (*tsah*, צח) is born.

The "purest" is none other than the fully fledged *yod*.

From the beginning the *yod*, in the shape of the horn of Ammon (I am inclined to say the horn of Amen!) was coiled in a seed shape within the depths of the archaic brain (rhinencephalon), in secret communion with the listening faculty and with vision, of course with smell, and doubtless with all the senses that were then but agents of the *sensorium dei* (sensory of God) essential to man.

The Horned Christ. There are also horned Christs, as we see in this drawing from the Basilica in Vaison-la-Romaine.

This *sensorium dei* seems to be the great architect of the body, fashioning everything around itself, for him, the *yod*. We can imagine this "purest," the incipient *yod*, piercing its matrixlike envelopes and springing forth a "horn of gold" from the skull of the accomplished man, who is attaining Keter, the Crown.

The horn of gold, present in the collective unconscious, is personified in Greek myths by Pallas Athene, who is born gold-helmeted from the head of Zeus. Athene, the immortal, is the fruit of Zeus's love for Metis, Wisdom, whom Zeus swallowed in order to marry her.

Nourishment and marriage are but one (see chapter 12, page 222). Here they signify the integration of the Tree's highest energy, Wisdom, which for the Hebrews is the last energy, Hokhmah, before Keter, the Crown.

The goddess Athene was carried for many months behind Zeus's forehead (מצח, *metsah*), matrix of the "all pure." When the time was ripe for delivery, the divine head of Zeus was seized with the pains of childbirth. Zeus begged Hephaestus, the celestial smith, to strike him with his axe. Hephaestus obliged; Zeus's forehead split open, and Athene came out, wearing a golden helmet and fully clad in shining armor. She gave a shout of victory and began to dance.

The son of Cronus (a son of Time, a mortal), having become a god, begets the immortal. He steps out of time. Arrayed in his garment of light, crowned with gold, he gives a shout of victory over death, over time, and henceforward feeds on the fruits of the Tree of Life.

Hephaestus's axe is the Hebrew letter *qof* (ק),[1] which designates the "cleaver." At one point in the evolution of the letter's design can be seen the shape of the double axe, a symbol dear to the Cretans. The double axe hangs over the head of the bull of Knossos. Between the animal's horns, it is a sign of victory.

The Hebrew *qof* corresponds to 100. On the cosmic plane it is unity. This letter is also a symbol of Wisdom.

The axe blow reinstates man in Divine Unity.

Zeus was nourished with the milk of the goat Amaltheia, one of whose horns had become the horn of plenty.

The first fruits of the celestial horn, the horn of plenty, in turn gave birth to the married woman's basket, which in the past used to be filled with presents, a sign of multiplicity within unity regained through marriage. The bride then used to be crowned with her husband. (In the Orthodox Christian rite of marriage, she still is.)

Horn and crown, at marriage, belong to the same deep symbolism. Every human marriage is, first, an image of the marriage of each one of us with himself, in order to give birth to the Divine Child, the *yod*, symbolized by the horn; and second, it is an image of the marriage of the created with the Uncreated, of man with God, symbolized by the crown.

In that sense, the horn is the highest manifestation of fecundity and power. It is the light Isaiah promised humanity in its accomplishment beyond all duality: "Thy sun shall no more go down; neither shall thy moon withdraw itself: for יהוה shall be thine everlasting light" (Isaiah 60:20).

Sun and moon, Divine Father and Mother, Wisdom and Understanding, are accomplished in יהוה, the horn of Israel, whose praises were already sung by the psalmist while it was still coiled in the depths of the Amen.

> Let them praise the Name of יהוה. . . .
> He also exalteth the horn of his people,
> the praise of all his saints;
> even of the children of Israel, a people near unto him.
> (Psalm 148:13–14)

In the line of King David, the chief and head of the people, the horn of Israel is lifted up. And when John the Baptist, the Forerunner, came into the world, his father, the high priest Zacharias, sings a song of rejoicing: "Blessed be יהוה Lord God of Israel; for he has visited and redeemed his people, and hath raised up a horn of salvation for us in the house of his servant David" (Luke 1:68–69).

The messianic horn concludes its course in the Person of Christ. Completion in the heart of a family is but a seed on the scale of a

The Unicorn. The unicorn symbolizes the highest
degree of fertility and power. It is light, linked with
threefold vision. (Cluny Museum, Paris.)

Forelock—or Horn? This American Indian has something of the unicorn about him. (Philadelphia Museum of Art.)

people—a seed that dies in the earth in order to rise to another dimension, a seed for the world.

This horn lies in the collective unconscious, under the name of "unicorn." It is another form of the third eye on the forehead.

At the top of the head it makes a unicorn (French: *licorne*); in a roof it is a dormer window. This skylight may be called a bull's-eye glass, which confirms the link between horn, eye, and light.

Hair and Crown

Hair and fingernails are made of the same biochemical elements as the horns of animals. They are the celestial rays, the roots through which Divine Energies and life-giving force descend into man. These rays become the branches of his tree's growth at the top.

Hair is the symbol of divine power, as the story of Samson magnificently illustrates (Judges 14–16).

Samson had been consecrated to God from birth, and there had not "come a razor upon [his] head" (Judges 16:17). His strength terrified the "adversary," here symbolized by the Philistines. Samson wed this adversary in order to dominate it. We again come across the law governing the black phase of the Work, and this is even clearer when Samson becomes blind. In the end he dies, pulling down the two columns on which the Philistines' house stood: they represent here the two poles of duality collapsing. Samson, enlivened by divine strength contained in his hair, an incipient crown, takes on in death one aspect of the first part of the marriage of Israel with its God.

During the passage through the Gate of Men, the loins (kidneys) symbolized strength, and for the Chinese, "the loins blossom in the hair" (see chapter 12, page 192). Western medicine is less poetic, but nevertheless makes a link between the activity of the suprarenal glands and the hair.

Hair is arborescence and flowering, burgeoning of the sap and the flower of sexuality. Speaking of woman's hair, the apostle Paul alludes to its perturbing effect on angels. Woman's hair is the glory of man, he says, while man's hair is the glory of God. He recommends therefore that man should uncover his head when praying, while woman should remain covered (1 Corinthians 11:3–15).

The word for "baldness" in Hebrew—*qereha* (קרה)—has homographs that are the words for "ice" and "frost." If hair on the head symbolizes the strength and crowning of sexuality, it is interesting to note that at the other extreme, in the depths of hell, certain travelers, like Dante, encounter a sea of ice, symbolizing utter destitution.

This experience must be similar to Samson's when, during the night of his black phase of the Work, he united with Delilah—a woman whose name is also linked with the night—and was shorn by her. She shaved off the "seven locks of his head" (Judges 16:19). Become bald, he was bereft of strength.

The *Bardo Thödol* advises the one who must rise from the abode of the dead and be reborn to "move away from the wheel of samsara"

The Bull of Knossos. Hair and horns are the celestial roots from which energy descends. (Heraclion Museum, Knossos, sixteenth century BC.)

and to go toward "the kingdom of supreme happiness," meaning "the kingdom of close concentration," or "the kingdom of the long-haired."

What is the Arab's "lock of Allah," the traditional braid of the Chinese, if not the ray of light linking them to heaven and the subtle continuation of the spinal column?

All rites concerning hair have a sacred meaning. These rites are amazingly frequent, historically and geographically, and go from a simple symbolic gesture to an arsenal of magical procedures linked with profane sexuality.

The single hair—*sear* (שׁער) in Hebrew—is the "prince," the principle (שׁר) implanted at the "source" (ע) of being. "Hair takes root in the loins" but blossoms in the Crown.

The word *sear* (שׁער), designating a hair, may also mean "fear," "trembling" (awe in the presence of the sacred), when pronounced *saar*.

When a human being feels fear—and fear is a distorted reflection of dread in the presence of the sacred—he feels his hair stand on end. All his antennae are alert; he seeks information that may save him from an event he cannot control. Biologists are aware that animals' bristles are antennae, which, when they stand on end, inform and make them sensitive to vibratory modes too subtle for what remains of modern man's receptive capacity, especially in the West.

This human being, such as we see him today, seems to have lost his bristle and his hair through the ages, gradually obfuscating his sense of the divine and hence of the worlds surrounding him, no longer aware that he carries them within.

On the other hand, cases have been observed where people with the gift of clairvoyance were very hairy on certain parts of their body.[2]

We know that the growth of nails and hair continues well after biological death and seems to follow a biogenetical stimulation different from the one governing the life of other tissues.

In view of the popular love for stories, there are many legends—which always carry a grain of truth—chronicling phenomena of this order, especially in the lives of the saints. "Is it not alleged," says Dr. Larcher, "that St. Hubert's beard continues to grow, and that every year on his feast day the sacristan shaves his chin?"[3]

Eastern Christians and Muslims could give many testimonies about anchorites discovered long dead in their caves. Even sometimes after many years, their hair and nails continued to grow.

Might this fairly ordinary phenomenon be more noticeable with certain beings who have attained a high degree of evolution, some of whom were found perfectly preserved after death? If so, could it be that abundance of hair is linked to saintliness (or perhaps, on the negative side, to satanic states)? This question deserves a separate study.

The word for "hair" among the Nazarenes, *pera* (פרע), is made up of the same letters (energies) as *afar*, the "dust," which is the state of man in his multiplicity at the start of his growth (see chapter 8, page 103).

At man's birth the kneecaps (small crowns) already foreshadow his single crown.

Hair is this crown at the level of the head; the dust-multiplicity has become unity.

The same word (פרע), pronounced *paro*, means "to uncover, to remove the bit, to unbridle." The crowned man is indeed wholly free because, transformed into the likeness of God, he has encountered his archetypes.

The anarchist thinks he is free because he has rejected all archetypes. His hair is wild, unkempt; nowadays even its color can be crazy. When he imagines he is embodying an archetype, his hair takes the shape of a crest. Unconsciously, this is a horn.

The reverse of this childish lunacy is a well-arranged hairdress with the tresses arranged like a diadem.

With her hair, Mary Magdalene wiped the feet of Christ, moistened by her tears, and anointed them with perfume (Luke 7:38). Again on Easter even she poured onto Christ's hair "an ointment of spikenard very precious" (Mark 14:3). She is humanity returning to its true Spouse. She lays her hair at his feet and breaks open the alabaster box, which is herself when, wholly accomplished, she dies and gives out her perfume.

From all eternity the Divine Spouse has been waiting for humanity, his Bride, in order to crown her.

"Plead with your mother, plead," he cried, speaking of her through the prophet Hosea, "For she is not my wife, neither am I her husband: . . . And I will not have mercy upon her children; for they be the children of whoredoms" (Hosea 2:4).

But his love is stronger than all, and in the words of the same prophet, the Spouse says: "Therefore, behold, I will allure her, and bring her into the wilderness, and speak comfortably unto her. . . . And I will betroth thee unto me for ever; yea, I will betroth thee unto me in righteousness, and in judgment, and in loving kindness, and in mercies" (Hosea 2:16–21).

He continues through Isaiah: "Thou shalt also be a crown of glory in the hand of the Lord, and a royal diadem in the hand of thy God" (Isaiah 62:3).

"Be thou faithful unto death," he says through the prophet of Revelation, the beloved John: "Be thou faithful unto death, and I will give thee a crown of life" (Revelation 2:10).

In his most sublime vision, John adds: "There appeared a great wonder in heaven; a woman clothed with the sun, and the moon under her feet, and upon her head a crown of twelve stars" (Revelation 12:1).

The Christian tradition, closing the liturgical year, celebrates the accomplishment of humanity, the Bride, by the crowning of the Virgin Mary.

Tradition says that the Virgin Mother, raised to heaven by the hands of angels, becomes the Bride. She is crowned by her Son, the Spouse.

She is accomplished humanity.

She is the beginning of each of us.

CHAPTER 21

The Mandorla

THE GREAT WORK IS ACCOMPLISHED.

The crowned bride enters the chamber of the Spouse, whose Spirit impregnates her. She is intoxicated with his delights.

We know nothing more except that man has gone beyond Keter. He has entered the transcendental darkness of the Ain. For such is his greatness: to be known to him who defines himself as Being (Exodus 3:14), but who lifts the Bride away from all definition, at the very heart, never reached, of Nonbeing.

From Yesod, the Divine Secret, to Tiferet, the "great darkness of the divine," and then beyond Keter in the royal chamber of which only the word "Nothing" can speak, man has known ever bolder and ever more mysterious marriages. They can be spoken of only by one who has experienced them. And we have seen how reluctant our ears are to hear the secret. If we receive something of it, we make fun or rebel.

Have we not, like Ham, betrayed Noah's secret? Have we not, like the crowd, been shocked by the intoxication of the apostles on the day of Pentecost, when they were penetrated by the Holy Spirit with tongues of fire?

Do we not smile when we hear the words "mystic" and "visionary," terms that have been totally devalued in our Western consciousness? For it is easy to mock and be shocked by people having the kind of experience that our own mediocrity prevents us from engaging with—especially if what they recommend is uncomfortably far from our need for security.

Laughter and anger are the only means at the disposal of the impure (i.e., those who are impervious to their true calling) to free themselves from the resonance encountered within by the mystery of union. But both laughter and anger can kill life.

Life, in its seed form, as well as in its becoming, is the union of contraries, "to accomplish the miracles of one thing," said Hermes Trismegistus in *The Emerald Tablet*—even before the apostle Paul, seeking to translate the same reality by speaking of Christ and the Church, exclaimed: "This is a great mystery" (Ephesians 5:32).

The miracle is accomplished, but the "mystery remains sealed for impure spirits."

The chariot of Israel transports the Bride up to the Divine Throne.

Elijah was taken up from the earth by "a chariot of fire and horses of fire. . . . Elijah went up by a whirlwind into heaven" (2 Kings 2:11).

And above the firmament that was over their heads was the likeness of a throne, as the appearance of a sapphire stone: and upon the likeness of the throne was the likeness as the appearance of a man above upon it.

And I saw as the color of amber, as the appearance of fire round about within it, from the appearance of his loins even upward, and from the appearance of his loins even downward, I saw as it were the appearance of fire, and it had brightness round about.

As the appearance of the bow that is in the cloud in the day of rain, so was the appearance of the brightness round about. This was the appearance of the likeness of the glory of the Lord. (Ezekiel 1:26–28)

Man's glory is symbolized by the mandorla, which is seen around the body of Christ in majesty, as it is around saints and Buddhas in different iconographical traditions.

The mandorla is the "festooned almond," which opens onto Light.

The two almonds (tonsils), which were man's first encounter at the entrance of the last palace, are revealed in this instance as "the miracles of one thing" surrounding the body of man deified.

The almond tree is one of many species of trees and shrubs that are venerated not only because they symbolize the Green Tree—that is, the Red Man attaining divine accomplishment—but also because they have their own distinctive virtues.

France and the Celtic countries regard the oak as sacred because it is robust and virile. They also venerate holly and pine because they are evergreen. Their leaf, which does not wither, symbolizes immortality. These three trees, and the orange tree, surround the "Dame à la Licorne" in each of the six tapestries sewn to the glory of this legendary animal, the unicorn (see chapter 20, page 367).

The fruits of the orange tree are the famous "golden apples" that appear in many tales and myths. As a counterpoint to the apple, which according to the oral tradition is the fruit of the Tree of Knowledge, the "golden apple" is the fruit of the Tree of Life.

In this perspective, the orange tree is the tree of the wedding feast of humanity and its God. The crown of flowers from the orange tree is the bride's diadem. The latter symbol was operative not so long ago, in the French countryside, where at every wedding the bride either wore a crown of orange blossoms on her head or, failing that, had a bouquet of the flowers in her basket, a symbol of the horn of plenty.

The almond tree has the same meaning as the orange tree in the sense that, being a monoecious tree, its flowers are both male and female. In the Green Man, that represents the conquest of androgyny. Man has gone beyond the duality of the sexes, gained Unity, and is introduced into the nuptial chamber.

The flower of the almond tree is a sister of the wild rose and garden rose. It shares their symbolism, exalted in the rose windows of our cathedrals: the marriage of the macrocosm and microcosm, of heaven and earth; they glow with the light and fire of Divine Love, which burns but does not consume.

Going to the center of the rose means returning to the One.

"Also when . . . the almond tree shall flourish . . . man goeth to his long home" (Ecclesiastes 12:5).

The Hebrew word for eternity, the east, is *qedem* (קדם: 100-4-600), which is the word for Adam (אדם: 1-4-600) on another octave (see chapter 3). The name of the almond tree—*sheqed* (שקד: 300-100-4), or rather that of its anagram, the Holy One, *Qadosh* (קדש: 100-4-300)—is very similar to it: the *shin* ש (300) has replaced the final *mem* (ם: 600).

If we introduce another *shin* at the heart of the almond, we will find the east, the immortal Adam (100-300-4 + 300). Here, it seems to me, is the deep meaning of the icon representing Christ in full glory surrounded by the mandorla, the almond: Christ is the living *shin*. As a Trinitarian symbol, but also as a "tooth," symbol of the "cornerstone" (see chapter 17, page 336), the *shin*, in the Risen Christ, meets its archetype.

This symbol was already contained in the Ark of the Covenant: the six-branched candelabra, whose shape represented two combined *shins*, had on each of its branches "three bowls made after the fashion of almonds" (Exodus 37:19).

Within the same text, we read that "he made the incense altar of shittim wood . . . the horns thereof were of the same" (Exodus 37:25). The *shittah* tree, or acacia, a sacred tree par excellence, is also monoecious and hence a symbol of the conquest of androgyny, bringing forth divine fruit.

If the almond is the divine fruit, symbolizing not just immortality, but above all man's eternity, then it is essentially a fruit of light. Hebrew has another word for the almond: *luz* (לוז, see chapter 9, page 121),whose homograph, *loz*, means "set apart." This meaning is the very foundation of the idea of the sacred.

The sacred is what has been set apart, separated from what is common (*for what has become common and profane is only what has become separate from the sacred*).

This is interesting: René Guénon, giving an account of a Kabbalistic tradition, tells us: "The word Luz is the name given to an imperishable particle of the body, symbolically represented as a very tough bone. The

The Mandorla. A "festooned almond," the mandorla is the fruit of light breaking out from the darkness of the shell. The angels rejoice and dance around the Son of Man, who has become total Light. (Cahors-en-Quercy Cathedral; photo by Theojac, Limoges.)

soul is thought to remain connected to this after death until the resurrection. When this area awakens, kundalini moves up through the various chakras, and then to the Third Eye."[1]

Israel as the spinal column of the world starts in Luz, the town where Jacob had the vision of the ladder during the night (the darkness of the Lower Triangle). One essential meaning among many symbolical interpretations of this ladder, which rises from earth to Heaven and descends from Heaven to earth, is the awakening of kundalini.

When Jacob awoke, he named the place where he spent the night *Bethel*, which means "house of God." (The same word, *bethyl*, means "the emerald.")

As for Luz, the original name of the town, it looks as though Jacob was to raise it to a higher rung of the ladder.

The root *luz* is linked with the root of words like *lux* (light in Latin), *Lug* (the name of a Celtic god), *Luc*, *Ludwig*, etc., derived from Occitanian and Celtic languages. These first names all convey the idea of light. The Evangelist *Luke*, in Christian symbolism, has the bull as emblem. *Luz*, the almond, a seed within a shell symbolically situated at the base of the spine, has climbed all the rungs of darkness; it has burst open its shell.

Like Christ coming out of the tomb, man has become Light.

The mandorla is the final manifestation of the body, at the frontier of the immaterial. The antecedents of this egg of Light are the successive begettings of man, born from himself to himself in the increasingly unknowable mystery of love.

He continues toward the Ain Sof Aor, the Ain Sof, the Ain, "No thing" . . .

Conclusion

SUCH IS THE BODY AS I HAVE SEEN AND FELT IT. THERE ARE important omissions in this book, resulting largely from my ignorance or inexperience, though also from the many "circumcisions" I have imposed on myself in writing it.

The book itself grew as a tree. In order to allow the sap to rise powerfully enough, without being drained off by the many subsidiary branches, I have obeyed the law according to which "the tree must be pruned that it may bear fruit." The great danger was to make a tree out of each and every branch and thus to present the reader with the inextricable undergrowth of a virgin forest.

Now that the trunk of the tree has blossomed and brought forth its fruit, I would like to think that each branch, lopped off, might be taken up again, by myself, or by others, to be directed in such a way as to bring out its abundant riches. For if each organ of the body has its profound significance—and I have only drawn out a few examples—the relationships between them are also significant, and this I have scarcely broached. Clearly the work remaining to be done is huge. Huge on the level of research, but infinitely greater and more urgent on the level of experience.

At this point, it seems crucial to remove the stumbling block that has weighed—and still weighs—so heavily on human society and on individuals in the West: the idea in a certain kind of religious teaching that makes of the body an instrument of perdition.

On the contrary: the body is the most marvelous tool we have for our realization.

First of all, it represents a language. This language, which we have just tried to decipher, informs us of a task to be accomplished. Through sickness, it tells us when we have taken the wrong path.

In our hands as journeymen, so to speak, it is the raw material with which we work, the tool and the vessel in which we operate.

But care is needed. If we stay solely at the level of this threefold perspective, we run the risk of reducing the body to the role of an object. While it is indeed this instrument, this language, this raw material, it is also man in his essence, a meeting of body, soul, and spirit. Each of us is, indissociably, his body at the same time as his soul and his spirit. And the least part of the body contains the totality of man, body, soul, and spirit, in the image of each sefirah, which, though distinguished from the other sefirot, contains the totality of Divine Unity.

Cutting off a part of the body means mutilating man's unity, his harmony. What could be more benign than extracting teeth, removing tonsils, etc.?

On the face of it, yes . . .

On the other hand, as already pointed out, it is clear that speaking of an organ means not just alluding to the organ itself but essentially to its function, and this is replayed on the level of each cell in the body, because each cell is potentially a whole body.

When an organ is removed, its function does not completely disappear, but this function has undeniably suffered considerable damage, up to the subtlest of levels.

Surgery hitherto has not realized that to remove a gall bladder affects the very heart of a human being's function of accomplishment. It has as yet no idea that an incision into the skin that severs a meridian as described by the Chinese tradition destroys the energy paths at a deep level.

It is not aware that certain pains are initiatory, meaning they are linked with the freeing of energies at that stage of the journey and that it is thus advisable not to intervene.

Western medicine, in general, has not yet understood the language of the body.

The doctor must become aware that the true physician watches over the gestation of the *yod* and assists man to give birth to man, and finally to the god that he essentially is.

Thirty Years Later

THIS BOOK WAS WRITTEN THIRTY YEARS AGO AND WAS THE fruit of my life experience up to then. I had looked after large numbers of sick people, wondering about the meaning of their suffering, as I had wondered about the meaning of life since early childhood, without ever receiving satisfactory replies to my questions.

From this childhood, I have the memory of my father returning grievously wounded from the 1914–18 war and yet seeming only to live by the memories of the carnage. In meetings of war veterans, re-living this tragic upheaval gave them all the impression, or rather the illusion, of being alive. My mother had difficulty recovering from the prohibition society placed on her study of medicine. In 1910, only five girls sat the *Baccalauréat* in France, but there was no question of their gaining further professional qualifications that might have threatened the social order! In chapter 13 I spelled out the important consequences this social environment had on me and how I was very young when confronted with absurdity. If my parents were living in the past, and my contemporaries were fleeing hotfoot toward the future, what was to be done with the present and its potential weight of meaning? I was riveted to such questions, which today are acquiring still more importance.

This is what I should like to discuss with my new readers now that this book is being translated into other languages. For I am much moved to realize that whereas in the past my elders could only encourage me to prepare for a good death within the iron collar of a destructive moralism, heaven has blessed me by opening up the symbolic dimension of the universe and of our sacred scriptures.

The symbol is the quality of any thing insofar as that thing is bound up with the Word that sustains it. The myth is the narrative that recounts the inner man—himself linked with God, in whose image he is—with the aid of these living and breathing "things" belonging to the outer man. As I discovered this dynamic, liberating side of existence, I began to escape from the prison of received ideas, which was stifling me, and to live in the present moment with the abundance its vertical dimension brought with it. Thenceforward I never left it, or rather him, for he revealed himself to me as being the "I AM," the Hebrew Holy Name YHWH, which Christ declares himself to be:

"Before Abraham was, I am" (John 8:58).

It was wonderful to discover, beyond our historical time, that other time that enabled me to expunge from our humdrum translations the classical but reductive "In the beginning" in Genesis and St. John's Gospel. *Bereshit*, the "principle" that opens these two books, is present within us at every moment. It is the divine image, the foundation of Adam—Adam being the whole of humanity—you, me, each human being, pregnant with the hidden Seed.

Christ himself was then freed from mere historicity and confinement within traditional religious categories. He was flesh of my flesh!

The biblical texts began to sing a tale with meaning. Focusing on the parts of the body to which there are abundant references, I discovered the ineffable experience granted to Moses on Mount Sinai where he saw the "shape" of YHWH (Exodus 33:23) and received the Torah from him "mouth to mouth" (Numbers 12:8).

In a kind of image of this kiss, I received in turn the "divine shape" passed on by Moses as a model of the human body. This meant that the body was also a symbol, closely connected to its divine archetype.

Such were the beginnings of *The Symbolism of the Human Body*.

I then began to understand the meaning of *ishah*'s heel, bruised by the serpent in the myth of the Fall (Genesis 3:15), and that *ishah* herself was Adam's inwardness, his "other side" and the "other side" of all of us, not the actual wife of a hypothetical first man. Jacob wounded in the "hollow of his thigh" (Genesis 32:25) spoke to me of a mighty inner struggle, which I could myself undertake, to open the way to a passage through an essential gate of life. The judge Samson, whose entire strength was in his hair (Judges 16), told of another kind of strength. The Greek myths agreed, speaking the same language of the soul, and I understood why there were so many wounded, swollen, and unshod feet, why Prometheus's liver was devoured by an eagle, why Oedipus was blind, and why the skull of Zeus was cleft by the divine smith to give birth to Pallas Athene, radiant with gold.

I also came to understand that the very shape of man's body was significant, that the name of its organs and limbs revealed a secret function, and that the whole body *was* a language and *possessed* a language of enjoyment or pain. When someone is suffering, classical medicine can do away with the sickness but does not take account of the message it is communicating. The sickness is then likely to come back in another way, because the problem has been displaced but not solved. I thus discovered the essential part played by the sick person when he takes responsibility for his symptom. For man's body is called to rejoin its model, which means it is programmed for a precise purpose: to make us men, then gods. Blocking the unfolding of this program means generating sickness. For the moment our humanity, collectively, has not yet understood this. It has remained at the animal stage corresponding to the state of confusion obtaining on the sixth day of Genesis. It is identified with the outside of things and has no idea that there is an inside governed by laws it knows nothing about and therefore transgresses, with untold suffering as the consequence!

The task of life, which is our vocation, is made present and played out from the divine kernel within us, the Son of Man. Each of us has the task of seeing to his growth within us by the combined strength of the Holy Spirit and our own spirit. With this in view, an extraordinary sum of potential energies is given us, which we have to actualize in the course of our lives; these energies are to become information and build the Tree of Knowledge; it remains for us to become the fruit of this Tree: I AM. To do this we have to be born to the new dimensions that are within us, from the first matrix of water at the urogenital level, then from the matrix of fire at the level of the chest, and finally from the matrix of the skull. The spinal marrow, which comes to a head here, is wrapped in the layers of the dura mater and the pia mater, whose names reveal their ultimate maternal and womblike function; as if the spinal marrow, in a secret marriage of water and fire, were the firstfruits of the "waters above," the unknowable divine world, of which man is nevertheless invited to partake in the unfathomable mystery of the wedding.

This upward dynamic is inscribed in every cell of the body and determines the essential function of each organ and each limb, which their physiological function reveals. When the physiological function is affected, the person is called upon to ask questions about the deep function that it expresses. In such a perspective, medicine can no longer have recourse only to a strategy of combat against the enemy (microbe, virus, etc.), that in any case has an extraordinary capacity for camouflage under yet more powerful appearances; we do nothing but go round in circles in a maze with no exit, and we reap the grim rewards. This law, which our sacred texts reveal, may be applied not only to the body of each human being, but to society, or to the body of humanity, the whole of Adam.

To illustrate this appeal to another dimension of being, I should like to recall the admirable reply given by a great spiritual leader, the Dalai Lama, to a group of rabbis and lay Jewish people who visited him at Dharamsala, India, in 1990. When they expressed surprise that the Dalai Lama had not raised an army to defend Tibet against the invader, he replied that the Chinese were only "the external factor."[1]

Since I wrote this book thirty years ago, such reflections have led me from one discovery to another, particularly where the beauty of the human body is concerned. I take back nothing I have written, but having thought still more, I feel strongly the need to add an appendix.

Hence the new appendix that follows, which bears on three essential points: the distinction we have to make among the body and the flesh, the symbolism of the white corpuscles in the blood, and the symbolism of the spinal marrow.

Appendix

The Body and the Flesh

These two concepts are difficult to distinguish. They appear to be two poles of one reality, but are not to be confused one with the other. Christian anthropology sees in man a triad of spirit, soul, and body, and yet the Hebrew language has no word to express the last of these, the body.

Jewish mysticism contemplates the "body divine" in the "shape" revealed to Moses on Mount Sinai. That is, the shape of the Word at the foundation of our being, that of YHWH, the sword הוה.

The divine Sword carves out man, whose ontological vocation is to "make," so that he allows himself to be "made" by it in the movement from image to likeness. In this collaboration of the human and divine for the growth of the Son of Man, man cannot settle down, he "hath not where to lay his head" (Matthew 8:20). He is then carved out in his total being, including his physical body.

This "making" takes place "in the principle," that is to say, when man—either the Adam of Genesis who remains faithful to this principle, or the man after the Fall who returns to the principle of his being and renews ties with it—leaves behind the situation of confusion belonging to the sixth day of Creation and enters into the seventh day.

In the sixth day, man created in God's image is unaware of the honor involved. He is still completely confounded with the animals that are revealed on the same day, or even those of the fifth; they make up his *adamah*, his animal psyche (group mind), and he has no conception of the wealth of his inner life. These "animals" surround the Seed of the Son in the heart of his *adamah*, like the ox and the ass round the crib in Bethlehem.

The body of this Adam unaware of his depths is an animal body and yet already determined by the shape of YHWH and able to become a spiritual body. The animal body of man has no Hebrew name, perhaps because this state belongs to a necessary stage of gestation for the dynamics of future development, but is fetal and hence nameless.

For man is made to enter into the fertile breath of the seventh day. In that holiest of days, Elohim withdraws in order that within man, his secret Name, his Person in its uniqueness, the divine image of the Word, YHWH (in Hebrew, the present form of the verb "to be," I AM), the Christ he is to become, may be enabled to grow. Elohim withdraws much as a father today (obeying an archetypal law) might take a back seat in order that his son may become his own person, without the father's shadow interfering or his power having an undue and estranging weight.

Until the seventh day, Adam was confounded with his "animals," the energies of his inner *adamah*, and was therefore unable to cultivate it; but in the gaping emptiness of the *shabbat* (Sabbath) the divine image within him receives the breath of the Spirit of God, and man becomes a "living soul"—no longer the animal group mind of the sixth day, but a personal soul. In the strength of the Holy Name he is now able to distinguish himself from the *adamah* within him, as from any human group outside him. He is now able to till his *adamah*, for his first "self," his ego, blessed at that moment above all, enters into resonance with another "I" within him. This corresponds to the divine image of YHWH, I AM. He becomes aware that he is "I am in a state of becoming"; and, like John the Baptist speaking of Jesus, the first "self" can say of the new "I":

"He must increase, but I must decrease" (John 3:30).

The ego is linked to the animal body; the "I" heralds the spiritual body. In every human being the "I" is the Son of Man, summoned to attain fullness of stature. With this in view, the great working field of the *adamah* is put into action, and man (that is, man or woman) carries out within it the "male" work of "remembering" her (the *adamah*) and the Son she bears. (As was pointed out earlier, the Hebrew word *zakhor* covers both meanings: the substantive "male" and the verb "to remember.") In the extraordinary power of his desire for God, which is given him with the image of God, he begins to penetrate the energies of his *adamah*, in the "garden of delight" (Eden) that is to become a garden of knowledge, for these energies become information (the Hebrew letters make links between these two words "delight" and "knowledge").

When the sap of the Tree of Knowledge begins to circulate, the sap of the Tree of Life, that of God's infinite love for Adam, comes and impregnates it, and "I AM" enters into his becoming.

The Son of Man grows within him through successive "lands" (earths, new fields of consciousness), until the "Promised Land," the land of the Name, is reached.

In this process, man grows upright. He had become upright in his physical body in order to speak (without the upright posture he could only make noises like animals), but he must now become upright in his inner being and in his subtle bodies in order to become Word. When the body of Adam expresses and glorifies the divine image sealed in his deepest depths, in his principle, in the dayspring of his being, which in its ultimate end is his Name, this body becomes living flesh.

Is not flesh what God has sealed in the depths of Adam's "other side"?

The Hebrew root *tahat*, which designates these depths, has been translated as "instead," in a quite superficial reading of the divine work performed upon Adam. In this reading: "And he took one of his ribs, and closed up the flesh instead thereof; And the rib, which the Lord God had taken from man, made he a woman" (Genesis 2:21–22).

The disastrous consequences of what follows in the story, according to this understanding of the text, are well known. Yet the immediate translation of the Hebrew is as follows: "The Lord God takes one of Adam's sides and seals the flesh in its depths; he builds the side which he has taken from Adam into a spouse and has her come towards Adam."

This side of Adam's self, which he knew not, is none other than his *adamah*, this side of the Tree of Knowledge, which corresponds to the pole of darkness of his being, known in Hebrew as "unaccomplished." This unaccomplished side is not that of evil, but is a huge potential of energies called to become light (knowledge) to form the Son. In order to accomplish the Son (Word) within him, Adam has to wed all the animal energies of his *adamah*, now called *ishah* in the sense of "spouse."

God has made a differentiation between Adam and that with which he was hitherto confounded. When Adam in a deep sleep (a sleep that is a "descent toward likeness," in other words, an awakening, or even an ecstasy) contemplates his *ishah*, he exclaims:

"This is now bone of my bones, and flesh of my flesh" (Genesis 2:23), which in Hebrew means:

"Here is she who is substance of my substance—she who is hidden within me—and my principle."

The flesh, thus glorified with the bone, the innermost part of Adam, this secret part, can only be the principle of his being.

The Hebrew word *basar*, translated by "flesh," is a kind of condensation of the word *bereshit*. It may be read "in the prince," but who is the prince in Adam if not what the Hebrew calls his Seed, the Seed of the Son-Word and the principle of his being? In *basar* we find the root *bar*, the Son, whose two letters surround the letter *shin*. The early ideogram of *shin* was a bow with a taut string, ready to release an arrow that will either hit or miss the target. (We recall that the word "sin," *hamartia* in Greek and *hata* in Hebrew, means to "miss the mark.") The mark is the Holy Name in the Promised Land, the Son completely accomplished and revealing the Father. To miss the mark is to transfer to the outer darkness (of which the Satan has become prince) the power of what the letter *shin* symbolizes, the power of the spirit of man, the power of the eros within him.

"Where the Son is, there is the Spirit also," to quote a saying of the Orthodox Church. As the image of God, Adam is Son and Spirit, God alone is Father. *Basar*, the flesh, thus contemplated, is revealed as the divine image in which the Adam is created, unique in each human being and revealing his Person, made up of the Son and the spirit of man.

Rooted in his Person, which alone breathes with the divine Trinity "on high," man's vocation is to make the Son grow in the formidable power of eros. He then transforms his animal psyche, his *adamah-ishah*, into a spiritual soul, and this lights up his body.

Man's body is the expression of the flesh when man has entered into his dimension of man—that is, when he goes through the Gate of Men and becomes a man of the seventh day.

Hebrew has no word for the body here either, for the body radiates, as it were, the flesh, according to the different levels of consciousness (knowledge) in which the flesh involves it as it moves toward accomplishment. These different stages of knowledge, reached in inner work, have corresponding levels in the Real, which weave the depths of all things. Each of these levels has its own space-time, and our situation in exile only allows us to perceive their most apparent aspect.

And yet today quantum physicists are discovering these different levels of the real by external scientific means: from what they call the implicate order, the very principle of the created world, to the last degree of the explicate order, which we are deceived into thinking is the only reality.

These physicists sometimes reach a degree of contemplation such that one can no longer say that their approach to this level of consciousness is merely external. (If it were, they would be reenacting the drama of the Fall, which may also happen quite often!) Considering, then, this implicate universe, this "principle"—Einstein had already called it the "elsewhere," and they call it the "universe of tachyons" (particles with no mass traveling faster than light)—they say that this universe, which is the source of all information, is that of consciousness. Were they to attain it, they would be in a continuous present—I AM. "Time is then completely transformed into space."[1] Are they not describing in scientific terms the resurrection body, the body of the Risen Christ in glory, I AM?

It becomes clear that "man created from nothing" (me-ain in Hebrew) is created from that universe. It may well be the outcome of kénōsis, the Greek word for divine "contraction" or "emptying," or of tsimtsum, the divine "aspiration" in Hebrew, from Nonbeing to Being, I AM, whose form man inherits and whose germ is his flesh.

Quite an adventure!

Still more moving is the adventure of the Son of God, Christ, I AM, continuing his self-emptying (kénōsis) to the extent of becoming the animal body of the one who is created by him!

For man in a state of sinfulness goes back to the state of the sixth day, remains confounded with the animal world of his adamah, is enslaved by his drives and a prey to the Satan. His Spirit gone astray invests eros only in the outside world, and the Son of Man within him (in this case the widow's son, for ishah is no longer wed) dies! His psyche is devoured by the Satan, who eats its "dust" (the multiplicity of what might have become fecundity); and his physical body, no longer sustained by his more subtle bodies, which have faded away, will fade away in its turn. Man abandons himself to a way of death. We can see why this animal body is called in Hebrew gof, corpse. Christ confirms this when he says to one of his followers:

"Let the dead bury their dead: but go thou and preach the kingdom of God" (Luke 9:60).

And the news of the kingdom is basorah. The proclamation of Christ's resurrection after the Son of God has joined man in the extremities of death to save him from it—this extraordinary proclamation is that of the inner kingdom reestablished and the flesh, *basar*, restored to the Divine Spouse. The arrow of eros has recovered its direction, says the word *basorah*; it flies irresistibly to the mark. The widow's son rises from the dead. And the delighted earth rejoices.

In conclusion I should like to say that man's body, reviled by some and idolized by others, has deserved neither such honor nor such disgrace. It is in constant resonance with the flesh, the principle of being, whose servant it is when man, led by the Spirit, seeks God, or seeks his true identity, not knowing for the time being that it belongs to the divine. *Man is only "incarnate" in the situation of the "seventh day" when he is turned by the grace of God in the direction of his ontological norms and goes through the Gate of Men. He then begins "to till his ground* (adamah)*" and to transform its energies into light (knowledge).* The bodily work that goes with this work on the internal earth can be a wonderful help if carried out rightly. If not, it can lead to mental derangement, as can spiritual development without checks.

In the logic of this situation, problems of reincarnation have no foundation, for one is not "incarnate" just because one has a body. Nor is one incarnate when seeking self-justification in the framework of sound morality. Energies are then thrust back behind the bars of prohibition and are not thereby accomplished. They leap out in aggression, or they undermine from within, but in both cases they are destructive. And sickness today—whether of society or of an individual—is still only treated in its external symptoms, not their deeper causes. Man in a state of unconsciousness is a prey to the enemy, the Satan, to whom he gives power even if he fails to realize it, for, as Christ says, "He that is not with me is against me" (Matthew 12:30).

His words call for a hearer with "ears to hear" and the ability to understand that he who does not receive the Sword kills with the sword.

Man's body is in the service of one or the other; there is no middle term. But when man receives the Sword of the Word of God, he is grasped in the wholeness of his being—spirit, soul, and body—in an enlightening breath of life, the breath of the Risen Christ.

The Symbolism of the White Corpuscle

I have spoken of the red corpuscle, its function related to breath, and the extraordinary adventure of the cell that, in a kind of *shabbat* (Sabbath), mysteriously loses its nucleus to leave room for the divine identity of Man-Adam on the seventh day of its life (see pages 203–214).

"The Spirit of God is in the blood" (Genesis 9:4), says God to Noah, and then to the children of Israel who have come out of Egypt:

"The life [breath] of the flesh is in the blood" (Leviticus 17:11), and later again:

"The blood is the life [breath]" (Deuteronomy 12:23).

This speaks of such a strong reality that the name of Adam (אדם), which is that of every human being, is:

א, *alef*, Elohim—דם, *dam*, (in) the blood. *God in the blood.*

Consequently, to shed the blood of another is the gravest of acts. It is shedding the divine power onto the outward earth, which becomes a focus of idolatry, while at the same time breaking still more the relation of the killer with his inner *adamah*. Furthermore, the "other," albeit distinct from the murderer, is one with him at a deeper level, so killing is "losing the breath (life)" *of both*:

"And now art thou cursed from the *adamah* (earth), which hath opened her mouth to receive thy brother's blood from thy hand [or: from thy *yod*, which is to say, 'from thy power as Word']" (Genesis 4:11).

But if the red blood cell carries this breath of life in a particularly significant way, what is the role of the white cells?

I am inclined to see in these two components of the blood the same dialectic as between the states of the sixth and seventh day of Genesis, and more precisely between the role of the first ego-self, necessary for the child and the adolescent, and that of the second self, the "I am in process of becoming" of the adult man.

I mean that the first self of the child and adolescent is constructed in a slow process of differentiation between the parental world—particularly that of the mother—and that of the child, closely linked with the progressive acquisition of mobility and language. In the latter we have the first manifestation of the functioning as Word, which is archetypal and peculiar to man. If the child did not become physically upright, he could not attain the function of language. In the second part of his life, he goes through the Gate of Men through a process of differentiation from his inner mother, the *adamah*, and enters into resonance with the divine image, which is at his foundation and whose secret she holds sealed (that of his true identity). At that time he begins his inner marriages with her and a more subtle process of becoming upright. This leads him to his function of creative Word.

I have shown how the red corpuscle plays a preeminent role in this second stage of life, to which very few beings hitherto have acceded: "Elohim withdraws, in a *shabbat*, so that YHWH may grow." Only in the seventh day of Genesis is this mystery of the emergence of the person in his unique identity played out.

As long as the child, adolescent, or man remaining in the sixth day has not gone through the Gate of Men, the red corpuscle retains its normal physiological function. The Spirit of God present in the blood provides for respiration through the lungs and for the being's animal life, but the presence of "YHWH in becoming" does not reach the subject's consciousness. It seems that throughout this period the white corpuscle plays a key role in the structuring of the first self in the child and the adolescent. It may be that when man overstrengthens this individualistic and narcissistic self and resists going through the Gate of Men, its role is more one of disintegration. But in its structuring phase—according to contemporary biological discoveries—the white corpuscle prepares the child psychologically for this process of differentiation. It teaches him to distinguish self from not-self at the same time as his blood actually recognizes what is foreign: the antigen. This antigen is treated as an adversary, not an enemy, for the adversary has no other aim than to call up within the white cell something corresponding to it. Without this no process of recognition could have taken place, since what is not carried inside can in no way be recognized outside the living being. This is why, more generally, the opponent does not so much take on the color of the object of his fight as discover that he carries this object within himself. In this sense, to "fight against" is self-destructive. The white cell teaches par excellence that any "war" should be a spiritual one! We have just seen that its recognition of what is other enables the first kind of immune reaction to take place. This kind is innate; it is part of the very nature of the white corpuscle; it takes place by phagocytosis, that is, by digestion of the other—the white corpuscle absorbs the foreign body.

The second kind of immune reaction is acquired and varies according to the nature of the danger presented. It may consist of antibodies, or mediation by transmitters, etc.

What is foreign may either be recognized directly or by the intermediary of a presenting cell, which receives it and associates it with the major immune grouping already set up. This brings in lymphocytes, some for attack, some for support or stimulation. It amounts to a veritable army, masterfully arrayed to struggle with the adversary, whose essential function here too is to reveal the warrior to himself and call up his power of assimilation. In Hebrew, war, *milḥamah*, is ontologically that which enables salt, *melah*, to accomplish its dual function: to separate the adversaries in order to unite them. *Milḥamah* is a "soldering iron," as it were.

With this in mind, my sense of the white cell's importance is that in microbiology it induces the structuring of the first self, or at least answers to the law requiring that this first self should be forged by contact with and in opposition to the not-self, both microbiologically and psychologically. The accompanying aggressiveness is necessary for the acquisition both of identity and of immunity.

In this context one can understand why obligatory vaccinations shortly after birth are tragic. They force the child to recognize the not-self at a moment when he cannot do so, not having the immune structures that go with the acquisition of mobility and language. Similarly the abuse of antibiotics in early childhood to prevent illnesses that appear as initiatory stages in the acquisition of the self and of immunity represents a grave danger. For one thing the immune system may collapse. For another, it seems doubtful whether this self, thus weakened, will be able to recognize the second identity waiting in the wings and to withdraw that it may step in.

That said, it may be that religious authorities seeking to curb the necessary aggressiveness of the child toward the other do just as much damage. Clearly this leads to the problem of violence, and the whole question of rightness in education consists in knowing how best to foster the growth of the first self of the child, while remaining ready to serve the second identity when its demand to grow becomes apparent. Aggressiveness is necessary for the child and the adolescent insofar as it is governed by the white cell in a game of understanding with the antigen, but the subject (child, adolescent) should gradually be made receptive to the quality of combat. In this sense the white corpuscle not only structures the first self but also induces the emergence of the subject's second identity by initiating him into the quality of genuine combat. The child and the adolescent (necessarily)—but also man, physically adult but arrested at the stage of the sixth day (sadly)—can only live by relations of power. By contrast, the man of the seventh day has his model in the patriarch Jacob.

When Jacob was commanded to go to his brother Esau, who at the time was bent upon killing him, he spent a whole night (of the soul) wrestling with a frightening man—the angel of life and death—who obliged him to transform into forces of light the energies that were hiding within him, eaten away as he was by fear, hatred, and other unaccomplished elements of the flocks in his soul. When morning came and he had prevailed, he saw his brother approaching, who came and embraced him. Wounded in the thigh, that day he passed through the Gate of Men (Genesis 32:24–32; 33:4).

Man at the stage of the sixth day, firmly fixed in his first "self," wrestles *against* the enemy, using ever more sophisticated arms and never suspecting that one day they will be turned against him. The man of the seventh day wrestles *with* the adversary, who is the objectification outside of the adversary he carries within.

His real concern is with this adversary and the many others, which together make up a huge potential of inner wealth.

If these potential energies are not transformed into forces of light by work on their integration, they turn against man and cause sickness, accidents, or waves of violence. The role of the white cell par excellence is teaching how to do this work.

Personally, I believe that after a long and painful journey in the labyrinth—which belongs with the sixth day—humanity today is being collectively and inexorably led before the Gate of Men. Hence the great identity crisis it is living through: peoples are demanding their independence; men and women no longer know who they are; governments, no longer having any archetypal reference points, set up homosexuality as a social norm; people identify with the compensatory elements of their as yet nonexistent "person"; and arms kill. In a word, human relations are becoming so tragic that it is not surprising that illnesses of the immune system, of which AIDS is one of the most serious, are coming to the fore. But perhaps it is thanks to AIDS that laboratory research has increased our knowledge of the white cell by a thousandfold. This research is beginning to penetrate the language of identity. Perhaps it is not far from summoning us to listen out for our genuine identity, "I AM in process of becoming," which calls us from the other side of the Gate of Men.

It is certain, though, that the man of the seventh day, who has entered into resonance with his secret Name and has received what Chinese tradition would call *ming-men*, his "mandate from heaven," is theoretically no longer preoccupied with the biologically foreign. If a foreign body appears, it will find a strong immune system in the white cell, a surety for his first identity and an initiator of the genuine "I." It will also find in the red cell a Presence that partakes ever more of the divine nature and brings it to join its opponent. The man of the seventh day is essentially concerned by what is foreign in the potential of energy within him, at his disposal with a view to its accomplishment (the animal psyche called to become the spiritual soul). Anything "foreign" in the blood is the objectification of this. When actualized, these energies illuminate the blood and become information. They build up the Tree of Knowledge and ripen its fruit, the Presence of YHWH. Such a man conquers within him "new lands" (earths, fields of consciousness), ever more spacious and governed by the law of time in inverse ratio to that of space. When "all is accomplished," space is infinite and time abolished. Man has become permanently "I AM." He reaches the likeness and becomes the fruit, YHWH.

In such a dynamic of conquest, it is understandable that laws relating to given levels of the Real may be upset or bypassed. One can understand healings that do not fit into the medical logic of the sixth day, accept "miracles," and enter into an understanding of these words of Christ:

"Verily, verily I say unto you, he that believeth on me, the works that I do shall he do also; and greater works than these shall he do; because I go unto my father" (John 14:12).

We can thus understand that our agnostic civilization, which has done away with God, has also done away with the Satan, the ontological adversary, without whom there is no life, for life is the integration of a potential of energies.

In biology, asepsis—the destruction of the microbe seen as enemy—has become an obsession with our fearful contemporaries and means death.

The Risen Christ, who at Golgotha took on the archetype of all integration, is life.

The Symbolism of Blood Platelets

When I was writing this book thirty years ago, I had a feeling that concealed within the blood, the noblest part of the body, was an image of the Holy Trinity. I dared not say this and was unable to show it. I spoke then of the red corpuscle, its breathing and its oxygenizing function in distributing light to the whole body. It seemed as though I could hear within the red cell the breath and song of the Holy Spirit, yet I was unable to speak of the white corpuscles or the platelets. At present the white corpuscle can be seen as the great defender of the organism, which integrates the adversary. It is the savior, the master of growth, and these functions establish it as corresponding to the divine work of the Son in his incarnation. The platelets for their part act to stanch the flow of blood resulting from man's exile and his turning away from the Father, the heavenly Spouse. (Cf. Mark 5:25–43, the Gospel narrative of the death of a twelve-year-old girl, into which is interwoven the story of a woman suffering for twelve years from an issue of blood. The little girl symbolizes the Divine Child in this woman. Jesus raises this child from the dead, which brings about the woman's healing.) They deal with the healing of wounds by joining their edges and forming scar tissue. This role corresponds clearly to what physicists are discovering today in what they call the "hidden third." It joins together the opposites of the world when they are raised to a higher level of the real. In the same way, if we turn toward the Father, we enter into the ontological dynamic symbolized by climbing Jacob's ladder. At the very top of this ladder, where it reaches its limit, is the "ultimate third," the Lord, who leads us to the Father—the One.

The Symbolism of the Spinal Marrow

With "the forge" I described the work that takes place at the level of the matrix of fire (see chapter 12, page 220). I made this description more

precise when writing my book *Alliance de feu*,[2] but today I feel the need
to go further still and to bring into this Great Work what I see as the
symbolic function of the spinal marrow.

The great breath of wind, which gives life to this forge, is the work
of the Holy Spirit, with which, at this stage of the work, the spirit of
man has become united. Man's flesh, *basar*, has come alive, and the
letter *shin* at its heart has begun to adjust the direction of its loving
"arrows." These are no longer scattered in the outside world only, hor-
izontally, as it were, but the fire of *shin* causes "the waters below" to
boil and draws forth from them a vapor, which is the desire of man
for his God. Hebrew, we remember, calls "water below" the potential
of energies given to man in order that the divine image, the Son of
Man, may grow in him; this potential makes up the "unaccomplished"
pole of the Tree of Knowledge. It is a quantity of energies peopling the
matrix of water, the *adamah*: these are the "fish" created on the fifth
day of Genesis, which play a quite special role in the two testaments.
On the seventh day, Adam is imbued with the Holy Spirit and seeks to
"till his *adamah*." From his depths he draws forth this "vapor," which
is a great driving force. In a way it acts like a pump, bringing the unaccomplished energies up to the matrix of fire (hitherto they had been
held back, symbolically, in the spleen and the pancreas). When they
are born from this matrix (womb) and are accomplished, they become
the building materials for a "new land (earth)." The waters have become "dry land," and this dry land calls for and receives its fecundity
from the "waters above." Until now the "waters below" represented the
"unknown" of man (today we should say the "unconscious"), and the
"waters above" the Unknowable of the divine. These are now available
to man become conscious, so that he may partake of them. They are
God's erotic response to his spouse, this Adam who now becomes a
vessel for God's desire for him. Adam, man, turns out to be the space in
which two desires meet, for his name, אדם, may be read אד-ם, "Elohim in the blood," but it is also *ed-mem* (אד-ם). *Ed* is the "vapor,"
the desire of man for God, and the letter *mem-mayim*, "waters," in its

position at the end of the word (ם), is a symbol of the "waters above," the desire of God for man. These two desires are respectively the sap of the Tree of Knowledge and that of the Tree of Life, both trees being in the middle of the Garden of Eden. From the middle of the human being in resonance with the divine kernel at his foundation springs forth the vapor, as well as God's response to man's love. This response streams forth in the river (of fire) described in Genesis 2:10. *Brit-esh* (another reading of the word *bereshit*) is "covenant of fire." This stream divides into "four heads," of which each becomes a source of life at a given level of "earth" built by man—and in just measure, for God only gives himself to the extent that man can bear. *Shaddai* (שדי), the Almighty, only strikes with his "arrow" (ש) sufficiently—*dai* (די, *dai*, "enough," is the letter *yod*, or the hand, *yad*, read backward). God holds in hand the arrow of his love in order to pierce the heart of man. What divine tenderness!

The reason for recalling this here is that this divine river seems to me to be symbolized in the body by the spinal marrow.

Although the two are distinct, Chinese tradition links the bone marrow and the spinal marrow in a common function of energy. In this tradition, both are among the marvelous entrails that are closer than others to the sacred, because their substance has to do with the unknowable nature of the divine. I have mentioned this in connection with the bone marrow, which gives rise to the red corpuscles of the blood and "spirits away" their nucleus.

The Hebrew word *moah* (מח), the marrow, is the root of the verb *mahoh*, "to rub out" or "spirit away." God's *shabbat* in the bone marrow is when Elohim (א) withdraws from אדם so that the blood can take charge of YHWH, the *yod* (י), man's identity, and he can go forward to the likeness, or even to rest, *dami* (דמי), for at this stage he will have become his Name. Is there not a *shabbat* of man in the spinal marrow? It may well be within it, in this river of fire, that man is "taken up," spirited away with part of himself that dies, in a sort of preassumption in one land, in order to rise in a new land.

The subject now is the mystery of the spinal marrow, which, like a river of life, runs the length of the spinal column and makes us participate in a universal joy. I am struck by the fact that the spinal marrow travels down from the head, where it radiates in the "shining crown," right down to the coccyx, but this only in the first three months of fetal life. At that stage, with the widening of the medullary canal, it goes up as far as the second lumbar vertebra, where it stops. This river of life therefore deposits a kind of memory at the base of the spinal column, a "secret" that may give its name to the "sacrum," to the first "sacred" vertebrae and to the sefirah Yesod, Foundation, since Yesod may be read י-סוד, "the secret of the *yod.*" It is genuinely the foundation of being. The secret of the Name is there, but is straightaway forgotten. When the adolescent, as his life subtly grows, enters into the matrix of water, whose door is the sefirah Yesod, his task is to complete the construction of his first "self," differentiated (or so it should be) from the parental self. The sacred vertebrae and the last lumbar vertebrae, which he or she forges during their labyrinthine journey in this matrix, remain unvisited by Divine Fire, unless it be by a discreet and secret memory sealed within him or her. This memory is registered outwardly in our sacred books with their four levels of meaning, which gradually become accessible to man according to the ascent of his consciousness. This memory does not force itself upon us. Man is free, free to increase his sensitivity to it and thus to prepare the meeting with his secret Name, his future identity, or to remain arrested in the structure of his first self (which is tragic, for it implies a deafness, a surdity that becomes ab-surdity). Becoming a prisoner of his exile, he makes his matrix into a tomb. Should this happen, the adolescent will never go through the Gate of Men and will not take on his Name, the YHWH, I AM, which he is called to become. There is, however, another divine call that takes place just as discreetly at this level, which does not force itself upon anyone either, but which the adolescent may hear. It comes from the last "head" of the river of the One, called at this stage the *frat,* reductively translated as a geographical entity: "Euphrates" (Genesis

2:14). The *frat* is like a divine fruit shown to the one who may be able
to taste it. What this means is that this river of fire, giving out its light at
the level of the second lumbar vertebra, as explained earlier, is present
in man's exile, but man is unaware of it. He does not realize that without
this presence, he could not even enjoy physiological life.

It seems to me that man drinks every night at the source of the
frat and receives from this divine breast not merely the information
necessary for his breath and life in the moment but also that which
encourages him to go toward the whole of his being, toward his Name.
This is particularly true of REM sleep, which occurs three or four times
a night, without which man would die and which maintains the function
of dreaming.

Dreams sometimes come from a source higher up than the *frat*; their
language challenges the everyday logic of outer man, and although they
use words and images from this world, they are charged with a symbolic dimension leading to uprightness:

"In a dream, in a vision of the night . . . [God] openeth the ears of
men" (Job 33:15–16).

When man (man or woman) hears and "remembers" (זכר, *zakhor*), he becomes spiritually "male," for the verb "to remember" has
the same letter-energies as the noun "male." He then begins the male
work within him, penetrating the energies of his mother-*adamah*, who
in this work is called *ishah*, spouse. He goes through the Gate of Men,
pierces his inner heavens, and drinks from the new source of the river
of the One, the *Hideqel*. This part of the river of fire is a subtle light,
daq, which feeds the prophets.[3] It runs symbolically with the spinal
marrow along the last dorsal vertebrae. This is the level at which man
genuinely takes root in his Name, begins to forge his new identity, "I am
in process of becoming," and receives from YHWH, the Lord, I AM,
his own charism. This is the meaning of the sefirot Glory and Power. If
he seeks first the Kingdom, "all these things shall be added unto [him]"
(Luke 12:31). Chinese tradition expresses the same reality by saying
that at this stage of his life, man receives by the *ming-men* one of the
infinite possibilities of manifestation of the One. This actualization of

the One by the *ming-men* is known as the shift from the Earlier to the Later Heaven. Beginning to draw from the unsuspected treasures of this "heaven," man is led to his true inner "place" and consequently to his outward place as well. He enters into the creative flow of his being, marveling at the way it bears him along and partaking of the same river of life, which breaks out into the sounds, colors, tastes, and smells of everything, which is naturally, in the universe, linked with the One. When studying the subtle function of the navel, called *tabor* in Hebrew (see chapter 12, page 219), I spoke of the numinous (and sometimes luminous) experience that man has on reaching this level of his being, the sefirah Tiferet, Beauty. Christ's transfiguration on Mount Tabor is the archetype of this experience. But Christ immediately links this pole of light with the pole of darkness, which is to follow and which could not take place without the experience on Tabor.

"Tell the vision to no man," he charged the three disciples who witnessed the light, "until the Son of man be risen again from the dead" (Matthew 17:9). The descent into hell, before Christ rose again, was not the same for him as for the three disciples chosen for this experience. Christ descended to the original source of the river of the One, having taken on the darkness of the world during his public life. The three apostles took on the hells of the matrix of fire, given substance by the outside world.

Their descent into hell took place in what we call Gehenna, which is none other than the *Gihon*, second head of the river of the One coming from God, third in man's rise up to God.

The *Gihon* is a "belly," *gahon*, a matrix of fire that purifies man in such a way that when he is born from it, he will have forged the *yod*, YHWH, his Name. The *Gihon* is symbolized by the spinal marrow flowing in the first dorsal vertebrae, and in these waters of fire man purified accedes to his "royalty." In the river of the outside world, which bears the same name, King David in his extreme age had Solomon go down to be anointed king (1 Kings 1:45).

This is the level of the heart, where the bellows of the heavenly smith's forge sends man down into his darkness to receive light and returns him to the light that he may acquire strength for a new wedding with darkness. The lungs are "wings," like those of the dove and the raven working in Noah's ark, which is a matrix of fire. Within it the patriarch is born in the intoxication of the fruit of knowledge, which is wholly his, and of his Name, which he has wholly become. This Great Work is only made possible by Christ's descent into other hells than that of the *Gihon*.

After his transfiguration on Mount Tabor, Jesus takes on the work of the final matrix, that of the skull (in Hebrew, *Golgotha*—liberation from *galut*, exile), where the first "head" of the river of the ONE, the *Pishon*, springs forth. *Pishon* is the manifestation (*panin* = countenance) of the letter *shin*. It is the theophany of the Holy Spirit at the springs of the Tree of Life.

The *Pishon* springs forth in a burning stream into which no one can go down unless he has taken on the whole of the matrix of fire and become I AM.

Having stated again—this time to the soldiers who have come to arrest him—that he is I AM, Jesus dies to this world symbolized by the horizontal bar of the Cross. "All is accomplished (it is finished)," he said as he died (John 19:30). He then went down into the last extremes of darkness to rise again in uncreated light, albeit veiled, in a double movement symbolized by the vertical of the cross.

In the darkness of *Pishon*, Christ takes back in hand the bow and arrow of the letter *shin* inscribed in the flesh, *basar*, of man and violated by the Satan. He saves the Spirit in man and frees the inner Son. This is symbolized by the release of Barabbas, whose name means "son of the Father."

To this end, he encounters the Satan. A terrifying confrontation. He, YHWH, "seed of *ishah*," accomplishes in history the eternal act by which he crushes the seed of the serpent, the Satan, who has usurped the function of *ishah*'s spouse, the spouse of all humanity and the prince of this world. Through his victory over this *enemy* in a final fight for integration, Christ confirms the Satan's ontological function as necessary *adversary.* In so doing he restores "the flesh," *basar*, to its original vocation. Christ's resurrection is also the resurrection of the dead, that of the flesh, *basar*; it is the "good news," *basorah.*

It may be that Noah partook of this great mystery when, after coming out of the ark, the matrix of fire, he entered the tent, אהל, *ohel* in Hebrew, a name built of the same letter-energies as the root of the divine name Elohim. This *ohel* may perhaps be an image for the matrix of the skull, where man, having unleashed the nuclear energies of his Name, becomes the Elohim he was called to be.

"I said, Ye are gods (Elohim)" says Christ to his disciples in confirmation of the Psalm sung by King David (Psalm 82:6; John 10:34).

Similarly, Job entered the matrix of the skull when YHWH, his guide in the last stage of his inner journey, asked him to gird up his loins like a man, to go down and confront the monsters of the hellish deep Behemoth and Leviathan (Job 40). Are we not asked to do likewise?

These lords are Cherubim and Seraphim, who keep with the flaming sword "the way of the Tree of Life" (Genesis 3:24).

Coming from the One, called upon to conquer the One, man is wholly stretched in the direction of his source, the very source of the *Pishon.* He can then be born from the crown of his head, the sefirah Keter. The spinal marrow, which from the crown downward lights up the whole nervous system, gives to the skin, which is similarly textured, its own light.

With this end in mind, before closing this chapter, I should like to ask the reader to rethink the ethics of his or her life in general and particularly the ethics governing the different stages of life's journey. Historical time is given us to accomplish the Great Work of our being, by a series of mutations; if they do not take place, the potential energies called to these transformations are converted into destructive violence against people or against society.

I should like to insist on that essential stage which, for women, is the menopause and, for men, the age of fifty or thereabouts. In the menopause, radical changes take place in a woman's body. These are reflected in men on the level of their energy. More than ever, at this time of life, men and women are called to go through the Gate of Men—if this has not already happened—for their bodies inexorably mark the transition from the lunar to the solar phase of their evolution, the transition from the phase of procreation linked with the first "self," to that of becoming the creative Word, linked with the real "I" of their being.

In the course of this work I named two glands situated in the matrix of the skull, one being the hypophysis, or pituitary body, corresponding to the lunar rhythm of the procreative phase, the other the epiphysis, or pineal gland, corresponding to the solar rhythm of the creative Word. The physiology of the first, which governs the growth of the physical body and the equilibrium of sexual life and procreation, is well-known to medical science. The physiology of the epiphysis is, however, still little known. This is partly because few human beings give a free rein to its function, which requires genuine spiritual growth, and partly because science, which is in principle agnostic (confusing "religious" and "spiritual"), recognizes in man no spiritual vocation, still less a vocation for deification. The epiphysis seems nevertheless to govern the actualization of this last engrammatic memory in the body. Called by the ancients "the sun in the head," and more popularly "the third eye," it appears as the visual center for the great depths in man, when he takes on the matrix of fire. A number of myths in all traditions tell how their heroes had access to this vision, usually through momentary blindness. The epiphysis has a more subtle role to play than microbiology can determine and a definite energy function, opening up different levels of the real until the Promised Land of I AM is realized (the universe of tachyons in the outer world).

On the way to this dimension, the final cessation of the menses seems to repeat what woman has already experienced on the level of procreation. When pregnant with an actual child, the "blood energy" of her periods is transformed into "milk energy" to feed her baby. At the time of the menopause, a corresponding transformation takes place for women and certainly for men, too, since this inner childbearing is something they share with women. Both have to see to the growth of

the Son of Man, who is present within every human being, and to
feed him.

Blocking this natural transformation and keeping the person in the
lunar phase of his or her existence means tragically maintaining humanity's unconsciousness. Agnostic medicine plays excessively on the fears
that come with the threat of old age and illness, but may well engender
graver illnesses still by instilling in the human body hormones of animal origin and hence regressive information from the animal world.

I invite all women who are on an inner path to refuse this medical
imperialism and to trust in the wisdom of the body, the temple of God.

I should like to have reflected here on bioethics. But it would be too
much for this chapter, and I refer the reader to the aspects of the subject
I have treated in works written after the present one.[4]

I will only say emphatically that cloning—making a man in the
image of man—destroys the power of mutation peculiar to man. The
clone would remain "continually living in the time (of exile)," as Genesis says, speaking of him who might dare to "put forth his hand, and
take also of the tree of life" (Genesis 3:22).

Taking of the Tree of Life seems to me to amount to the sin against
the Spirit which "shall not be forgiven" (Luke 12:10; Mark 3:28–30),
for the Spirit alone is the giver of life. Manipulating life, making a man
in man's image for narcissistic satisfaction, could well amount to pro-
gramming the clone to stay at the stage of development at which the
parent is arrested, a purely animal stage unvisited by the Spirit and its
power of evolution. The clone might then be condemned to stay perpetually in time, rather than becoming "eternal," for it would be unable to
recover eternity.

No less emphatically, I confide to the reader the experience of my
whole life. Traditions, in the depth of their message, speak the language
of the One from before the tower of Babel. They have deposited their
secret in the heart of our being and in their sacred books. Our body is
the repository of this secret; it has also been granted the infinite power
of love to realize it.

Notes

Foreword

1. "Poor aim" is the sense of a Hebrew word often translated as "sin."

Chapter 2

1. "Metahistory": beyond history, that is, belonging to ontological reality.
2. Annick de Souzenelle, *La lettre: chemin de vie; le symbolisme des lettres hébraïques* (Paris: Albin Michel, 1993), chap. 2.

Chapter 3

1. This is the foundation of the Orthodox theological courses taught by Mgr. Jean de Saint-Denis at the Saint-Denis Institute of Paris (1954–59).
2. The usual translation, "Behold, the man is become as one of us," is questionable. "Of us" can be read as "because of it" (the Tree of Knowledge). This comment, along with several others that will follow, are explained in Annick de Souzenelle, *Alliance de feu: nouveau regard sur la Genèse* (Paris: Dervy, 1986, 4 volumes), a study of Genesis.

Chapter 4

1. Léo Schaya, *L'homme et l'absolu selon la Kabbale* (Paris: Buchet Chastel, coll. La Barque du Soleil, 1958), 19–20.

2. *Ain* (אין), "nothing," should not be confused with *ayin* (עין), "source" or "eye."

Chapter 5

1. Karlfried Graf von Dürckheim, *Hara: The Vital Center of Man*, trans. Sylvia-Monica von Kospoth (Rochester, VT: Inner Traditions, 2004).
2. Mgr. Jean de Saint-Denis, theology course, 1969.

Chapter 6

1. Dr. Jean Schatz, "Réflections sur la gauche et la droite selon la pensée énergétique chinoise," *CoEvolution*, no. 4 (1981).
2. "Existential" is used here in its etymological sense, "outside of being," that is, in our skin-coated nature, acquired as a consequence of the Fall.
3. These two terms, "accomplished" and "not yet accomplished," render the two essential aspects of the Hebrew verb: the perfect and imperfect, which represent completed and noncompleted actions, respectively. They join the two poles of the Tree of Knowledge, *tov ve-ra* (טוב ורע). *Tov* (טוב) is the accomplished, and *ra* (רע), the not yet accomplished: that which has become light, and that which is still in darkness. See the Glossary.

Chapter 7

1. Pausanias, *Description of Greece*, vol. 2, bk. 26, 3–5.

Chapter 8

1. In Gabriel Monod-Herzen, *L'Alchimie méditerranéenne* (Paris: Adyar, 1963), 142ff.
2. *Kalevala: The Land of the Heroes*, trans. W. F. Kirby (London: Everyman's Library, 1977): 6–7, lines 209–36.

Chapter 10

1. Gilles Andrès, *Principes de la médecine selon la Tradition* (Paris: Dervy), 112.

2. *Nehemod*, here translated as "desirable," has an etymology implying warmth, energy, and desire as well as comfort and rest. [The Hebrew *shakal*, here translated as "success," can also mean the ability to be prudent or wise. The latter is more common in English translations.— *Ed.*]
3. See René Guénon, *The Reign of Quantity and the Signs of the Times,* trans. Lord Northbourne (London: Luzac, 1953).
4. Hilaire de Poitiers, *Traité des mystères* (Paris: Cerf, 1947) bk. 1, chap. 13, 99.
5. *Mer* (sea) and *mère* (mother) are homophones in French. —*Trans.*
6. De Souzenelle, *La lettre: chemin de vie*, 168.
7. See chap. 11, p. 165 and chap. 12, p. 202 ; also De Souzenelle, *La lettre: chemin de vie*, 245.
8. The French is *"dare-dare,"* an expression of unknown origin that corresponds phonetically to the Hebrew above. —*Trans.*

Chapter 11

1. Luke 6, between present verses 4 and 5. This is absent from most of our current editions but is found in the fifth-century Codex Bezae in the collection of the University of Cambridge.
2. C. G. Jung, *The Archetypes and the Collective Unconscious*, trans. R. F. C. Hull (London: Routledge, 1959), 29–30.
3. Ibid., 32.
4. See Vincent Bourne, "La divine contradiction," Église Catholique Orthodoxe de France Web site; http://eglise-orthodoxe-de-france.fr/la_divine_contradiction_II.htm; accessed March 9, 2015.
5. In Hebrew, the verb for "to look" is formed with the same four letters as the name of Jesus, the Savior. In a sense, then, the first divine look upon man after the Fall is that of Jesus.
6. See above note.

Chapter 12

1. Genesis 2:6–7 and De Souzenelle, *La lettre: chemin de vie*, 61–62.
2. See chap. 11. Response, as responsibility, is "the thing that has weight" (*pondus*) and thus what one carries, to which one *responds*. Also, in Hebrew, the word for bride (*sponsa* in Latin) is *nessuah*, literally, "she who is carried." To espouse is to respond to the inner bride and to carry her.

3. De Souzenelle, *La lettre: chemin de vie*, 309.
4. Ibid, chap. 21.
5. Ibid., 272.
6. See chap. 20, p. 359. Also, in the Chinese tradition, on the energy level bone marrow and spinal marrow are closely related. See p. 402 for the symbol of the spinal marrow.
7. Jean-Marc Kespi, *Acupuncture* (Moulin-lès-Metz, France: Maisonneuve): 224. Cf. Kespi, *Acupuncture: From Symbol to Clinical Practice* (Seattle: Eastland Press, 2013).
8. Rudolf Steiner, *Triades*, bk. 1, no. 4: 66.
9. Ibid., 59.
10. De Souzenelle, *La lettre: chemin de vie*, 88.
11. Marcel Jousse, *L'anthropologie du geste* (Paris: Gallimard, 1969).
12. Did this *sidēros* come from Mars, the "red planet," which shares a name with the god of war? There may be something here that is worth studying in more depth.
13. René Guénon, *The Lord of the World*, trans. A. Cheke and Carolyn Shaffer (Ellingstring, North Yorkshire, U.K.: Coombe Springs Press, 1983).
14. Kespi, *Acupuncture*, 112.
15. Ibid., 168.
16. De Souzenelle, *La lettre: chemin de vie*, chap.11.
17. Ibid., 200.
18. Kespi, *Acupuncture*, 117.

Chapter 13

1. Sri Aurobindo, *The Life Divine* (Pondicherry, India: Sri Aurobindo Ashram, 1955), 46.
2. De Souzenelle, *La lettre: chemin de vie*, 157. I refer here to the word *nagod* (נגד), which also means "face to face." In this word the *nun* (נ) faces the *dag* (דג). There can only be information if man becomes fish and marries a new sum of energies, symbolized by the *dag* in the depths of the unaccomplished.
3. In G. Monod-Herzen, *L'alchimie méditerranéenne* (Paris: Adyar, 1963), 138.
4. Cf. Jacques Duchaussoy, *Le bestiaire divin* (Paris: La Colombe, 1957).
5. Friedrich Husemann, *Aenigmatisches aus Kunst und Wissenschaft* (Stuttgart: Die Kommende Tag, 1922).
6. Eric Daviller, *Le schizophrène, le yogi, le chaman, et le commissaire*

(Doctoral thesis in medicine: University of Nancy, 1977), vol. 1, 128.

Chapter 14

1. In Paul Vulliaud, *La Kabbale juive* (Paris: Nourry, 1923), vol. 2, 48.
2. Dante, *Purgatory*, canto II, verses 28–39.

Chapter 15

1. Gershom Scholem, *Major Trends in Jewish Mysticism* (London: Thames & Hudson, 1955), chap. 2.
2. Kespi, *Acupuncture*, 130 (see chap. 12, n. 7).

Chapter 16

1. See Paul Nogier, *Traité d'auriculothérapie* (Paris: Maisonneuve, 1969).
2. Alfred Tomatis, *L'oreille et le langage* (Paris: Seuil, 1963), 70.
3. Alfred Tomatis, *La nuit utérine* (Paris: Stock, 1981), 134.
4. Ibid.: 81, 87.
5. René Guénon, *Man and His Becoming according to the Vedanta*, trans. Richard C. Nicholson (New Delhi: Munshiram Manoharlal, 1981), chap. 16.
6. René Guénon, *Symboles de la science sacrée* (Paris: Gallimard, 1962).
7. Swami Nityabodhananda, *Mythes et religions de l'Inde* (Paris: Maisonneuve, 1967), 84.

Chapter 18

1. Hubert Larcher, *Le sang peut-il vaincre la mort?* (Paris: Gallimard, 1957), 209.
2. Makali-Phal, *Narayana* (Paris: Albin Michel, 1942).
3. Larcher, 212.

Chapter 19

1. De Souzenelle, *La lettre: chemin de vie*, 175–76.
2. Swami Nityabodhananda, *Myths et religions*, 84 (see chap. 16, n. 7).

1. De Souzenelle, *La lettre: chemin de vie*, 207.
2. Alain Assailly, "Contribution à l'étude de la médiumnité," *La science et le paranormal* (Paris: I. M. I.,1955).
3. Larcher, *Le sang*, 151 (see chap. 18, n. 1).

1. Guénon, *The Lord of the World*, chap. 7 (see chap. 12, n. 13).

Thirty Years Later

1. Rodger Kamenetz, *The Jew in the Lotus: A Poet's Rediscovery of Jewish Identity in Buddhist India* (San Francisco: Harper San Francisco, 1994), 185.

1. Brigitte and Régis Dutheil, *L'homme superlumineux* (Paris: Sand, 1990), 87–93.
2. De Souzenelle, *Alliance de feu*, vol. 1, 282–339.
3. Ibid., vol. 2, 209–11.
4. Annick de Souzenelle, *La parole au cœur du corps* (Paris: Albin Michel, 1993), 119–179; *Le féminin de l'être* (Paris: Albin Michel, 1997), 255, 287–289; *Oedipe intérieur: la présence du Verbe dans le mythe grec* (Paris: Albin Michel, 1998), 167 to end.

Index

cornerstone, 137, 376
corpse, 394
correspondences
  in acupuncture, 313–14
  of bodily parts, 41, 55, 312(i), 318
  of Cinnabar Fields, xxv–xxvi
  of elements with body, 99
  of heavenly bodies, 41
  of Hebrew alphabet, xix
  of numbers, xix
  of Old and New Testaments, 336
  of stages of knowledge, 393
  of symbols and archetypes, 7
  of twins, 57–58
cosmic consciousness, 258
cosmos, 49
covenants, 115–17, 137–38, 223, 330, 404
cranial respiration, 359
cranium, 319, 358–59
create/creating, xxvi, 124
Creation, 2–3, 9, 15–16, 71–73, 258
creatures, in Ezekiel's vision, 18–19
Cronus (Titan), 65, 287, 353, 364
Cross, symbolism of, 408
cross(es), 63, 236
crossing, 47, 78, 177–78
crown chakra, 62, 311, 334
crown(s). *See also* Keter
  of bride and groom, 365, 371–72
  dental, 337
  hair and, 192, 370–71
  of head, 338
  kneecap as, 100–101, 101(i)
crucifixion, 272, 409
crutches, 27(i), 44–45, 64, 92–93, 155, 162–63
cry, 315, 351
curse
  Ararat as removal of, 135
  divine, 60–61, 104, 316–17, 352
  of sterility on Corinth, 84
Cybele (goddess), 259
Cyclopes, 65, 221, 353
cymbals, 233–34

D

Daat (eleventh sefirah; Knowledge), 134, 307
daat (knowledge), 47
Daedalus, 44, 146, 152, 282
dag ha-gadol (great fish), 348
dai (enough), 404
Dalai Lama, 386
dalet (door), 46–47, 62, 120
dalet (ד), 46
dam (blood), 70, 193, 193(i), 205, 326, 340
Damascus, 304, 340–41
Damesheq (Damascus), 340
dami (to rest), 404
damot (likeness), 340
Dana (goddess), 259
Danaids, 178
dance and dancing, 157, 201, 206–7
Dante, 260, 262, 265, 285–87, 311, 368
dantien (*belly*), 182
daq (subtle light), 406
darkness, 51, 61, 89, 266
Daughter-Bride, 217
David (psalmist), 211–12, 330, 407
Daviller, Dr., 269
Day of Atonement, 211
dead, 187
Dead Sea, 160
deafness, 321, 405
death
  Gate of Men and, 184–85
  as initiatory, 132
  love and, 236
  mystery of, 183–88
  of physical body, 132
  second, 186–88
  state after, 265–67
decapitation, 40
deification, 41
delight, 112–13
Delilah, 368
Delphi, 83

vision
egg and, 350
gall and, 228, 349–51
hand and, 278
lungs and, 279
owl and, 354
pulmonary tree and, 239
Visitation of Our Lady, 205–6
vital knot, 361–62
vitriol, 232
vocation, 81, 82, 103, 385–86
volcano, 65
Vulcan (god), 221

W

wandering, 217, 348
warrior, kneeling, 80
water(s)
blood and, 120, 193
breath and, 124
elemental principle of, 99
feet and, 99
filtering of, 193
Helle linked with, 292, 294
leaking vessels and, 178
primordial, 2–3, 139
purifying, 9, 184–85
returned to source, 160
salt and, 195
as symbol, 8–9
as unaccomplished, 120, 129
uterus and, 227
vapor, 120
"waters above," 386, 403
"waters below," 403
wavelengths, 8–9
weak/weakness, 54, 56–57
wedding, xxvi, 6, 112, 307. *See also*
marriage
wedding banquet, 95, 194, 375
Western Christian mystics, 35
Western world, 32, 144, 281, 298, 380

whale, 257, 259, 348
wheat, 329
wheel, 18–19, 81–82, 215, 287
white corpuscles
in children's identity, 397, 400–401
as defenders, 203, 402
symbolism of, 396–401
White Dragon, 287
white phase of the Work (albedo)
blindness following, 346
counterfeit, 282, 292–98
dove as, 133
as light, 327
White Dragon and, 287
widow/widowed, 75, 77, 97, 394
wilderness, 194–95
wind, 403
wine
at crucifixion, 272
enjoyment and, 194–95
fruit as forerunner to, 222
as Holy Spirit, 250
symbolic wavelength of, 8–9
wings, 153, 157, 276, 282, 408
wisdom teeth, 338
Wisdom/wisdom, 9, 26, 54–55, 291, 362.
See also Hokhmah
withdrawing
alef, 204–5, 236
Eliahu, 252
Elohim, 71, 109, 204, 390, 397, 404
John the Baptist, 252, 390–91
parents, 44
within and without, 2
wolf, 171, 343
woman/women. *See also* ishah
compared to men, 179
divine curse and, 60–61
enmity with serpent of, 91, 244
as face of Sphinx, 83–84, 89(i)
at fifty, 120–21, 409–11
impurity of, 119–20
as inventor and creator, 181
as symbol of restoration, 88